CHRISTOPHER D. KOLENDA
(Editor and Co-Author)

Leadership: The Warrior's Art

With a Foreword by
General Barry R. McCaffrey
(U.S. Army, Retired)

Introduction by
Lieutenant General
Walter F. Ulmer, Jr.
(U.S. Army, Retired)

The Army War College Foundation Press

Copyright 2001 by Christopher D. Kolenda

ISBN 0-9709682-1-3

Manufactured in the United States of America

Second edition.

Recommended by the

ASSOCIATION OF THE U.S. ARMY

"A remarkable collection of contributions by highly-qualified practitioners. For those wishing not just to understand the challenges of leading soldiers in ground combat but also to understand contemporary issues of rebuilding the US Army after VietNam, this book is a must. The authors are important rebuilders explaining what, how and why. Other authors are those now creating the future Army. Yet others are excellent historians. Simply the best leadership collection I have seen - bar none."

——Lieutenant General Frederic J. Brown,
US Army Retired, *Amazon.com*.

"*Leadership: The Warrior's Art* will likely become a longstanding leadership reference throughout the Army, and should become so throughout the Navy and other services as well... Themes on leadership that run throughout the book include elements of finesse, structure, discipline, adaptation, creativity and versatility. The editing, in its simplicity and creativity, is the book's mastery, as lessons are delivered subtly... I shall keep it close at hand."

——Commander Gene Moran, US Navy.

"This book is an absolute must have for any military leader, regardless of rank. Chris Kolenda takes leadership to the next level and challenges readers to expand their beliefs about the most precious art of our time. By reading this book, you will not only learn more about leadership, but of yourself as well. Every leader should have this book in his kit bag. It's the best collection of thoughts on leadership I have ever read."

——Major Larry Reeves, US Army,
BarnesandNoble.com.

"... *Leadership: The Warrior's Art,* living up to [General Barry R.] McCaffrey's commentary in the book's Foreword, provides "an enormous contribution to understanding how organizations can produce extraordinary success by building teams capable of heroic behavior." This interesting, thought-provoking, and intellectually challenging anthology is highly recommended to military and civilian readers — and especially to the Army's current senior officers as a reminder of the characteristics of and the need for genuine leadership in the Army today."

——Lieutenant Colonel Harold E. Raugh, Jr.,
US Army Retired, *Armor*.

TABLE OF CONTENTS

To the Men and Women of the Armed Forces
of the United States —
World-class warriors who deserve
world-class leadership.

FOREWORD

by General Barry R. McCaffrey
(US Army, Retired)

The purpose of leadership boils down to one central reality: human organizations produce extraordinary success where they create teams capable of heroic behavior. The study of leadership has been the preoccupation of business leaders, military commanders and political elites since Plato wrote *The Republic*. Major Chris Kolenda has produced a broad, valuable, and comprehensive addition to the study of leadership in this superb anthology entitled *Leadership: The Warrior's Art*. On one level this volume is an intensely interesting and readable textbook for a college level course. On a higher level, this collection of essays defines a coherent, history-based theory of effective military leadership for both combat and the peacetime training environment.

Chris Kolenda, the editor, poses as his central thesis the notion that the best way to study leadership is from three perspectives: theory, history and the insights and experiences of others. He has organized nineteen brilliant essays under the themes. The chapters are written by experienced military professionals who have had to put their ideas through the crucible of practical experience, as well as by nationally known civilian scholars who are experts in the study of leadership. The military authors range in rank from full general to major. The recognized civilian scholars are highly respected and well published in their fields. These essays are intensely gripping and hard to put down. Fortunately, each chapter stands alone and can be read in a single sitting — an aspect of the book that makes it attractive given the pace of military and civilian professions. The format is well suited to support personal and organizational professional development programs.

This leadership anthology presents rich intellectual fare written by authors with dramatically varied experiences and perspectives. The presentation begins with a sophisticated introduction by retired Lieutenant General Walt Ulmer, who was a model and mentor to a generation of young Army officers and West Point cadets before he went on to spend a seminal decade as President and CEO of the Center For Creative Leadership in Greensboro, North Carolina. Chris Kolenda and other chapter authors, to include the inspirational former Army Chief-of-Staff Gordon Sullivan, provide an excellent conceptual framework in the opening section.

This foundation is followed by seven fascinating historical case studies in Section II in which we gain insights from analysis of past leaders and organizations. We penetrate into the genius and the tragic hubris of Alexander, and the quirky leadership of Frederick the Great, King of Prussia. We witness the devastating failures of the ill-trained and hastily selected American officer corps on the WWI battlefields of France, and then the unbelievable heroism and effectiveness of US Army WWII noncommissioned officers and company grade tactical leaders. We learn of the *Wehrmacht's* incredible battle performance, leadership flexibility, and ethical emptiness during years of hopeless struggle under the immoral and evil Nazi regime. We grapple with the ethical dilemma presented by General Curtis LeMay whose powerful leadership, organizational skills and technical innovations resulted in the slaughter of hundreds of thousands of Japanese civilians with massed firebombing attacks on urban areas, but which arguably helped knock the Japanese Imperial Government out of the war and possibly saved a million US Army ground casualties. We study the brilliance of revolutionary Soviet military doctrine and concepts of initiative created by Red Army generals whom Stalin then had exterminated just prior to the Nazi attack on Russia. This historical analysis is an extraordinary set of essays that provide tremendous teaching lessons to leaders charged with the responsibility for people, resources, limited time, and demanding outcome expectations. The reader should also not miss the lengthy and carefully researched endnotes that add enormous depth and credibility to the main chapter essays.

The final section on Contemporary Experiences and Reflections On Leadership is the real payoff in this monumental work for the developing leader in the military, business or government. Here are some of the most penetrating and varied approaches to understanding leadership that I have encountered in a lifetime of personal study and experience. Chris Kolenda has crafted a superb balance beginning with the modern Army's most brilliant and broadly gauged officer, Lieutenant General Dan Christman, the current Superintendent of Cadets at West Point, who correctly argues for a broadened and more compassionate officer to handle the complexities of 21st Century leadership. The colorful and legendary Doc Bahnsen boldly tackles the question of charisma and why it remains so vital. The widely experienced and courageous Dick Potter speaks to the questions of the unique leadership requirements of command in elite Special Forces military units. Mark Hertling addresses the frequently unstated fundamental prerequisite to battlefield or team sports success: physical and mental training, toughness and stamina. Retired three-star General John Woodmansee discusses crucial concepts associated with creating high performing units — organizations capable of heroic performance because leadership has unleashed human potential. Doug Lute and Robert Cone provide valuable lessons on leadership from the front, vision, character, and training. These essays are classic stuff. They are fun to read and incredibly helpful to understanding leadership.

Forty years ago at age 17, I entered West Point and began the practical study and practice of leadership. It has been a long trail of experiences, pain, the thrills of hard won success and the confidence that develops from the privilege of serving and leading Americans in war and peace. You mostly learn from your own experiences and what you observe in others. If you're fortunate, you are turned on to the study of history, and you gain perspective, maturity and judgment from vicariously living the lessons of both inspired and failed leaders in other places and times. Out of all this you cobble together a set of fundamental leadership convictions, principles and techniques that can embrace the challenges of new environments, changed missions, dynamic crisis situations and slowly evolving American social mores. At the end of the day, you treasure leaders with technical expertise and competence. You recognize that all soldiers and organizations are capable of greatness if their leadership creates an expectation of mutual respect and trust. And finally you understand that leaders must have a coherent vision, form a simple and sound plan, and then lead to the objective.

These intriguing nineteen essays on leadership pulled together by Major Chris Kolenda, US Army, are an enormous contribution to understanding how organizations can produce extraordinary success by building teams capable of heroic behavior. This book is also an intellectual challenge that will pay off with enhanced organizational behavior when leaders apply the ideas, lessons, and insights contained herein. The authors have given us an extraordinary piece of analysis.

Barry R McCaffrey
General, USA (Ret)

EDITOR'S PREFACE

The purpose of this volume is to enhance the education of leaders. Education, according to Plato, is not the practice of putting sight into blind eyes; it is the art of turning the soul from the shadows of ignorance toward the light of truth. While the value of this book is not nearly so weighty, Plato's theory of education offers an important insight on the study of leadership. Too often aspiring leaders turn to quick-fix formulas as easy solutions to complex leadership problems. The idea is an attractive one – provide a set of charts and rules tailored to general situations for the leader to put into a "kit-bag" and pull out when the situation arises. Attractive, but entirely wrong-headed. An equally attractive and troubling idea is to provide a list of hidden, mystical leadership secrets and aphorisms that leaders can place on calendars, placard on walls, and quote *ad nauseum* in the hope that such feel-good phrases will eventually sink in and make all problems go away. If only it were that easy.

Unfortunately, leadership does not conform snugly into diagrams, models, and flow charts. Similarly, leadership does not fit neatly into the straitjacket of a single personal experience, theory, or historical study. The education of a leader requires a broader perspective.

Experience is the great teacher of leadership, but even the most privileged crowd but a relative few experiences into a lifetime. Personal experience, however, is also the school of hard knocks. The limit of our own experiences and powers of perception suggest that even this school is incomplete. Valuable to be sure, but as Otto von Bismarck once commented: any fool can profit from his own mistakes – the wise man profits from those of others. Experience is valuable only if it is imbued with meaning from which one can draw salient conclusions. Otherwise, experience becomes imprisoning.

Intellectual development is the key that opens the door to meaning. The education of a leader must move beyond personal experience and draw on the boundless experience and insights of others. These opportunities for education lie in the pages of history, philosophy, theory, and the reflections of past and contemporary leaders. Personal experience, therefore, must be augmented by the records of others and synthesized by the insights of history, philosophy, and theory. Such an approach broadens one's mind and the richness of one's perspective, and leads ultimately to a much greater understanding of leadership.*

Developing the vibrant intellectual core from which a leader can draw insight into the art of leadership requires the courage and humility to immerse oneself in the ideas and experiences of others. Such an approach differs significantly from the intellectual comfort of the notion that leadership is only a process to be mastered rather than an art to be developed. Process, to be sure, is vitally impor-

---

*I am deeply indebted to Colonel Charles F. Brower IV for helping me frame the ideas in this and the preceding paragraph.

tant to the art of leadership and there is much discussion of process in these pages. But process cannot stand alone. As with any art, leadership has processes that provide certain guidelines, fundamental skills, and principles or rules that make it intelligible as a concept. Writing a good essay, for instance, contains several elements of process: rules and formats regarding argumentative structure, paragraph and sentence construction, grammar, punctuation, and spelling, and the reporting of evidence. Unfortunately, even with the most meticulous attention to the details of the format, an essay bereft of insight, analysis, and spirit remains a poor one. No refinement of the process can make the essay worth reading. On the other hand, a person unable to communicate complex insights in a coherent manner following the fundamental rules of the writing process will ensure his ideas are lost to the reader. In either case the result is a bad essay.

Process without art is empty and lifeless. Art without process is unintelligible. The one is form without substance; the other is substance without form. The pursuit of one to the exclusion of the other is incomprehensible. Art is the catalyst that brings animation, purpose, and spirit to process; process offers form to art, lending structure that enhances meaning to the beholder. Leadership is no more confined to process than writing is to format. Leadership is an art that is made comprehensible by process.

The shelves are filled with books about improving the process of leadership; discussions of how to hone its art are few. Checklists and processes do not challenge our ability to think, they do not force us to defend our ideas or look new ones in the face. They demand no depth. Defining leadership as an art rather than as a process does not mean that leadership cannot be taught. It merely means that gaining a greater understanding of leadership requires intellectual courage. Just as we develop physical courage by experiencing and functioning under physical fear and moral courage by making the choice of right amidst the pressure to do otherwise, so we develop intellectual courage through the discomfort and ambiguity of experiencing ideas that challenge our depth and perspective. Leaders develop intellectual courage by continuously sharpening the saber through education, and in doing so they hone within themselves the art of leadership.

This book is designed to be part of such an education. It does not propose anything particularly new or flashy. These are not ready-made solutions to complex problems. This book explores arguments about leadership, as well as its experiences; it cuts across temporal lines as well as those of genre and levels of organization. It seeks not to be the pinnacle of the leader's education, but rather a complement to an existing program of development or the beginning of a new one. Its goal is to generate reflection, stimulate curiosity, provoke thought, and inspire passion for further study.

The increasingly impenetrable prose in the leadership literature over the past few years stems in part from confusion over exactly what leadership is. Pick up nearly any leadership book and you will find many descriptions of leadership behaviors, many theories on process, and a plethora of adjectives (visionary, transformational, transactional, charismatic). Rarely will you find a precise definition of leadership.

Many scholars assume that leadership is ultimately a process to influence people to do something that they would not ordinarily do to accomplish organizational objectives. This concept hinges on the notion of influence. If by influence we mean "to get someone to do what we want them to do," then we are left with the very significant problem of legitimizing coercion as an appropriate method of leadership. Since such a coupling is unacceptable, scholars have had to invent modifiers to clarify the difference between good and bad leadership. "Transactional" leadership, for instance, is coercive because it relies upon simple reward and punishment for influence, while "transformational" leadership relies on such things as charisma, inspiration, intellectual stimulation, and/or individual consideration. With the good and the bad forms carefully separated, scholars now argue about the specific behaviors, traits, and processes that make up the good forms, and then use complex statistical analyses to support their theories.

While the contributions of such scholarship to behavioral science and to many aspects of leadership are critically important, I am reminded of Tolstoy's poignant statement that "there is no greatness where simplicity, goodness, and truth are absent." To recover some clarity in the study of leadership we need to begin with a sound definition. Leadership is the art of inspiring the spirit and the act of following. The following must be voluntary. The individual and the group of individuals must want to be guided by that person for the latter to be called a leader. Certainly leaders use rewards and punishments when appropriate; some are charismatic in the Weberian sense, some are not. Some stretch others intellectually, some inspire devotion by their simplicity and genuineness. Some possess an expertise far greater than that of their followers, some are merely competent. Some devise unconventional solutions to problems, others implement conventional solutions with sound plans. That the list can go on forever perhaps suggests the limits of the behavioralist approach to leadership.

A more comprehensive approach exists in the realm of ideas. Leadership is about trust – trust in the leader's vision, trust in the leader's competence and character, trust in the leader's respect and care for those under his or her charge. Every effective bond between people has trust as its bedrock. Every failed relationship is ultimately an actual or perceived breach of that trust. Leadership is so difficult because earning that actual and perceived trust is so challenging. Successful leaders earn the trust of others, and in doing so inspire that voluntary spirit and act of following.

Good leaders have an understanding of the human condition. While a number of recent studies have sought to explore the specific behaviors of leaders to which people respond most favorably and thereby gain insight into the motivations of followers, I believe that Thucydides, the fifth century B.C. Greek historian, provided a more profound insight into human motivation. Thucydides tells us that prior to the outbreak of the Peloponnesian War an Athenian citizen informed the Spartan assembly that Athens was animated by three of the strongest motives – fear, interest, and honor. Among other things this is a statement on the enduring motivations of humanity. Fear and interest are understandably compelling; the idea of honor is less clear. Honor can be expressed in terms of reputation, respect, prestige, fame, pride, and esteem. When the ideas of fear, interest, and honor intersect people become exceptionally motivated. Fear of punishment produces only so much effort as to alleviate the threat of punishment. Monetary or other material interest engenders only enough effort to achieve the reward. When the ideas of honor become involved people are motivated to exceed expectations — they go "above and beyond the call of duty." Upholding moral and ethical values, maintaining standards of excellence, developing, fostering, and sustaining personal and collective pride, these all represent interests and fears that go beyond the merely physical. The most effective leaders are able to motivate people to operate above the material plane. They do so not by appealing to fear and interest alone (the "transactional" approach), but by appealing to ideas more lasting, more meaningful, and ultimately more human. Such leaders can inspire exceptional performance because they understand both human nature and human motivation. You will find the ideas of fear, interest, and honor offer an interesting sub-text to the chapters in this volume.

Leadership is indeed the warrior's art. And like leadership, the definition of "warrior" has also become obscured. The term is contested in contemporary discourse. Those who believe the military is suffering through a sort of "moral crisis" and loss of martial spirit lament that the hard edge of the fierce and courageous warrior has been blunted by the forces of political correctness. They point to the numerous "chain-teaching" mandates about sexual harassment, equal opportunity, homosexual policies, and consideration of others, as well as declining readiness rates, inadequate performance at combat training centers, and the discussion of women in the combat arms as evidence of such softening. They argue that America's military must recapture the warrior spirit.

On the opposite side of the argument are those who believe the notion of "warrior" to be inherently savage and antithetical to a military befitting 21st Century America. They see the celebration of a warrior ethos in terms of unbridled, bloodthirsty *machismo*, and the perpetuation of such ethos as responsible for sexual harassment, racism, hostility to and violence against homosexuals, domestic violence, etc. In combat or on peacekeeping missions, they argue, the ethos will result in war crimes and violence against civilian populations.

Each side points to the other as part of the problem. The first group regards the second as misguided social engineers with little to no military experience who have placed the readiness of the military at risk. The time spent on hours of human relations training will have severe consequences on the battlefield, they claim, resulting in needless casualties and the potential jeopardy of American interests and security. A "soft" military, the argument goes, cannot measure up to the ferocious "barbarians" of the world. The second regards the first as angry critics at odds with society and contemporary reality. The military cannot protect society if it is divorced from its values. As the military is called increasingly to humanitarian and peacekeeping operations, consideration and gentleness are more desirable than ferocity and martial ardor. If the military cannot protect its own soldiers and families from violence within the ranks, how can it possibly protect our own society and others?

What is really at stake here is more than the definition of the warrior — it is the identity of the military both in the eyes of itself and society. Recovering the true idea of the American warrior is thus part of the answer to the question of identity. Plato, perhaps, put it most simply and most eloquently when he spoke of the "guardian" in the *Republic*. The guardian, he argued, must be fierce toward the republic's enemies and gentle toward its friends. The guardian must at the same time be gentle and spirited. The true guardian, he claimed, is philosophic, spirited, swift, and strong. The simplicity and wisdom of Plato encapsulates the idea of the American warrior. One who possesses the highest ethics and morals, who is kind, respectful, and caring toward society, comrades in arms, and non-combatants, and yet fully trained and ready to fight and win against any enemy who threatens our interests, our Constitution, and our way of life represents the American warrior.

Stephen Ambrose, the renowned historian, illustrated the idea powerfully in a 1999 lecture to cadets and faculty at West Point and in his critically acclaimed book *Citizen Soldiers*. Whenever German or Soviet or Japanese soldiers advanced into a foreign town during the Second World War, the population would hide as the presence of those soldiers meant rape, pillage, and destruction. When American soldiers entered a town, children and adults lined the streets because the presence of Americans meant freedom. Freedom from fear, freedom from tyranny and oppression, and the promise of a better life. While that story is certainly over-simplified, those American soldiers in what Tom Brokaw calls our "Greatest Generation" represented the idea of the American warrior. They were fierce toward their enemies and gentle toward their friends.

The pages of this volume contain the examples and insights of American warrior leaders, as well as those from other countries at other times. They demonstrate the criticality of true leadership and the consequences of incompetence, poor character, and immorality. The American warrior leader is trustworthy, inspires others through character and competence, vision and coherent plans, and serves and protects America, its allies, and non-combatants. As American warrior leaders, we cannot do more than our duty with honor for our country; we must never do less.

A number of common themes emerge from this anthology. Trust is the most critical leadership principle. It is gained through character and competence, and through a coherent vision and a rational set of programs designed to attain that goal. Trust provides the fundamental bedrock in the relationship between the leader and the led. Only when people trust their leaders will they follow them voluntarily. Trust is crucial across the unit as well; trusting relationships between peers and teams form the basis for organizational excellence. Mastering the fundamentals of skill competency and organizational values, primarily through training, establishes a level of discipline that enables the organization to mature. Mastery and maturity set the conditions for versatility, independence of thought, and initiative which sustain the vitality of an organization and keep it centered on its core competencies and values.

Mutual respect and a genuine sense of caring add fiber to the culture of trust, and thereby solidify the relationships between leaders and subordinates, as well as among peers. They enhance discipline and cohesion, and reinforce the environment of trust throughout the organization. Respect and caring are best transmitted by those "little things" that become so important in developing people's perceptions of the leader and the organization. Treating others with dignity, having a sense of humility, understanding the importance of people's contributions, and letting everyone know that they are valued members of the organization add to a leader's trustworthiness. No large training program, sensitivity session, or policy statement can substitute for the level of sincerity that a leader must demonstrate through action. Deeds are more important than words.

The best intentions, however, may not be enough. A gulf of perception can develop between leaders and followers. Leaders seeing things one way while the followers see them differently is a circumstance which no set of authoritative behaviors can predict, prevent, or rectify. Ultimately the leader's authority and success rests with the perception of those being led, and it therefore becomes the leader's responsibility to identify and rectify the problem. Providing a forum for subordinate feedback and assessment, when coupled with the trust that leaders will act to resolve the problems and not resent constructive criticism, is the surest way of getting such contrary perceptions into the open and taking steps to solve potential problems.

Leaders and organizations can never attain perfection. Development involves a series of trials and errors, triumphs and mistakes, steps forward and back, in a long journey toward becoming better through learning. This anthology suggests some frameworks for leadership and organizational effectiveness — the way things ought to be — as well as providing critical analyses of leaders' and organizations' efforts to work through the challenges. Each chapter will provide insight for leaders who wish to undertake the journey and make a difference.

Human interaction is chaotic. A multitude of ideas, agendas, and wills, sometimes competing subtly, sometimes at odds, coupled with external pressures and the uncertainty and ambiguity of the future, form the fog and friction of the human endeavor. The art of leadership is the ability to move an organization through that fog with direction and purpose. Navigating the fog successfully requires the development of a penetrating intellect. Learning how to think about leadership forms an important part of that intellect. This book is designed for those leaders who have the courage to think, the humility to read the ideas, perspectives, and experiences of others, and the passion to challenge themselves to sharpen their saber and hone their own art of leadership.

This book comes at an especially important time for the Armed Services. In an era of declining resources and benefits that is coupled with a dramatic increase in overseas deployments, morale in the armed services has reportedly sagged significantly. At the time these pages were written, the current solutions to these problems seem to be structural in nature – increase pay and benefits, or at least arrest their decline, and perhaps limit the number of deployments. However, it would be unfortunate to pursue such an approach exclusively. General Bruce Clarke once remarked that morale is the result of three concepts: knowing what you are doing is important, doing it well, and knowing it is appreciated. General Frederick Franks, discussing the Army in the early 1970s as it tried to restore its morale in the post-Vietnam era, argued that bringing the Army out of its malaise during those traumatic times was "an act of command will." Such insights alone suggest that the real solutions to problems of morale lay squarely in the realm of leadership. The pages of this book are filled with examples of leaders who recovered flagging morale and sustained battlefield effectiveness in conditions far more difficult and deadly than the environment in which we find ourselves today. The insights and reflections from and about such leaders are timeless. Furthermore, I hope a better appreciation for the idea and identity of the American warrior leader emerges from this volume. As fewer and fewer Americans have experience in uniform, it is incumbent upon military leaders to define and articulate our role and ethos as the guardians of our Republic.

ACKNOWLEDGEMENTS

When I asked one of my graduate school professors how his book was coming along, he replied it was going so well that it was practically writing itself. Perhaps that's part of the meaning of the old saw about inspiration and perspiration. I am not nearly as gifted as my professor, so this book never wrote itself. It is, however, the product of the inspiration and perspiration of many very talented people. I owe them a great debt.

I have had the good fortune to work with some of the Army's finest soldiers, and from those leaders, peers, and subordinates has come a great deal of inspiration. The list of those great people is entirely too long to record here. I had a number of mentors during my cadet days, and their example is what brought me back for a tour to teach at the Academy. In the 11th Armored Cavalry Regiment in Europe, 1st Squadron, 7th Cavalry at Fort Hood, University of Wisconsin-Madison, the Department of History and West Point and now in the 2nd Armored Cavalry Regiment I developed a passion for the military profession that was inculcated by those guardians of our Republic, both military and civilian. Great leaders, whether senior, peer, or subordinate leave a legacy in us that time cannot erase. This book is a product of their inspiration.

Regarding the inspiration and perspiration of this work in a more specific sense, I first and foremost need to thank the authors for so generously devoting their ideas, time, and energy to their chapters. Anyone who knows these authors can appreciate readily how very selective I was in seeking contributors, and necessarily so given the subject. I have gotten to know each of them as the book has evolved; at the beginning I knew several of them only by reputation. I began this project as a captain, and remain the junior member by measures of both military and academic rank. As the editor I was in the seemingly difficult position of providing feedback and criticism to my seniors, and had to do so with equal vigor to each chapter. Although we had plenty of discussion over some points of contention, never once did anyone, from major to professor to general, take issue with getting feedback from a subordinate. The willingness to listen and argue the issues rather than the collar is part of the reason why they are such great leaders. I sincerely appreciate their patience and their mentoring. I have certainly learned more from each of them than I have returned. The ideas herein are theirs; the errors remain the sole responsibility of the editor.

I must thank Colonel (Retired) Scott Wheeler for getting me in contact with so many of the authors and for his continuous support and friendship. Generals Bahnsen and Ulmer have been terrific mentors throughout this process. Alfredo Mycue and Kevin Farrell, in particular, helped my own ideas take shape through our many conversations and arguments together. Colonel Robert Doughty, Professor Linda Frey, and Professor Dennis Showalter provided invaluable feedback and advice on the early drafts, forming it into something a publisher would accept as a manuscript. I also want to recognize the authors of essays that, for reasons of overall length or subject, did not make the final version: Eugenia Kiesling, Kim Kagan, Paul Krajeski, Brian DeToy, and Stephen Biddle.

I am deeply indebted to the Army War College Foundation Press. Specifically, I would like to thank the "dream team" – Major General (Retired) Edward B. Atkeson and Colonel (Retired) Zane Finkelstein – for the countless hours they have spent on reading, proofing, and editing the manuscript, as well as the good humor, advice, insight, patience, and friendship they have brought to this project. It has been a sincere pleasure working with both of them.

Most importantly, I would like to thank my family: Christine, Lauren, Michael, Zachary, and Jacob, for their love and support. The balance between family and work is always a delicate one, and one at which I fall short routinely. This project has been in addition to an already heavy work-load, and the vast majority of my work on this volume has been during the wee hours after all of them have gone to bed. Nevertheless, their love knows no bounds. Their steadfast joy, love, and enthusiasm for life serve as a constant example of what is truly important: faith, family and friends, service, and the legacy we leave in the lives of those we touch — all of which must be balanced and unified by the principles of right living.

The views expressed herein are entirely those of the authors of this book and do not purport to represent any official statement, policy, or view of the Department of Defense, Department of the Army, United States Military Academy, or any other government office.

INTRODUCTION

by Lieutenant General Walter F. Ulmer, Jr.
(US Army, Retired)
former CEO of the Center for Creative Leadership

When Michael Shaara's award-winning depiction of the defining moments of the Battle of Gettysburg was first published in 1974, some historians wondered what more of value could be gleaned from yet another analysis of those terrible days in July 1863. Yet his *Killer Angels* proved again that issues of human character and temperament could be revisited dramatically and usefully through the experience of the battlefield. The motivating behaviors we describe as "leadership" obviously occur in a wide variety of settings. The PTA meeting in the high school cafeteria, the directors' session in the corporate boardroom, and the daily activities on the floor of the industrial plant all include leadership of one form or another. In our democracy, in particular, we prize widely distributed leadership, remain serious about local responsibility and initiative, and are rightly skeptical about the role of kings and chieftains. And modern businesses are discovering the wonderful efficiency of a workplace where hierarchical structure accommodates individual and team innovation, and where an informed sense of responsibility for organizational productivity is widely shared.

But the essence of leadership may be revealed conspicuously through individual actions in times of crisis. The battlefields of history provide a unique opportunity to examine key aspects of the leadership phenomenon. This is true even though an odd debate continues in some circles about whether or not such a thing as leadership exists at all. The central question in that discussion is whether circumstance produces leaders or individuals significantly influence events. After more than twenty centuries (under our current calendar, and many more before that) one might conclude that a mix of situation and individual personality together craft events and outcomes. However, the evidence is strongly in support of the thesis that leaders make history more than history makes leaders. Our continuing analysis of who leaders are, how they got that way, and why their examples and actions make a difference are surely relevant topics for the 21st Century.

All kinds of leadership are ultimately about results. Leaders of all seasons have focused the energy, commitment, and intellect of their followers or constituents on the problem at hand. Leaders traditionally have described an appealing vision of the desired future, developed trusting relationships, facilitated essential decision-making, set standards of performance, exemplified courage, kept hope alive, and rationalized sacrifice.

In his first chapter of this book (which represents one of many good reasons for adding this very diverse collection to our libraries) Christopher Kolenda sees as the essence of leadership "To inspire the spirit and act of following, regardless of external circumstances." The "external circumstances" surrounding military leadership are notoriously demanding, and not infrequently geopolitically consequential, but are not so different in context as to preclude the transference of concepts to other leadership environments. These chapters may highlight activities more dramatic and urgent than those of most "peacetime" occupations, but the competencies and passions of the effective military leader are essentially universal attributes of accomplished leaders in all walks of life.

Just as the Bible, Shakespeare, and Tolstoy collectively might be seen as covering adequately the whole gamut of human behavior, we might conclude that studies of Alexander, Caesar, and Frederick comprise a sufficient library on the subject of military leadership. However, this collection validates the utility of melding the lessons of the Romans and Greeks with the insights of recent practitioners such as Bahnsen, Cone, Christman, Potter, Sepp, Sullivan, and Woodmansee (there are some great leaders here!), combined with the special perspectives that the students of military history and leadership theory bring to the table. The mixing of these venues offers an opportunity for readers to continue to explore, to learn, and to evaluate. We read military examples that illuminate concepts and theories while reflecting on the most and least noble modes of human behavior.

For some reason it is easy to forget that there cannot be leaders without followers — or whatever term describes those who are inspired and moved by the character and behavior of others. In Douglas Lute's discussion of "followership," there is the observation that "In practice the authority on leadership rests with the led." This is both a seminal and a controversial point within leadership studies. Its controversial element stems from a lingering ambiguity in the definition of "leadership." If by "leadership" or "leader" we are referring to all individuals who are appointed or elected to positions of authority, then "leadership" is a noun and "leading" may have nothing to do with motivating potential followers. If we adhere to the definitions of Kolenda and others such as John Gardner where respect and trust are crucial, then indeed the only reliable assessment of the leader comes from the followers. It is this latter definition that permits us to report that some CEO's and presidents and kings and superintendents and generals were leaders, and some were definitely not. And it is this latter definition that confounds many observers of the leadership scene who are troubled by the criterion problem. How in fact can we assess accurately the effectiveness of a leader in his leadership role? This issue is particularly germane in hierarchical organizations such as most businesses and all militaries.

The issue of definition is present in one form or another within the various chapters of this book. Perhaps we should discriminate more clearly between an executive's roles as leader (motivator/visionary), manager (resource allocator), and responsible authority (commander/CEO). Or maybe we should simply admit that except in the most unusual cases, individuals who are "leading" something must integrate their roles and adapt their styles and select their motivational or coercive source as fits the situation at hand. Military "leaders" are provided awesome decisionmaking and punitive powers, and nobody who has a whit of practical experience on the battlefield would change that. Increasingly, however, because of advances in technology and the expectations of individuals in modern societies, the use of positional power is becoming a more delicate matter in formal organizations. The described "decimation" of the ranks of failed Roman units is not only illegal (and in fact unthinkable) for today's commanders, but the notion that such techniques would produce sustained effectiveness in battle have long ago been discarded. Both societal and technological change place more demands on today's military leaders than in any prior time in history by a clear order of magnitude.

Still, there is both a penchant and a utilitarian requirement to evaluate leaders' effectiveness. How can we select, or elect, or implement plans to develop leaders if the criteria for their success is vague? We have contributed to the complexity of this issue by our insensitivity to the criticality of the span of time over which we evaluate leader success. If we value only the outcome of the immediate battle, or merely the next quarter's report of profit and loss, then our yardstick will be set to disregard long-term consequences of whatever methods were used to attain immediate results.

Certainly there are situations in which the criteria for instant results take precedence over any concern for the future posture of the organization. The war cannot be won if all battles are lost — although we know that the contrary is not true. So there is reason to expect immediate, discernible, measurable results from a leader's performance. Most of our institutions focus almost exclusively on such measures, implicitly justifying a wide range of "means" to gain specific "ends." And if the followers are considered relatively expendable compared to the perceived criticality of the immediate goal, there is little extrinsic reward for the leader in preparing for the future. The issue here is not the need to accomplish today's mission, but that it is usually imperative that we do so while conserving resources for tomorrow. Possibly our inattention to the intricacies of measuring leader success is stimulated in part by overuse of the battlefield analogy. Preparing for battle, which consumes most of the time of military formations, carries a different alignment of priorities of leadership methods than does battle itself. Yet it is important to note that Farrell comments on the *sustained* excellence of German small units in World War II; there is no doubt that from the inside of the unit there is limitless appreciation for the leader who minimizes casualties while meeting mission requirements. Showalter concludes that in Frederick's army "Compulsion in its various forms might keep men in the ranks. It could not make them fight. More precisely, it could not keep them fighting."

Nevertheless, it is easy to rationalize short-term, marginally productive or dysfunctional leadership styles in non-battle situations when that style might be appropriate during the heat of a firefight where time is really of the essence and hopefully trust and the leader's credibility have already been established. It is also noteworthy that the erosion of organizational effectiveness can be a quiet cancer, initially difficult to discern amid the noise of current events, and so subtle that only the most discerning observer can catch the change until too late in the game. This reality — the difficulty in assessing strategic results in a world captivated by instant winning — may be the principal cause for the lingering presence of the leader-versus-tyrant issue.

Another issue within contemporary discussions of leadership concepts is whether or not the term "leadership" includes automatically a moral component. In other words, can one be a "leader" if he is not concerned with the moral or ethical outcomes of his leadership? Recent dissertations on the subject of transformational leadership by such authorities as Burns and Bass provide a construct that requires us to explore the question of "leadership for what societal good?" before determining whether or not one deserves the appellation of "leader." Ethical issues always are entwined with leadership, either on the smaller scale in terms of the propriety of a leader's options to "manipulate" followers, or on the macro scale such as in the chapter reviewing Curtis LeMay's strategic bombing. No doubt what is considered ethical depends in part on historical context, but it is notable throughout these readings that the authors both civilian and military are clearly cognizant of the inherent moral and ethical issues associated with leadership. As this book goes to press public discussions are ongoing regarding the relevance of a leader's general character to job performance. With us since Greek and Roman times as we read in these chapters, the "character issue" is not resolved to everyone's satisfaction. We can say with certainty that "character flaws" are significant in practice if they lead to erosion of follower trust in the judgment or loyalty or commitment of the leader.

Physical courage, physical capacity, remain essential attributes of military service, and the description of Special Forces training reminds us of that reality. It is one of the realities that continues to distinguish the military from most other professions, since fat lawyers or frail professors do little automatic disservice to their professions. Kingseed's description of American soldiers under fire in the Normandy invasion of 1944 could translate to the heroics of Alexander or of the U.S. Army Rangers in Mogadishu. Neither the immediate ferocity of land battle nor the elements of heroism have much changed in the past 2000 years. But moral courage may be even more priceless to the military profession — not a substitute for, but a necessary companion to, physical courage. These pages are full of conspicuous examples of selfless behavior and unconditional devotion to duty that should inspire all of us in our own work.

The more we read into history, the more justification we have for being very humble about our discoveries about leadership. The notions of command climate, subordinate initiative, and organizational culture were not lost on the ancients, although such concepts were not formalized by them. We probably have advanced the state of the art in this regard, as the chapter on the creation of command climates thoughtfully indicates. A conscious model for attending to the organizational environment has been one of the constructive products of behavioral science research over the last couple decades. Unit cohesion growing from trust and shared values, and obedience entwined with creativity are the keys that perceptive leaders pursue relentlessly. Sullivan's neat metaphor of the jazz combo plays directly into the subject of orchestration of command climate. We now have in the American and other militaries an increasing use of surveys assessing the organizational climate, a companion trend to that of industry. We also have more routine use of psychometric instruments in deciphering the components of personality that push us toward one or another style of leadership. These chapters provide a memorable excursion into the personalities of formidable leaders. We see some of the dark sides as well as the possibilities that altruism and selflessness can bring, knowing that the specters of despair, arrogance, and rigidity lurk over the shoulders of all men of power and position.

There is some discussion in the current literature on American military futures about a predicted "Revolution in Military Affairs." As noted in this book, it derives from the recent and continuing application of technology to information collection, processing, and dissemination. At issue is the impact of this technology on the battlefield and on the military personnel who will be more and more supplied with machines for handling data. Soon nearly all the soldiers in a line company may "see" the battlefield as well as and simultaneously with their senior commander. Information will pass up, around, and down at unheard of speeds, engulfing commanders and staffs and small teams in floods of data. So, can information circuitry replace leadership? Can remote sensors and digitized command posts somehow render courage, candor, and commitment irrelevant? Many careful observers of organizational change have concluded that the future battlefield, full of speed and enhanced lethality and smaller operating units and an urgency for local decisionmaking to adapt to rapidly changing conditions, will require more and better leadership, not less. The thinking is that with routinely widely dispersed information combined with the need for local innovation to move inside the enemy's own decision cycle there must be particularly strong mutual trust between leader and follower. There will be less latitude in acceptable leader style because expectations for high quality leadership in all sectors are growing, despite periodic public episodes of leader misbehavior.

This book addresses these issues and more. There is a full meal here, and some of it is deep stuff. The assembly of people and ideas presents a pocket library of notable deeds and adventures of the past along with what should be reassuring words from the current generation of scholars and practicing leaders. It is just worth more than the price of admission to roam through these pages and once again be captured by the heroics, prodded by the mistakes, and motivated by the best parts of leadership.

Section I

Ancient and Modern
Concepts of Leadership

Chapter One

What is Leadership?
Some Classical Ideas

by Christopher D. Kolenda

Strong commanders are those who can impress upon their troops that they must be followed even through fire or danger of any kind . . . people follow because they recognize his qualities; it would be reasonable to say that a man like this goes to war with strength in his hand, since so many hands are prepared to obey his mind's directions; and great indeed is the man who can use his mind rather than his physical might for great achievements.[1]

Xenophon

It may seem a bit curious to discuss ancient Greek and Roman ideas of leadership as we move into the twenty-first century. After all, haven't things changed a bit over the last two millennia? Aren't new ideas on leadership necessary for the new millennium? The answers to both questions are yes and no. Certainly advances in technology and organization have made the challenges and techniques associated with leader competencies somewhat different. Yet, while the technologies have changed, the very human dimension of leadership has remained constant. The task of a leader, then and now, is to inspire the best in others so they can contribute meaningfully to the overall good of the organization. True leaders touch the soul of others, turning the souls (as Plato put it) toward a good purpose. By doing so, leaders can inspire in others a devotion toward that purpose that enables people to overcome any odds, face any dangers, to achieve it.

Anyone who has studied those leaders who have motivated others to win in the face of overwhelming odds can begin to comprehend that special magic of leadership. They also know that the inspiration of such spirit cannot simply be boiled down to a process of aligning resources to accomplish a certain task. They find unsatisfying the attempt to reduce leadership to simplistic formulas, step-by-step models, "mystical" leadership secrets, or maddening diagrams and flow-charts. While such devices can be read quickly and make for neat cards that one can place in a pocket and produce in time of doubt, such simplifications miss that very special spirit that everyone calls leadership although they may find such essence difficult to quantify. What makes the study of the ancient Greeks and Romans so satisfying and important is that many of them sought to explore the essence of that spirit in all of its depth, complexity, and beauty. They sought to understand human nature and in doing so they arrived at ideas on leadership that transcend time and context.

Other objections to the study of the classics might be that the rapid pace of change brought about by the "information age" renders them out-of-date, and that the contextual problems of human sensitivity require fundamentally new approaches to leadership. I suspect the ancients would differ with both suppositions. First, while the consequences of failure to keep pace with change today might result in lost business opportunities or technological obsolescence, failure to anticipate and adapt to change for the ancients meant the collapse of the government or the destruction of the state. Dealing with the rapid pace of change was a necessity of survival. Second, the issues of human sensitivity and meaning have never been separated from the art of leadership. Today we tell a leader to be himself; the ancients told him to "Know Thyself." Today we highlight the ideas of character and competence; the ancient Greeks taught the same but called it *areté* (excellence, moral virtue). Today we discuss vision; the ancients discussed the end (*telos*) and the idea (*eidos*). Today we demand respect and caring from leaders; the ancients conceptualized the moral equality of all humanity and the duty of the leader to be the caretaker of the people. Today we use values to inculcate identity and appropriate behavior; the ancients used laws.

This essay will focus primarily on the concepts of leadership articulated by Xenophon, Plato, Aristotle, and Cicero, each of whom devoted considerable attention to the idea. Leadership to them was the art of inspiring the spirit and act of following, regardless of external circumstances. In more metaphysical terms, it was the art of turning the soul toward some purpose. Leadership required an understanding of human nature. Armed with this understanding, these ancient philosophers argued that the foundations for effective leadership were *areté* and vision — excellence in skill and character and an understanding of the idea of the end-state. Leadership was the bridge between the personal, interpersonal, and cosmological (visionary) levels. These ancient philosophers sought to articulate principles that, when applied consistently, would enable a leader to be effective as that bridge. They did not offer checklists or recipes. They sought to establish a standard for what leadership *ought* to be. This essay will synthesize the major components of their thoughts, and in so doing will illustrate the lasting value of the classics in the study of leadership.

DEFINING LEADERSHIP: SOME CLASSICAL AND MODERN PERSPECTIVES

Xenophon, a pupil of Socrates who led the retreat of the ten thousand from Persia to Greece in 400 BC, was the first to record a definition of leadership in the western world. According to classical historian Neal Wood, Xenophon "was apparently the first western thinker to be deeply concerned with both political and military theory. One result of the dual concern was a momentous intellectual discovery: the idea of an army as a community to be founded and maintained by the general."[2] For Xenophon the central political problem revolved around how to create a rational, orderly, and effective community while respecting the freedom and dignity of the individuals within it. In *Oeconomicus* (Estate-Manager), Xenophon tells us that he regards "it as highly indicative of good leadership when people obey someone without coercion and are prepared to remain by him during times of danger."[3] The true test for a leader, according to Xenophon, is whether people will follow of their own *free will* even during times of immense hardship.[4] The reliance upon force is antithetical to Xenophon's ideal leader because coercion causes a subordinate to perform a task against his will; tyranny, in other words, replaces leadership.

In a similar vein, Lord Moran, a British Army doctor in the First World War and Churchill's physician during the Second, argues in *The Anatomy of Courage* that leadership in the practical sense is "the capacity to frame plans which will succeed and the faculty of persuading others to carry them out in the face of death."[5] Success, according to Moran, is the bridge between the two. Once people are convinced that the leader can "build for victory" they will gladly commit themselves to carrying out the leader's orders even under extreme circumstances.[6] In essence, the ability to persuade others to risk their lives voluntarily rests implicitly in the trust they have in the leader's character and ability to win.

James MacGregor Burns, in his Pulitzer Prize winning volume, *Leadership*, makes more explicit what is implicit in the definitions offered by Xenophon and Moran. For Burns, leadership is the process of "leaders inducing followers to act for certain goals that represent the values and motivations — the wants and needs, the aspirations and expectations — of both leaders and followers."[7] The relationship remains purposeful, but Burns adds the assumption that the values and motivations of both the leader and the followers must be identical, or at least similar enough to avoid conflict, for the inducement to work. Missing, however, is the crucial variable suggested by both Xenophon and Moran: that leaders can persuade others to perform an arguably counterintuitive act, placing their lives in jeopardy, voluntarily.

The issue of persuasion deserves further treatment. If leadership is purposeful, if it is the act of influencing others to accomplish a mission, then what role does coercion play? Does the use of force fit into the notion of ideal leadership? Is the concept of voluntary obedience, as suggested by both Xenophon and Lord Moran, a necessary precondition for true leadership, or is the accomplishment of the mission, regardless of means, the proper standard?

The ancient Greeks and Romans developed a framework to deal with this very problem: *pietho* (persuasion) was opposed to *bia* (force). Persuasion was the "natural" medium for a "statesman" or leader to influence human beings, since humans were separated from animals by the gift of reason. Force, the absence of reason, was the way of the tyrant — it was unnatural in human relationships and fitting only for beasts. As Xenophon explains through the mouth of Socrates in *Memorabilia*, "persuasion produces the same results without danger in a friendly spirit," while "violence is not to be expected of those who exercise reason; such conduct belongs to those who have strength without judgment."[8] Plato, in his *Republic*, develops the *pietho/bia* discourse further to account for the difference between the philosopher-king and the tyrant:[9]

pietho	*bia*
persuasion	force
leading	coercion
follower/free	subject/slave
just	unjust
human	beast
natural	unnatural

According to Plato, people erred if they coupled the king or statesman and the tyrant. "And if we call the art of those who use compulsion tyrannical or something of the sort and the voluntary care of voluntary [people] political, may we not declare that he who possesses this latter art of caretaking is really the true king and statesman?"[10]

Cicero, the first century BC Roman politician and philosopher, shares the sentiments of Plato. In *De Re Publica* (The Republic), Cicero argues that only the true statesman, the "good, wise and skillful guardian and protector," who rules for the practical interests and self-respect of the citizens can truly be called the guide and pilot of a nation.[11]   Once the ruler ceases using persuasion and merely uses the threat of punishment, the government is no longer one fitting for rational human beings.   This is not to say that a leader should never use coercion under compelling circumstances or when principles are at stake, but that in the ideal sense a leader would not have to do so.   Once a leader uses coercion rather than persuasion, he or she is no longer, by definition, leading.

For these ancient Greeks and Romans, as they struggled philosophically to define the nature of a ruler who could harmonize the need for order with the freedom and dignity of the citizens, the standard was quite clear: the true statesman appealed to reason to *persuade* others to follow.   The citizens would follow willingly because they trusted the statesman to rule for their benefit. The relationship was natural and thus ideal.   The tyrant, who ruled for himself and to the detriment of the community had to resort to coercion — treating humans as beasts — to compel them to do his bidding, thus fostering a relationship that deviated from "nature."[12]

The standard for leadership was grounded in the use of persuasion to accomplish a mission rather than the use of force.   In this sense, leadership was the art of inspiring the spirit and act of following, regardless of external circumstances. People who could gain the willing obedience of others, even in the direst of circumstances, met the standard of leadership. They did so by appealing to the best that was in others. As such, the leader was a force of positive integration, one who, through his or her character, ability, and vision earned the admiration of others, inspired them to develop the best in themselves and motivated them to accomplish a clearly defined goal.

ARETÉ AND VISION: THE PAIDEIA OF LEADERSHIP

To define leadership as the art of inspiring the spirit and act of following may be simple enough in theory, but what enables a leader to accomplish this? How does a person develop the ability to become a leader? Are leaders born or made? Ultimately a theory of leadership begins with an assumption about human nature. While it is commonplace to discuss human nature in terms of fundamentally good, fundamentally bad, or a "blank slate," a number of ancient philosophers had a slightly different perspective. They saw people in terms of what they can be and should be. Etched in the rock alongside the stairs that one traveled up to visit the oracle at Delphi were the words, "Know Thyself." The study of leadership necessarily begins with a concept of humanity.

Plato explored the nature of humanity from the perspective of the soul (*psyche*). In the *Republic* he argued that the human soul is divided into three parts, the rational (*logos*), the spirited, and the desirous. Most critical to Plato was the rational part, since reason is what separated humans from animals. Operating from the assumptions that the cosmos is governed by pure reason (*Logos*), and that reason is the part of the soul that enables human beings to bring order to their lives, to discipline their desires, and to think and persuade, Plato came to the conclusion that reason is something shared between the human and the divine. Since we had the gift of reason, and reason was good, then a person's *telos*, or ultimate purpose, was to assimilate as far as possible to the *Logos*.

In Book VII of the *Republic*, Plato uses the allegory of the cave to illustrate the concept of movement toward the *Logos*. Human beings, he argues, have a confused understanding of the good because they do not see things as they really are. People are bound as if by chains in the bottom of a cave. A light is behind them, and objects pass between them and the light. All people see are the shadows of things on the wall of the cave. Since people know no other reality, they take these shadows to be what is real. Although he uses objects to illustrate his point, what Plato really means is that people have a confused understanding about what is good. They do not know what the cardinal virtues of wisdom, justice, courage, and moderation really are, and since they cannot grasp these, they are content to define the good as the objects that they can comprehend. This problem opens the path to materialism and, more problematically for Plato, to relativism. The subtext of the allegory is that, being utterly confused about the good, people are utterly confused about themselves. It is impossible to "know thyself" if all one sees is a shadow of the self and others.

Education, primarily through philosophy, promotes a change to this condition of unreality. According to Plato education is not putting sight into blind eyes, it is the art of turning the soul from bondage to freedom, from darkness to light, from ignorance to truth. The turning of the soul toward the light is painful and blinding at first. The ascent is long and steep and difficult. But once there, the soul can see what "is" rather than what "seems" to be. In this "realm of the forms" the person can see wisdom, justice, courage, and moderation as they are and thus can apprehend the good. The journey, however, is not yet complete. The soul, seeing things as they truly are, has the duty to return to the cave and help other souls break the chains of ignorance and make the journey up. The opening lines of Plato's *Republic*, "I [Socrates] went down to Pireaus," symbolizes Socrates' return to the cave to lead others up. Socrates' sense of duty is magnified by the certainty that, while he will help others make the turn, he himself will be executed for doing so.

Plato's *Republic* has long been regarded as one of the greatest educational treatises of all time. The Greek word for education is *paideia*, but the Greeks meant more by the term than just schooling. *Paideia* encapsulates the development of a person from childhood to maturity, from living in a *polis* (city-state) to becoming a citizen of it. People, for the Greeks, were biological facts. Citizens were social artifacts. *Paideia* represented the construction of an individual into a person worthy of citizenship and able to strengthen the *polis* and the members in it. Man, to use Aristotle's famous phrase, is a political animal. People reach fulfillment not as individuals in the "state of nature" but in the context of political life in service to the state and to others. Only in the social and political arena could people exercise their *areté* (excellence, moral virtue), their character and abilities. Such a life of meaningful service, contributing to the common good, enabled a citizen to reach his *telos*, his end-state. A person reached human completeness as a citizen of the *polis* through the exercise of virtue.

For these particular Greek and Roman political and moral philosophers, the concepts of "know thyself" and human nature were seen from the perspective of the end-state. Human nature was not simply what one was, but what one *ought* to be. Whether from the start point of reason (*logos*) in the soul, the social instinct, or the "seeds of virtue," the full development of these endowments was the *paideia* of humanity. To paraphrase Johann Wolfgang von Goethe, treat a man as he is and he will remain as he is; treat him as he can be and should be, and he will become what he can be and should be.

"Know Thyself" in other words was not simply understanding your own weaknesses and strengths and arriving at solutions to overcome the former and highlight the latter. To know thyself meant to know *what* you are, to know human nature. It is only with an understanding of human nature that a person could begin to develop a coherent moral philosophy and idea of leadership. From their concept of human nature, the ancient philosophers were able to develop the concepts of *areté* and vision they believed were so central to the idea of leadership. Indeed, it was only a person

with *areté* and vision who could begin to inspire in others the willingness to follow voluntarily.

Areté is best translated as excellence or moral virtue. According
to Aristotle *areté* is the combination of what a person can do (competence), and what a person invariably is (character).[13] Competence,
a particular expertise in a subject matter or duty, while difficult to
acquire is nevertheless a simple concept to understand. Character,
however, is problematic on both counts. While both ancient and
modern scholars have underscored the importance of character as
a fundamental prerequisite for effective leadership, defining the
nature of character is a difficult endeavor.

Aristotle, for instance, considered moral virtue (character) a habit
— the sum total of our daily choices of right over wrong, and not
something implanted by nature. People are equipped by nature
with the ability to cultivate the moral virtues, but only habit can
make them moral.[14] The development of character thus had an
educational and an experiential component. One had to both
understand the difference between right and wrong and form the
habit of choosing right to be called a person of character.

Cicero, in a slightly different vein, believed that all human beings
possessed "certain seeds" which, if nurtured, would enable one to
develop moral virtue.[15] Delving deeper into the subject, Cicero
argued that a person's complete character was the result of four
interactions. Two of the elements were implanted by "Nature." The
first was universal — people were all endowed alike with the gift of
reason and hence an innate regard for the "good" and the four cardinal virtues (wisdom, justice, courage, and moderation). The second was assigned to individuals in particular in the form of various
qualities or aptitudes: mental, physical, emotional, etc. The third
element was the result of external circumstances or chance such as
a person's upbringing or social and economic background. The last
was a person's own choice: the type of person he or she strove to
be. Together, these four coalesced to form the total character.[16]

Character, he believed, could be positive or negative, depending
upon whether the person chose the right path in life (to cultivate
the cardinal virtues). It could also be strong or weak — the forti-

tude to follow a set of convictions or merely to drift with the current of opinion.[17] As a result, character can be divided, although somewhat simplistically, into four types: positive and strong, positive and weak, negative and weak, negative and strong. The first embodies what should be expected of leaders (a force of positive integration), the middle ones generally lack the ability to lead, while the latter is antithetical to the type of person who should be in a position of responsibility.

Moral virtue, or what we would consider today as "character" in the strong, positive sense, formed a critical foundation for the leader. Aristotle, in his advice to orators, considered *areté* to be the most effective form of persuasion. Along with intelligence and goodwill, moral virtue was essential in winning the trust, confidence, and conviction of others.[18] Achieving *areté* was a person's *telos* (end-state or goal in life), the fullest expression of what it was to be a complete human being. Character, as a result, has a sort of magnetic effect; people are naturally drawn to those who have cultivated this ability in themselves. Xenophon, in fact, considered that Socrates made those who spent time with him hope that by following his example, they would develop the same character.[19] Moral character, best expressed in the four cardinal virtues, wisdom, courage, justice, and moderation, formed what Cicero called the "principles of right living," that enabled one to move toward what Plato referred to as the "good."[20]

It would be a mistake to assume that the development of *areté* was purely self-interested and had little to do with the obligation to defend one's state and way of life.[21] *Areté* was political virtue; its development and use hinged upon social and political interaction. One could be "innocent" by living the secluded life of a hermit, as the Cynics advocated, but such a person could not attain virtue because that required an understanding of right and wrong and the choice to do right in the face of the option to do wrong. One could also live a social life detached from civic life, as the Epicureans maintained, but this would demonstrate a lack of courage and a dereliction of the duty to promote and defend justice in the state. Virtue was the moral order of the soul; justice was the moral order of the state. The two concepts of order were inextricably bound together. The tumultuous context of the ancient Greek city-states and the Roman Republic (especially in Cicero's time) made political and military service to the state a necessity for survival. Perhaps no better example of this sense of duty was the death of Socrates (who did fight as a soldier of Athens in his younger days). When his followers offered to help him escape after he was sentenced to death for "corrupting the youth" and "introducing false gods," Socrates refused. To escape would be a violation of the principles Socrates sought to instill in his followers; doing so would also deprive Athens of the greatest proof of how far the city had fallen from justice.

The notion of *areté* as the *telos* of an individual allowed for an expanded sense of the end-state in the form of vision. Vision was not a word the Greeks used, but the concepts of *telos* and *eidos* – end-state and idea – express the term nicely. Believing that the order of the city and the order of the soul were linked conceptually, Plato argued that an understanding of divine order would offer a pattern or guide for the proper order in political and individual life. The task of the leader was to separate out the idea from all other things and be able to distinguish it in argument (dialectic) with others so that it would meet the test of "being" rather than that of mere opinion.[22] The journey up into the "Light" in the allegory of the cave to comprehend what really "is" represents the attempt to discover the "Idea" of order as the end-state. "But in heaven . . perhaps, a pattern is laid up for the man who wants to see and found a city within himself on the basis of what he sees. It doesn't make any difference whether it is or will be somewhere. For he would mind the things of this city alone, and of no other."[23] The journey back down into the cave to turn the souls of others can be seen as the effort to articulate the "Idea" of the end-state to others and inspire them to make the journey up as well.

Aristotle and Cicero endeavored to bring Plato's abstraction to more concrete form. Aristotle regarded the state as an association for some purpose, and this purpose was "political" because it aimed at securing the "good life" for its citizens. The aim and the end of the state was perfection, and so an understanding of the good life expressed the vision of the state. As Aristotle puts it, "The well-being of all men depends upon two things: one is the right choice of target, of the end to which actions should tend, the other lies in finding the actions that lead to that end."[24] The function of the rulers of the state was to define the good life and then develop laws and make decisions that contributed directly toward it.

While Aristotle sought the good life in terms of what was possible for humans to accomplish, Cicero pursued a different path. Arguing that the state was an association of justice, Cicero sought to define the just state as an extension of the Natural Law by which the Divine *Logos* (Reason) ordered the cosmos. "True law is right reason in agreement with nature," he claimed, and this law is unchanging and everlasting.[25] For a state to be just, it had to align its laws with Natural Law or else the state would deviate from nature. Cicero thus sought in his *Republic* and *Laws* to define Natural Law and illustrate the link between divine and human order and reason. With the whole universe as a commonwealth united in justice, Cicero saw Natural Law as the vision for justice in the state.[26] While the laws of each particular state would vary over time and by culture, Natural Law remained the absolute guide, the vision, for determining justice in each.

What emerges from these arguments is that vision is a mental creation, an idea of the end-state. Whether in the form of the "Idea," the good life, or Natural Law, vision serves as the guiding light that directs the actions of leaders, subordinates, and organizations. A successful vision "turns the soul." To do so it must express a meaningful link between the individual, the organization, and the idea that inspires a spirit of devotion and duty.

Areté (moral virtue, excellence) and vision thus form the *paideia* (education) of leadership for Xenophon, Plato, Aristotle, and Cicero; a *paideia* that operates on a number of different levels simultaneously. The idea of humanity linked by reason to the divine led to the concept of *areté* as the goal of the individual.[27] The leader had to possess the four cardinal virtues of wisdom, justice, courage, and moderation, the virtues that most closely resembled the human ability to reach the good; knowledge of the virtues and experience in choosing right over wrong were the schools of *areté*. Such a leader became the model that inspired others to follow. At a higher level, intellectual development enabled a leader to understand and formulate the idea of the end-state. Without such vision as a start point, *areté* at the individual and collective levels was not possible. Ascertaining vision, the leader's journey back down into the cave to lead others up by helping them turn their souls represented the *paideia* of individuals and organizations from darkness to light, from ignorance to truth, from infancy to maturity, from chaos to order. The leader was the bridge between the individual, collective, and cosmological (visionary) levels.

PRINCIPLES

From this brief sketch of some ideas on leadership from Xenophon, Plato, Aristotle, and Cicero, it is possible to deduce some principles that they believed should guide the relationship between the leader and the led. These ancient philosophers clearly believed in the existence of transcendent principles that provided order and stability in the chaotic and dangerous times in which they lived. The principles of trustworthiness, respect, and caring provided the link between the personal qualities of *areté* and vision and the interpersonal nature of leadership. They served as a guide toward resolving problems of conflicting loyalties, and provided a consistent method for action in situations in which right and wrong were not clearly defined. In short, using principles as the guide for decision-making rendered the choice of the one versus the many irrelevant. Decisions based upon principles would naturally result in what is best for the one and the many.

Trustworthiness was the dominant principle that expressed the two-fold conception of *areté* (competence and character), and the credibility of the leader's vision. It combines the ability and willingness to act in good faith, regardless of circumstances, toward the right purpose. The leader must demonstrate the skill and competence to instill in others the confidence that the leader knows what he or she is doing. Also, the leader must have the foundation in character to distinguish right from wrong and have the moral courage do what is right. Certainly, a person of good ethics who is nevertheless incompetent in a given duty inspires as little trust as a competent scoundrel. Competence and character must co-exist in a leader. In essence, the concept of trustworthiness is the art of setting the example on both counts.

In terms of interpersonal relationships and in ethically problematic situations, these ancients argued that a leader must make decisions based upon the cardinal virtues rather than out of favor to a specific person or group. Only by upholding those virtues and practicing them consistently could the leader do what was best for everyone. Trustworthiness meant the application of the virtues as the principal guide in resolving interpersonal and ethical dilemmas.[28] The trustworthy leaders, Cicero and Xenophon believed, were those who were simple and genuine, and who set the example in terms of skill and the cardinal virtues — "there was nothing that men did not think they could accomplish under such leadership."[29]

Critical to building the inner substance of trustworthiness for these ancient philosophers was the notion of *sophrosyne* (moderation). *Sophrosyne* means the wisdom of self-mastery and self-discipline, what Cicero calls "the science of doing the right thing at the right time."[30] According to Neal Wood, the Socratic principle of self-discipline is central to Xenophon's conception of leadership.[31] For Xenophon, those who lack self-discipline are absolutely slavish, and no "slave" to money, luxury, glory, sex, etc. could become a trustworthy leader.[32] Slavishness showed a lack of courage, the inability to discipline the desires, and thus an absence of the inner strength to choose right from wrong. Only a person, according to Cicero, who was free from worries produced by "slavishness" and indifferent toward outward circumstances could lead the dignified and consistent life fitting for a statesman.[33] Trustworthiness results, in part, from the self-discipline to acquire the skills and moral virtue necessary for competence and character plus the courage to choose right from wrong. Only in this way could the leader properly serve the followers and the state.

The concept of vision is also a part of trustworthiness. Quite simply, people will follow the person who knows best what ought to be done and can communicate that intention in a practical and meaningful way to each member of the organization.[34] To inspire the spirit and act of following the leader must articulate a credible and understandable vision of "the good" that touches the soul of others and infuses them with a common spirit. By linking the concepts of God, human beings, and civilization through reason, these philosophers believed that they had developed a framework for the creation of such a vision.

The second principle, *Respect*, was the genuine regard a leader shows for others. Such regard is only possible with the recognition that all people share a common humanity and as a result command a level of respect as morally equal human beings. Although the notion of moral equality might seem like a late twentieth century concept due to the social Darwinism and racism that has plagued the world, only Aristotle of the four philosophers discussed in this essay held a decidedly ethno-centric view. He still maintained the importance of respect within that framework, however. In his advice to political leaders, Aristotle counseled that by treating others with dignity the statesman would inspire in them respect instead of fear.[35] Plato, Aristotle's mentor, never ventured beyond the context of the Greek world in his philosophy, but when he argued in Book VII of the *Republic* that the power to turn toward the light was in the soul of each, the intellectual foundation was set for the concept of a common humanity. Xenophon, Plato's fellow pupil of Socrates, was not far from the mark in the *Cyropaideia* (Education of Cyrus the Great of Persia) as he described the ability of the Persian King to unite different peoples willingly into a single empire.

The concept of moral equality came to fruition with the Stoic philosophers after the conquests of Persia and parts of India by Alexander the Great (336-323 BC). The political problem of how to unite different peoples into a single kingdom fostered the development of the "brotherhood of humanity." Consistent with this idea, Cicero argued that true leaders ("kings") hold all people in an equality of right and show reverence toward them because all are bound by a natural fellowship and union. There is no difference in kind (nature) between people, he asserts, for they share reason in common with each other and with God. In fact, "there is no human being of any race who, if he finds a guide, cannot attain to virtue."[36]

The notion of humility was also imbedded in the principle of respect. For the ancient Greeks, hubris (overweening pride, arrogance) meant the folly of equating oneself with the gods. Hubris preceded ruin; the one guilty of hubris moved outside the bounds of reason and thus set himself up for the fall. If a person equated himself with the gods, then the advice and counsel of others was neither needed nor desired. Furthermore, elevating oneself to the level of the gods opened the way for abuse and tyrannical practices. The centrality of the problem of hubris in ancient Greek culture is evident in Greek tragedy. The so-called "tragic flaw" of most tragic heroes and heroines centered primarily on hubris. Moreover, the histories of leaders such as Alcibiades, Alexander, Julius Caesar, and a number of Roman Emperors are designed to illustrate the consequences of hubris. Leaders, the ancient philosophers believed, must have the humility to listen to the arguments of others, take in their advice, and arrive at reasoned decisions.

Caring for the needs of others formed a third principle of leadership. Plato saw leadership as the shepherd's art; the leader was the human caretaker whose duty it was to provide for the needs of the flock over the needs of himself.[37] Xenophon argued that everything a leader does must demonstrate to his subordinates that he constantly thinks of their welfare and works for their benefit. Securing the happiness of one's followers was the critical test of the ideal leader, for "those who are well looked after turn out to be grateful and grow in their loyalty."[38] True caring, for Xenophon, came in the form of providing for the physical, mental, and spiritual well-being of others through justice and generosity; discipline went hand-in-hand with caring.[39]

Cicero also argued that caring was a component of justice. The leader should be a steward or trustee, conducting his affairs for the "benefit of those entrusted to one's care, not of those to whom it is entrusted." Only in this way — by winning the hearts of men and attaching them to his service — could a general or statesman accomplish great things for the benefit of the state.[40]

The art of genuine caring forms a critical pillar in the art of leadership. Words are not enough. People must come to believe by the virtue of the leader's actions that he or she is willing to act for their benefit. A benefit, however, should not be confused with a short-term change in mood at the expense of long-term happiness. A benefit by nature cannot be injurious to its recipients. Caring, in essence, is the art of doing what is best for those whom the leaders serve.

The concepts of *areté* and vision form the foundations of effective leadership. The principles of trustworthiness, respect, and caring add consistency to the leader's decision-making and behavior, acting as the guidelines for interpersonal relationships. Principles become the catalyst for the credibility of a leader's *areté* and vision. The ideal leader (or the "real" leader in Plato's conception) inspires the spirit and act of following by "turning the soul" of others toward some good purpose. According to Plato:

> *This, then, is the end, let us declare, of the web of the statesman's activity, the direct interweaving of the characters of restrained and courageous men, when the kingly science has drawn them together by friendship and community of sentiment into a common life, and having perfected the most glorious and best of all textures, clothes with it all the inhabitants of the state . . . holds them together by this fabric, and omitting nothing which ought to belong to a happy state, rules and watches over them.*[41]

While Plato expressed the statesman in abstract terms, Xenophon used historical romance. *Cyropaideia* (the Education of Cyrus the Great of Persia), admirably illustrates Xenophon's concept of what a leader ought to be. Xenophon begins the book with the initial premise that herds of animals are far easier to manage than people, because "animals more readily than men obey their rulers." In fact, he asserts, men "conspire against none sooner than those whom they see attempting to rule over them."[42] But when he reflected upon the fact that Cyrus, the Persian, commanded the obedience of a vast number of men, cities and nations, he felt compelled to change his opinion. People followed Cyrus willingly, even though some were distant from him by many days of travel, others had never seen him, and most of the peoples of his empire were not Persians. "Nevertheless they were all willing to be his subjects." He decided, from the example of Cyrus, "that to rule men might be a task neither impossible nor even difficult, if one should only go about it in an intelligent manner."[43] To discover why Cyrus was so deserving of admiration and obedience, Xenophon sought to investigate "who he was in his origin, and what sort of education he enjoyed, that he so greatly excelled in governing men."[44]

Xenophon's *Cyropaideia* is historical fiction. The Persians he presents are more akin to the Spartans that he so admired than the Persians of his day, and the person of Cyrus comes off as being a little "too good." Nevertheless, his purpose in writing the account was to give people a picture of what he considered the ideal leader – a leader who was guided by Socratic principles and could apply them in everyday life. The picture of Cyrus that emerges from the account is one of a leader who inspires devotion in his friends and fear in his enemies. Cyrus became the embodiment of *areté*: he possessed wisdom, justice, courage, and moderation. He set the example in piety and generosity, and in skill and bravery. He formulated intelligent ends, and directed his actions and those of others toward those ends. He established a lasting, unified empire made up of diverse peoples by appealing to and exemplifying the transcendent principles that bonded different people together for a good purpose.

CONCLUSION: LEARNING FROM THE PAST

The idea of leadership was central to the political and moral philosophies of Xenophon, Plato, Aristotle, and Cicero, because leadership functioned as the nexus in maintaining the delicate balance between order and freedom. Working from the assumption that "human nature" is best understood from its *telos*, and that people had an innate desire to achieve that condition, these ancient philosophers constructed a theory of leadership founded on the notion that the most fitting leader must embody that *telos*. In doing so, the leader functioned as a bridge between the personal, inter-personal, and cosmological (visionary) levels.

Ancient concepts of leadership are certainly not without their problematic assumptions and flaws. Most critical to the ancient philosophers was their concept of human nature, an assumption that remains difficult to prove. Niccoló Machiavelli and Thomas Hobbes, writing in the context of disorder, corruption, and internecine warfare in 16th century Italy and 17th century England, came to the opposite conclusion regarding human nature in *The Prince* and *Leviathan*.[45] Their theories of leadership followed logically from their assumption that man in the "state of nature" was nasty, brutish, and self-centered. To be sure, the "darker" side of humanity is never far from us, and yet there is much to be said for the fact that a Socrates is held in much high-er regard than a Nero. The assumption regarding the complete-ness of the four cardinal virtues can also be called into question, as can the existence of a divine controlling force in the universe through which humans can comprehend transcendent principles and the good.

The ancients did live in a slave society, and although they skirt-ed the issue by arguing that the "true slave" was a person controlled by their passions and desires instead of by reason, the philosophy of human freedom and the practice of slavery are difficult to rec-oncile. The Romans made famous the practice of "decimation" – the execution of every tenth man in a failed formation, although the value of such treatment was questioned even at that time. Furthermore, only Plato discussed in depth the role of women as guardians of the state, arguing that men and women, though bio-logically different, have equal abilities to live according to the car-dinal virtues and apprehend the good.

While the ancients did encounter and argue persuasively against much of the above criticism, the assumptions upon which they based their theories of leadership can never truly be proven or completely refuted. We must also bear in mind that these ancient philosophers were not discussing "the way things were." Instead, they were articulating "the way things ought to be." In doing so, they offer a concept of humanity that uplifts and inspires us to cultivate the best that is in us and in others. They do indeed "turn the soul."

What can we learn from the ancients? Here are a few thoughts. Any coherent philosophy of leadership begins with an assumption about human nature. Leaders must study human beings from the perspectives of theory, philosophy, and history and arrive at some conclusion about what they are in a universal sense, as well as what they can be. Certainly not all people will match that conclusion, but such a start point and end-state (if we accept that definition) enables a leader to appreciate people as individuals with all of their virtues and vices and work from there. Their concept of human nature adds much needed substance to the ideas of respect and caring; ideas so often talked about yet so infrequently practiced. Such study also offers the leaders insight into themselves, for it is only when we know what we ought to be that we can begin to understand how to get there.

If we accept the ideas presented in this essay about human nature, the importance of character becomes readily apparent. Certainly the fact that no one will trust an incompetent, especially when lives are at stake, remains true regardless of how we view humanity. It is the issue of character, however, that comes through most eloquently. If the leader is supposed to be a model of the end-state, someone others look up to, then both character and competence are critical to earning trust. There is a difference between the various desires individual people possess and the "character flaws" that the undisciplined practice. People who cannot control their desires, these ancients argue, will erode the fabric of the relationship between leader and led, and are thus unfit to lead. Those with good character, on the other hand, draw others toward them and uplift them. The pursuit of excellence demands both character and competence.

A leader with character and competence who is trustworthy, treats others with respect, and cares for them can inspire the spirit and act of following through the creation and relentless pursuit of vision. On the one hand, the leader embodies vision at the individual level by demonstrating what one ought to be. A leader of an organization, however, is more than just an individual mentor. A vision for an organization requires the discovery and articulation of an idea that infuses all with a common spirit and excites the imagination. Vision tells an organization "why." It defines duty.

The creation and pursuit of vision requires intellectual courage; the commitment to developing wisdom and making wise decisions that lead to accomplishing the goal. The pursuit of vision, to paraphrase Carl von Clausewitz, is like movement in a resistant element (friction). The complex interaction of a multitude of competing ideas and wills, the impersonal factors that inform and shape the ideas, the confusing, contradictory and overwhelming information, and prevailing uncertainty are but a few causes of friction. A leader must have the intellectual courage to make decisions in the midst of such chaotic ambiguity to keep the organization oriented on the proper azimuth. Experience alone is not sufficient. Leaders who have not taken the time to cultivate the mind and develop intellectual courage become prisoners of their own experience. Leaders without the intellectual courage to make decisions in the realm of uncertainty rapidly become crisis managers, only making decisions in the intellectual comfort of simple necessity. Finally a brief moment of clarity arrives in which a decision is required, and experience will enable one to make what appears to be a good choice. Unfortunately the choice in crisis is often the selection of the best of several bad options. Since the nature of a crisis is that which threatens the purpose of the organization, even if the crisis manager happens to choose the best of these bad options, the choice will only relieve the problems of the moment. Once crisis management becomes a habit, the organization becomes rooted in the labyrinth of short-term decisions, moving in many different directions but no closer toward achieving the organizational purpose. The undeveloped mind, when bombarded with information and external stimuli, quickly loses the ability to decide and the courage to act until the moment of crisis. The developed mind can part the shadows of chaos, disorder, and confusion to create a vision and pursue it with conviction, keeping the organization on the proper azimuth to achieve its purpose. We can learn from the ancients that acquiring the full spectrum of courage (intellectual, physical, and moral) requires the continuous development of the mind, body, and soul.

The ancients, and not these four alone, provide us a wealth of ideas about leadership that transcend time and context. Their concept of leadership was personal. They did not have television sound-bytes, e-mail distribution lists, or the capacity to mass-produce memoranda and policy letters. They did not fool themselves into thinking that they could develop a kit-bag full of magic formulas to rescue themselves in the disturbingly frequent times of immediate danger and doubt. Ancient leaders had to stand before their citizens and soldiers and touch them personally or face the immediate and severe consequences. They had to turn their souls. Many ancient philosophers and historians explored leadership at its most fundamental, complex, and stimulating levels. The very lasting, human intimacy of their ideas on leadership earns them the distinction, classics.

Chapter Two

Teaching Combat Leadership at West Point: Closing the Gap between Expectation and Experience

by Charles F. Brower, IV and Gregory J. Dardis

"The battlefield is the epitome of war," Brigadier General S.L.A. Marshall concluded in his classic study of the behavior of American soldiers in battle. "All else in war...exists but to serve the forces on the battlefield and to assure final success in the field."[1] The Department of Behavioral Sciences and Leadership (BS&L) at the United States Military Academy offers a senior-level seminar open to cadets that seeks an interdisciplinary examination of leadership in combat at the tactical level. PL470, Leadership in Combat, starts with the premise that experience—broadened vicariously by the records of others and leavened by study and reflection—breeds an enhanced under-

27

standing of the nature of combat and the essence of successful combat leadership. Of course cadets have no direct access to a battlefield laboratory; they rely instead upon the recorded experiences of others and the recollections of veterans willing to share their perspectives with us. Fortunately, a considerable body of relevant knowledge about human behavior also informs the study of leadership and behavior in combat. BS&L's course brings this disciplinary power to bear on this most essential of the tasks of members of the profession of arms.

Taught jointly by two officers on the BS&L faculty, one a Vietnam combat veteran with a doctorate in history and the other an infantry officer with extensive experience in infantry units and a doctorate in organizational behavior with emphasis in leadership, the course first provides cadets with a theoretical foundation based upon contemporary behavioral science theories and concepts, and then explores some of the factors that influence the leadership of soldiers in combat through a collection of readings, film, and first-hand discussions with combat veterans.

COURSE DESIGN

The course is organized into three areas. Area I, ***Theoretical Perspectives on Leadership in Combat***, provides an interdisciplinary foundation for the course using the disciplines of psychology, social psychology, sociology and history. Two books, Anthony Kellett's *Combat Motivation* and Richard Holmes' *Acts of War: The Behavior of Men in Combat* are explored in this area.[2]

Area II, ***Factors Influencing Soldiers in Combat***, examines a selection of factors influencing behavior in combat. The selection is not, of course, comprehensive. Its intent is to allow cadets the opportunity to reflect upon a variety of such influences—in this case we chose fear, courage, cohesion, stress, killing, death and the enemy—although many other possibilities certainly exist. Readings, film and special classroom visitors inform the class discussion during this area. Gerald Linderman's wonderful *The World Within War: America's Combat Experience in World War II*, Stephen

Ambrose's remarkable analysis of the cohesion of an airborne rifle company in the European Theater of Operations, *Band of Brothers: E Company, 506th Regiment, 101st Airborne Division from Normandy to Hitler's Eagle's Nest*, Lord Moran's classic *The Anatomy of Courage,* John Dower's account of the savagery of combat in the war against Japan, *War Without Mercy: Race and Power in the Pacific War*, and Dave Grossman's *On Killing: The Psychological Cost of Learning to Kill in War and Society* are the center of gravity of this area.[3]   The readings have been supplemented by the films "Red Badge of Courage" and "Paths of Glory" and by special visitors Major Dick Winters, Stephen Ambrose and Dave Grossman.

Area III, ***Case Studies in Combat Leadership at the Tactical Level***, gives cadets the opportunity to develop more deeply into the nature of combat leadership. Four case studies—infantry company command in the European Theater of Operations in World War II, the battle of the Ia Drang in Vietnam in 1965, leadership in expeditionary combat in Somalia in 1991, and prisoner of war experiences in Vietnam or Operation Desert Storm—are the centerpiece of this area. Assigned readings include Charles B. MacDonald's introspective account of his combat experience in Europe, `Company Commander*, Lieutenant General Hal Moore's and Joseph Galloway's riveting *We Were Soldiers Once...and Young*, Mark Boden's commentary on expeditionary warfare and the battle of Mogadishu, *Blackhawk Down,* and either Rhonda Cornum's engrossing *She Went to War* or John S. McCain's poignant *Faith of My Fathers: A Family Memoir.*[4] Classroom visits by one of Moore's company commanders on LZ X-Ray (and BS&L alumnus) Colonel (Retired) Ramon Nadal, Colonel Rhonda Cornum and Admiral Jim Stockdale, a class viewing and discussion of Steven Spielberg's award winning D-Day film, "Saving Private Ryan," and cadet interaction with a panel of combat veterans from World War II, the Vietnam War, and Desert Storm supplement this part of the course.

The course is organized as a seminar with two-person cadet discussion leader teams assigned throughout the course. Discussion teams meet with the seminar advisors one week before their session to review proposed strategies and discussion questions. Following that meeting, the discussion questions are shared with the seminar electronically. Discussion leaders also integrate additional film clips, handouts or other visual aids to supplement their presentations. Following the session the instructors provide detailed feedback on their performance as discussion leader. This event is a significant part of the seminar's overall value and it constitutes 20% of the total course grade.

Any course so designed lives or dies depending upon the preparation of seminar members and diligent preparation is absolutely vital. The instructors consider that the assigned readings form the basis of seminar discussions, not the start and end points, and thus warn cadets of their intention to use seminar discussions to explore a wide range of issues. Participation is graded both qualitatively and quantitatively and constitutes 30% of the overall grade. A peer evaluation is also used as part of the data to determine the seminar participation grade. Cadet participation in class and in the presentation team enhances their mastery of the course materials and also improves their small group leadership and followership skills. Effective cadet participation also contributes to an active learning environment and contributes to the learning of other seminar members.

WRITING REQUIREMENTS

Two major writing requirements complete the design of the course. The first requires cadets to read S.L.A. Marshall's classic work, *Men Against Fire: The Problem of Battle Command in Future War* and then to analyze Marshall's conclusions regarding any one of the factors addressed in Area II: fear, courage, cohesion, stress, loss, killing or the enemy. Cadets draw on the materials covered in the course to that point (about a third of the way through the course) and submit a short paper of three typed pages worth 10% of the course grade. The intent in this initial writing requirement is to give them an opportunity to reflect on one of several factors that influence the human dimension of combat and to do so in a paper of reasonable length. The requirement also provides a vehicle to introduce cadets to the Marshall thesis and to have the opportunity to analyze it. *Men Against Fire* is very effective for these objectives, being an easy read and of manageable length.

The second writing requirement is significantly more imposing and is worth 40% of the final course grade. In this fifteen page paper cadets comparatively analyze the combat leadership of two tactical leaders of their choice. Cadets must first develop and justify their own analytical framework for their analysis, including both psychological and organizational factors in the framework. Here cadets are to thoughtfully lay out the reasoning underpinning their framework. What elements constitute their definition of successful and unsuccessful combat leadership? Why were the chosen factors for analysis included? More important, cadets have to illustrate that they appreciated in what ways the chosen factors relate to each other and to the larger framework, what their relative weights were, and why cadets assigned that weight. Cadets find this part of the requirement not only the most difficult but also the most rewarding. Regular mentoring sessions with their assigned professor assist them in thinking through the various factors, weightings and interrelationships.

Cadets then examine the two chosen combatants. Who were they? Why were they chosen? What about their background and experience is significant in terms of their success or failure as a combat leader? In answering these questions cadets are required to avoid assertion and to carefully lay out the evidence from their reading and research which supports their conclusions. In this section of the paper cadets are trying to get at the question: What personal, experiential, and institutional factors appear to have contributed to developing the chosen combatants into successful or unsuccessful combat leaders? Using their derived and justified framework, a comparative analysis of the two combat leaders is the logical next step. Cadets seem to attack this portion of the paper with relish, aiming to draw conclusions about the psychological and organizational factors that influence successful leadership in combat. Finally, cadets summarize the implications of their conclusions in terms of their personal preparation for leading soldiers in combat. Their efforts have direct relevance to their preparation for officership and reflect on what they have learned from their research that will better prepare themselves for "the epitome of war."

———————————————

From this seminar's study of leadership in combat emerged the conclusion that successful combat leadership was in large part a function of the ability of the leader to understand the nature of the human dimensions of combat and to build and sustain the cohesion of their units in battle. We recognized that the complex challenges arising from the factors making up the human dimension of combat were many and that their influence varied over time and experience. The seminar sampled some of these human dimensions—courage, stress, fear, loss and killing, perceptions of the enemy, cohesion—recognizing that the list was not exhaustive and expecting that we were modeling for the seminar members approaches for exploring dimensions not addressed. The seminar concluded, however, that combat effectiveness seemed to be significantly improved when leaders understood these human factors and applied them in building and sustaining cohesion in their units.

As our course title suggests, our approach is to close the gap between the expectation and experience of combat by exposing cadets to various perspectives on the phenomenon, joined with the opportunity for them to study and reflect upon leadership within that fascinating and foreboding field. Because combat presents problems that cannot be duplicated precisely in training, and because anxieties about combat and the resultant stresses of actual combat pose serious problems in terms of combat effectiveness, any investment in closing this gap reaps potentially large dividends on the battlefield.

COURAGE AND FEAR

Courage and fear are perhaps the most natural of the human dimensions of combat. The record shows again and again that soldiers worry significantly about how they will perform in battle. Whether soldiers in blue and gray or khaki or olive drab, soldiers more often as not view battle as a test that will reveal and intensify their basic nature.[5]   Indeed, Anthony Kellett concludes that "the fear of fear" is a more potent influence upon them than the fear of danger.[6]   This is the fear of letting one's fellow soldiers down; the fear of not measuring up; the fear of dishonoring oneself or one's unit.   Bravery is mental, but courage is mental and moral.   In *The Anatomy of Courage*, Lord Moran terms this "the idea greater than fear," the notion that such things can be more feared than the high risk of death.[7]   We found that the simple explanation of why many soldiers will risk death in combat is that they do not wish to face the approbation of comrades in arms.

In battle danger paralyzes.   Soldiers seek reassurance by bunching up and taking cover.   Inaction and passivity are the norm.   In our reading and study we found that most soldiers in battle fought when called upon to do so, but without much enthusiasm.   This seemed to be the case whether in our study of courage in Easy Company, 506th Infantry Regiment in World War II, the First Cavalry Division in the Ia Drang Valley or Rangers and Delta Force soldiers in the Battle of Mogadishu.   More often than not in these cases, a minority of better motivated, more aggressive soldiers carried the fight to the enemy and raised the combat effectiveness of the unit as a whole.   Anthony Kellett concludes that in such situations the power of example is controlling and that soldiers will almost instinctively follow almost any kind of lead—flight or fight— or anything in between.   Leading by example thus remains a basic tenet of combat leadership.   The willingness of leaders to show "a demonstrable acceptance of risk and sacrifice" will draw soldiers to do their duty and fight.[8]   We discovered innumerable evidence of this phenomenon's powerful influence on successful leadership in combat throughout the course. Perhaps the best illustration was found in the actions of Captain Dick Winters of Easy Company, 506th PIR, while clearing the Utah Beach causeways on D-Day.[9]

The principal mission of the 101st Airborne Division on D-Day was to secure the series of causeways that allowed the American forces landing on Utah Beach to cross the inundated land to the west of the landing beaches and penetrate into the interior.   Near Brécourt Manor, a large Norman farmhouse to the north of Ste.

Marie-du-Mont, a German battery of four 105mm cannon, well cam-
ouflaged and linked by an extensive trench system defended by
fifty German infantrymen, controlled Causeway No. 2 from Utah
Beach. The strong German position was connected by wire communications to a forward observer positioned to adjust fire on the
4th Infantry Division a mere four kilometers away on Utah Beach
and had the potential to significantly disrupt the Utah Beach operations. Winters' sadly under-strength company, badly scattered in
the night drop, was given the mission of neutralizing the battery.[10]

With only twelve men initially present for duty in his company
(five others would join the attack in progress), Winters carefully
scouted the German position and then organized a quick frontal
assault supported by covering fire from two machine guns placed
to deliver flanking fire along the hedgerows. He personally led the
attack, not by charging the guns head long but by disciplined fire
and maneuver supported with well-aimed rifle fire. "We fought like
a team without standout stars," one member of the company later
recalled. "We were like a machine…We had learned that heroics
was the way to be killed without getting the job done, and getting
the job done was more important." The attack moved forward
relentlessly, systematically killing the defending Germans and
destroying the guns in turn with blocks of TNT and phosphorus
incendiary grenades.[11]

Winters' casualties were four dead and two wounded; German
losses included fifteen dead, many others wounded, and twelve
prisoners. The guns, of course, were destroyed and Causeway No.
2 was opened.   Winters was recommended to receive the
Congressional Medal of Honor, though only one man per division
was to receive that award during the Normandy campaign and he
subsequently was awarded the Distinguished Service Cross. Four
members of the company in that attack received the Silver Star and
the other eight received Bronze Stars.[12]

Stephen Ambrose's oral history interviews of the members of
Easy Company provide an engrossing perspective of the combat
experiences of a remarkable collection of American soldiers. What
is most striking about the stories that emerge is the unanimity of

opinion regarding the leadership and character of Captain Dick Winters. He emerges as the paragon of the combat leader—physically fit, brave, technically competent, genuinely interested in the welfare of his men, friendly yet distant. "He was an officer who got the men to perform because he expected nothing but the best," one of his soldiers told Ambrose. "You liked him so much that you just hated to let him down." Ambrose's conclusion naturally followed: Dick Winters "was, and is, all but worshipped by the men of E Company."[13]

In case after case, we found that the force of example and the enthusiasm of a few leaders like Dick Winters often affected the combat performance of their units in extraordinarily disproportionate ways. These leaders were influential because their men had confidence in their tactical and technical competence; because they cared for their soldiers emotional and physical needs; because they persuaded their soldiers that they would not be reckless or wasteful with their lives; because they sought to make order out of chaos; and most of all, because they led by example. These leadership attributes helped soldiers overcome the real enemy—their fear— and perform their soldierly duties in combat. The normal state of the soldier is one of fear and fatigue, however. General George S. Patton, Jr. claimed that "no sane man is unafraid in battle."[14] As a consequence, soldiers live with continual conflicts between the desire to conquer the enemy and the fear of combat, between the desire to escape the situation and the fear of being considered by his comrades or others a poor soldier, or worse, a coward. Fear is ever present, however, and it is important for leaders to appreciate just how it may be manifested.

Fear is an emotion involving the whole physiological pattern induced by the action of the sympathetic nervous system. The characteristics of fear are unpleasantness, fatigue, and a desire to escape. It involves such individual symptoms as violent pounding of the heart, a sinking feeling or sickness in the stomach, trembling, and, in extreme situations, a loss of control of the bowels and bladder. Fear thrives upon frustrations, and it will persist and grow when the individual can do nothing to lessen the threat. The soldier, beset by fear, vacillates between a desire to escape danger and a pride that makes him want to fight. In great fear, soldiers may be captured by inertia—incapable of doing anything—either to satisfy their desire for safety or their motives for fighting. The soldier in whom fear overrides all other emotions is an unwilling fighter, hesitant to advance against the enemy, inefficient to the point of uselessness and a detriment to his unit. Fear on the battlefield will be ever present, but it can be conquered by the emotionally stable and well-adjusted soldier who has been prepared to face it. Soldiers should be taught to expect fear and to recognize it as a psychological phenomenon common to all men in combat.

Fear, in itself, is no enemy—only uncontrolled fear becomes detrimental to the behavior of a soldier. The courageous soldier is not one without fear, but one who conquers his fear and performs in spite of it. Besides fear, the soldier must be disciplined, trained, confident, and informed. He must be disciplined so that he will fight off the initial effects of fear; trained to protect himself in combat and to function as a member of a team; confident of the power of his unit and himself; and informed as to what the situation is and what can be expected in the immediate future. In this way, he keeps fear from becoming the major influence on his behavior in combat.

When the soldier himself cannot overcome the effects of fear, directed activity may do it for him. Many combat leaders have testified to the fact that they have been successful in overcoming fear in their men by making them do almost anything physical—-moving from one position to another, even if not towards the enemy, assisting other men in carrying equipment, administering first aid to a comrade. Action appears to be a great steadying force and a successful cure for fear. In fact, the sensation of fear often disappears entirely in the exhilaration and excitement of actual close combat.

ISOLATION AND STRESS

"The battlefield is cold," wrote S.L.A. Marshall about the isolation of combat. "It is the lonesomest place which men share together." This sense of isolation, of learned helplessness, dominates the battlefield. Soldiers experience "tunnel vision," the inability to see but their own small part of the battle; they cling to their comrades for psychological support, instinctively bunching up when under fire and anxiously seeking to decipher a familiar voice from the clamor of the battle. "In battle you may draw a small circle around a soldier, including within it only those persons and objects that he sees or believes will influence his immediate fortunes," Marshall wrote. It is this "presence or near presence of a comrade" that enables the soldier to keep going in battle. It is, he concludes, "one of the simplest truths of war."[15]

How to moderate and deal with stress on "the painful field" has preoccupied combat leaders since the dawn of warfare.[16] The anxieties of soldiers about how they will perform in battle and the threats to their survival directly influence individual performance. The cumulative effect of this stress leads to combat exhaustion in individuals and units. The tolerance of "normal" soldiers is finite. Richard Gabriel claims that in the American wars of this century, "the chances of becoming a psychiatric casualty—of being debilitated for some period of time as a consequence of the stresses of military life—were greater than the chances of being killed by enemy fire."[17] Good leaders find ways to mitigate the stress associated with combat, often through rotational practices. Soldiers need the prospect of rest and escape from the immediate danger of the battlefield to cope with stress; they need the ability to identify a short-term goal around which to plan for personal survival. Nothing drove this point home more to the seminar than the comparison of Captain Dick Winters' Easy Company, 506th PIR, and Captain Charles MacDonald's Companies I and G of the 23rd Infantry Regiment, 2nd Infantry Division. Long front line service without the prospect of rest and escape from daily danger manifested itself in diminished group cohesion and combat exhaustion in the latter, while regular rotation of the 101st off the line to prepare for subsequent airborne operations allowed Easy Company to renew itself and to justify Stephen Ambrose's claim that "it was as good a rifle company as there was in the world."[18]

KILLING

Considerations of how soldiers and their leaders dealt with the phenomenon of killing were naturally not far from the forefront of the cadets' thinking about leadership in combat. In few other occupations do individuals deliberately take actions bringing themselves into contact with other humans whose primary objective is to kill them and whom, in turn, they seek to kill. Yet war demands the taking of human lives. In *On Killing*, cadets explore Lieutenant Colonel Dave Grossman's provocative explanation of how soldiers are motivated to kill and what the effects are of having done so.

Grossman considers the alleged aversion of American soldiers to battlefield killing. In *Men Against Fire*, S.L.A. Marshall concluded that not more than 25 percent of American infantrymen in World War II engaged the enemy when they should have.[19] Grossman's analysis is largely based on these findings. Studies of infantrymen in Vietnam indicated that the enemy was engaged at much higher rates than Marshall found during World War II. In Grossman's view, this increase was a direct consequence of the desensitization and conditioning of American trainees; more significantly he sought to investigate the effects on these soldiers of having killed after such training. Grossman finds the soldier's humanity diminished. Indeed, the act of killing frequently had significant negative repercussions that were closely related to postwar psychiatric problems. The conditions under which the killing took place also influenced many post-conflict reactions.[20]

Prompted by Marshall's reports that up to 75 percent of soldiers chose not to fire their weapons, after World War II the American armed forces revolutionized their training methods by integrating strictly behavioristic methods: classical conditioning, imitation of models, and rewards and punishment. Grossman argues these techniques were so successful that the soldiers who fought in Vietnam were temporarily conditioned to overcome their natural inhibitions to kill. The result was a 95 percent rate of fire. A heavy price was paid afterwards, he concluded, as the soldier's instinctual proscription to kill usually reasserted itself, and he experienced horror and guilt.

From the stories of soldiers he interviewed, Grossman deciphers a universal sequence of stages: concern about killing, the actual kill, exhilaration, remorse, and rationalization and acceptance. He poignantly notes that Vietnam veterans were the first to be "psychologically enabled to kill" and then cruelly denied the "psychologically essential purification rituals" that would have provided absolution and permitted the sequence to reach the rationalization and acceptance stage. Instead, for nearly two decades, these veterans languished in the remorse stage because they perceived that their country reviled them as much at they loathed themselves. To this, he adds a riveting twist: because these soldiers had been so deeply conditioned to think the unthinkable, those who did not kill ultimately shared the burden of guilt and self-recrimination with those who did.

Military deployments for missions other than war may involve such diverse purposes as humanitarian aid and peacekeeping, but when America sends its soldiers to war, it understands that they are going there to kill. Despite this essential feature of war, killing is more often viewed by military training schools as an act to perfect rather than an act to discuss.

Most people are not sociopaths and hence are reluctant to kill another human being. Without attempting to speculate on the idiosyncratic personality factors that create such resistance, Grossman discusses the direct relationship between distance-to-victim and willingness to kill. Artillerymen who rarely see the deaths they produce have been shown, for example, to be more willing to fire their weapons accurately than infantrymen who can distinguish more precisely the human nature their target.

Cadets in the seminar also learned of the role of pressure from others in influencing a willingness to kill. How effectively an authority figure, such as a company commander, can exhort his men to kill is influenced by the intensity of his demand, the degree of respect his men hold for him, and how close he is to the men squeezing triggers. The strength of a person's identification with a unit influences the amount of the pressure the unit exerts to kill and the quality of absolution it bestows on the person who killed in its name. For the combat leader, Grossman helps sharpen command- ers' awareness of the ethical challenges they face and their role in producing soldiers who will and can kill, and who must live with themselves afterwards.

THE ENEMY

John Dower's account of the kill-or-be-killed nature of the Pacific war starkly captures the brutish and primitive nature of that "war without mercy" on both sides. Both sides dehumanized their enemy in order to make more acceptable their extermination. To Americans, the Japanese were apes, "monkeymen," and primitives; to the Japanese the Americans were brutes and wild beasts—"the bestial American people." This kind of psychology was a kind of self-perpetuating vicious circle, of course. Japanese soldiers fought to the last man, it was believed, and did so for many and complex reasons—honor, duty, mass psychology, and even to avoid social ostracism for their families. But countless numbers also died because they saw no alternative—they simply expected to be killed by the Americans if they were taken prisoner. And Dower argues persuasively that they were right to believe so in many, many instances.[21] "The fierce struggle for survival," wrote Marine veteran E.B. Sledge, "eroded the veneer of civilization and made savages of us all."[22] And Colonel Tony Nadal, a veteran of the Seventh Cavalry's 1965 battles in the Ia Drang Valley, emphatically under- lined the same point while addressing the seminar. "The thin veneer of civilization is easily scraped away in combat, unless the leader is on guard," he emphasized. "The enemy is the enemy until he is under my control. Then he's my *responsibility*."[23] Combat wears down ethical standards; it takes leaders to know their ethical duty and to make a difference.

The seminar started with the proposition that successful leadership in combat was a function of the leader's ability to understand the nature of and human dimensions of combat and the ability to build and sustain "the mysterious fraternity" representing the cohesion of combat units.　Combat effectiveness resulted when leaders successfully closed the gap between the expectations and the experience of combat.　Successful combat leaders understood the factors that influenced soldiers in battle—fear, courage, stress, loss, killing, the enemy and cohesion, all of which were explored by this seminar.　Leading by example emerged again as a basic tenet of combat leadership.　Because the group processes of combat make it a particularly emulative activity, the power of example proved compelling over and over in combat situations—Lieutenant Colonel Hal Moore's steadying calm on LZ X-Ray; Captain Dick Winters' heroic action in the hedgerows on the outskirts of Utah Beach; Major Rhonda Cornum's stoic resolve as a prisoner of war in the Gulf War; the list continues.　Leaders understood that the power of example was most influential in such situations and their willingness to accept risk and sacrifice was often necessary to stimulate their soldiers to do the same.　Such leaders by their actions conferred a sense of protection on their soldiers.　Leaders who took care of their soldiers, who met their tactical needs through their own competence and skills, who provided them the administrative and logistical means for soldiers to do their jobs well (especially the prompt medical support to justify their willingness to assume risk of wound and injury), and who allayed their soldiers anxieties that they would respect their lives by avoiding wasteful casualties—these leaders led units that were the most combat effective.

Chapter Three

Leadership, Versatility, and All that Jazz[1]

by Gordon R. Sullivan

Versatility has become the hallmark of America's Army. Our capstone doctrinal manual, US Army Field Manual 100-5, *Operations*, explains that "versatility implies a capacity to be multifunctional, to operate across the full range of military operations, and to perform at the tactical, operational and strategic levels."[2] We consider versatility to be one of the five fundamental tenets of Army operations. It is a recent addition to that short list, but hardly a new concept. It is an attribute that has often been essential in our past, and I expect it to be central to our future.

We strive for versatility in our units. We have designed forces and developed command and control procedures that permit the rapid creation and employment of task-organized units tailored to achieve success under diverse conditions. Employment of those forces also requires leaders with the ability to enter one situation and rapidly adapt to another. We must understand the fundamentals: the capabilities and vulnerabilities of our weapons, our soldiers and our subordinate units. And we must have the ability to read a changing situation and react faster than our opponents. Versatility in leaders, to a large extent, is the ability to improvise solutions in uncertain and changing battlefield conditions.

In battle, versatility allows a commander to act with certainty and decisiveness amid the fog and friction of mortal combat. In training, it spurs us to press the edge of the envelope, to try new ideas, to dare great things and to grow as individuals and as an army. It is a characteristic that springs from a certain knowledge of the basics of our craft. And that certain knowledge gives great leaders the confidence to improvise solutions — to move well beyond the situations we may foresee today. No one can predict precisely what the Army of the future will look like. But based on what is already happening to us, we can say this: Tomorrow's wars and operations other than war (OOTW) will require leaders versatile in mind and will, their perspectives uncluttered by preconceived notions or cookie-cutter solutions.

As I have contemplated the relationship between versatility and leadership, I have been drawn to a simple metaphor. The skill and talent required of military leaders is in many ways akin to the virtuosity of the best jazz musicians. Our military plans have the complexity of orchestral scores, but the certainty of that sheet music does not parallel the changing conditions under which the military leader performs his tasks. Versatility-the improvisation of the jazzman-has been a hallmark of great leaders in our past and is in even greater demand today. Our challenge today is to build on our traditions and to develop a generation of leaders experienced in their craft, alert to an ambiguous environment and confident in their ability to improvise and win.

We may not yet see clearly the face of future war, but we have seen the face of our future brand of leaders. As the commissioned and noncommissioned officers of America's Army look ahead toward the 21st century, we would do well to consider the examples of two Americans of this century who demonstrated the versatility to which we all aspire. Their fields of endeavor differed greatly, perhaps as widely as one could imagine. Yet, the two men shared a common approach to their respective pursuits, and it is that style, that disposition, which demands our consideration.

The first man followed in the footsteps of his father. After studying at several of the more notable institutions of higher education that defined his profession, he also had the opportunity to learn from a pair of recognized masters. So schooled, and in consequence of his own noteworthy abilities, he achieved notoriety as a team builder, known for molding uniquely capable groups under stressful situations. Rising to the top ranks of his calling, he achieved his greatest renown for his performance in a novel environment, one about which he had never been taught, and yet one that perhaps only he could resolve. Truly, he was the right person at the right place and the right time, a point often noted by modern historians.

We can say much the same thing about our second subject. He hewed to the strong example of his mother and older brothers. Following formal education in his chosen vocation, he had the opportunity to deepen his understandings in the company of two distinguished elders, both of whom greatly influenced his early professional development. Well-grounded, conscious of his growing talents, he formed several distinctive, highly capable teams that attained remarkable success in all aspects of their efforts. Singled out as one of the key innovators in his field, he demonstrated consistent ingenuity, devising works so unusual that, in many ways, they now define the outer limits of his profession. He directly affected the course of recent American cultural history.

We know these two men as Matthew B. Ridgway and David W. Brubeck, battle commander and jazz impresario, respectively. You might say that this is an unlikely twosome, the soldier and the musician. But that ignores the deeper ties, the pronounced similarities in how the pair have carried out their lives' works. To understand the connection between Ridgway and Brubeck, it helps to measure the difference between the artistic practitioner and the practical artist, between the conventional general and the master of the battlespace, between the classical orchestra musician and the stylings of the dedicated composer, spinning out clear, cool jazz.

FIRM FOUNDATIONS

Everything, especially the creation of great art (whether operational or musical), takes study and work. People come into this world with varying degrees of talent, but few achieve much without a great deal of diligent effort. It is an old truism that you cannot get something for nothing. This is especially true in trying to develop a versatile intellect. It does not "just happen."

The first step in becoming a leader in any walk of life is easy to say but not easy to do-become an expert. In professional life, knowledge is power, and the capacity to gather, interpret, organize and use available information is one of the major features distinguishing the versatile leader from the time-server. Good leaders, real artists, are experts. They know the fundamentals of their craft.

Ridgway certainly measures up in this regard. Raised in a military family, a 1917 graduate of West Point, a good student at Fort Benning's Infantry School, Fort Leavenworth's Command and General Staff College and the Army War College, Ridgway spent nine of his first 46 years in military educational establishments. He knew the theory behind his job very well.[3]

Brubeck reflects a similar pattern. With his mother teaching piano lessons and his older brothers working as music educators, young Brubeck began playing the piano at the age of 4. By the time he was 13, he was playing regularly in public and earning some money, too. He studied classical music at the College of the Pacific in Stockton, California, and also took music theory courses at nearby Mills College. Brubeck learned the details of classical music, a background unusual among many jazz players.[4] But Brubeck would be more than a jazzman. He would be an innovator. And it started with knowing the great classics-cold.

Along with a strong grasp of the nuts and bolts of one's chosen profession, it also helps to learn everything you can from those who have already been there. In the Army, we often discuss this under the concept of mentorship, the idea that a more experienced soldier should share the fruit of experiences with younger professionals. A prudent leader seeks such insight.

Ridgway definitely acknowledged the value of such personal contacts. His two great mentors could not have been more different. Lieutenant Colonel George C. Marshall, the reserved tactical mastermind of General John J. Pershing's World War I American Expeditionary Force, first met Ridgway when they served together in the 15th Infantry Regiment in Tientsin, China. Ridgway later attended the Infantry School, and under Marshall's tutelage, he learned the latest in combined arms tactics and combat leadership from a colonel determined to go well beyond "the school solution."

If Ridgway perfected his infantry skills under the uncompromising eye of Marshall, he gained invaluable exposure to the political aspects of the warrior's role courtesy of Brigadier General Frank McCoy, who asked Ridgway to accompany him to monitor the 1928 Nicaraguan elections. Fluent in Spanish since his Academy days, Ridgway learned much about the interactions of soldiers and diplomats, the doings of guerrilla chieftains such as Augusto Sandino and the usually porous membrane between politics and military affairs.[5]

Many American generals could claim proudly to be "Marshall Men." Only Ridgway had the benefit Of McCoy's unique political-military insights. Coupled with his military course work and inquiring mind, these experiences laid the foundation for later success in very delicate, dangerous political-military situations.

Brubeck, too, sought the wisdom and counsel of mentors. He attended several presentations by Arnold Schoenberg of Austria, a giant of early 20th-century classical music. Working with Schoenberg, Brubeck learned to discipline himself to read and write complex music, to understand melody, harmony and rhythm, the basic components of musical construction.

At Mills College, Brubeck also had the good fortune to meet and work with a composer who went beyond purely classical music-Darius Milhaud of France, a contemporary of Maurice Ravel and Igor Stravinsky. Milhaud had been so unimpressed by the American jazz movement that he produced some early works of jazz-classical fusion, and he enthusiastically encouraged Brubeck to continue in this relatively uncharted realm of musical experimentation. Schoenberg honed Brubeck's classical, symphonic instincts, but Milhaud showed him how to build on those ideas, to pioneer the uncharted boundaries that had previously separated American jazz and the likes of Beethoven or Brahms. The Frenchman so impressed Brubeck that the American named one of his sons Darius, a tribute to Milhaud.

Just as Ridgway was both a well-educated infantryman and a budding soldier diplomat, so Brubeck saw himself as "a jazz musician who wanted to learn composition."[6] Both men refused to be dabblers or dilettantes. Rather, they started at square one, learned their respective trades and sought the advice and assistance of sympathetic older professionals to expand their horizons. There would be plenty of ingenuity to come, but for these two gentlemen, it all arose from a solid bedrock of expertise. Versatility starts here.

BUILDING GREAT TEAMS

It is one thing to be a solo performer, a single man or woman out on the wire or ahead of the pack. It is quite another to translate singular excellence to a group, to impart a vision and a style so completely that, after awhile, the body begins to act in concert with its leader. In the Army, we say such an outfit is cohesive and combat-effective. And in today's difficult world, sure to be at least as challenging tomorrow, all our forces must truly "be all that they can be." Again, Ridgway and Brubeck show us the way.

Ridgway's organizations always showed a character much like his own: driving, tenacious and imaginative. He imparted his way of thinking to America's airborne formations in World War II and on the Eighth Army in Korea. Paratroopers groused that "there's a right way, a wrong way and a Ridgway," but their combat record demonstrated that the "Ridgway" amounted to applying brain power and aggressiveness, not outdated rule books, to wartime challenges.[7] Units trained and led by Ridgway from the 82d Airborne Division of 1943 and 1944 to the entire Eighth Army in

1951, consistently displayed a high degree of battlefield savvy. All of that started from the top, with Ridgway's example, the chief team builder of them all.

Ridgway left plenty of room for others with character traits as unusual as his own. Indeed, he sought them out and encouraged them. He did not allow conventional wisdom to stand in his way. The Army grapevine grumbled that James Gavin was too young to command a division and that Maxwell Taylor was too cerebral. Ridgway thought otherwise, and their superb performance as commanders of the 82d and 101st Airborne divisions in 1944 and 1945 proved him right. In his time, Ridgway selected and trained a generation of Army leaders, most thoroughly imbued with their leader's regard for versatility in action.

It might seem strange for soldiers to look at Brubeck as a team builder, but jazz by definition builds around the session, the small collection of musicians who experiment, practice and perform together. No composer can accomplish much if a viable session does not come together. Brubeck, as a pianist, followed in the tradition of Jelly Roll Morton and Duke Ellington, and assembled a series of sessions to pursue his interest in introducing classical elements to jazz. Brubeck's more famous bands include his eight-man Jazz Workshop Ensemble (1946- 1949), his trio of 1949-1951 and his quartet of 1951-1967, usually considered to be the classic Brubeck-inspired session. He has formed others since, including a partnership with sons Darius, Chris and Danny. But always, the bands featured Brubeck's determination to mix in classical melody and harmony with what he termed "rhythmic experimentation."

Brubeck's sessions emphasized teamwork and team learning, as his scores were always heavily influenced by classical forms and thus not easy to learn. Surely a "Brubeck way" existed, and just as the "Ridgway" sought to maximize the diverse talents of others, the jazz composer encouraged the abilities of his fellows. Brubeck stretched all of the old borders and did so deliberately.

He recruited an African-American, the brilliant double-bass, guitarist Eugene Wright, in the middle 1950s, a move that segregationist diehards claimed would ruin Brubeck, then ascending in popularity. Brubeck stood by his fellow musician, even canceling numerous lucrative dates in Southern states rather than work without his bassist. Wright played bass with the session for a decade, including his work on *Take Five*, the first jazz record to sell a million copies.

Most Americans have heard *Take Five*, in many ways the signature Brubeck piece. Yet, in fact, Brubeck did not compose it. The group's superb alto saxophonist, Paul Desmond, actually wrote the music, yet the work is so essentially Brubeck that only a few aficionados know this.[8] That is the Brubeck style, to pass the lead as jazz players must do, but to pass on his knowledge and perceptions to others, as well. Today's jazz has a lot of Brubeck in it, and that is no accident. The artist saw to it.

The greatest mark of team building is to create an organization that can continue to function without a hitch when the originator moves onward. Both Ridgway and Brubeck accomplished this repeatedly over their careers. Despite their ambition-and both had it, as do most true artists-neither man inflated his own ultimate importance. Both willingly deferred to others when that made sense, "passing the lead,"; in jazz technology. To those who inflated their own role, Ridgway offered this advice: "When you are beginning to think you're so important, make a fist and stick your arm into a bucket of water up to your wrist. When you take it out, the hole you left is the measure of how much you'll be missed."[9]

Brubeck might have said much the same thing. Our legacy is not what we do today, but what we teach those who follow us, those who will lead our Army into the future. You know, the battalion commanders of 2010 are today's lieutenants. Like Ridgway and Brubeck, we owe them our most candid, consistent coaching. We must pick the best and not let ourselves be bound by outmoded ways or "the conventional wisdom." Building tomorrow's Army, our future team, is already under way. Ridgway and Brubeck offer us some good ideas on how to get this right.

IMPROVISING ON A THEME

At some art schools and in sports, one hears talk of "compulsory figures," the equivalent of blocking and tackling, of mortar crew drill or of basic arithmetic. Interestingly, many prominent people, including some in uniform, never get beyond the school figures, the approved solution. A decade ago, against a relatively predictable foe in a fairly obvious theater, a soldier could get by with that sort of behavior. Today, tomorrow and the day after tomorrow, pat answers and the "way we have always done things" will not cut it.

Both Ridgway and Brubeck proved to be adept at improvising around a basic theme. Ridgway practically invented modern airborne operations out of whole cloth, building on rumors from hostile Germany and small-scale efforts by the British. Marshall trusted him to carry out his ground-breaking airborne campaigns in company with a galaxy of tremendous subordinates, and Ridgway proved eminently suited for this daunting task. His later service as the commander of Eighth Army in Korea electrified a dispirited multinational force, instituting tactics and techniques to address the specific frustrations which marked that difficult conflict.

In some ways even more deserving of credit, Ridgway left the field of battle to assume overall command in the Far East during a critical period in the Korean War. General of the Army Douglas MacArthur had been removed from command, and American soldiers, citizens and political leaders all looked to Ridgway. Did he, too, favor a wider war against Communist China, a World War II-style insistence on total victory? MacArthur had lost his job over this issue. Now Ridgway stepped up to the plate.

The school solution learned at Forts Benning and Leavenworth and practiced in northwest Europe in 1944-1945 would have argued for a drive to victory or withdrawal. But Ridgway understood that nuclear weaponry made such a finish fight impossible, at least without severe damage to America itself. He recognized the need to prosecute a limited war, a fight to be settled at the truce table, not in the hills of Korea and definitely not in Manchuria. Just as important, he knew he had to limit America's losses in "this kind of war," in T.R. Fehrenbach's memorable phrase.[10]

That Ridgway did so reflected well on his broad-mindedness, his willingness to deal with each new reality as he found it. The same general who had once personally stalked German snipers in the Normandy hedgerows also arranged armistice talks with his ruthless enemies in Korea. It was a different war and a different time. Ridgway knew that. More important, he was conditioned by years of study, thought and practice to respond that way, to improvise on a theme rather than stick to the same old dirge.

Brubeck, of course, epitomizes the concept of improvising on a theme. As you listen to his music, especially various recordings of the same compositions, you hear subtle nuances and distinctions as Brubeck modifies his musical score to match the audience, the skills of his other players and his own continuing exploration of rhythm, melody and harmony. He knows how to compose and he and his partners know how to play-not *what* to compose, and not *what* to play.

Woven throughout any reflective thought pertaining to these two men in their roles as creative leaders composing is the importance of vision in their work. Each of them could probably have explained with precision and clarity their expectations or their vision for their organization.

Visions and expectations are what carry us forward in a productive way. Brubeck and Ridgway have provided us a perspective on how it is possible to bring a group into the future in a purposeful and productive way. Visions relate to themes, expectations and goals in a very powerful way.

This explains Brubeck's incredible longevity as an entertainer. Working from his classical repertory and his jazz evolutions, Brubeck has been in the public eye since 1933. His works include two ballets, a musical, an oratorio, four cantatas, a mass and countless jazz pieces. He has made the cover of *Time* (1954), participated in great jazz festivals at Monterey (1962 and 1980) and Newport (1958, 1972 and 1981). He and his session played at the White House in 1964 and 1981. These varied marks of public acclaim tell us something. This artist is no flash in the pan. Even a cursory review of musical literature reinforces Brubeck's distinctive place in our culture.[11]

He earned every bit of his reputation, the same way as Ridgway earned his-by improvising on a theme. The world has changed tremendously since he began playing during the Great Depression, but Brubeck has had the perception to stay current, to adapt, to pay attention to his surroundings. He never does the same thing twice, because situations are never quite the same-yet, his work always displays his own unmistakable style.

Many people think that improvising in the Brubeck way simply means doing something different, whatever that something may be. But a closer look at the examples of Ridgway and Brubeck suggest otherwise. Uneducated improvisation, trying things on a whim, represents gambling, shooting in the dark, which is not wise when American lives are involved. Like all real professionals and genuine artists, soldiers must have the discipline to build on a theme, to work from the known to the unknown. As we improvise solutions in our operations around the world, our goal is constant-not merely to do something, but to do the right thing.

LEADERS FOR A LEARNING ORGANIZATION

The Ridgway and Brubeck stories remind us of what can spring from the diverse richness of the American people, an ever-fresh well of vitality, ingenuity and boundless enthusiasm. While Ridgway clearly reflects that part of our populace which serves the Republic in uniform, we should note that Brubeck also answered his country's call as a soldier in 1944. He and his band played in Europe, no doubt entertaining some of Ridgway's paratroopers and glider forces in the process.[12] Both have worn Army green, and they and the men and women like them tell us much about the quality of the citizens who served in our ranks in the past, those who serve now and those who will join our Army in the days to come. We have a lot of great talent in America's Army.

Ridgway and Brubeck, of course, are exceptional personalities, historic figures of some prominence. At least in that respect, they are far different from most of us who carry out our duties without any particular public notice, let alone fanfare. While we can rightly attribute part of the pair's performance to the workings of individual chemistries, we should also be clear about some of the things that make them so outstanding among this century's Americans.

Absolute expertise in professional matters, commitment to team building and a preference to improvise based on known concepts-the general and the composer share these three traits. As Margaret J. Wheatley points out, America's Army is a learning organization, "rich in connections and relationships that make it possible to *know* what it knows."[13] Ridgway and Brubeck showed that degree of situational awareness; they developed it over years of study and effort. They understood themselves, their professions and the world around them. Equally important, they knew how to translate those insights into positive action.

When you think about it, that is what Army leaders strive to do every day as they meet the challenges of our volatile world. Without doubt, we are already making great strides in creating a leadership climate that nurtures organizational and personal growth. When we sent American soldiers into Kurdistan in 1991 and when we deployed the 10th Mountain Division into Somalia in 1992, we asked them to function in very ambiguous, dangerous and difficult environments. Our leaders in these operations, and many others, reinvented their forces to meet changing situations. We call that "tailoring" or "task-organizing based on METT-T (mission, enemy, troops, terrain (and weather), and time available)." It is a fundamental aspect of our current professional education.

That kind of approach would be very familiar to Ridgway or Brubeck. It reflects the Army's institutional, doctrinal manifestation of versatility. Our Army teaches this concept in our schools, practices it in our training centers and encourages it in our leader development process. We are working to inculcate versatility, endeavoring to infuse all of our men and women, all potential leaders, with the characteristics that made Ridgway and Brubeck so effective. Their examples light the way to our 21st-century force, an Army characterized by a commitment to learning leadership, with a premium on operational versatility and the improvisational genius that defines our military equivalent of jazz artistry.

Chapter Four

Living on the Edge: Building Cohesion and the Will to Win

by Robert W. Madden

Preparing soldiers and units to withstand the stress of combat has occupied the thinking of theorists and great battle captains alike. They have echoed throughout the centuries Xenophon's assertion: "You know I am sure that not numbers or strength bring victory in war; but whichever army goes into battle stronger in soul, their enemies generally cannot withstand them."[1] This is further supported by the oft-quoted Napoleonic maxim, "in war, the moral is to the material as three is to one."[2] Writing early in the 19th century, Prussian military theorist Carl von Clausewitz clearly understood that moral factors were among the most important in war. "One might say that the physical seem little more than the wooden hilt, while the moral factors are the precious metal, the real weapon, the finely-honed blade."[3]

Given the importance of the moral dimension in war, the readiness of soldiers and units must include psychological preparation for combat. This is especially important for our force projection Army — an Army in which soldiers live on the edge of peace. Soldiers must be prepared to make rapidly a psychological transition from peace to conflict, potentially without forewarning or in-depth knowledge of the situation.

The irony of the United States' post-WWII military experience is that the Army found itself fighting in places far different from those our soldiers had been led to expect. Soldiers comforted by the concept of deterrence, confident that there would be weeks, perhaps months, of build-up as diplomacy failed, found themselves fighting desperately, virtually without warning. Desert Shield and Storm aside, American troops have faced North Koreans, Chinese communists, Vietnamese peasants, Cuban construction workers, Panamanian Defense Forces, Somali warlord factions, and forces from the Former Republic of Yugoslavia in Bosnia and Kosovo. In fact, the United States has demonstrated a willingness to employ ground combat forces on a contingency basis no less than ten times since 1958.

Since 1990 our National Security Strategy has emphasized a shift to a more global framework, highlighting force projection as one of its primary military components. Coupled with a significant decrease in forward-deployed Army units, this strategy has necessitated an enhanced capability to employ forces on short notice to anywhere in the world from the continental United States as well as from the remaining forward-deployed locations. Force projection is increasingly the model for the likely employment of Army elements.[4]

> *They [US forces] must be able to respond quickly, and*
> *appropriately, as the application of even small*
> *amounts of power early in a crisis usually pays sig-*

nificant dividends. Some actions may require con-
siderable staying power, but there are likely to be sit-
uations where American focus will have to succeed
rapidly and with a minimum of casualties.[5]

In preparation for such operations, soldiers and units will have to maintain unprecedented physical and mental states of readiness. The transition from peace to war may only be a matter of days or weeks, not months or years. National Military Strategy and US Army doctrine are based on the premise that the Army in peace must consist of disciplined, cohesive units that possess the will to fight and win with little notice in an environment of ambiguity and uncertainty.[6] The will to fight must carry the individual soldier through the entire spectrum of conflict from humanitarian relief efforts in operations other than war to combat in a high intensity environment.

THE CASE FOR UNIT COHESION AS A FORCE MULTIPLIER

Comparing the number of combat stress casualties a unit suffers to its overall wounded provides compelling evidence that cohesion directly correlates to a unit's combat effectiveness. That unit cohesion, or a lack of it, can have a dramatic impact on battlefield effectiveness is demonstrated in Figure 1 (page 58), which compares casualty data for four U.S. infantry divisions during six weeks of combat operations in the European Theater of World War II.

The 82d and 101st Airborne Divisions had a unique mission which lent them a distinct unit identity, and they had been together for a considerable period of time before finding themselves in the heat of battle.[7] The impact of the cohesion that these units developed is evidenced by the low rate of combat stress casualties they sustained during a period of high intensity. The 85th and 91st Infantry Divisions, however, were mobilized quickly and had little time to train and work together as units prior to deployment for combat. Their stress casualty rates rendered these units nearly combat ineffective.[8]

CASUALTY DATA FROM WW II

UNIT	WIA	LOSS DUE TO COMBAT STRESS	%
85th ID (Gothic Line, Italy: 44 days)	3600	817	22.7
91st ID (Gothic Line, Italy: 44 days)	2700	919	34.0
82d Airborne Div (Normandy: 38 days)	4197	238	5.7
101st Airborne Div (Battle of the Bulge: 42 days)	4992	100	2.0

Figure 1

A more recent example of the correlation between unit cohesion and combat effectiveness is illustrated by the Israeli experience. The Yom Kippur War in 1973 and the Lebanon War in 1982 were conducted suddenly and unexpectedly. In these conflicts, psychiatric casualties accounted for 30.0 and 23.0 percent, respectively, of all wounded.[9] It was difficult for the individual soldier to prepare his psychological defenses. Studies conducted by Israeli psychologists concluded: "Soldiers who were confident in their military skills and in their leader, and who were members of stable, cohesive units ... showed themselves more resistant to combat neuroses, even under the most severe stress situations."[10] A greater number of soldiers maintained their will to fight in cohesive units.

US Army doctrine suggests that the foundation of success is based on creating cohesive, disciplined teams that can withstand the stress of combat and maintain the will to win under the most adverse conditions. Cohesion is defined by the Army's leadership manual, *FM 22-100*, as "the existence of strong bonds of mutual trust, confidence, and understanding among members of a unit."[11] DA PAM 350-2 defines unit cohesion as "the feeling of belonging to a team of soldiers who accept a unit's mission as their mission."[12]

To combine the two definitions, a unit becomes cohesive when its members feel a sense of belonging that is developed through shared unit values and relationships of mutual trust and confidence. Unit cohesion, however, does not occur by happenstance. Leaders must develop cohesion deliberately within their organizations in order to foster the will to win in their soldiers.

COHESION THEORY — VEGETIUS TO SLA MARSHALL

Writing in the late 4th century, Flavius Vegetius Renatus (Vegetius) recorded the traditions, tactics, military customs, and virtues that made the ancient Roman Army the premier of its time. His work, *The Military Institutions of the Romans*, was intended to be a "bottom up review" which included recommendations to the Roman Emperor, Valentin, on how to reform the deteriorating army and return it to its former greatness. "Victory in war," he wrote, "does not depend entirely upon numbers or mere courage; only skill and discipline will insure it."[13] Vegetius stated that the Roman Army of the past did not go out of its way to select the best and brightest for service, rather it relied on arduous training programs to make its soldiers reliable and confident in combat.

> *They [The Roman Armies of the past] understood the importance of hardening them by continual practice, and of training them to every maneuver that might happen in line and in action ... The courage of a soldier is heightened by his knowledge of his profession, and he only wants an opportunity to execute what he convinced he has been perfectly taught. A handful of men, inured to war, proceed to certain victory, while on the contrary, numerous armies of raw and undisciplined troops are but multitudes of men dragged to the slaughter.[14]*

Vegetius' work became the most influential military treatise in the western world from Roman times to the 19th century. In fact, as late as 1770, the Austrian Field Marshal, Prince de Ligne, called it magnificent and wrote, "A God, said Vegetius, inspired the legion, but for myself, I find that God inspired Vegetius."[15]

If Vegetius was the most influential theorist until the Napoleonic era, the post-Napoleonic era was dominated by the writings of two theorists: Baron Antoine Henri Jomini and Prussian General Carl von Clausewitz. Both had participated in the Wars of Napoleon on different sides. Though they did not particularly agree on much, they concluded, based on their experience, that moral superiority is an extremely important factor in the effectiveness of units and in the outcome of battles.

Jomini mentions Vegetius in his work, *The Summary of the Art of War*, when discussing the importance of cultivating a military spirit in one's citizens and the impact of morale on the outcome of battle.

> *This seems to be due to a certain physical effect produced by the moral cause. For example, the impetuous attack upon a hostile line by twenty thousand brave whose feelings are thoroughly enlisted in their cause will produce a much more powerful effect than the attack of forty thousand demoralized or apathetic men upon the same point.*[16]

Jomini believed that there were two means of encouraging the military spirit. First, those who serve in the military should receive special consideration from the public and government so they know they have public support. Second, he believed that the key to maintaining a high military spirit was arduous training which would expose armies to labor and fatigue, keep them from stagnating in garrison during peacetime, exult their superiority over their enemies, and arouse their enthusiasm by all means available in harmony with their frame of mind.[17]

Clausewitz, on the other hand, believed that an army gained its discipline and will to fight from an internalized military spirit.

> *An army that maintains its cohesion under the most murderous fire; that cannot be shaken by imaginary fears and resists well-founded ones with all its might;*

that, proud of its victories will not lose the strength to obey orders and its respect and trust for its officers even in defeat; whose physical power, like the muscles of an athlete, has been steeled by training in privation and effort...such an army is imbued with the true military spirit.[18]

Clausewitz stated that the true military spirit can be created only in war. "Discipline, skill, goodwill, a certain pride, and high morale are the attributes of an army trained in times of peace."[19] These command respect but they are fragile in war and have no strength of their own. He advised that we should be careful not to confuse the real spirit of an army with its mood.[20] Further, he embellished: "No general can accustom an army to war. Peacetime maneuvers are a feeble substitute for the real thing..."[21] Though he stated that the military spirit can only be created in war, Clausewitz conceded that it may endure for several generations, even under leaders of average ability and through long periods of peace. In other words military leaders must capitalize on traditions and lessons of the past to maintain spirit in the present. Military spirit springs from two interactive sources: a series of victorious wars and frequent exertions of the army to the utmost limits of its strength. "Nothing else," according to Clausewitz, "will show a soldier the full extent of his capacities. The more a general is accustomed to place heavy demands on his soldiers [and subordinate leaders], the more he can depend on their response."[22]

Clausewitz identified danger, physical exertion, intelligence, and friction as the elements that form the abrasive nature of war. Only one lubricant exists to reduce the abrasion — combat experience. If we accept this assertion as true, then it raises a significant issue. If we cannot realistically duplicate the element of danger in peacetime training, what mitigates the psychological impact of combat for inexperienced troops?

Clausewitz's concept of training focuses on preparing the army to endure great hardships. As war is the realm of exertion and suffering, he states that these alone will defeat us unless we can make ourselves indifferent to them. Indifference by birth or by training provides a certain strength of body and soul.[23] He strongly believed that exertions must be practiced in peacetime to prepare the mind, even more than the body. Habit hardens the body for exertions and trains soldiers and leaders to deal calmly with adversity. Finally, he believed that friction must be incorporated into training to exercise the officers' judgment, common sense, and resolve.[24]

Clausewitz clearly understood the value of the individual soldier to unit effectiveness.

> *An army's military qualities are based on the individual who is steeped in the spirit and essence of this activity; who trains the capacities it demands, rouses them, and makes them his own; who applies his intelligence to every detail; who gains ease and confidence through practice, and who completely immerses his personality in the appointed task.[25]*

Thus, according to Clausewitz, tough realistic training which closely simulates the stresses of combat serves to mitigate the psychological impact.

The effects of battle on the individual soldier became a career-long study by French military theorist Colonel Ardant du Picq. Writing prior to the Franco-Prussian War (1870), his work, *Battle Studies*, reflected the insights of a soldier who had experienced first-hand the demands of war. Du Picq pointed out that while all other circumstances change with time, the human element remains the same, capable of finite levels of endurance, fear, sacrifice, effort, and no more. He recognized that the increased lethality on the battlefield resulted in greater dispersion which, in turn, hindered supervision. Decisions now were gained by action in open order, where each soldier was expected to act individually, with will and initiative to attack the enemy and destroy him. Additionally, the soldier seemed to fight alone in the smoke, dispersion, and confusion of battle. Unity was no longer assured by mutual surveillance.[26] He believed these conditions created a greater need for cohesion than ever before.

Du Picq's concept of cohesion is best illustrated by this analogy: "Four brave men who do not know each other will not dare to attack a lion. Four less brave, but knowing each other well, sure of their reliability and consequently of mutual aid, will attack resolutely."[27] This unity and confidence springs from mutual trust which is fostered by discipline to orders, living together, obeying the same leaders, and shared experiences of fatigue and hardship. Mutual trust also develops from the cooperation among men who quickly understand one another in stressful situations. "It is that intimate confidence, firm and conscious, which does not forget itself in the heat of action and which alone makes true combatants."[28] Perhaps Du Picq's legacy is his recognition that unit effectiveness is enhanced within "an organization which will establish cohesion by the mutual acquaintanceship of all,"[29] that is a knowledge of comrades, a trust in officers providing visible leadership, a sense of duty, discipline, and pride. This sustains the soldier in combat and prevents fear from becoming terror.

His concept of discipline bears further elaboration. Du Picq stated that, "The purpose of discipline is to make men fight in spite of themselves."[30] He acknowledged that the customs of a democratic society did not permit draconian discipline whereby soldiers advanced forward in battle because of the fear of death from behind if they fell back. Other techniques had to be applied in order to instill discipline. He believed that the cohesion resulting from the mutual trust among men and officers is what creates discipline. "Today, why should not the men in our companies watch discipline and punish themselves. They alone know each other, and the maintenance of discipline is so much to their interest as to encourage them to stop skulking."[31] He also pointed out that as wars become shorter and more violent, cohesion must be created in advance.[32]

Almost a century later, SLA Marshall echoed the views of du Picq. Increased lethality and battlefield dispersion had reached new proportions during WWII, and his interviews with soldiers fresh from the front lines reaffirmed du Picq's insights on the necessity of mutual trust. Marshall also argued for the value of instilling unit cohesion during peacetime: "It is from the acquiring of the habit of working with the group and of feeling responsible to the group that his thoughts are apt to turn ultimately to the welfare of the group when tactical disintegration threatens in battle."[33]

The landmark study by Samuel Stouffer, et al, *The American Soldier*, offered extensive insights into the social psychology of WWII soldiers. They concluded that the primary or informal group served two principal functions in combat motivation: "It set and enforced group standards of behavior, and it supported and sustained the individual in stresses he would otherwise not have been able to withstand."[34]

The various theories regarding the moral domain of battle have greatly influenced American doctrine. The architects of US Army doctrine acknowledged Patton's admonition, "Wars are fought by men, not machines. The human dimension of war will be decisive in the campaigns and battles of the future, just as the past."[35] The US Army recognizes that the increased lethality of modern battle requires the dispersion of forces. This in turn requires a command and control system that emphasizes decentralized execution within the framework of a commander's intent. Units will find themselves isolated on the future battlefield which "will place a premium on sound leadership, competent and courageous soldiers, and cohesive, well-trained units."[36]

US Army doctrine is based on certain key assumptions.[37] First, the concept of decentralized execution is predicated on Anthony Kellet's assertion that "on the battlefield, self-discipline plays a much greater role in modern combat than discipline imposed from without."[38] It assumes that the individuals composing the primary group and formal unit structure will, in the absence of higher authority, actively seek to defeat the enemy. Individuals will pursue a course of action contrary to human nature, forsaking relative safety and comfort to risk their lives in actively seeking to engage and destroy the enemy. It supposes that soldiers and leaders have so internalized their concepts of discipline and will to fight, that their actions in the face of the enemy will conform to the expectations of doctrine. As Lord Moran argues, "discipline, control from without, can only be relaxed safely when it is replaced by something higher and better, control from within."[39]

Many of the motivations that influence soldiers in battle clearly have peacetime roots. The brief survey shows that unit cohesion is derived from leadership, training, and individual readiness, and that it must be attained in advance of combat. In light of this, several questions require further investigation: What are the individual characteristics of today's US Army soldier? What are the combat characteristics of force projection operations (what stressors can our soldiers expect to face prior to engaging the enemy)? What unit characteristics are essential to prepare soldiers to deal with the combat characteristics?

A PROFILE OF THE US ARMY SOLDIER

Despite the Army's efforts to instill the will to fight and win in its soldiers, a certain tension exists between the expectations of the Army and the influence of society. SLA Marshall probably best described the social conditioning and moral restraints placed upon the modern American soldier.

> *He is what his home, his religion, his schooling, and the moral code and ideals of his society have made him. The Army cannot unmake him. It must reckon with the fact that he comes from a civilization in which aggression, connected with the taking of life, is prohibited and unacceptable ... It stays his trigger finger even though he is hardly conscious that it is a restraint upon him.*[40]

Based on his experiences of warfare in 400 B.C., Sun Tzu, recorded in his treatise, *The Art of War*, "Know your enemy, know yourself, and in a hundred battles you will never be in peril."[41] In order for our leaders to "know themselves," they must understand the motivation of young Americans who volunteer to serve in the Armed Forces. The following facts profile today's US Army soldier fresh out of basic training. He is typically 20 years old. 92% are high school graduates.   12.4% of first term enlistees are married. 38% come from broken homes as a result of divorce.   94% come from homes whose parents had a combined income of less than $50,000.[42]   They are all volunteers.

Since 1973, the US has relied on an all-volunteer force. However, to sustain this policy, it has had to resort to numerous incentives to enlist and retain quality officers and soldiers.   The results of a survey of infantry recruits conducted by George C. Wilson and published in *Mud Soldiers*, indicate that 70% joined the Army to obtain money for college, a steady job, discipline, or adventure and travel.   Ten years later in a FY97 New Recruit Survey, education benefits increased in importance as did a recognition that the Army provides job opportunities and potential for advancement (Figure 2).

The U.S. Army Soldier

Profile	Reasons for Entering the Service	1989[43]	1997[44]
o A volunteer	o Money for College	27%	33%
o Typically 20 years old	o Adventure/Travel	16%	8%
o 12% of first termers are married	o Wanted to be a soldier (something to be proud of)	15%	12%
o 38% from broken homes	o Challenge: Prove I Can Make It	15%	7%
o 94% w/parent incomes <$50,000 yr	o Better job opportunities and potential for advancement	14%	21%
o 92% high school graduates	o Serve My Country	5%	9%
	o Unemployed: nothing better to do	6%	4%
	o Enlistment bonus/ Retirement plan	2%	6%

Figure 2

These recruits joined the Army in the belief that it would get them somewhere in life and provide them with some fun and adventure along the way. "They were looking for a sliver of America's good life and would risk their lives for a chance to get it."[45] A majority of these recruits, by their own admission, did not join the Army to be soldiers. During the Gulf War, cartoonist Gary Trudeau traced the adventures of two of his characters who were Army Reservists and whose unit had been activated and deployed to the Gulf (Figure 3).[46] Perhaps this cartoon is illuminating.

Figure 3

As the profile of today's soldier indicates, it is up to the Army to instill the soldierly values and live up to its promise to enable these new soldiers to "be all you can be." While basic training is the starting point for shaping these soldiers, the actual commitment to organizational values does not occur until they report for duty to their first unit.

STRESSORS OF THE FORCE PROJECTION ARMY

In addition to knowing basic profiles and initial motivations of soldiers, it is important to understand the types of stress they may face during a deployment from the alert phase through the actual execution of the contingency operation. Deployments under contingency conditions are often undertaken in crisis avoidance or crisis management situations that are time-sensitive, and in which the mission of the force and the enemy situation are still being developed. Military forces are employed to make a political statement of resolve, and soldiers may or may not receive popular support prior to deployment. In the case of the Falklands, British forces knew the nation was behind them. In Grenada, US forces did not know how the nation would react. In the Gulf War, the public firmly supported the deployment.

Today's soldiers may be expected to fight and win without a clear understanding of their purpose. Colonel A.J. Bacevich (USA, Ret) explains how the political nature of contingency operations changes the moral justification for military involvement.

> *Engaged in dirty wars where moral certitude may be in short supply, these professionals will fight not for ideals but to advance the interests of the state. Their effectiveness will stem less from having the right cause or even the right hardware, than from the toughness, resilience and cohesion of individual units.*[47]

Political restrictions in the form of rules of engagement will usually be placed on combat forces. These rules can become a source of frustration to soldiers who are trained to maximize combat power. The strategies of massive and indiscriminate bombing against German and Japanese cities during WWII, or the more limited bombing campaigns such as those against Iraqi and Serbian cities and forces during the Gulf War and Kosovo crisis, might not be acceptable uses of force for contingency operations, as in the case of Somalia. The soldier with his M16 becomes the precision tool to surgically remove an enemy in order to reduce the risk to the local population. Additionally, limiting US combat losses to retain public support is a strong consideration. Increasing television and other media coverage of Third World conflicts reinforces the decision-maker's concerns about minimizing noncombatant and US soldier casualties. These constraints weigh heavy upon the minds of soldiers and leaders who grew up in the shadow of the My Lai incident. In many cases, as in Somalia, the only way to distinguish an enemy soldier from a noncombatant is when he or she opens fire.

The soldier's preconceptions about the combat characteristics are an important part of mental preparation. Beforehand, he assesses the risks, hardships, intensity, duration, etc., based on training, information from the chain of command, and popular conceptions from books and movies. This allows him to measure in advance the amount of inner strength he will need. The potential, therefore, exists for the soldier to become demoralized if actual combat differs substantially from his mental image.[48] As arms sales and weapons of mass destruction proliferate, Third World may not necessarily mean lack of capability – particularly in the contexts of the fighting in Iraq, Somalia, and Chechnya. Forces deployed in future contingency operations may face adversaries who possess significant heavy force capabilities, ballistic missiles, artillery, chemical weapons, etc., or who have the ability to fight a series of fierce asymmetrical engagements with some degree of initial success. Additionally, adversaries may harbor a strong, perhaps even fanatical, resolve to defend their national or sub-national objectives.

Furthermore, rapid deployment places unique stresses on individual soldiers. The circumstances surrounding the deployment may be unforeseen and unanticipated by the soldier, who may be deployed without a clear understanding of national interests or of the enemy situation. In order to maintain security, soldiers are alerted at the last minute and are restricted from making outside phone calls prior to their deployment. For example, when soldiers were alerted to deploy to Grenada in 1983, few believed it to be the real thing even after being issued live ammunition. Most thought they had been alerted to reinforce the Marines in Beirut after the terrorist attack on the Marine Barracks.

The sudden shock of family separation or no-notice deployment may impede the psychological readiness of US soldiers. Having been rapidly alerted and deployed under conditions of enforced secrecy, soldiers preparing for the invasion of Grenada were concerned about the notification and support of their families. Questions arose such as: How will they pay the bills? How will she manage with her pregnancy? How will my son finish his science project? Single soldiers worried about other issues: How will my girlfriend and parents find out that I have been deployed? Did I remember to roll up my car windows? Many of the men wrote "last letters" just in case something might happen. Officers began to wonder if they had trained their men properly.[49]

Predeployment activities also affect the soldier's sleep cycle and contribute to the biological tension that leads to fatigue and exhaustion even before actual combat. Studies have shown that soldiers are likely to become combat ineffective after 48 to 60 hours without sleep. The effects of sleep loss are mainly psychological — mental ability deteriorates and tasks requiring cognitive ability, such as vigilance on the perimeter or planning and decision-making, are significantly impaired.[50] In the case of the Division Ready Brigade of the 82d Airborne Division during the invasion of Grenada, leaders had been awake for almost 30 hours by the time they disembarked the C130s on the Salinas air strip at 1330 hrs, 25 Oct 1983, and began to expand the lodgment area. It was not until after midnight on the first day that leaders were able to sleep, not by design, but by physical necessity. They could not stay awake. Fortunately, there was little to no resistance during the first night.[51]

In addition to overcoming physical demands, contingency operations are more dependent upon the initiative of the individual soldier who fights isolated actions in small groups. "Decisions in combat that once were reserved for the aristocracy of battle — the commanders — were pushed down to the ranks of the ordinary soldier. Do I advance? Do I take cover? Do I fire now? Do I retreat? Do I surrender?"[52] The fear of isolation on the battlefield is a major factor in maintaining the soldier's will to fight. Napoleon realized the importance of this when he stated this maxim: "Make the enemy believe that support is lacking; isolate; cut-off, flank, turn, in a thousand ways make his men believe themselves isolated."[53] Du Picq also theorized, "Today the soldier is often unknown to his comrades. He is lost in the smoke, the dispersion, the confusion of battle. He seems to fight alone. Unity is no longer insured by mutual surveillance."[54]

A soldier need not be located apart from his comrades to feel isolated. He can be isolated by his own fear and a perceived lack of support from his primary group. Studies done from the Yom Kippur War found that men who suffered such reactions reported little or no identification with their unit or team, no trust in their leaders, and frequent transfers or rotations.[55]

Having described the individual characteristics of typical US Army soldiers and the stresses they are likely to face during the course of a deployment, it is now time to discuss how leaders may develop cohesion within their organizations to help soldiers counter their concerns and fears.

ENTER THE LEADER

While basic training is the starting point for shaping soldiers, the actual commitment to organizational values does not occur until they report for duty to their unit. It is the responsibility of the leader to develop cohesion based upon a commitment to unit values, which will psychologically harden the soldiers to the exertions and danger posed by the expected nature of combat. According to US Army doctrine, "The most essential dynamic of combat power is competent and confident officer and noncommissioned officer leadership. Leaders inspire soldiers with the will to win. They provide purpose, direction, and motivation in combat."[56] In essence, unit leaders set the conditions for the development of lethal, cohesive units that can function effectively in the physical and psychological stresses of combat.

Leaders can design unit activities that generate the kind of bonding or behavior they want to encourage. First, they should decide which values, both general and unit specific, they want to instill in their soldiers.[57] Next, these values should be integrated into all facets of unit operations using elements of spirit such as unit mottoes, symbols, traditions, history, records for high performance, and marching cadences to maximum advantage. Essentially, they are a means by which a unit displays its identity.[58]

Another means of quickly instilling unit values into soldiers is through a bonding cycle. This is a carefully selected set of experiences designed to make the soldiers into family.[59] The bonding cycle begins with the integration of the soldier into the unit. This is the stage when a soldier is most impressionable as he is transferring his loyalty from his old unit or finding out where he fits into the unit's mission. Early on in his assignment, he forms his opinions and attitudes toward the unit that could last for the remainder of his tour. He should be welcomed with open arms and made to feel a valued member of the team from the very start.

Loyalty is further developed by ensuring that soldiers understand the importance of their role in combat and how they fit into the big picture. As Field Marshall Bernard Montgomery said, "Every soldier must know, before he goes into battle, how the little battle he is to fight fits into the larger picture, and how the success of his fighting will influence the battle as a whole."[60] This is accomplished by keeping soldiers informed through command information periods and informal training evaluations.

To enhance the bonding of soldiers, leaders must strive to reduce personnel turbulence by maintaining continuity of job assignments. US personnel assignment policies hinder the development of unit cohesion as soldiers and leaders are rotated frequently. Therefore, we must not add to the turbulence by continually reassigning subordinate leaders and soldiers to different jobs and sections. According to FM 22-100, "Bonds of respect, trust, confidence, and understanding take time to develop. When soldiers or leaders are shifted, bonds are broken, and new ones must be built."[61] Turbulence tears at the fabric of unit cohesion, degrading a unit's combat effectiveness. Maintaining unit integrity whenever possible creates an environment for sharing experiences and enhancing teamwork.

It is foolish to believe that a soldier's loyalty, trust, and commitment belong to his leaders and organizations alone. Leaders must also be sensitive to the needs of the family. FY99 figures show that approximately 35% of the young soldier population, 80% of the NCO's, and 83% of the entire officer Corps (lieutenants at 44%) are married. Families, who often feel isolated and lack a sense of belonging, need both a formal and informal support structure, especially when the unit is deployed.[62] Likewise, soldiers need to know that their families are being taken care of during deployment.

Soldiers also feel more secure in facing combat when they possess confidence in their leaders. This places a heavy psychological burden on leaders, who realize that their actions are greatly scrutinized by their soldiers and who are afraid of showing weakness or indecision. Major Chuck Jacoby, Commander of the first infantry company of the 82d Airborne's Division Ready Brigade to arrive at the Salinas Airfield in Grenada, stated that "My soldiers looked to me more than usual for guidance and strength. Failing as a company commander was more threatening to me than the fear of enemy action."[63] Most likely, leaders at the lower levels, who will not have had combat experience, have to build their credibility during peacetime. How the leader reacts in the first few critical minutes of exposure to hostile fire is directly related to how his soldiers will react. If he exudes confidence and aggressiveness, then so will his subordinates. In the Mediterranean Theater in 1944, infantrymen rated "leadership by example" as the most important attribute of officers who had done a particularly good job of helping their men to feel confident in a tough or frightening situation.[64]

Leaders gain confidence and become more tactically and technically proficient by planning and conducting realistic training. Likewise, through the conduct of challenging training, soldiers gain confidence in themselves, their fellow soldiers, and their leaders, as well as in their weapons and equipment. The expression, "train as you will fight," is more than just catchy rhetoric. If leadership is the heart of developing cohesion in organizations, training is the blood that enables all parts to work in synchronization with one another — physical fitness, tactics, doctrine, technology, logistics, medical care, and discipline. As such, leaders must focus on replicating the combat characteristics unique to contingency operations — predeployment conditions, uncertainty, political constraints (rules of engagement), etc. Dr. Roger Spiller contends:

> *Armies have had a great and abiding faith in the idea that military training can prepare a soldier for combat, and many soldiers have testified that training can physically toughen the man destined for the fighting lines ... However, even the best training is never equal to combat. When training is deficient or indifferent or misguided, based upon an ill-founded idea of what combat may be like, it is as dangerous to the fighting soldier as an enemy bullet.[65]*

Training must harden soldiers to fear, fatigue, exertion, and privation. FM 22-100, *Military Leadership*, advises, "Put soldiers through significant emotional and physical experiences in which they do things they did not believe they could do as individuals or as a unit."[66] Clausewitz believed that the frequent exertion of the army to the utmost limits of its strength must be practiced in training, "A soldier is just as proud of the hardships he has overcome as of the dangers he has faced."[67] This is further illustrated by Guy Sajer's experience in the German Army in WWII. His training for acceptance into the elite *Gross Deutschland* Division stretched the limits of his endurance. When he completed training, he was extremely proud of his accomplishment:

> *[I] joined the ranks of those who had already completed the ceremony, in a high state of emotion. . . Despite all the hardship we had been through, my vanity was flattered by my acceptance as a German among Germans, and as a warrior worthy of bearing arms.*[68]

As Sajer's experience suggests, a Rites of Passage exercise followed by an official acceptance ceremony is a good method of rapidly integrating a new soldier into the unit. The ceremony clearly shows other members of the unit that the new soldier is now qualified to be "one of us." Bonding activities that can help further build cohesion include the "Ten Foot Tall" experience that is usually some physical feat that associates good performance with the unit's mission.[69] Physical fitness programs must also be tailored to prepare the soldier to perform combat skills in the specific geographic and climatic conditions of the unit's assigned contingency mission.

Arduous training expands the boundaries of a soldier's endurance giving him both a sense of accomplishment and confidence. Response to various combat situations must become automatic, "Routine, apart from its sheer inevitability," argued Clausewitz, "also contains one positive advantage. Constant practice leads to brisk, precise, and reliable leadership, reducing normal friction and easing the working of the machine."[70] Battle drills help reduce the level of anxiety as soldiers develop a high degree of self-confidence about their ability to handle themselves when exposed to danger. Additionally, the level of fear is reduced once the soldier begins to execute the specific drill in a skilled manner.[71] Rehearsals prior to deployment give the soldier greater confidence that his mission can be accomplished. Still, training should not be too rigid. As most combat situations in contingency operations are characterized by uncertainty and sudden change, leaders must inject the unexpected into each training situation.

Realistic training must also expose soldiers to battle stimuli such as the noise and shock waves of explosions. In this way, soldiers sense the imminence of annihilation and develop an expectation of what combat is like. Stouffer asked WWII veterans the question, "Is there any particular kind of training you did not get that you wish you had received before you went into combat?" The most frequent response was, "Yes ... training under live ammunition, under realistic battle conditions."[72] In a study of the Falklands, indirect fire was more stressful to the soldiers than direct fire, but the former, proportionally, did not account for many casualties.[73] This confirms Stouffer's finding during WWII in North Africa that the threat of certain weapons evoked exaggerated reactions of fear among those soldiers who had been in combat only a short time. Although the German dive bomber elicited the most fear, it accounted for a small percentage of overall casualties.[74] In Grenada, the Rangers attributed their superior performance to the fact that they continually trained with live ammunition in realistic training scenarios at least twice a month. Numerous soldiers stated in interviews afterwards that they fought as they had trained.[75]

The conclusion from this section is obvious. Leaders must decide what type of behavior and what kind of commitment they want from their soldiers. Subsequently, leaders can systematically design programs that will inspire soldiers to internalize the values of the unit, often without being aware of it.

Figure 4 presents a proposed system for deliberately instilling unit cohesion into an organization. By employing a leader-designed program for deliberately instilling cohesion, soldiers

A PROPOSED SYSTEM FOR INSTILLING UNIT COHESION:

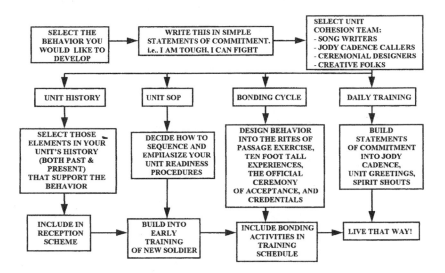

Figure 4

become loyal members of the team and gain a great deal of confidence in themselves, their weapons, and their leaders in the process. This system is applicable to all levels from squad through the Corps level to include high level staffs. The implementation of a cohesion strategy is only limited by the leader's imagination and initiative.

CONCLUSIONS AND IMPLICATIONS

Contingency operations place difficult psychological demands upon soldiers. The circumstances surrounding the deployment are shrouded in secrecy. Predeployment activities disrupt the soldier's sleep cycle and do not allow him to inform loved ones. The requirement for a rapid response to a remote country often does not allow time to develop a thorough intelligence picture, contributing to an environment of uncertainty. The political nature of the conflict may not provide the soldier the moral justification for his involvement, or even the knowledge that the nation is behind him.

In most cases he will have to fight more from a sense of duty rather than from outrage against threats to vital national interests. Finally, the soldier's leadership and training establish certain preconceptions about the nature of contingency operations. If the combat characteristics are considerably different than what the soldier has been led to expect, the preconditions for demoralization are set.

The research analyzing contingency operations such as the Falklands and Grenada indicates that cohesion is a force-multiplier as Napoleon, Clausewitz, and du Picq had theorized. Units that had sewn the seeds of cohesion in peacetime had greater battlefield success. Additionally, they were better able to maintain their will to fight and withstand deprivations of climate and deficits of supply compared to less cohesive units.

Developing cohesion and the will to fight in individual soldiers and units is a dynamic process. Leadership and training are the two most essential components contributing to unit characteristics. They enhance and strengthen the bonds of trust and mutual respect between soldiers and soldiers and their leaders. The soldier's willingness to fight reflects the leader's efforts to shape the soldier's character and to solidify his commitment to unit values. As Lord Moran stated,

> *Character . . . is a habit, the daily choice of right instead of wrong; it is a moral quality which grows to maturity in peace and is not suddenly developed on the outbreak of war. For war, in spite of much that we have heard to the contrary, has no power to transform, it merely exaggerates the good and evil that are in us, till it is plain for all to read; it cannot change, it exposes. Man's fate in battle is worked out before war begins.*[76]

Unit values are built into and derived from the elements of spirit. The leader must develop cohesion through activities designed to instill unit values into the individual soldier. If these factors are to be effective motivators, they must be made an integral part of a soldier's training and a part of daily life.

Additionally, soldiers must know that their families are being looked after. Efforts must be made to deal quickly and efficiently with legal issues of divorce, alimony, child support, indebtedness, and sole parenthood as they arise in peacetime. Pre-established support programs such as family support groups and deployment information briefings will relieve the concerns of soldiers and reduce their psychological baggage.

Training must harden soldiers to the factors of fear, fatigue, and physical exertion that limit combat effectiveness. Arduous training expands the boundaries of endurance giving soldiers a sense of accomplishment and confidence in their own abilities, their fellow soldiers, and their leaders. Training must also replicate the combat characteristics of contingency operations. This can be done by frequent (semi-annual) Emergency Deployment Readiness Exercises (EDRE). Training for executing the deployment cycle must also include a disciplined sleep plan so that soldiers and leaders are alert enough to fight once deployed.

Every unit in the US Army is assigned a priority contingency mission or a role in a major regional theater of war. This should provide the focus for tailored training programs that address the specific physical and psychological demands of a particular geographical region. Efforts must be made to stay abreast of political situations in likely areas where contingency operations may be conducted. War plans should be updated accordingly. The elements of uncertainty and surprise should be reduced by giving soldiers training on the geography, culture and military capabilities of potential adversaries in these areas.

While the US Army teaches military history to its officer corps, there is little emphasis on military history within the training cycles of the individual soldiers. Using the British example, the US Army should also inculcate soldiers with a sense of military history. In so doing, the soldiers' pride in their unit's traditions is enhanced, as is their determination to be worthy of them.

Unfortunately, stabilization is required to solidify allegiance and loyalty to the unit, and US Army peacetime personnel policies hinder the development of unit cohesion by creating personnel turbulence. All theories of cohesion development include stability of unit members and their leaders as a pre-condition. The attempt to regimentalize the Army seemed to be a step in the right direction, but there no longer appears to be a concerted effort to do so. Nevertheless, personnel policies should be developed that allow a soldier stability and identification with a specific unit for a prolonged period of time.

The major implication from the study is that force projection operations are likely a "come as you are" affair. Therefore, the will to fight and win must be developed in peacetime. Some soldiers may find themselves decisively engaged in as few as eighteen hours after they were alerted, others in as little as ninety-six hours. The tactical units that will conduct future contingency operations must take deliberate steps to instill in their soldiers an aggressive will to fight and win. As du Picq stated, "what must be inculcated [in the soldier] is a will of his own, a personal impulse to send him forward."[77]

The contingency soldier on the battlefield of tomorrow wins or loses the battle based on the level of unit cohesion developed in peacetime. Confidence in himself, in his weapons, in his comrades, in his leaders, virtually his entire psychological readiness, is a result of the efforts of his leaders and the quality of training he has received in advance.

Chapter Five

Discipline: Creating the Foundation for an Initiative-Based Organization

by Christopher D. Kolenda

Discipline, for members of a mature organization, means to understand the difference between right and wrong in terms of performance and behavior, and to do what is right in the absence of supervision.[1] Leaders who value versatility, independent thought, and initiative require this level of discipline, because it forms a foundation of trust that permeates the organization. Once the members of an organization have demonstrated mastery and internalization of the fundamentals, once they perform routine skills to standard and behave within the framework of organizational values without supervision, the leaders can move from detailed method of control to a directive one.[2] In doing so they can foster that versatility, independence, and intiative that gives an organization vitality: the ability to maintain effectiveness and dictate change in a fluid, uncertain situation while remaining centered on its core competencies and values. Organizations that build this level of discipline are lasting. They master changes in technology and context without being mastered by them; they maintain the intiative against their adveraries over the long-term rather than react to them; and they respond to problems and crises in a predictable, coherent manner.

That discipline has become a misunderstood quality and often regarded as taboo is not surprising. Part of the stigma comes from the frequent coupling of discipline with sanction; to "discipline" people implies punishing them. Another, more salient reason is that discipline as a method of gaining compliance comes in a variety of forms. Models range from the unquestioning automaton who performs precise bodily movements under the direct threat of physical coercion[3] to the professional self-discipline described above.

Coercive discipline is most appropriate for immature organizations: those whose members have a low level of skill competency or have yet to internalize specified behavioral norms. Mass conscript armies with little time to train and build cohesion naturally fall into this category as do typical basic training units. Relying primarily on the tools of reward and punishment and constant, direct supervision, these organizations must employ the "carrot and stick" approach to establish and enforce standards and reward compliance.

Naturally, this coercive model tends to foster a level of dependence which can be anathema to independence and intitiative. While independence and intiative are not sought after in conscript or basic training units, sole reliance upon coercion is not an appropriate method for organizations that need innovation and creativity to sustain their vitality. The general result in organizations that emphasize punishment to gain compliance is a sullen minimalism. Their members will only put forth enough effort to keep them out of trouble, and only then when the "boss" is watching.   As a result, they can never "push the envelope" of higher performance. The cost to a business is profit and productivity; an army pays its price in blood.

The true test of discipline, therefore, is functionality. Discipline must directly contribute to the accomplishment of the organization's goals and objectives or else it is meaningless. For organizations such as the military that operate routinely in chaotic and uncertain situations against a thinking, uncooperative adversary, discipline must contribute to skill performance and appropriate behavior as well as subordinate leader independence and intitiative. Self-discipline serves as a nexus of trust between the individual and the collective. In this way, a military organization maintains its versatility and ultimately its effectiveness over the long-term.[4]

This level of discipline does not occur by happenstance. It must be developed within the organization. As Lord Moran, a British front-line doctor in the First World War and Churchill's personal physician during the Second, suggests in his classic study, *Anatomy of Courage*: "If discipline is relaxed when it has not been replaced by a high morale, you get a mob who will obey their own primitive instincts."[5]   In essence, Moran argues that discipline is at first imposed externally and can be relaxed or tightened at the discretion of the leaders depending upon the morale of the soldiers. High morale, he asserts, will eventually create the same effect as discipline; after a period of training soldiers can develop a high level of professionalism and perform without supervision. In his assessment of the Guards, the elite of the British Army, Moran claims that "they must submit to the creed that there is another discipline besides the discipline of movement — the self-discipline that drives a man to the mastery of his art through long, laborious days, eschewing pleasure."[6]

Once this level of discipline has become inculcated within the culture of the organization, the foundation is established for an initiative-based organization — one that values and promotes versatility and independence of thought in the absence of orders or in the context of a rapidly changing situation. This essay will discuss some theories on how this mature level of discipline is developed and how leaders can use it to build an initiative-based organization.

INSTILLING A HIGHER FORM OF DISCIPLINE

According to Lord Moran there are two types of discipline: the discipline of movement which is externally imposed on the physical activities of soldiers, and self-discipline which springs from a sense of professionalism inside the individual fostered by what he terms the "discipline of persuasion."[7] Taking Moran's argument a step further, once discipline is internalized throughout the organization, the result is an environment in which people can regulate themselves and their comrades, because they know that doing so will keep the organization functioning effectively.[8] The result is a high-performing unit that will continue to function effectively in the absence of supervision.

Moving from a form of discipline based on the presence of supervision to an internalized discipline must begin with education and training. Confucius, the classical Chinese philosopher, when asked how to inculcate in people an enthusiasm for excellence, replied, "Rule over them with dignity and they will be reverent; treat them with kindness and they will do their best; raise the good and instruct those who are backward and they will be imbued with enthusiasm."[9] Education and training form the foundations for discipline because they inculcate the difference between right and wrong in terms of organizational values and professional skills.

Character is a habit,[10] and the same can be said for competency. Education and training must be based upon clearly articulated standards of perfomance and behavior as well as the reasons why they are important. Values education should center ideally upon well-defined ethical principles that provide an appropriate guide for just decision-making and help prevent these values from becoming mis-applied in problematic situations.[11] Skill training must begin with clear expectations about performance as well as an understanding of how that particular competency fits into the larger scheme of the organization. Together, education and training define the difference between right and wrong in a rational, coherent manner and establish the foundations for discipline. This is what Lord Moran defines as the "discipline of persuasion" — the inculcation of standards in such a way that people become convinced that compliance will ultimately lead to the desired outcome.

Xenophon, a pupil of Socrates, an experienced military commander, and the first great thinker in the western world to articulate a theory of discipline, provides a useful approach toward creating a functional discipline. According to Xenophon, an army, just like an estate or a *polis* (city-state), is a social organization. A leader, therefore, must create an organization that will be able to execute his commands.[12]

According to Xenophon, the first step on the path to discipline begins with the leader, who by definition possesses the *arete* (moral virtue, excellence) to gain willing support from his followers even in times of great danger.[13] The leader's primary responsibility in forming his organization is to teach his followers the difference between correct and incorrect performance and behavior, thereby establishing a coherent, attainable set of expectations.[14] Implicit in the articulation of what is right are clearly defined standards of ethics and performance, as well as an explanation of why these standards are important. The leader must choose these performance and behavior standards with great discretion. If they are chosen haphazardly and without a clear link to the accomplishment of organizational goals and objectives, people will have difficulty differentiating between which standards are important and which ones are not. By selecting standards and expectations judiciously, the leader has begun to form a rational foundation for the "society." For Xenophon, the leader, not the followers, is to blame if the expectations are unclear.

Once the standards have been established, internalization begins. Integral to this process is the enforcement of standards to underscore their importance. As such, the leader must both punish inappropriate and reward good behavior. The guiding principle, however, is persuasion rather than coercion. The leader must maintain the credibility that punishment is in the interest of those being punished. Xenophon, like his mentor Socrates, believed that tyranny was unfitting for human beings. Given that people are all endowed alike with the gift of reason, Xenophon argues in *Oeconomicus* that they "can be made more obedient by force of argument [persuasion], by proving that it is their interest to obey."[15] He must, therefore, reward and punish in a predictable and discriminating fashion in order to avoid the hatred or contempt of his subordinates.

To illustrate this principle, Xenophon provides an interesting account of two commanders he observed on his expedition with Cyrus against the Persian king, Xerxes, in 401 BC.[16] Both failed but in different ways. Clearchus, a Spartan commander, took pride in his severity, believing that soldiers should fear their superiors more than they feared the enemy. Because his rule was considered arbitrary rather than reasonable, Clearchus lost a great many men on the expedition due to desertion. By contrast Proxenus, a Boeotian and a friend of Xenophon, sought to win the love of his soldiers by withholding praise from wrongdoers instead of punishing them. In doing so, he became an object of contempt.[17]

Enforcing high standards of conduct and performance is critical, and this necessitates the thoughtful application of rewards and punishments to indicate that the expectations are important rather than arbitrary. Lacking the courage to punish in a discriminating fashion is just as damaging to an organization as a failure to reward outstanding performance. As Xenophon explains, "Good workers get depressed when they see that, although they are the ones doing all of the work, the others get the same as they do, despite making no effort and being unprepared to face danger, if need be."[18]

Mutual respect is critical to this process, asserts Xenophon: soldiers and leaders must interact in a friendly, professional spirit.[19] These sentiments have provided a foundation as well for the thoughtful inculcation of discipline in a more modern context. While admonishing the United States Military Academy Corps of Cadets to end the practice of hazing in 1879, Academy Superintendent General John M. Schofield crafted what is now referred to as "Schofield's Definition of Discipline" which still must be memorized by all West Point Cadets, and ideally internalized as a standard for leadership:

The discipline which makes the soldiers of a free country reliable in battle is not to be gained by harsh or tyrannical treatment. On the contrary, such treatment is far more likely to destroy than to make an army. It is possible to impart instructions and to give commands in such a manner and such a tone of voice to inspire in the soldier no feeling but an intense desire to obey, while the opposite manner and tone of voice cannot fail to excite strong resentment and a desire to disobey. The one mode or the other of dealing with subordinates springs from a corresponding spirit in the breast of the commander. He who feels the respect which is due to others cannot fail to inspire in them regard for himself, while he who feels, and hence manifests, disrespect toward others, especially his inferiors, cannot fail to inspire hatred against himself.[20]

Discipline, for Schofield, is the natural consequence of good leadership and a positive, healthy, command climate.[21] Leaders who are trustworthy and treat their subordinates with respect create an environment in which discipline can result. Soldiers will not have any regard for leaders who fail to respect their own subordinates and cannot uphold their own standards.

While rewards and punishment are key initial foundations for establishing the importance of standards and maintaining a healthy, consistent relationship between leaders and subordinates, they alone, argues Xenophon, "do not constitute a sufficient means of instituting and maintaining discipline. . . [t]o achieve this, obedience must be given voluntarily rather than under compulsion."[22]   In other words, standards must be internalized. This means more than merely avoiding punishment. Internalization occurs when expectations are established rationally, enforced consistently and respectfully, and result in successful outcomes. The "discipline of persuasion" inculcates appropriate habits upon which the leader can develop a culture that promotes initiative and independence.

A leader establishes this culture by aligning expected performance results with healthy, shared, ethics-based values. A results-only environment is dangerous. A culture of results without values quickly devolves into selfish individualism and dysfunctional behavior which will doom the organization to hostility and strife. A focus solely on values without regard to results, on the other hand, while not dysfunctional, will lead to an inept organization. People might work well together, but they will not be any good at what they do.

Only when results and values exist in a complementary relationship will the organization develop a healthy culture and a positive command climate. When leaders, peers, and subordinates possess the discipline to function within these standards, an environment of trust is forged. This allows Aristotle's notion of "reciprocal equivalence" to take place: the principle of mutually supporting diversity of function which establishes a practical unity within an organization.[23]   Vision provides the focus; performance results and values furnish the necessary boundaries within which an organization and its members will operate.

This form of discipline and the organizational culture it fosters occupies a critical place on the modern battlefield. As Anthony Kellet, a scholar of combat motivation, asserts, "self-discipline plays a much greater role in modern combat than discipline imposed from without."[24] Whereas the pre-twentieth century battlefields were marked by tight formations of soldiers who could be constantly under the watchful eyes of their leaders, modern combat emphasizes a much greater spatial separation in which a platoon leader, never mind a general, might not even see a large part of his force until the battle is over. The advent of digitization, the ability to send burst transmissions of data throughout the depth and breadth of the battlefield, enables an even greater dispersion, making the issue of discipline even more crucial.[25] Trust, the implicit understanding that senior, peer, and subordinate alike are doing their absolute best to accomplish the mission in the right way, forms the bedrock of organizational effectiveness for any profession. Discipline forges the foundation of trust at the organizational level, bringing with it a level of maturity necessary to develop and practice independence and initiative.

FROM DISCIPLINE TO INITIATIVE[26]

Since discipline plays such a critical role in forming a healthy organizational culture, the question for the leader now becomes one of selecting an appropriate method of control over decision-making given the existing level of discipline within an organization. The two, control and discipline, have an interesting inverse proportionality. An organization which possesses a low level of discipline requires a stricter method of external control over decision-making than does a unit with a high degree of discipline. Trust is the operative concept: a higher level of trust results from a higher degree of discipline, which in turn requires less control from the leaders. Trust, which springs from discipline, forms the basis for initiative-based organizations that have historically performed at a higher level than those based upon external control.

Leaders of an immature organization generally employ a "detailed" method of control.[27] Detailed control is a strict approach, appropriate for an organization which has yet to develop a sufficient level of trust. Resting on the assumptions that those at the top are more likely to make better decisions than their subordinate leaders, and that people will generally stray when left to their own devices, detailed control places decision-making authority strictly in the hands of the senior leaders. In this environment, the senior leader clearly states the goal and the means each subordinate will employ to attain that goal. The focus is not just on what to do, but how to do it as well, which leaves subordinate leaders little latitude to deviate from the plan. Unity of effort in this case results from strict adherence to a detailed plan fed from the senior to the junior leader. Because the organization is immature, the senior leader's focus is on mitigating the risk of mistakes and failure by strictly controlling decision-making. Subordinate leader initiative is neither required nor expected. As long as the subordinates adhere to the plan, the organization will usually accomplish its mission.

While this method of control may seem safe, it has several inherent problems. First of all, while few plans ever survive the chaos of interaction with a thinking, uncooperative adversary, detailed control demands that the plan be carried out anyway. When the situation changes unfavorably or an opportunity presents itself to achieve the goal in a different way, subordinate leaders, being either untrained to recognize the opportunity or not trusted to exercise initiative, are not allowed to deviate from the original plan because that would throw the entire organization out of synchronization. Instead, detailed control requires subordinate leaders to report the new situation and await further instructions from the senior leader. To speed the cumbersome process the senior leaders may plan for myriad contingencies to deal with fluid situations, but the decision to implement any "branch" plan nevertheless rests with the senior leader alone. Since opportunities are often fleeting, detailed control bears with it the acceptance that these will be missed and must be made up for by new plans from the top. The only way to gain or regain the initiative is to make good decisions more quickly than the enemy. Naturally, in the face of an opponent who is capable of exercising lower-level decision-making, the more cumbersome organization will quickly lose the initiative.

While detailed control organizations must accept the burden of being unable to capitalize upon opportunities, the context of an immature organization makes this a necessity. Without the bedrock of discipline in place, senior leaders simply cannot grant latitude to their junior leaders. Initiative in the hands of an undisciplined subordinate is a dangerous weapon. Incompetent leaders, or those who operate outside the organization's framework of values, will likely make poor decisions that can result in the disintegration of their unit and might jeopardize the mission of the larger organization. Until an environment of trust is established, the organization is doomed to a cumbersome decision-making cycle.

By contrast, a mature organization can practice "directive" control. This method of control assumes that in a period of rapid change, subordinate leaders who are in touch with the situation can best make decisions that will capitalize upon fleeting opportunities.

Since initiative vis-à-vis the enemy is the key to successful battle-field outcomes, the side that can make the best decisions more quickly usually wins. The senior leader develops this initiative-based organization by providing direction to the subordinate leaders who are armed with decision-making authority. The senior leader is responsible for clearly articulating the goal, providing guidance and resources to subordinate leaders, and offering a plan that has the best probability of success given the current situation and anticipated variances due to enemy reactions. The subordinate leaders are responsible for adhering to the plan until it no longer conforms to the reality of a changed situation. Once this occurs, subordinate leaders are both expected and required to use their own decision-making authority to modify the plan in order to cap-italize on the changed situation. The subordinate leaders should exploit the opportunity initially and determine chances for success, then report their actions and recommendations so the senior leader can capitalize on the new situation on a larger scale. Anticipating the change, other subordinate leaders adjust their plans to allow for greater exploitation at the critical point and monitor the situation to see if an enemy reaction will open another opportunity. As these decisions are implemented, a new reality is forced upon the enemy, who must then react to the change. If the opponent has a slower decision-making process, adjustment to the new situation will be awkward and inappropriate, thus opening up greater opportunities. The initiative rests with the side that can make the better decisions more quickly, because that side dictates the terms of the battlefield to which the other must conform.[28]

Discipline forms the foundation which allows an organization to practice lower-level decision-making. Initiative means the courage to act on independent decisions in the absence of orders, or when current orders no longer make sense in the context of a changed situation. Such independent decisions, however, must facilitate the accomplishment of the larger mission. Precise guidance during the initial planning sets the goal for the organization and establishes the framework in which initiative can take place, but the cultural con-text of an initiative-based organization must be established well before the conflict.[29]   To develop independent thought and initiative, training must move beyond the fundamentals of job performance and into decision-making.

Directive control bears with it the inherent risk that junior leaders will make mistakes while exercising initiative in training. Honest mistakes, however, enhance the learning process and should not serve as a basis for punishment or castigation. For junior leaders to take initiative, they must trust that the senior leader will support the exercise of it, and that an inappropriate decision made in good faith is a training opportunity, not a mark against them. Junior leaders will rarely take the initiative if they do not trust their senior leaders to have matured beyond a zero-defect mentality. Training mitigates the risk of mistakes on the battlefield. For initiative to become a reality, leaders must train their subordinate *how* to think, not just *what* to think, and to use their creativity to solve complex problems on their own. Initiative without the underpinning of fundamental skill can be disastrous, but once this skill has been established, the key to unleashing the creativity of an organization is to develop the decision-making capabilities of junior leaders. Once leaders, peers, and subordinates not only believe in each other's skills and ethics, but also understand how each other thinks, the organization is ready to practice initiative.

CONCLUSION: PAVING NEW GROUND

Discipline fosters contextualized creativity, which allows training to occur at a deeper level. The intellectual growth that results from thinking in depth through complexity opens the way for innovation and creative solutions to problems, but it is the mastery of the fundamentals that allows new levels of ideas to grow.   Plato and Copernicus, Albert Einstein and Heinz Guderian, to name just a few, mastered the fundamentals of their professions before they were able to enter into a new realm of thinking, seize the initiative, and attack a problem from a completely different direction or in a new manner altogether.

Notions such as discipline and lower-level initiative might seem like dated concepts in the digital age. Information technology will give senior leaders access to overwhelming amounts of information, enabling them to monitor friendly as well as enemy movements.   Equipped with the capability to peer "cybernetically" through the thermal sights of a tank or aircraft, to zoom in and observe a junior leader moving forces over the battlefield, or to observe remotely a routine staff meeting, senior leaders have the potential to achieve levels of control over their organizations as never before.   As satellite imagery and digitized information provide continuous, "realtime" situation updates at the stroke of a mouse-key in the "twenty-first century" battlespace command post, higher echelon commanders can arguably access more information in a matter of seconds than their counterparts fifty years ago could get their hands on in a lifetime.   "Information superiority" has become a reality with the advent of the microchip.

The dawn of the information age seems to suggest that discipline and initiative can now be replaced by supervision.   The de-personalization of leadership via digital communication has the potential to truly "redefine" the way in which people control their organizations.   Unfortunately, this redefinition would constitute a backward-looking, reactionary method.   Impersonal, centralized, digital control would merely revitalize a traditional approach characterized by an external shamanistic authority.   For the twenty-first century absolutist divine anointment would be replaced by the gift of increased hard-disk space and expanded random access memory.

Good leaders, however, select their methods of control based upon organizational maturity, not on their capability to micromanage a subordinate's actions.   Witnessing a communications revolution not entirely unlike our current one with the invention of the telegraph in the mid to late nineteenth century, Helmuth von Moltke the Elder, the Chief of the German General Staff, remarked: "The advantage . . . which a commander believes to achieve through continuous personal intervention, is mostly an apparent one.   He thereby takes over the functions whose fulfillment other persons are designated.   He more or less denigrates their ability and increases his own duties to such a degree that he can no longer fulfill them completely."[30] As Moltke understood so well, combat is a human endeavor, and no amount of technology can mitigate the fear, courage, chaos, and personal bonding that occurs when people are placed in an uncomfortable or threatening situation. The side that possesses disciplined soldiers and employees who are trained to exploit fleeting opportunities have historically proven more successful than their rigid counterparts.

The magic of great leaders such as Alexander and Caesar, or Erwin Rommel and George Patton, lay not in their ability to exercise total, impersonal control, but in their ability to unleash the creative excellence of their subordinate leaders and channel that energy in the right direction. In their heydays, each of their organizations was built upon a foundation of trust. Discipline formed the bedrock, while training developed the ability of their subordinates to exploit fleeting opportunities. Darius III of Persia, Varro,[31] and Adolf Hitler, among so many others, stand as monuments to the ineffectiveness of rigid, centralized control founded upon what Lord Moran calls the "discipline of movement."

The current information revolution *can* result in an order of magnitude increase in the effectiveness of organizations by returning to the primacy of lower-level initiative. With the capability to educate and train subordinates to an increasing degree of excellence, why reduce people to automatons and repeat the same failures of a previous age? Battlefield dispersion in the next conflict and the increasing amount of information generated by reconnaissance, direct combat and logistical platforms will rapidly exceed the ability of one person or staff to control them all rigidly. To avoid being choked by a pathological consumption of information, senior leaders will need to rely upon the initiative of junior leaders in a magnitude never before experienced. With decision-action cycles becoming ever more rapid, the successful prosecution of armed conflict will lay squarely on the shoulders of subordinate leaders who understand the difference between right and wrong and can make decisions in the absence of orders to exploit increasingly fleeting opportunities. The current revolution in lethality makes this need even more critical, as a breakdown will result in casualties at an unprecedented scale and pace. The long-term investment in creating a disciplined organization will build the level of trust necessary to make initiative-based operations a reality. This initiative and independence of thought will help foster a new generation of leaders who, like the great ones before them, will have the depth and creativity to make technology their servant and not their master.

Section II

Historical Cases Studies

Chapter Six

Alexander the Great: A Study in Vision, Character, and Perception

by Christopher D. Kolenda

INTRODUCTION

Cyrnus, this city is in travail, and I fear she may give birth to a proud and violent man, to be leader of sore discord; for albeit her citizens be discreet, their guides are heading for much mischief.

Theognis

"There have been many Alexanders," writes historian C. B. Welles, but there will probably be no definitive Alexander.[1] Indeed, the complex historiography of Alexander the Great reflects the complicated nature of the man. On the one hand, Sir William Tarn offers a gentlemanly Alexander, a model humanitarian who envisioned mankind as a brotherly fellowship and inspired the Stoic philosophy of Zeno.[2] Another historian, Ernst Badian, on the other hand, argues that "on the personal level, the story of Alexander the Great appears to us as an almost embarrassingly perfect illustration of the man who conquered the world, only to lose his soul."[3] To be sure, the nature of Alexander lies somewhere between these two extremes.

When analyzing Alexander III of Macedon, historians, in general, have focused on Alexander either as a statesman or as a military commander. Few have chosen to offer more than a tangential study of Alexander as a leader. The assumption seems to be that since Alexander, despite his personal flaws and idiosyncrasies, conquered a greater part of the "known world" and was an effective military commander, he must have been an outstanding leader. As N.G.L. Hammond asserts, "We can see that it was Alexander's leadership and training which made the Macedonians incomparable in war and in administration and enabled them. . .to control the greater part of the civilized world for a century or more."[4] British General J.F.C. Fuller, in his classic study of Alexander's generalship, writes: "Whether on the battle or in camp, Alexander dominated his companions. Through his overmastering personality and his genius for war he won their trust and devotion." Despite the opposition of the Macedonians to many of his policies, argues Fuller, "it redounds to Alexander's leadership that. . .he was able to carry out his conquests with so few internal dissensions as those recorded."[5]

According to John Keegan, Alexander was the embodiment of "heroic" leadership: "exemplary, risk-taking, physical, passionate."[6] Martial virtue, he asserts, defined heroic leadership in Alexander's day; it was the display of courage, the more reckless the better, that proved the worth of the leader in the eyes of his soldiers. "To keep the regard of such men," claims Keegan, "the war leader had constantly to excel — not only in battle but in the hunting field, in horsemanship or skill at arms, in love, in conversation, in boast and challenge, and in the marathon bouts of feasting and drinking that were the hero's *repos du guerrier*."[7] The heroic leader, in short, was a man of action; a great warrior with a disregard for danger and a contempt for the future, a man who sustained his position through victory whether on the battlefield or in the camp.

There is much to be said for the above conclusions regarding Alexander, but they seem to render only a superficial view of the Macedonian's leadership. Alexander did conquer a vast amount of territory and was without doubt the most accomplished warrior of his day. Nevertheless, despite these qualities, Alexander's own soldiers repudiated him on several occasions: the Thessalians and other Greek allies revolted near Bactra (330 B.C.), and his own Macedonians refused to cross the Hyphasis (326 B.C.) and then mutinied again at Opis (324 B.C.). On top of these problems, there was the argument with, and subsequent murder of, Cleitus — the commander of his famed Companion Cavalry (328 B.C.), the "conspiracy" of Philotas (330 B.C.) and the "Pages' Revolt" (327 B.C.). These important issues must be accounted for in any assessment of Alexander's leadership.

Fuller and Keegan, however, ignore these problems when they evaluate Alexander as a leader. Keegan, in fact, seems to blame the soldiers and conspirators rather than Alexander: "Power corrupts, but its real corruption is among those who wait upon it. . . Significantly all three plots postdate the great battles: they formented in a period when Alexander had come into the plenitude of his power, not while he was striving after it. Alexander the young general was not troubled by conspiracy."[8] Keegan would be correct if these conspiracies and revolts were about power, but they each revealed that there was something fundamentally different at stake. Each involved a rejection of Alexander's vision and character as they understood it. In essence, a rejection of his leadership. If Fuller and Keegan were correct that genius on the battlefield and unparalleled courage were the quintessence of leadership in Alexander's day, then these problems would never have occurred. That they did suggests the inadequacy of our picture of Alexander's leadership.

This essay will examine Alexander's leadership by analyzing his vision and character primarily from the point of view of his soldiers and the cultural context of his day.[9] Doing so will provide a different avenue of analysis into some of the factors that made Alexander a great commander on the battlefield as well as some insight into why, despite his martial genius, many of his subordinates no longer wanted to go where Alexander wished to lead them.

VISION, COURAGE, CARING: AN ARMY OF LIONS LED BY A LION

In addition, you have Alexander commanding against Darius. Alexander's speech before Issus
(Reported by Arrain)

Although Keegan asserts that Alexander embodied "heroic leadership," the Macedonian's skill as a battlefield commander and leader went far beyond his vast reservoir of personal courage. Alexander's success, argues Fuller, lies in his genius as one of the Great Captains. Alexander was both a brilliant strategist and tactician, possessing a genius for defining his strategic and tactical aims, an intuition for when and where to strike the decisive blow against his enemy who vastly outnumbered him, and doing so in a manner which limited the casualties in his own force.

While the aim of Alexander's tactics was to win great battles, the aim of his strategy was to pacify and not antagonize his enemy, thereby hoping to limit the number of battles he had to fight. According to Justin, when "marching forward in quest of the enemy, he kept the soldiers from ravaging Asia, telling them that they ought to spare their own property, and not destroy what they came to possess."[10] Alexander wished to achieve a bloodless conquest as much as possible, and thus drew a distinction between the Persian army and the Persian people: his aim was to defeat the former and win over the latter.

When Alexander did have to fight, his genius as a tactician was translated into decisive victories by his ability to articulate coherently his vision and plans for battle. Although one may believe that commanding the Macedonian army was a fairly simple and centralized affair, due to the fact that Alexander could see all of his troops and all of his enemy's troops, the reality was much different. Alexander could indeed observe the array of both forces prior to the battle, but once the engagement began this was no longer the case. Alexander always placed himself on the right-wing of his force with the Companion Cavalry and personally led the decisive charge into the enemy's ranks. Once this occurred it was all but impossible for Alexander to direct anyone except for those in his immediate vicinity — the dust resulting from the cavalry charge as well as the general melee forced Alexander to fight his own individual battle. While Alexander was delivering the decisive blow on the right, Parmenion, his second-in-command, would be holding the left, preventing the enemy from penetrating and enveloping the Macedonians.[11] Despite being hard-pressed on the center and left in the battles of Granicus, Issus, and Gaugamela, Parmenion and the Macedonians (as well as the other Greek allies) never broke. This was only possible through discipline, a thorough understanding of Alexander's plan, and faith that it would ultimately work.

Through his coherent vision and precise planning, Alexander's army was capable of executing complex maneuvers in the face of the enemy. A salient example was the battle of Gaugamela. The Persian line extended beyond the flanks of Alexander's force and the Macedonians risked being enveloped on both sides. To reduce the positional advantage of Darius, the Persian King, Alexander angled both of his flanks inward and created a rear phalanx. Correctly foreseeing that Darius would try to use his positional advantage to attempt a double envelopment, Alexander planned for his "refused" flanks to bend under the Persian pressure until they made contact with the rear phalanx, thus forming a box which was defended on all sides.[12] To relieve the pressure on his right, from which he would deliver the decisive blow, Alexander marched toward the Persian line in oblique fashion, thereby enabling him to keep his Companion Cavalry out of contact until a gap opened in the Persian line. As the Persian satrap, Bessus, attempted an envelopment of the Macedonian right, Alexander shot into the gap in the Persian line, wheeled right to destroy Bessus, then returned to the left of the formation to bol-

ster Parmenion.[13]   Darius fled the battlefield and Alexander
became master of Asia.

Turning his sights on the Persian capital, Persepolis, Alexander
executed what Fuller regards as one of the most brilliant mountain
campaigns in history (330 B.C.).[14]   After launching an ill-advised
assault on a heavily defended mountain pass known as the Persian
Gates,[15] Alexander regrouped, leaving a detachment at the pass to
hold the Persian attention while conducting a night movement with
the rest of his force through the mountains and around the Persian
flank. Alexander then split his maneuver force three times in order
to turn Ariobazarnes out of the pass and prevent his escape to
Persepolis.   Once in position, Alexander sounded the attack; the
Persians, seeing that they were trapped, fled in panic and were
slaughtered by the Macedonians.[16] As A. B. Bosworth explains,
Alexander "had once more displayed a genius for rapid and incon-
spicuous movement and had attacked at the time the enemy was
most vulnerable both physically and psychologically."[17] Alexander's
precise planning and genius for maneuver defeated an enemy who
was in a position considerably stronger than his own.[18]

Alexander's genius on the battlefield was matched by his personal courage. He was always at the most dangerous point on the
battlefield, showing a disregard for his own personal safety and
inspiring, through the force of personal example, the same bravery
in his soldiers. As Hammond observes, Alexander's courage "added
a special dimension to his power of leadership; for he was the first
to do whatever he asked his men to do, and his survival of danger
after danger created the myth that he personally was invincible in
war."[19] During the protracted siege of Tyre (Jan-July 332 B.C.), in
which the Macedonians were forced to construct a 1000 yard
"mole" or causeway to the island which was protected by the
Phoenician fleet as well as a garrison inside the fortress.[20] Arrian
reports that Alexander was repeatedly at the front with the engineers and construction crews, risking with them the attacks and
missiles from the island and the fleet, "taking a strenuous part in the
action itself and keeping his eyes open for any conspicuous display
of courage and daring by others in the danger."[21]

A striking example of Alexander's personal daring occurred during the siege of a Mallian town near the Hydaspes River in the winter of 326-325 B.C. After the Macedonians declined to cross the Hyphasis River during the previous summer, Alexander may have begun to doubt the fighting spirit of his soldiers who looked forward to returning home after ten years of constant campaigning.[22] The Mallians refused to submit to Alexander, so he ordered a siege of the fortress. Once the storming party had mounted ladders on the walls of the citadel to begin the dangerous assault, it appeared to Alexander that they either hesitated or refused to scale them. Alexander then seized a ladder himself and scaled the wall with a handful of bodyguards.[23] His soldiers, ashamed by their hesitancy, rushed forward to emulate their commander, the ladders collapsing under their weight.   Meanwhile, Alexander and his bodyguards leapt down from the wall and began to fight the Mallians alone — Alexander receiving a near-fatal chest-wound from an arrow in the process — until the Macedonians succeeded in scaling the walls and slaughtering the defenders.[24]

While Alexander's battlefield exploits were remarkable, two of his finest acts of personal courage occurred away from the battlefield. In August 333 B.C. Alexander fell ill after bathing in a cold spring near Mount Tarsus, so Alexander's physician and long-time friend, Philip, had prepared a purge for the king. As Alexander was about to drink, he received a letter from Parmenion warning that Philip might try to poison him.   According to Arrian, Alexander read the letter and while drinking the purge, handed the letter over to Philip. Through this act "Alexander showed Philip that as his friend he trusted him, and his suite in general that he was resolute in refusing to suspect his friends and steadfast in the face of death."[25]

Perhaps Alexander's most celebrated act of personal courage occurred during the grueling march through the Gedrosian Desert in October 325 B.C. On his return route from the Indian Ocean, Alexander decided to follow the coast in order to supply his fleet, which was to navigate the coastline once the autumn monsoons subsided.[26] Alexander then intended to leave the coast and march through the desert with his army — a feat which had been attempted by Cyrus and Semiramis, but both had failed to bring their armies through intact.[27] The march took an enormous toll on his army and the mass of camp followers that accompanied him.[28] Water was a precious commodity, and at one point the supply of it was nearly exhausted. Some of Alexander's soldiers had found a small spring of water and gathered it into a helmet which they offered to the King. According to Arrian, Alexander "took it and thanked them, but then poured it out in the sight of everyone; and at this action the army was so much heartened that you would have guessed that all had drunk what Alexander had poured away."[29] Alexander never asked his men to do what he himself was unwilling to do, nor did he allow himself material goods which his soldiers were denied.[30]

Another hallmark of Alexander's leadership was the care he showed for his soldiers. Alexander no doubt realized that his success was dependent upon the goodwill and spirit of his men, but it would be incorrect to regard this caring as merely a ploy for future self-aggrandizement. Soldiers, then as now, can spot a hypocrite fairly quickly and will rarely follow one. This was especially true in the Macedonian army which prided itself on a culture of respect between leader and led.[31] Alexander's care for his soldiers was genuine and it motivated his entire army. After his first great battle with the Persians at Granicus (334 B.C.), Alexander, according to Arrian, "took great care of the wounded, visiting each man himself, examining their wounds, asking how they were received, and allowing them to recount and boast of their exploits."[32] After taking Halicarnassus that same year, Alexander decided to send home his recently married soldiers so they could spend time with their new families in Macedonia over the winter. Arrian tells us that Alexander gained as much popularity by this act among the Macedonians as by any other.[33]

Alexander's regard for the worth of each individual was apparent in the speeches he gave his soldiers prior to battle. While never shying away from mentioning his own exploits, Alexander would take the time to acclaim previous acts of bravery performed by his soldiers. Before the battle of Issus (333 B.C.), Alexander rode up and down the ranks of his soldiers, reminding them of their previous successes, and "cited any noble act of personal daring, naming both the deed and the man."[34] After the battle, despite a sword wound in his thigh, Alexander again went around to see the wounded. He then collected all of the dead and gave them a splendid military funeral. In the funeral oration he cited "all whom he knew, from his own eyes or from the agreed report of others, to have distinguished themselves in the battle."[35] Alexander's exhortations were infectious, for citing acts of a soldier's personal courage had the effect of making every other soldier wish for that same kind of acclaim. Through his care of the wounded and dead, Alexander demonstrated a genuine regard for his soldiers, and they in turn trusted him to make his plans for battles and campaigns which assured their victory with a minimum loss of life. Alexander's Macedonians were truly an army of lions led by a lion.

The story of Alexander's leadership, however, is not confined to his battlefield genius, personal courage, and caring for his soldiers. Just as Alexander's vision and personal character enabled him to conquer the greater part of the known world on the battlefield, so his inability to articulate his vision of empire coupled with the increasing number of troubling questions concerning his character outside the framework of the battlefield served to erode the foundation of trust which is the primary sustaining value between leader and led.

ALEXANDER'S SUPPOSED COSMOPOLITANISM: THE 'CIVILIZING PROCESS' IN REVERSE

For Delusion, with semblance of fair intent, lureth
man astray into her snares, whence it is not possible
for him scatheless to escape.
—Aeschylus (Persians, 111-114.)

Alexander's "cosmopolitanism,"[36] his desire to integrate the different peoples of the empire, has been a subject of much historical debate and has become somewhat of a yardstick for many scholars in their evaluation of his reign. Tarn, for instance, sees Alexander as a humanitarian and the inspiration for Zeno's Stoic philosophy.[37] The "unity of mankind," argues Tarn, formed the foundation of Alexander's conception of empire; he dreamt that "the various races of mankind, so far as known to him, becoming of one mind together and living in unity and concord."[38] Ulrich Wilcken, however, views Alexander as a pragmatist who developed a "policy of fusion" in order to intermingle the Persians and Macedonians into a sort of "dominant people to whom he could entrust the defense of his Asiatic Empire."[39] In this same vein, Ernst Badian argues that there was no evidence for such a cosmopolitan dream on the part of Alexander. For Badian, Alexander's gestures of unity were not humanitarian but merely "carefully calculated for political effect." This alone, he believes, reveals the "unmistakable Alexander of history" who did not attain his empire by "well-meaning muddle-headedness."[40]

There are plausible arguments for both positions,[41] but in terms of Alexander's leadership, a different avenue of analysis is warranted. Alexander left no philosophy of empire or of statesmanship, so discovering the "unmistakable Alexander of history" is a delicate endeavor. A historian can merely evaluate Alexander's actions and draw some conclusions from them. In analyzing Alexander's leadership, however, what may be of more importance is not so much what was "inside Alexander's head," but what his subordinates *believed* was inside the king's head. On this issue the conjectural accounts and historical scholarship are all in agreement: whatever may be said of Alexander's supposed cosmopolitanism, the vast majority of Greeks and Macedonians both in the army and at home rejected it completely. Their refusal to follow this "vision" bears substantive analysis.

In the fifth and fourth centuries B.C. the Greeks divided the world into Greeks and non-Greeks; the latter they regarded as barbarians — men who said "bar-bar," or men whose speech could not be understood. "Barbarian" did not necessarily imply "sub-human." The characterization simply referred to a lesser stage of civilization than what was enjoyed by the Greeks. In the late fifth century B.C., the Athenians saw themselves as the agents of civilization. Diodorus, recounting the speech of Nicolaus the Syracusian who recommended mercy to the Athenian captives of 413 B.C., writes, "The Athenians it was who first introduced the Greeks to cultivated food, which they had received from the gods for themselves and offered for the common use. They are the inventors of laws, through which our common life was transformed from a savage and wicked existence into a civilized and just society."[42] According to Isocrates (436-338 B.C.) Athens "took over the Greeks living in scattered groups, without laws, some groaning under tyranny, others perishing for lack of leadership, and rid them of these evils, taking some under her protection and acting as an example to others." The Athenians had invented many arts and techniques, tested others, and then "handed them over to the rest of mankind to use."[43] Athens had received gifts from the gods which civilized her, and then did the work of the gods by bestowing these gifts on other Greeks and the rest of mankind. Athens was the agent of civilization, the catalyst for bringing men from a "beastlike" state into a higher form. Greece was now civilized, enjoying a more advanced form of existence than those who uttered "bar-bar."

Among the many polarities which separated the Greeks from the barbarians perhaps the most important was the *peitho/bia* dichotomy. As R.G.A. Buxton contends, the superiority of the Greeks, in their own self-conception, lay in their use of *peitho*, persuasion, as opposed to the barbarian use of *bia*, force.[44] *Peitho* was specified as a type of *logos*, rational discourse, which was associated with men, but not beasts.[45] Through this power of rational speech, men could communicate moral values, act politically, teach, and persuade. *Peitho* characterized the conduct within a civilized community, *bia* characterized conduct outside such a community.[46] Greek statesmen, as rulers of equals, used persuasion to lead their *poleis*. Barbarians, who ruled their subjects as masters do slaves, used force and tyranny. Barbarians, however, were not beasts, they possessed the *potential* for persuasion through rational discourse, they just needed to be civilized by those who actually exercised it.

Thus, in their self-conception, Greek: *peitho*: civilized was a higher form than barbarian (Persian): *bia*: beastlike. In the civilizing process the barbarian would become like the Greek.

Alexander initially did not intend his campaign against the Persians to be a means of extending Greek civilization. This was to be a punitive expedition; the official pretext of the war was to avenge the sacrilege committed by Xerxes who had burned Athenian temples and insulted her gods. Philip, Alexander's father, had first conceived the mission, perhaps to strengthen the Corinthian League,[47] but upon his death the task fell to Alexander. For the Greeks this was purely a war of revenge and they understood it as such. Alexander, however, may have had different thoughts in mind. As he sailed to Asia Minor, the young king cast his spear into the ground — a symbolic gesture that this was to be spear-won territory, a war for conquest.[48]

That the difference between Macedonian (as well as Greek) and Persian was distinct in the eyes of Alexander and his officers is apparent in the speech recorded by Arrian on the eve of the battle at Issus. "We Macedonians. . .are to fight Medes and Persians, nations long steeped in *luxury*, while we have now long been inured to danger by the exertions of campaigning. Above all it will be a fight of *free men* against *slaves*."[49] The speech reveals the popular perception of the dichotomy between the two peoples; a notion similar to the polarity represented in Aeschylus' famous tragedy, the *Persians*. The Persians teemed with luxury and gold, symbols of softness and decadence, while the Greeks were characterized by strength through virtue. The Persians worshipped their king and queen as peers of the gods, performing humiliating obeisance (*proskynesis*) in their presence as slaves to a master, while "Of no man are [the Greeks] called the slaves or vassals."[50] While the Macedonians and Greeks in Alexander's army may or may not have known Aeschylus' tragedy, this perception was entirely consistent with the historical context of Alexander's time.

After Alexander's victory at Gaugamela, the sack of Persepolis (including the burning of its temples) and the subsequent death of

Darius in 330 B.C., the official purpose of the war had been ful-filled in the eyes of many Greeks.[51] The Persian empire was van-quished and the last of the Achaemenid line had perished. At this point, Alexander was forced to release the Greek allies of the Corinthian League and allow them to return to Greece.[52] The acquisition of empire replaced the war of revenge as the "official" driving force for Alexander, but he was faced with the problem of insufficient manpower for further conquest. C.A. Robinson argues that Alexander, out of sheer military necessity, moved toward "ori-entalism" in order to gain the support of his former enemies to expand his own empire.[53]   To bridge the gap between the Hellenes and Persians, Alexander began to adopt Persian customs and dress. Persian flatterers were welcomed into the court and Alexander's personal attire reflected a mixture of Macedonian and Persian. With this change in appearance, according to Arrian, came a change in Alexander's conduct. "Alexander was carried away into imitation of Median and Persian opulence and of the custom of barbarian kings not to countenance equality with sub-jects in their daily lives."[54]

These developments were alarming to the Macedonians who began to resent the king's growing "orientalism." Rifts began to grow between the "new" Alexander and the "old" Macedonians who Alexander saw as his father's officers, not his.[55] The problem came to a head in the autumn of 328 B.C., when a drunken argu-ment developed between Alexander and Cleitus at an evening ban-quet. Cleitus, alienated by the increasing trend toward oriental des-potism at the court, gave expression to the general unrest by con-demning the eastern practices of Alexander and claiming that the king's lust for glory was becoming parasitical.[56]   Outraged, Alexander ran Cleitus through with a spear in what Balsdon regards as a typical act of a story-book tyrant.[57]

Deeply troubled by this murder, Alexander reportedly brooded in sorrow for three days. Anaxarchus, one of the court flatterers, visit-ed Alexander and informed him that as all acts of the gods were con-sidered just, so all the acts of the great king should be held as just.[58] Whether Alexander actually believed this specious line of argument is difficult to tell, but according to Arrian this set the stage for the introduction of *proskynesis*. Alexander had now become "divinicized" — his father was no longer Philip, but Ammon (Zeus).[59]

Proskynesis, prostration or obeisance, was common practice in the Persian court. The king's subjects would perform this act as a symbol of homage to the exalted status of the ruler.[60] For the Greeks, however, *proskynesis* was an act of abject servility to be performed only before the gods. For a mortal to require this act from another mortal was to equate the former with the gods — the ultimate manifestation of hubris (overweening pride) according to the Greeks. When Alexander and his court sycophants attempted to introduce this practice at a banquet in Bactra in 327 B.C., it understandably evoked widespread abhorrence from the Greeks and Macedonians.[61] D.G. Hogarth's argument that "nothing was intended by the *proskynesis* exacted at Bactra except the assimilation of the habit of two peoples before the king"[62] may be plausible, but it misses a central point. To the Greeks and Macedonians, who regarded themselves as "civilized" because the relationship between leader and led was based on equality of respect, this display of submission was a violation of their personal dignity wholly inconsistent with the standards of Greek political culture. To the Macedonians, Alexander was equating himself with the gods. He was puffed up with hubris, and in Greek tragedy those filled with hubris were always vanquished by the gods. "Zeus, of a truth, is a chastizer of overweening pride and corrects with a heavy hand."[63]

Needless to say, the attempt to exact *proskynesis* from the Greeks and Macedonians was a complete fiasco. Alexander summarily dropped the requirement for prostration from his Hellenic subjects, but still received obeisance from his Persians. According to Badian, "it was clear that Alexander had lost the sympathy of thinking Greeks — even those who had once hailed him as a divinely appointed leader."[64] *Proskynesis*, for the Greeks, was a barbarian practice. It was a submission to *bia* and a rejection of *peitho*, for "civilized" persuasion only existed among equals.

To most Hellenes Alexander had begun to operate at odds with any standards of respectability. However laudable Alexander's "cosmopolitanism" and efforts to integrate the races of the empire may have been, the Greeks and Macedonians viewed it as "orientalism" — a rejection of Greek and civilized and a preference for barbarian and uncivilized. If Alexander truly had a humanitarian dream, he utterly failed to articulate this vision to the Greeks and mobilize support for it. The same genius of vision he used to establish the conditions for victory on the battlefield was now found wanting in establishing the foundations for a lasting, integrated empire. To the Greeks Alexander had become barbarian in dress and manner, puffed up with hubris like Xerxes and Darius of Asia before him. To the self-appointed agents of civilization, Alexander's actions must have appeared as the civilizing process in reverse.

THE WAR WITHOUT END: INTERNAL REVOLTS AND THE EROSION OF TRUST

For presumptuous pride, when it has burgeoned, bears as its fruit a crop of calamity, whence it reaps a plenteous harvest of tears.

—Aeschylus (*Persians*, 821-2.)

By 330 B.C. the breakdown of trust between Alexander and his officers was rapidly becoming apparent, ultimately setting the stage for Alexander's only "defeat" at the Hyphasis and the subsequent mutiny at Opis. As Balsdon perceptively asserts, Darius was not the only victim of Gaugamela; tragedy was brewing among the victors too.[65] The first of these problems was an attempt on Alexander's life, the alleged "Philotas plot" of 330 B.C. The conspiracy failed, resulting in the execution of Philotas, the commander of the Companion Cavalry, and the assasination of his father, Parmenion.[66] To prevent a recurrence, the increasingly despotic Alexander reorganized the command of his army by splitting up the leadership of the Companion Cavalry into two parts so no one single man would have the command and loyalty of such a large and potent force.[67] Assuming direct control of the army, Alexander also refrained from appointing a second in command. Alexander had in a sense atomized the army, fostering competition for favor among his subordinates while never allowing one to become too powerful.[68] It was a clever way of preventing any sort of unification against him around a single figure.

The strategy worked for a time among the soldiers, but the next conspiracy came from an unlikely source: the sons of the Macedonian nobles who traveled with Alexander's entourage and were educated by the court historian, Callisthenes. These "Pages" were afforded the honor of accompanying Alexander on hunting expeditions and guarding the king's tent at night. Apparently during one such hunting expedition, one of the pages, Hermolaus, violated protocol by killing the first boar before Alexander had a chance to do so. This apparently outraged the king who ordered the young page to be beaten in the presence of his peers.[69]

This precipitated a plot by Hermolaus and some of the pages (327 B.C.) to murder the king at night when it was their turn to guard his tent. The plot, which was foiled when Alexander failed to return to the tent after yet another night of feasting and drinking, was revealed to Alexander the next day. In confessing his guilt Hermolaus claimed that "no free man could longer endure Alexander's hubris" and inveighed against the unjust deaths of Philotas and Parmenion, the drunken murder of Cleitus, "the Median dress, the plan not yet abandoned to introduce *proskynesis*," and Alexander's excessive drinking and strange sleeping habits. Hermolaus claimed he could bear it no more and sought to liberate himself and the other Macedonians.[70] Significantly, this plot was not about power but about concerns over Alexander's *arete*: his arrogance, orientalism, and alleged barbarism. Hermolaus evidently saw his act as a sacrifice for freedom for himself and the Macedonians in the face of a tyrant. Hermolaus and his fellow conspirators no longer believed in Alexander's character or vision and were probably not alone in this belief.[71]

Although the disaffection in the army was approaching the breaking point, Alexander continued to campaign towards the Indus over the next year. One campaign seemed to lead to another. Alexander never articulated at what point he considered the empire "secure" and when the Macedonians could expect to return home. He merely offered the worn out and vague explanation of reaching the "Ocean" which was supposedly just beyond yet another "next" river. A *pothos* seized him, argues Victor Ehrenberg, a longing for adventure and exploring the unknown.[72] Alexander seemed content to continue the campaigning, but at the Hyphasis River in 326 B.C. his soldiers had had enough — his *pothos* for conquest and their *pothos* for home and family had diverged.

Bosworth argues that frustration since Gaugamela and seventy days of monsoons combined to make the soldiers revolt; the demand to stop, return, and enjoy the fruits of conquest had become irresistible.[73] While these factors certainly contributed to the breakdown of the Macedonian morale, long campaigning and the elements were not the root cause of the revolt, for people throughout history have endured enormous privation and hardship when pursuing an important, common goal. For Alexander's soldiers in 326 B.C. this belief had vanished. When they demanded that Alexander define for them the purpose of continuing, the king invoked the familiar nebulous themes of reaching the mythical Ocean, and securing the empire against internal revolt and external conquest. He then told his Macedonians: "For my part, I set no limit to exertions for a man of noble spirit, save that the exertions themselves should lead to deeds of prowess."[74] The campaign, instead of being a necessary means to a logical end, had become an end in itself. Alexander's explanations were no longer good enough. With no clear direction from their king and no attainable or discernible end to the campaigning in sight, Alexander's soldiers simply refused to go on unless Alexander forced them.

The reply to Alexander's explanations are attributed by Arrian and Curtius to Coenus, a commander of cavalry who had distinguished himself in the victory over Porus during the Hydaspes campaign in India (326 B.C.). His ingenious counterargument to Alexander reflected themes at the heart of the soldiers' disenchantment with their king's enterprises, and Alexander knew it. According to Arrian's account, Coenus asked Alexander to respect the wishes of the soldiers, "seeing that you, Sire, do not yourself desire to lead the Macedonians as a *dictator*, but say that you will *lead* them by *persuasion*, and that, if they persuade you, you will not *coerce* them."[75] Using the semantic field of *peitho/bia*, Coenus had presented Alexander with an interesting dilemma. On the one hand, if Alexander considered himself a "Macedonian" he would have to lead through persuasion, convincing the army to continue the campaign of their own free will. Failing to do so, he, as a Macedonian leader, must be persuaded by them and turn back. On the other hand, if Alexander wished to continue the campaign, the soldiers would go with him, not of their own free will but through coercion (*bia*). In choosing this path, Alexander would be renouncing the Macedonian tradition and following the Persian or barbarian tradition. He would become a tyrant over slaves. In effect, Coenus was asking Alexander to decide whether he was *peitho*/Greek/civilized or *bia*/Persian/barbarian.[76]

Alexander understood very well the implications of the choice Coenus and the army had offered him.[77] After initially informing his officers that he would go on himself with whomever would volunteer, Alexander retired to his tent and kept to himself for three days hoping for a change of heart from the soldiers. When none was forthcoming, Alexander found the only way out of the dilemma possible. Sacrificing to the gods and seeing that the omens were unfavorable, Alexander informed his soldiers that he would turn back.[78]

Despite their elation at the prospect of returning home, Alexander's resolution of the dilemma had most likely left some lingering doubts among his soldiers. While the king had not forced them to go on, he had also not completely renounced his perceived conversion to orientalism. Trust still remained an unresolved issue in the eyes of the Macedonians. After the disastrous march through the Gedrosian desert and the eventual arrival in Babylon, the soldiers' suspicions of Alexander had by no means subsided.[79] The issue came to a head at Opis in 324 B.C. when Alexander elected to release those soldiers who were unfit for war. To replace them, he decided to fill the ranks of the phalanxes and Companion Cavalry with Persians and to introduce a new formation, the *Epigoni* (inheritors), made up of Persians trained in the Macedonian style.[80]

These changes exacerbated the frustrations of the Macedonian soldiers who, Arrian tells us, were aggrieved "that Alexander was going totally barbarian at heart, and treating Macedonian customs and Macedonians themselves without respect."[81] The soldiers did not endure the perceived affront in silence, but "called on Alexander to discharge them all from the army and to go campaigning himself with his father, referring in mockery to Ammon."[82] Alexander pointed out several of the most vocal and had them summarily executed, then railed against the soldiers for their ingratitude.

He began the harangue by referring to his own father, Philip, who "took you over when you were helpless vagabonds. . .He gave you cloaks instead of skins, he brought you down from the mountains to the plains. . .He made you city dwellers and established the order that comes from good laws and customs."[83] These services, according to Alexander, were great when considered by themselves, but were small in comparison with his own. "Yours are the wealth of the Lydians, the treasure of the Persians, the bounty of India and the outer sea."[84] After inveighing against their ingratitude for the gifts he had bestowed upon them, Alexander bid them begone, telling them to inform their families back home that "you deserted him and went off, handing him over to the protection of the barbarians he had conquered."[85]

This was evidently too much for the Macedonians who begged Alexander to forgive their transgression. In doing so, Alexander arranged for a massive reconciliation banquet to be attended by the Macedonians and Persians as well as other members of the empire. Hammond argues that this celebration signified that the integration of the various races into the army had been accepted by the Macedonians.[86] This conclusion is plausible to a point. According to Arrian, the source which Hammond and Tarn cite as evidence of this acceptance, Alexander "seated all the Macedonians around him, and next to them Persians, and then any persons from the other peoples who took precedence for rank or any other high quality."[87]   The Macedonians clearly had precedence in this seating arrangement.[88] While the Macedonians may have accepted Persians into their ranks, it was clear to them that they stood atop the hierarchy of the empire.

Alexander died a year later on 10 June 323 B.C., leaving no philosophy of statesmanship or of empire and delegating no successor.[89] The arranged marriages between the Macedonian officers and Persian women, which were designed to help intergrate the two peoples, were dissolved and the empire was partitioned among the ranking generals.   Whatever cosmopolitan vision Alexander may have entertained quickly vanished in the ensuing struggle for hegemony. Tarn argues, correctly, that the true unifying force for the empire was lacking; there was no common idea or ideal that the Greeks and Macedonians, let alone the Persians, could believe in.[90] If Alexander had such a vision he was unable to persuade his subordinates of its wisdom.[91]

ALEXANDER AS PROMETHEUS: "HUBRIS" OR "PHILANTHROPEIA"

For if a man take great wealth violently or perforce
or if he seize it through his tongue...the gods soon blot
him out and make his house low and wealth attends
him only for a little while.

—Hesiod

In the celebrated Greek tragedy, *Prometheus Bound*, Aeschylus portrays the plight of Prometheus, the Titan who revolted against Zeus and saved mankind from destruction.   For such insolence Zeus had Prometheus chained to a rock until the latter comprehended his own folly and paid for his offense. The tragedy itself consists of a series of dialogues between Prometheus, who tries to justify his actions, and his visitors, most of whom are gods.   In Prometheus' self-conception, he is the agent of civilization and *philanthropeia* who bestowed technical gifts to man: "Every art possessed by man comes from Prometheus."[92] Prometheus, however, is the only one who speaks highly of Prometheus. The rest see

Prometheus as the epitome of hubris, a defier of the wisdom and laws of Zeus, and now an example of his justice. As Oceanus explains, "Thy plight, Prometheus, is my instructor."[93]

The tragedy of Alexander can be seen in a similar vein. In Alexander's self-conception he was also the agent of civilization and *philanthropeia*, conquering the world not for himself (Alexander never hoarded the wealth he attained) but for his Macedonians and Greeks. Alexander's speech at Opis is instructive in this respect. While crediting Philip with giving the Macedonians good laws and customs, Alexander claimed to do much more, bestowing the wealth of the Lydians, the treasure of the Persians, the bounty of India and the outer sea upon them. He had given them gifts; all wealth they owed to Alexander.

To the Macedonians, however, Alexander had become puffed up with hubris. Instead of ruling as a king over equals, Alexander had become barbarian in custom, manner, and dress: seeing himself, like Xerxes and Darius, as a peer of the gods, enjoying the flattery of the sycophants, demanding *proskynesis*, and ruling as an intolerant despot. Alexander had ceased to be one of them. He may have given the Greeks and Macedonians great wealth, but as Curtius has Coenus explain to Alexander, "victors over all, we lack everything."[94] Philip had given them the *polis* and the good life; Alexander, in their perception, had given them only warfare and luxury.

When analyzing the leadership of Alexander, what rapidly becomes apparent is the manner in which the convergence and divergence of fundamental, core interests help shape the relationship between leader and led. The young Alexander was never troubled by conspiracy and revolt. While there were certainly many differences of opinion over plans and policies, both military and administrative, between the king and his generals and the Greek allies, Alexander was generally able to persuade them to believe in the direction he wanted to pursue. Their interests in the early years were seemingly convergent. They wished to avenge the sacrilege of Xerxes and eliminate the perceived threat posed by the Persian empire to the Greek world. The vision was well-defined, the differences in the means to achieve it were overcome in a manner consistent with Greek and Macedonian political culture.

This coalition of vision, however, began to unravel between 331 and 330 B.C. To many of the Greeks and Macedonians, the victory at Gaugamela, the sack of Persepolis, and the death of Darius had fulfilled the purpose of the campaign. They could return home and enjoy the stable, secure, political life they considered good. Alexander, on the other hand, had an entirely different definition of the good. As Arrian tells us, "while Alexander was not wholly beyond comprehension of better courses, he was fearfully mastered by love of fame."[95] A life of noble deeds on the battlefield defined the good life for Alexander, a definition which placed him, as king, squarely at odds with that of his followers.

Competing, irreconcilable visions of the "good life" formed the core of Alexander's leadership problems with the Greeks and Macedonians and ultimately broke down the trust between them. While Alexander's trustworthiness as a battlefield commander was unquestionable, his trustworthiness as a king in the eyes of his followers became suspect. Alexander wanted a great empire and was willing to adopt Persian customs and dress in its pursuit. Had he pressed on into India, there is little doubt that he would have tried to bridge the cultural gap there in a similar fashion. In the eyes of his Greek and Macedonian followers, however, Alexander was becoming an oriental, rejecting the "civilized" customs and norms of the Hellenes in favor of barbaric despotism and *hubris*. His vision and character had become anathema to what they regarded as important and even respectable. For this reason they revolted at the Hyphasis and again at Opis and finally rejected his vision altogether after his death. Alexander had become Prometheus, seeing himself as a bestower of great gifts, but perceived by the Greeks and Macedonians as one who, despite the gifts, had failed to deliver the good life.

Chapter Seven

Calculation and Circumstance: The Leadership of Frederick the Great

by Dennis Showalter

In an anthology on leadership Frederick the Great seems at first glance badly misplaced. This is the man who during his reign as King of Prussia from 1740 to 1782 insisted that common soldiers should fear their officers more than the enemy, and who so closely monitored his generals that none of them could be trusted to perform independently. This is the man who carried grudges against entire regiments for decades, and whose capricious evaluation of performances at reviews and maneuvers broke careers like matchsticks. Frederick lacked panache. He aged quickly and unattractively; his unprepossessing personal appearance was further diminished by his indifference to dress. In an age when raw physical courage was taken for granted in senior officers, Frederick twice, at Mollwitz and Loboswitz, left major battlefields under dubious circumstances. Nor was his post-battle behavior such as to impress warriors. He spent the first hours after the defeat of Kolin aimlessly drawing circles in the dirt with a stick, then left his army and turned responsibility over to his brother on the grounds that he needed rest. After Kunersdorf he again turned command over to a subordinate and grandiloquently declared he would not survive the disaster. A later, kinder generation may speak of post traumatic stress. Eighteenth-century armies had other, blunter words for such conduct.

As a ruler too, Frederick seems a master of *dirigisme* rather than inspiration. His archetype was a "well ordered police state," requiring not even the personal interventions familiar in the reign of his father, Frederick William I, whose royal cane directly chastised not a few slackers and wrongdoers between 1715 and 1740.[1] Frederick's principal contribution to the practice of war similarly invites presentation as focusing on drill and discipline at the expense of initiative and inspiration, restricting leadership to the narrowest manifestations of front-line courage.   Even there Frederick tended to favor hard-bitten field soldiers in the mold of Moritz von Dessau and Johann von Huelsen over Leopold von Dessau, who emphasized motivating men instead of driving them, or the courtly and humane Kurt von Schwerin, who at Kolin fell at the head of his own proprietary regiment shouting "come on, my children!"

Frederick the Great had no children, biologically or emotionally. His father not only brutalized him for his "unmanly" interest in the fine arts, but was perfectly ready to sentence him to death as a deserter when, in 1730, the 18-year-old Frederick sought to flee the country. Forcing his son to witness the execution of his friend for complicity in the attempt was humane only in relative terms. Frederick grew into a full-fledged misanthrope, whose ill-treatment of his close associates was too consistent to be casual. His older sister, Wilhelmina, was the only person he did not keep at arm's length — and his respect for her declined as his misanthropy became more misogynistic after a marriage that does not merit even the polite phrase "of form only." In short, the familiar picture of Frederick the Great is of someone whose character and career can at best be interpreted as illustrating the mechanistic rationalism of the high enlightenment and the top-down authoritarianism of enlightened despotism.[2] At worst they suggest someone who, had he not become King of Prussia, would be a viable candidate for an eighteenth-century madhouse or a twentieth-century talk show.

Frederick's approach to leadership nevertheless owed much to his experiences as a young adult. The direct consequences of his attempted flight could not be mastered by either the provocative behavior or the "passive aggression" Frederick had previously directed against his father. Instead, in his court-martial Frederick impressed the judges with his forthrightness and his willingness to accept responsibility for his actions. He appealed to Frederick William I for clemency in a similar tone. Frederick learned, in short, the importance of presentation. This skill must not be confused with dissimulation, despite their similarities. Frederick did not assume the mantle of *gravitas* merely as a cloak to save himself from a firing squad and restore himself to royal favor. He seems rather to have accepted his position and resolved to develop its possibilities. Until he succeeded to the throne he behaved as a model Crown Prince, applying himself assiduously to the study of administrative and military matters, embarking as well on a comprehensive reading program intended in good part to compensate for his lack of practical instruction in the craft of monarchy.[3]

This was an act of will informed by reason in the best traditions of the Enlightenment. It was also a process rather than an event. There is no indication of an epiphany, a defining moment when Frederick's life changed. There is, however, a developing pattern of behavior indicating awareness of the aphorism that "if you act like food, you will be eaten." Frederick was twenty-eight when he assumed the throne — a young twenty-eight in terms both of his preparation and his experience. He was correspondingly convinced that any show of uncertainty would mark the beginning of his downfall, whether at the hands of foreign powers or in the minds of senior councilors who wondered whether the new king would ever be the man that his father was. These factors in turn encouraged him to an approach based on the projection of expertise. Frederick had to appear as The Man Who Knew How, depending neither on a personal charisma he above all knew that he did not posses, nor on an inherited position his fitness for which all Europe was aware had been challenged by the one best placed to know—his own father.

Inexperience and uncertainty were not the only factors shaping Frederick's initial approach to leadership. Frederick regarded himself as an intellectual, able to take counsel of history, evaluate moral and political claims, then form rational and appropriate judgments. As Crown Prince he had developed, in conscious contrast to his father's pragmatism, an academic approach to questions of statecraft. Beginning with an assertion that Prussia needed a systematic, long-term foreign policy to secure its interests, he proceeded by traceable stages to the conclusion that expansion by annexation was Prussia's ultimate necessity.[4]   Frederick's. *Anti-Machaviel*, published in 1740, developed the related argument that law and ethics, while vital to the conduct of international relations, were based neither on the interests of the ruler nor the desires of the people. Instead they structured "reason of state," a necessity outside the moral frameworks applying to individuals, whether kings or commoners.[5]

Frederick correspondingly interpreted the behavior of states as subject to rational calculation, governed by principles that could be learned and applied in the same way one repairs a clock.[6] This trope remained central to Frederick's conduct of foreign policy throughout his reign despite the stubborn refusal of his neighbors, Austria in particular, to accept Frederick's definition of rational behavior in the context of such issues as Prussia's seizure of Silesia in 1740. Its application during his early years as monarch and general had a practical advantage as well by enabling Frederick to compensate for his lack of experience in either role. If in fact particular events were less important than general axioms, then youth mattered less than knowledge, and experience less than judgment. In such a context Frederick was not merely King of Prussia by inheritance, but a *roi-connetable*, a leader who understood the requirements of his position without requiring on-the-job seasoning.

This concept of leadership recognized as well a perspective just beginning to become coherent as Frederick assumed the throne. Since the emergence of the early-modern state in the fifteenth and sixteenth centuries, the crucial functions of its rulers had been representational and heroic. Neither can be subsumed under Max Weber's paradigm of "traditional" leadership that rests on long-standing customs and behaviors. Europe's principalities were overwhelmingly either ad hoc creations or amalgams of otherwise-discrete territories, and were under princes whose patents of sovereignty were often too new or too questionable to bear close scrutiny. The "traditions" of a given ruling house were largely constructions, modified or invented *de novo* in response to circumstance, will, and whim. In that context a crowned-head ruler was expected above all to look and act the part, sustaining a life-style and maintaining a court system that would both reflect and enhance his state's *gloire* while sustaining its *gravitas*.[7] In particular this concept spread from the France of Louis XIV across the Rhine, shaping, as the 18th century progressed, the behaviors of rulers of small and middle-sized states whose competitions for status increasingly focused on symbols rather than policies. Building palaces rather than making war, patronizing artists rather than paying soldiers — this was the raw material of prestige as the Baroque Age segued into the Rococo period.[8]

At the same time, rulers were expected to play a heroic role. This should not be understood in John Keegan's paradigm of "heroic leadership." It tended towards the symbolic as opposed to the functional. Some notables from lesser states, like Victor Amadeus of Savoy or Baden's Markgraf Ludwig, the *Tuerkenlouis* of song and myth, were active field commanders. Sweden's Charles XII was, however, the last true warrior-prince of the old style, and his impact on his kingdom did much to discredit the archetype. Louis XIV, on the other hand, presided over sieges because they posed the lowest risks to the royal person and the royal dignity. Britain's George II likewise accompanied his army into the field in 1743, but did no more at the Battle of Dettingen than show courage under fire.

On assuming the throne Frederick eschewed both representation and heroism—a denial aphoristically expressed in his self-characterization as "Field Marshal and First Minister of the King of Prussia." Nor was this mere rhetoric. Among the most consistent elements of his policy during the Seven Years' War was the King's insistence that should he be captured, the war must continue, without efforts being made to rescue or ransom him. It would be an error, however, to present Frederick as an example of Weber's "bureaucratic" leader. That style depends heavily, if not quite exclusively, on the synergy of developed, complex systems that have been in place for a sufficient length of time to make their functioning predictable if not always smooth or competent. Eighteenth-century Prussia was a long way from that condition. The system inaugurated by Frederick William I was still raw, still working itself in. Its developing status precluded as well an "anti-heroic" leader in the mold of the Duke of Wellington as interpreted by John Keegan. Wellington was the product of a self-confident ruling elite, well-established yet not so secure that it could afford complacency.[9] Frederick instead understood himself as being responsible for making leadership redundant by fostering an administration and an army that would be institutionally responsive not to the ruler's character or personality, but to his expertise.

Frederick's concept of fine-tuning from the top depended as well upon his conviction that Prussia must fight only short, decisive, brutal wars — partly to conserve scarce resources, partly to convince the losers to make peace and keep it, partly to deter other potential challenges. This meant developing a forward-loaded military system, an army able to go to war from a standing start with its effectiveness highest in the beginning. It meant that nothing should be wasted on secondary concerns. Skirmishing, scouting, and all the other elements of "little war" increasingly present in the 18th century, in Frederick's mind above all wasted time. And time was the one thing Prussia did not possess.

Frederick developed as well a strong awareness of the randomness of battle. At Mollwitz in 1740, the day seemed thoroughly lost until the final advance of the Prussian infantry turned the tide. Soor in 1745 began when the Austrians surprised his camp and ended when Frederick, "in the soup up to my ears," improvised victory from the fighting power of his men. Hochkirch in 1758 was an even more comprehensive surprise that Frederick dismissed as an outpost fight until taught better by rounds shot from his own captured guns. These experiences were hardly unique, and the collective wisdom of eighteenth-century warmaking responded by minimizing Fortuna's opportunities via marching and fighting only under perceived favorable conditions. Frederick's grand-strategic and strategic concepts, however, required him not merely to seek battle, but to hold nothing back once the fighting started. He became correspondingly committed to minimizing what Clausewitz would call fog and friction by developing an army impervious to shocks.[10]

The best illustration of this approach is the King's use of maneuvers. Most eighteenth-century armies concentrated on individual and company drill—a pattern facilitated by the absence of permanent units above regimental level. In the aftermath of the Silesian Wars (1740-1748), Frederick institutionalized annual field exercises in the autumn, after the harvest cleared the fields. Involving as many men as a fair-sized battle — 44,000 in 1753 — and correspondingly expensive, the maneuvers were intended not for display. They were meant to test formations and tactics, to practice large-scale movements the effectiveness of which depended on many regiments acting in precise concert, and to accustom senior officers to handling large bodies of troops under stress. This last, though Frederick never made the point explicit, may well have been his justification for the devastating, and career-destroying critiques that accompanied the exercises. To a degree they replicated the unpredictable, high-risk conditions of command in an eighteenth-century battle.[11]

By a combination of intention and circumstance, Frederick's approach to leadership was congruent with two basic aspects of Prussian culture. The first was Pietism. This eighteenth-century religious impulse challenged the quietism of traditional Lutheranism by emphasizing service to and reform of the community. While less austere than the Calvinism to which it owed much of its theological substance, Pietism cultivated a sober, level view of the world and of mankind's place in it. It offered little room for exaltation or inspiration, and less for the kind of public posturing that confused status with hubris and performance with visibility. The Prussian state justified itself not by divine right in the manner of Louis XIV, or on prescriptive grounds of the kind later articulated by Edmund Burke, but in instrumental terms with protection and stability being exchanged for service and obedience. It was the kind of social contract, no less firm for being unwritten, that Pietists were most likely to affirm. And Frederick, whose rejection of formal religion went almost as deep as his misogyny, nevertheless fit the Pietist template of an ideal ruler as well as any mortal was likely to fit it.[12]

The second cultural parameter was patriarchy. That concept has been so often defined in a model of overt dominance and submission that it merits examination in an alternate context as suggested by Klaus Epstein. Conservatism, according to Epstein, is most effective when unarticulated. When it responds to "the party of movement" by describing, let alone defending, itself, conservatism is playing on the other party's home field by its rules.[13] A similar point can be made about patriarchy. Whether in the context of family, village, or Junker estate, it was most functional when least obtrusive. For those in charge, both collective wisdom and individual experience indicated the counterproductivity of throwing one's weight around, of directly intervening in the routine course of events except when absolutely necessary. That which disrupted the least was also likely to be the best. And while the Frederician state was by no means invisible, it did not interfere at random or change its mind at whim.[14] The proverb "there are still courts in Berlin," quoted in many eighteenth-century contexts, highlights the developing image of Prussia as a *Rechtsstaat*, a state of laws and practices with the force of law that not even the King himself could ignore.

Not bureaucracy, but Pietism and patriarchy, underpinned the central feature of Prussia's army, the canton system. This systematic tapping of Prussia's native manpower in peacetime enabled the state to maintain a force large enough to sustain its great-power pretensions without emptying the treasury. It succeeded less by direct compulsion than because of the willingness of families and communities to furnish a proportion of their sons each year—and because the system allowed both institutions a significant role in deciding precisely which individuals were furnished. Public, official authority, in other words, reinforced its social, unofficial counterpart in a specific area that directly impacted large numbers of people. Considered in that context, the "police states," the enlightened despotisms of the eighteenth century, may have been more congruent with traditional societies than has been previously conceded—and correspondingly more acceptable.[15]

The Pietist concept of duty provided a moral dimension to the subject of service that was by no means artificial. Self-discipline and social discipline are significant contributors to self-awareness and self-esteem: pride in tasks consciously and conscientiously performed in an environment validating those tasks.[16] Discipline's positive aspects may also be enhanced by an environment that, like Frederick's Prussia, has little surplus to sustain hedonism and few attractive prospects for self-indulgence. Not a few officers, for example, turned to self-improvement and professional improvement from disgust or boredom with the opportunities for vice offered by a garrison town.[17]

Between 1740 and 1756, Prussia's achievements in war and government were sufficient to justify the King's initial concept of leadership. The paradigm's limits, however, emerged during the Seven Years' War — specifically within the army. The Prussian military system replicated Prussian society in having a strong contractual element, but was problematized by the large number of "foreigners" in its ranks — around forty percent once mobilization was complete.[18] These men are also frequently called mercenaries, but the term had a much looser definition in the eighteenth-century than it does today, in which "mercenary" connotes a ruthless cosmopolitan who fights for any paymaster. In the Prussian army a "mercenary" was anyone who was not a conscripted cantonist.

Many of the "foreigners" were, legally at least, Prussian subjects. Some were discharged apprentices and underemployed day laborers who joined the army for security. Others were men who saw no prospects of improving their lot in civilian life and sought, if not liberty, at least a new form of servitude. Not a few were "true volunteers." One seventeen-year-old Alsatian traveled as far as Aachen to join the Prussian army because of its high reputation. His account, while written from a perspective that often confuses positive experience with the general vigor of lost youth, nevertheless describes even his recruit days as full of fun and horseplay, spent in more interesting company than that of his home village.[19]

The Prussian "mercenary," in short, did not consider himself part of a legion of the lost ones. His self-image was likely to be that of a professional, following the honorable profession of arms by his own choice. And while the official contracts of enlistment might be both one-sided and absolute, a mercenary could always invoke the escape clause of desertion. The draconian penalties instituted in the Prussian army to prevent this alternative affirm its relative ease even in peacetime, to say nothing of active service conditions.[20] Malcontents could, moreover, have a significant effect on morale among the cantonists, who were usually too well integrated into their home communities to make desertion a feasible option. And Frederick's army depended for its effectiveness on its fighting spirit far more than on its formal discipline. Compulsion, in its varied forms, might keep men in the ranks. It could not make them fight. More precisely, it could not keep them fighting. Drill and training were designed in part to condition the individual soldier by inculcating automatic physical responses: loading and reloading by the numbers, moving according to orders. But neither conditioned reflex nor external force, together or separately, could keep men in the ranks at the height of a Frederician battle that resembled nothing so much as feeding two candles into a blowtorch and seeing which melted first.

To a certain degree loyalty was generated by what might be called a commitment-dependence cycle. The soldier of early-modern Germany had identified himself to a significant degree in terms of individuality. Becoming a soldier involved being able to carry a sword, to wear outrageous clothing, and swagger at will among the women in ways denied to the peasant or artisan. The introduction of uniforms and the systematic enforcement of camp and garrison discipline did much to remove the patina of liberty from a life that, while not solitary, was likely to be nasty, brutish, and short. In its place emerged a pattern in which the state demonstrated concrete concern for the soldier's well being as a means of increasing the soldier's dependence on the state, a process that began in France during the seventeenth century.[21] The Prussian state was less lavish, but its uniforms were regarded as among the best in Europe. Its medical care in peace and war was superior to anything normally available to commoners. Its veterans had good chances of public employment or assignment to one of the garrison companies that combined the functions of local security and soldier's home.

Providing tangible benefits for uniformed service became more critical as warfare grew increasingly deadly. A soldier's relationship to the state differs essentially from that of a civilian because it involves a central commitment to dying, as opposed to death as a byproduct of other activities like fire fighting or law enforcement. In western societies that commitment is not absolute — a fact that can surprise even students of military history when they discover what "fighting to the last man" means in practice.[22] Moreover, for most soldiers the "death clause" is inactive much of the time. An individual can spend thirty honorable years in any uniform and face only collateral risks. But all armies possess a sense of what it is legitimate to expect under given circumstances. Regardless of the receipt or promise of material sustenance, as casualty lists mount or administration collapses, soldiers of any time and place are increasingly likely to begin scrutinizing the moral fine print in their agreements, written and unwritten, with state and society.

Maintaining an effective Prussian fighting force, therefore, required something closer to what F. Scott Fitzgerald called "a whole-souled spiritual equipment." It required leadership. Inspiration, however, was unlikely to be provided by an officer corps whose dominant Junker element had only been integrated into the military system by Frederick William I. Whatever personal leadership they provided was likely to be "traditional" in the Weberian sense; depending heavily on patterns of deference and authority established in civilian life, and correspondingly unappealing to mercenaries who had often enlisted to escape such patterns and increasingly unlikely to resonate with cantonists for whom doffing one's hat in the road did not equate with losing one's head to a round shot.[23]   Nor was Frederick willing to brook "charismatic" subordinates. He inherited some senior officers like Schwerin and Leopold von Anhalt, the "Old Dessauer," who were respected in their own right by the army's rank and file. But no successors to them emerged during Frederick's reign.   Even Seydlitz and Ziethen were identified with a particular branch of service, the cavalry, rather than with the army as a whole.

Prussia's latent crisis in leadership came to a head at Kolin in 1757. In one of the final desperate attacks against the Austrian line, Frederick attempted to inspire his men directly for the first time in his military career. His shout, "Bastards! Do you want to live forever?" did not turn the tide. Nor was it in a class with the inspiring battle rhetoric of a Julius Caesar. It struck, however, at least one responsive chord. A musketeer allegedly answered, "Fritz, we've earned our fifty cents for today!"   While almost certainly apocryphal, the exchange was nevertheless significant. The war, instead of ending quickly, decisively, and positively, was dragging on into unpredictability. The army suffered heavy and irreplaceable casualties at Loboswitz, Kolin, and in front of Prague. Russian troops invaded East Prussia in August, while a massive French army supplemented by contingents from the Holy Roman Empire advanced against Frederick from the west. Frederick's unprovoked attack on Saxony and his subsequent, systematic plundering of that state's human and material resources had deprived him of whatever sympathy he might have possessed elsewhere in Germany. If the army had now decided that it had earned its pay, Prussia's prospects for survival, let alone victory, were grim indeed.

The victory at Rossbach on November 5, 1757, began a process of giving Frederick a new image. The phrase allegedly uttered by a French officer to his Prussian captor: "Sir, you are an army; we are a traveling whorehouse," epitomized a *Schadenfreude* at the French misfortune that extended well beyond Prussia's frontiers. The elaborate baggage train of the Allied army did indeed include "valets, servants, cooks, hairdressers, courtesans, priests and actors...dressing gowns, hair nets, sun shades, nightgowns and parrots."[24] Its capture offered corresponding opportunities for propagandists to trumpet the purported Prussian and Protestant virtues of simplicity and chastity. Frederick became a symbol, unwittingly lending his name to taverns, streets, and towns as far away as Pennsylvania. But Rossbach generated no bandwagon effect among the lesser German states, Protestant or otherwise. Nor did it deter the Silesian city of Breslau, annexed by Prussia in 1740, from politely informing Frederick's garrison that its room was preferable to its company when an Austrian army appeared outside the city walls.

Breslau's surrender on November 25 marked the nadir of an ill-conducted campaign under the Duke of Bevern that left the way to Berlin wide open for an Austrian army that seemed well able to exploit the opportunity. It also marked a change in Frederick's philosophy of leadership. When the King arrived in Silesia on December 2, he had only one option: fight — and win. His behavior in the next days laid much of the foundations for the myth of "Old Fritz." Account after contemporary account describes a sick, exhausted monarch moving from bivouac to bivouac, warming himself at the men's fires, listening to stories and hearing complaints, promising promotion and reward for future good service. To senior officers, instead of the expected tirades, Frederick offered fellowship, implying that future deeds would cancel past misfortunes. The King did not rely solely on personal efforts. He relaxed a usually-stringent camp discipline to allow his veterans of Rossbach to mingle with their fellow soldiers and tell their stories of victory and plunder. He issued extra food and extra liquor as far as resources allowed. And he capped his performance on December 3 when he invited his generals as well as the regimental and battalion commanders to his headquarters.

Such an invitation was itself unusual. And when Frederick appeared the officers saw not a battle captain radiating confidence and vitality, but a tired, aging man whose uniform was more threadbare and snuff-stained than usual, and whose voice was too weak to be audible beyond the immediate audience. The army, Frederick declared, would attack. Its only alternatives were victory or death. "We are fighting for our glory, for our honor, and for our wives and children...those who stand with me can rest assured I will look after their families if they are killed. Anyone wishing to retire can go now, but will have no further claim on my benevolence." Lest anyone think he had gone soft, Frederick concluded by announcing that any cavalry regiment failing in its duty would lose its horses; any infantry battalion that flinched faced the loss of its colors, the ceremonial braid from its uniforms, and the swords carried by the rank and file.[25]

The "Parchwitz speech," named from the campsite, blended sincerity and artifice in a way impossible to separate. It lost nothing in the retelling. Years afterward men could remember every detail of what they saw and heard even if they were nowhere near the ground. Two days later the Prussian army smashed the Austrians at Leuthen. One regiment did so well that Frederick donated 1500 thalers from his own pocket for distribution among the rank and file — a gesture that, given his ascetic parsimony, was as close to public emotion as he was ever likely to get.

Was Frederick's behavior in the days of Leuthen contrivance or charisma? He continued to harass his senior subordinates by mixtures of advice, warnings, recriminations, and orders—the latter sometimes mutually contradictory. Almost two decades after Zorndorf he reminded one regiment that it had broken on that day, and such behavior could neither be corrected nor forgotten. After the defeat of Kunersdorf he sneered that his troops had suffered from a fear of being transported to Siberia.[26] After Leuthen, moreover, there were no more easy victories, no more brilliant maneuvers — just the close-gripped massacres in East Prussia, at Hochkirk, and at Torgau. Observers like Horace St. Paul, an English colonel in the Austrian army, criticized Frederick for predictability: "As He (Frederick) always launches his attack against one of the two wings of the army he attacks, it is simply necessary to plan a suitable response." [27]

This was a far cry from the *roi-connetable*, the King who mastered the battlefield by the force of his will and the power of his intelligence. Yet the army under Frederick's immediate command endured part of the winter of 1759-60 not in cabins as usual, but in tents pitched on the Silesian plateau. On short rations, racked by dysentery and respiratory diseases, it neither exploded in mutiny nor dissolved in desertion. In the summer of 1760 many of the same men took part in a month's worth of forced marches that produced high rates of straggling but limited numbers of deserters. The thirsty, the blistered, and the exhausted staggered into their camps at each day's end without benefit of cavalry — the patrols detached to bring in stragglers before they could make their absence permanent.

Nor were these the soldiers that had filled Prussia's ranks in 1756. If in the spring of 1761 three-fifths of the army's replacements still came from the regimental depots, many of them were cantonists by courtesy. The rest were foreigners, prisoners of war cajoled or pressured into taking new colors, or men brought in by recruiting parties increasingly difficult to distinguish from press gangs: the flotsam of five years' "hard war." Some were integrated into regular units whose cadres were considered still strong enough to shape the newcomers instead of vice versa. Others were organized into separate "Free Battalions" whose quality and performance ranged from barely adequate to miserable.[28] Almost half the pre-war officer corps was gone as early as 1759. Some of their replacements were as young as thirteen. Yet this unpromising amalgam continued to stand its ground against steadily-improving enemies, until Frederick was able to take advantage of the death of Russia's Empress Elizabeth to exit from the war in 1763 with his kingdom still intact and his reputation higher than ever.

What kept the Prussian army to its task in the war's final years was Prussia's King. To a degree "Old Fritz" was a construction, a projection of the desire to find a tangible focus for the sacrifices demanded by army service in a drawn-out war in the absence of general ideals like patriotism or religion. But the campfire tales and tavern legends did not rest on a phantasm sustained by the gallows and the firing squad. Frederick demonstrated the same qualities of endurance that he demanded of his men. On the march and in camp he was present and visible. Men who understood nothing of the oblique order of maneuver had seen Frederick rally his broken ranks at Hochkirch, and knew he had been hit by a spent ball at Torgau. They knew of his insistence on personally overseeing details of administration that had traditionally been beneath the notice of heroes. This was no Alexander, no Henry of Navarre with his white plume in the van, but a warrior for the working day who commanded respect by not demanding it.

Frederick's behavior arguably struck as well a deeper common chord in his soldiers. Warfare in the eighteenth century was increasingly becoming a matter of endurance rather than performance. What contemporary military writing describes as "warrior traits" found little place in a line of battle. Even in a cavalry charge, victory — and often survival — depended on the ability to keep ranks and rally promptly when the trumpet sounded. If battles seldom lasted longer than a day, their close-gripped nature made increasing demands on a soldier's capacity to stand — to control fear without the anodyne of activity. Campaigns as well, particularly in the relatively barren expanses of central Europe, were exercises in survival, without even the limited pleasures of rapine and pillage that had persisted during the wars of Louis XIV.[29] In such contexts someone who shared the general lot of his private soldiers might indeed emerge as a focus of loyalty as well as admiration.

Despite his poisonous rhetoric on the subject of their qualities, Frederick in practice was by no means indifferent to the well-being of his men. Before the Seven Years' War, training was on an individual basis, with the instructors enjoined to use harsh methods only when appeals to the recruit's "better nature" went unheeded.[30] In garrison, the soldier off duty was very much his own man, free to seek part-time employment or to practice the arts of idleness until the next parade. That ease carried into the field. While expecting clockwork precision on parade, he refused to drive his men hard on active service, conducting only periodic refresher exercises as opposed to regular, lengthy drills. What twentieth-century armies call "bull" or "chickenshit" was also remarkably absent from a Prussian camp. Pickets and sentries were kept to a minimum — sometimes to Frederick's cost, as at Soor and Hochkirch. Fatigue duties were functional — foraging, hay-cutting, latrine-digging — and shared within the companies. The army's march behavior was casual. Frederick increasingly enjoyed riding along the ranks, joking with the men in dialect and occasionally being chaffed back — a liberty seldom taken with lower-ranking officers and noncommissioned officers. It was only when making camp that he resumed his commander's role and "it was as if our Lord God had descended to earth in a blue coat"—the same coat as the soldiers wore.[31] A familiar German military cliché originated in this period: *"Dienst ist Dienst und Schnapps ist Schnapps."* By 1763 Frederick's army understood the difference.

When that understanding lapsed, Frederick provided reminders. At the siege of Dresden in 1760, a regiment broke during an unexpected sortie by the city's garrison. Frederick stripped the men of their distinctive hat braid and their swords. These were seldom used for anything beyond camp duties, but the men of the 3rd Infantry saw their removal as a shame that could only be drowned in blood. Two weeks later, at the battle of Liegnitz, the regiment surged forward on its own initiative. Shouting "honor or death," its musketeers broke through the Austrian line in a hand to hand brawl of musket butts and bayonets. That evening, army legend had Frederick riding to the regiment's camp to say "boys, everything will be restored to you. All is forgotten." It was an event that should have happened even if it did not. Certainly the army believed the story; certainly the King did not deny it. And in his evening orders he announced his intention to pay for the 3rd's new hat tresses from his own pocket. Hermann the Cheruscan or Pompey the Great could have done no more; the *roi-connetable* had become a warrior-prince as well.[32]

Frederick applied similar methods in his officer corps. Prussian officers were not courtiers or bureaucrats in uniform but men of war, assertive by experience and conditioning, often with the kind of economic and social independence fully enabling them to leave the service should their honor be challenged even by the King himself.[33] Frederick's insistence on maintaining the aristocratic identity of the officer corps was only partly motivated by the need to keep a fractious nobility identified with the state. It reflected as well his belief that the nobility's core value of honor made them best suited to a career whose essence was not subject to rational calculation. It also made them responsive to Frederick's definition of officers as a fellowship of service in arms. Common identity was facilitated by limited emphasis on distinctions of rank and uniform. Here again the King's well-known indifference to dress set the tone. Insignia of rank were not introduced until after the war, and Frederick offered lieutenants the same direct access to his person that he did generals. Most contemporaries agreed as well that Frederick's unpredictable harshness contributed not a little to the *Korpsgeist* of his officers by making membership in the community a thing neither lightly achieved nor easily sustained.

After the Peace of Hubertusburg in 1763, Frederick's image as general, statesman, and *Landesvater* flourished without his cultivation. A professed indifference to public opinion, manifested in his later years by behavior ranging from erratic to eccentric, had the paradoxical result of enhancing his appeal to what Paul Hollander has called "political pilgrims" who came to Berlin prepared to admire the King for their own varied reasons. The men of the *Aufklaerung* saw Frederick as a focal point for intellectual perspectives challenging those emanating from Paris, in spite of his indifference to such authors as Lessing and Winckelmann. The King's very inaccessibility rendered him attractive to proto-Romantics who saw hidden depths in Frederick's denial that he possessed or valued such depths. An embryonic nationalist movement was even built on the legacy of Rossbach to interpret Frederick as an embodiment of German virtue on a level with Martin Luther. In more concrete terms, the reputation of Prussia attracted soldiers and administrators from everywhere in Germany who wanted to be part of the best — and to make it even better.

For Frederick this was the kind of nonsense that justified his increasing alienation from all forms of direct human interaction. He nevertheless utilized his status to facilitate Prussia's recovery from a war that had brought the state to the edge of collapse. Frederick personalized the distribution of seed grain and draft animals, the payment of officials' back salaries, and the opening of royal land to emigrant settlers. His wartime-generated reputation for controlling everything in person was sustained by the energy and detail with which he conducted inspections throughout his kingdom. In particular Frederick's first tour of Prussia's ravaged provinces was like the Parchwitz speech, remembered for years even by people a hundred miles away from the royal coach when it passed through. For awhile it seemed that the King's identity as a personally-caring focal point might extend from the army to the entire Prussian state. Centralization, however, worked increasingly against such a development. The administrative apparatus became more self-referencing, more remote, as it grew more complex. A similar process took place in the legal system. Throughout his reign Frederick was increasingly committed to creating a general law code. In the event Prussia's *Allgemeines Landrecht* was not published until 1794, and, far from being a coherent compendium, its complex combination of general principles and specific qualifications did much to bring lawyers to an equal footing with soldiers and clergymen among Prussia's functional elites.[34]

The army was no exception to the postwar process of abstraction. Its reviews and maneuvers developed from testing grounds for war to public displays of power, designed to deter any state thinking of trying further conclusions with Old Fritz and his faithful grenadiers. The brotherhood of endurance faded in peacetime, as discipline became an end in itself instead of a means of making war. The fellowship of arms eroded as the King's capriciousness broke careers without hope of redress. By the mid-1770s the army was focused on Frederick not as king, not as commander in chief, but as totem. It was a paradigm incorporating the disadvantages of personalization without its compensations.   Raising questions of procedure or substance within the system became increasingly difficult, not only from fear but from awe.   A certain parallel might be drawn with the status of Robert E. Lee in the Army of Northern Virginia by the end of 1862.   In both cases autonomy gave way to a comfortable feeling that the "old man" knew what he was doing even if the wisdom of a particular course might not be apparent. In both cases as well dissent was easily equated with disloyalty, whether by the central figure in the construction or by his entourage.   Frederick II did not even have a James Longstreet. Postwar adulation of his military genius was by no means universal among senior officers who remembered the fiascoes as well as the triumphs.   But while the King lived his veterans kept silent. With the passage of time, moreover, the Seven Years' War came to play a role for them similar to that of the American Civil War for its participants a century later.   It was the defining event of their lives, and as such not to be lightly trivialized.   Perhaps after all, things had not been as bad as dreams remembered.[35]

It is a paradox that a king who began his reign with an image of a state and an army in which charismatic leadership was superfluous should by the time of his death have become the center of the first modern cult of personality.   The *roi-connetable* of 1740 and the warrior prince of 1763 alike gave way to the icon of 1780 — an icon that in turn crumbled under Napoleon's cannon in 1806.   Here, as in the rest of his life, Frederick was a "kingdom of contradictions." His synthesis of institutional and personal leadership, of competence and charisma, was in part a response to changing circumstances and in part a reflection of abstract principles.   To a significant degree as well, "Old Fritz" was the creation of his soldiers and his subjects, a "teflon monarch" to whom nothing stuck because he was a projection of needs, desires, and myths independent of the real Frederick.[36]   His legend and his model nevertheless endured in Germany until 1945, defied all efforts of the German Democratic Republic to dismantle it before 1989, and has by no means vanished at the century's turn.   For good and for ill, Frederick II of Prussia remains Frederick the Great.

Chapter Eight

Hard Knocks, Hubris and Dogma: Leader Competence in the American Expeditionary Forces

by Richard S. Faulkner

On 4 July 1918 Colonel Harold Fiske, the staff officer responsible for coordinating and standardizing the training of Americans in France, reported to the American Expeditionary Forces (AEF) Chief of Staff his belief that, "Berlin cannot be taken by the French or the British armies or by both of them. It can only be taken by a thoroughly trained, entirely homogeneous American Army."[1] Despite his bombastic pronouncements, after four months and over 36,000 battlefield deaths, Fiske's Berlin-bound American army was still very far from the German homeland. Worn and blunted by a series of costly frontal attacks and a hopelessly tangled supply system, by late October

1918 the AEF had reached a state of crisis. Faced with as many as 100,000 soldiers straggling behind the lines, a skillful German defense of the region, and the impossibility of replacing its unexpectedly high casualties, the AEF had virtually stalled in the forests and rolling hills of the Meuse-Argonne. While a myriad of interrelated systemic problems had led the AEF to its unfortunate situation, the poor leadership of many of the Army's officers was a major factor in the Americans' lackluster performance in the Meuse-Argonne Campaign.

Combat leadership is the art of getting soldiers to do willingly what instinct and society has programmed them not to do: place themselves at mortal risk and kill others. To be effective, battlefield leaders must always show a genuine concern for their subordinates' welfare and demonstrate a level of tactical competency that assures soldiers that their lives will not be placed at unnecessary risk. Ultimately, battlefield leadership rests on a foundation of mutual trust and confidence between the leader and the led. The cornerstone of that confidence is the subordinates' faith that their leaders have mastered the technical and tactical aspects of their jobs. Without this basic foundation, units cannot build the cohesion necessary to overcome the survival instincts and social strictures regarding killing other humans. Due to hasty and often unrealistic training and uncertainty of the duties and responsibilities of their positions, far too many officers in the AEF were unready for the challenges of modern warfare and their roles as combat leaders. This dearth of battlefield "know-how" caused the Army an inordinate amount of casualties, which in turn, lowered morale and created suspicion and distrust between senior and junior officers, and between officers and enlisted men. This chapter examines these factors and how the Army's officer training program failed to prepare the leaders of the AEF for battle. To highlight the consequences of these blunders the chapter will also explore the effects of poor leadership on the combat experience of the 82nd Division during its operations in France.

When the United States entered the First World War in April 1917, the Regular Army and National Guard numbered only 17,750 officers and 200,000 enlisted men.[2] War Department planners faced not only the daunting task of raising a large expeditionary army, but also the more complex burden of procuring and training officers to lead the rapidly expanding force. While the Selective Service Act of 1917 ensured a steady supply of able-bodied enlisted men, the general staff anticipated a shortfall of 150,000-200,000 officers. Recognizing the importance of securing competent commissioned leaders, Army Chief of Staff Peyton March later noted:

> *The quality of troops and their value as an effective force depends to a very large extent upon the character and sufficiency of their training, which in turn is dependent upon the officers who are designated to instruct them in camp and lead them in battle.[3]*

While most of the senior Army leadership agreed with March's assessment, the press of events and the unsettled Allied military condition in 1917 demanded an immediate solution to the officer shortage problem. This "quick fix" was the establishment of sixteen Officer Training Camps (OTC) at thirteen army posts across the United States to induct, train, and commission qualified candidates from regional civilian populations, the direct commissioning of select civilians with technical specialties, and the early graduation of the West Point Classes of 1917 and 1918 (later expanded to the Classes of 1919-1921). The vast majority of the Army's Officer corps came from the OTCs. By the war's end, over 48% of the Army's officers had been commissioned through the Officer Training Camps, as opposed to 6% from the National Guard and 3% from the Regular Army.[4]

The Officer Training Camps were closely modeled upon the pre-war civilian military preparedness "Plattsburg camps" and were designed to produce junior officers after three months of training. Unfortunately, the training of the OTCs' "90 day wonders" was too rudimentary and unfocused to prepare the young officers for their future tactical missions or the responsibilities of leadership. While the OTCs were designed to draw "civilians who were by education, experience and natural aptitude especially qualified for leadership," the training camps had no uniform system of evaluating the candidates' leadership ability or to accurately test their reactions under stress.[5]

The War Department assumed that being white, college educated, middle or upper class and experienced in business or the professions somehow indicated an innate ability to lead soldiers. Building on this dubious assumption, the role of the training camps was mainly to impart basic soldier skills and transition the candidates from civilian to military life. Training at the OTCs generally consisted of close order drill, basic rifle marksmanship, route marches, courtesies of the service, basic military law and the fundamentals of infantry tactics. While this training should have given the officers a sketchy but sound foundation of military knowledge, insufficient and poorly trained instructors, shortages of ranges, and equipment and a lack of time further undermined the quality and effectiveness of candidate indoctrination. While AEF commander John J. Pershing proclaimed that the tactical doctrine of the American Army would be built upon individual rifle marksmanship, the officer candidates received only thirty-six hours of marksmanship training; an amount considered the bare minimum for a pre-war regular army recruit.[6] The OTCs shortcomings were apparent even to the candidates. One later recalled, "I have never seen such pathetic attempts at instruction as I saw in the First Officers Training Camp."[7] Though Ralph Perry, the Secretary of the War Department Committee on Education and Special Training, admitted that "the men who were finally commissioned were not trained officers," he argued that the camps had produced "picked men who had mastered the rudiments and knew how to profit by the experience and ordeal that awaited them."[8] Perry's assessment was far from accurate. The fledgling officers leaving the OTCs took with them flaws and gaps in their leadership knowledge that began to snowball once they arrived in their units. The OTCs produced two-thirds of the Army's company grade line officers; yet, the pre-commissioning training of these platoon and company commanders left them unprepared and ill-equipped to face the challenges of leading soldiers.

The Army expected the officers leaving the OTCs and the early graduating classes of West Point to round out their tactical and leadership skills once they arrived in their units. The Army generally placed inducted enlisted soldiers directly into the combat units in which they would serve. The new soldiers then received the equivalent of basic training under the direction and tutelage of the noncommissioned and company grade officers who would eventually lead them in combat. Unfortunately, the training and experience of the company level leaders had not adequately prepared them to accomplish this mission. The Regular Army and National Guard were far too small to provide training cadres to the rapidly expanding force. The officers who developed and implemented the training in the new battalions, companies and platoons were often little better than that of their recruits. While the Army had traditionally relied on noncommissioned officers to instruct and "whip into shape" new recruits, the promotion and training of sergeants and corporals proved even more haphazard and fragmentary than that of the officers. With no set criteria for enlisted advancement, most NCOs gained their stripes solely on their ability to impress their officers, pass simple examinations or over-awe their fellow recruits. As with the majority of the recruits from which they were drawn, few sergeants and corporals had previous military service. While a post-war board of officers studying the problems and achievements of the AEF lamented the "poorly trained and rather dull non- commissioned officers" of the American Army, the board members failed to grasp that the American NCOs generally received no special training, and little incentive, for their assignment.[9] Their positions carried few privileges in terms of pay and utilization and even fewer responsibilities. Without a strong cadre of competent NCOs to draw upon, the junior officers were left to "sink or swim" in the training of their units. As one infantry captain recalled:

> *[The] training of non-commissioned officers [was]*
> *slighted almost to the point of neglect. Officers, from*
> *the Company Commander down, [were] obliged to*

*spend fifty percent of their time and energy in doing
the work of non-commissioned officers.*[10]

The Army's belief that junior officers could round out their skills
with "on the job training" within their units was incompatible with
actual conditions in the companies. With their own experience
and knowledge barely above the level of a pre-war private, the
junior officers found themselves suddenly responsible for the basic
instruction of their soldiers. This left little time for the officers to
concentrate on developing their own tactical competence. The
under-trained lieutenants and captains frantically scrambled to
learn the basics that they were expected to impart to their subordinates. For example, W.A. Sirmon, a lieutenant in the 82nd
Division's 325th Infantry, recalled spending much of his time at
Camp Gordon, Georgia, in ad hoc classes just to turn around and
give the same lessons to his soldiers later on in the day.[11] The officers' lack of training thus permeated the ranks of the AEF; without
a solid basis of experience and knowledge, the combat training of
the forming divisions degenerated into a tragi-comic case of the
"blind leading the blind."

The nation's lack of preparation to fight a large scale war also
hindered the instruction of the new army's officers. This resulted
in both a shortage of weapons and other equipment with which to
fight and train and an insufficient understanding of the complexities of modern warfare. Scarcities of training ranges and equipment
added extra levels of stress to already overburdened and unsure
company level leaders. The acute shortage of weapons in the 82nd
Division forced officers to contract with local saw mills for the production of wooden rifles. While the "Camp Gordon 1917 Model
Rifle," as the doughboys derisively called the wooden weapons,
allowed units to conduct limited instructions in the somewhat obsolete battlefield skills of close order marching and the bayonet exercise, it had few other useful purposes. Though the 82nd Division
was formed in August 1917, some of the unit's infantry regiments
were not completely armed with rifles until the first week of
February 1918.[12] Rifles were but one of the shortages that ham-

strung the division's training.   The Division Chief of Staff, Colonel
G. Edward Buxton, recalled:

> *The training of specialists in the United States was*
> *necessarily of a theoretical character. The Divisional*
> *Automatic Rifle School possessed about a dozen*
> *Chauchat rifles; the regiments had none.   Colt*
> *machine guns were issued to machine gun compa-*
> *nies, although this weapon was never to be used in*
> *battle. The Stokes Mortar platoon never saw a 3-inch*
> *Stokes Mortar while in the United States, and the 37-*
> *mm gun platoons possessed collectively one of these*
> *weapons during the last two or three weeks of their*
> *stay at Camp Gordon. A limited number of offensive*
> *and defensive hand grenades were obtained and*
> *thrown by selected officers and non-commissioned*
> *officers at the Division Grenade School. The men of*
> *one regiment witnessed a demonstration where four*
> *rifle grenades were fired.*[13]

These shortages not only hindered the training of the unit's weapons
specialists, but also prevented the junior officers from understanding
the employment and potential of the new military technologies.

Even after units overcame shortages of equipment, they still
faced the daunting task of using inexperienced officers to teach
their soldiers the skills necessary to perform and survive on the
modern battlefield.   The majority of the American soldiers who
landed in France could be considered only half-trained.[14] Training
time in the United States often centered on subjects which the
novice officers understood and could easily teach, such as close
order and bayonet drill. Looking back on the training he gave and
received, one lieutenant confessed, "Too much stress [was] put on
form, ceremonies, close order drill and other West Point relics of
the Roman phalanx age...too much valuable time [was] spent teaching "squads right" and not enough making every man able to use
any type of machine gun."[15] Without their own base of experience
to draw upon, the junior officers often found it difficult to instruct

their men in the more complex tasks of soldiering. Despite the time and effort that his unit devoted to marksmanship training, the 82nd Division's famous Alvin York remembered that his comrades remained "the worstest shots that ever shut eyes and pulled a trigger," and that their shooting "missed everything but the sky."[16] Unfortunately, as American units prepared to deploy overseas, the experiences of Alvin York and the 82nd Division were the rule rather than the exception. While motivated and well-intentioned young officers had attempted to transcend the host of training problems that confronted them, their greatest obstacles were their own limitations and inexperience.

Adding to the training problems that plagued the American Army was its inexperience with modern warfare. In 1917 the Army was still a small imperial constabulary force with a frontier mindset. In 1916, while the European armies were involved in titanic struggles at Verdun and the Somme, the American Army debated the merit of providing each infantry regiment with four machine guns. Despite the fact that the European war had shown the effectiveness and lethality of machine guns, modern artillery, tanks and air power, the Americans maintained an ostrich-like indifference towards the changes taking place in warfare. Thus, when the United States entered the war, the officer corps found itself not only dealing with the problems of mobilization, but also "playing catch up" in terms of formulating a coherent tactical doctrine for use in France. This lack of a coherent and realistic idea of how the Army should fight on the battlefield further exacerbated the problems of training competent junior officers.

Although American observers had reported on the new conditions of warfare on the Western Front, many regular and temporary officers clung to overly "romantic" visions of war. A graduate from a 1917 Officer Training Camp wrote that America's entry into the war would return, "the warfare of the old days, the warfare of our own West and South, when sabers flashed to the beats of galloping horses, and men went miles over the top instead of yards."[17] Tied to this romantic vision was a widespread faith in the innate superiority of American methods and skills over those of the Europeans.

Pershing insisted that the American Army's superior drive, morale and marksmanship would force the Germans out of their trenches. Once free from the trenches and into "open warfare," the Americans' greater skill and ability at maneuver would allow them to corner and destroy the inferior German Army.[18] Many Americans, from Pershing to the most junior lieutenant, convinced themselves that years in the trenches had blunted the offensive edge of the Allies and had sapped their aggressiveness, initiative and will to win. As one senior GHQ staff officer argued:

> *In many respects, the tactics and techniques of our allies are not suited to American characteristics or the American mission in this war. The French do not like the rifle, do not know how to use it, and the infantry is consequently too entirely dependent upon a powerful artillery support. Their infantry lacks aggressiveness and discipline. The British infantry lacks initiative and leadership.[19]*

Given this perception of the situation, the senior officers of the AEF maintained that only fresh American soldiers, superior American tactics and better American "know how," could beat the Germans. Unfortunately, Pershing's failure to understand both the brutal effectiveness of modern weapons and the lack of training of his own officers and men doomed the "open warfare" doctrine to failure. The General declared that despite the use of trenches and technological advancements, "the basic principles of warfare had not changed," and it was his view that "the rifle and bayonet still remained the essential weapons of the infantry."[20] While Pershing spoke of dominating the battlefield with superior American marksmanship, his Inspector General discovered that a number of the AEF's doughboys had never fired a rifle in training, and some did not even know how to load their weapons.[21] Though GHQ exhorted line commanders to train for open warfare, Pershing's staff never established a workable and realistic training program nor a set of battle drills for converting the AEF commander's rather nebulous ideas into a coherent doctrine. Pointing out this problem,

Colonel George C. Marshall reported, "the mass of tactical instructions which were printed and issued were beyond the grasp of all concerned."[22]   An artillery officer summed up the experience of many Americans in France by noting, "The system of training...was obsolete, showing that our Army had learned no lessons of modern warfare as developed in Europe in the two years that the war had been going on."[23] Within the AEF, "open warfare" remained not a doctrine, but rather a dogma; a mere mantra to "marksmanship and maneuver" to be sung in the presence of Pershing, but always in the end, mysterious and elusive to the officers who had to execute it in combat. Chained by an unwillingness to adhere to the advice of the Allies and set adrift without a reasoned and logical doctrine of their own, the AEF's line officers were forced to learn about war the hard way: through the hard knocks school of personal experience. Unfortunately, this proved a poor method for improving leader competence and instilling trust and confidence between the soldiers and their officers.

Although Pershing never fully appreciated the seriousness and degree of his army's lack of training and doctrinal focus, he understood the AEF's inexperience and tried to sharpen its war fighting abilities before committing Americans to battle. The AEF implemented a training policy that rotated American divisions through combat instruction with Allied units and then service on a quiet sector of the front. Pershing also established an extensive network of schools to introduce American officers and NCOs to modern weapons. In the long run, the rotation policy and schools system did little to improve American readiness, and actually worked against building strong junior leadership and unit cohesion. In the case of the 82nd Division, it trained behind the lines with the British 66th Division in Flanders and later occupied trenches in the relatively tranquil Lagny sector under French control. After a month of training with the British and 58 days of front-line service with the French, the division was neither proficient in trench warfare nor ready for open combat. The British broke the division into battalion sized units and scattered it widely around Flanders for training. This prevented battalion, regimental and divisional commanders and staffs from learning how to control and supply the unit as a whole. To ease supply problems, the British also collected all the American's weapons and reissued British small arms and machine guns. Most of the division's time with the British was spent learning bayonet fighting, physical fitness and the marksmanship and maintenance of weapons that the doughboys would never use in combat.[24]

The 82nd Division's experience with the French Army was little more rewarding. For nearly two years a tacit truce between the French and Germans had kept the Lagny sector relatively calm. Neither the French nor the Germans were particularly enthusiastic at having the raw and rambunctious Americans disturbing the region's "live and let live system." The French officers assigned to the American units did everything within their power to control and divert the aggressiveness of the newcomers. In the end, the doughboys' combat experience in the Lagny sector amounted to little more than a few trench raids and exposure to German shell fire.[25] The sector was so quiet that Lieutenant W.A. Sirmon recalled that he shot quail and gathered plums and apples in no-man's land.[26] Despite the relative peace of the trenches, the division still suffered casualties. While serving on the French front, the division lost 44 men killed in action and another 327 wounded. Many of these casualties can be traced back to the lack of training of both officers and men. Seventeen of the 44 soldiers killed were lost in a single incident after a German shell slammed into an overcrowded trench. Most of the division's wounds resulted from exposure to gas and could have been prevented by more thorough training in chemical warfare and better supervision of the soldiers by their officers.[27] As with many other AEF units, the 82nd Division left its front line service with the Allies with little to show for the experience. As the unit prepared for its combat debut during the St. Mihiel offensive, the 82nd's doughboys had still not received realistic training for the fighting they would face, and the division's officers had not greatly improved their tactical competency. Their service with the French and British had also prevented the division's senior officers from learning and practicing how to maneuver, supply and fight as brigades and as a division.

While the lack of focus and realism proved a major failing of the Americans' instruction with the Allies, the AEF's own policy towards schooling further aggravated the total training of competent officers. While Pershing intended his elaborate school system to produce officers familiar and comfortable with the new weapons of the war, the system degenerated into an ever expanding bureaucracy which stripped line officers from their units for long periods of time at critical points of platoon and company cohesion-building. Though the officers became technically proficient in a weapons system, they were often missing from their units when their soldiers were learning to rely on one another and to work as a team. Due to misguided War Department policies of taking huge levies from forming divisions to build up a reserve of specialists or to round out the manpower for other divisions, many of the units departing from the United States did not receive their full contingent of troops until a few weeks before they sailed for France. For example, the 82nd Division was hit with three such levies between the time it formed in August 1917 and the time it sailed in April 1918. Many of the division's soldiers joined the unit only days before it departed, and thus lacked both training and a sense of inclusion.[28] Given this friction, junior officers should have been busy honing their leadership skills and working to integrate the members of their units into a close knit organization. Unfortunately, the AEF's draconian schools quota system yanked the leaders from these evolving platoons and companies at the key point in the units' development: when the soldiers were gaining trust and confidence in their own and their leaders' abilities. Generally, a young captain or lieutenant in the AEF could expect to attend at least two schools during his time in France and lose approximately two months of time with his soldiers. In July 1918, one disgusted 82nd Division officer commented, "The Germans begin a great offensive, and we retaliate by starting another school."[29] The schools' length and over emphasis on technical aspects of the weapons rather than their tactical employment served to limit their usefulness. As one infantry officer pointed out:

> *Specialty schools for officers were overdone. Three weeks courses were given in courses that any reasonable man ought to learn in three days. If he couldn't learn grenade throwing, for instance, in three days, he ought not be an officer...Somebody's obsession regarding the necessity for schools kept about 50% of officers away from their units all the time, when they ought to have been giving their time to their men.[30]*

The AEF's policy of retaining talented students to teach in the army's school system further exacerbated the problems of leadership by stripping combat units of their most experienced and able young officers. The blow that the schools program dealt to unit cohesion and leader development never equaled the benefits of the instruction.

The junior officers' obvious lack of tactical and leadership competence strained their relations with both their superiors and soldiers. The vast majority of the AEF's division commanders (all but one) and most of its brigade and regimental commanders were regular soldiers with rather patronizing attitudes towards their newly commissioned subordinates. The regulars saw the "temporary officers" as nothing more than an undisciplined bunch of amateurs with no understanding of military matters or the proper "Army way" to accomplish tasks.[31] Along with the well established disdain of "temporary officers" by the regulars came a corrosive lack of trust which frequently ate away at the bonds of mutual respect that hold units together in combat. Voicing a sentiment shared by many senior officers, the AEF Inspector General placed the fault for much of the American Army's problems on the lack of responsibility and initiative on the part of the junior officers.[32] In a vicious cycle of mistrust, suspicion, and blame, senior commanders acted to limit the decision-making and discretionary powers of their junior commanders. This only served to retard the authority and ability of captains and lieutenants to exercise their leadership and better learn their jobs. It also undermined the confidence of the enlisted soldiers in their leaders, thus further eroding unit cohesion. Rather than devote attention to professional development and correcting the flaws and gaps in their officers' knowledge, senior leaders micro-managed their subordinates, thus ensuring a self-fulfilling prophecy of junior leader incompetence.

Much of the senior leaders' distrust and micro-management of their subordinates stemmed from their fear of being relieved of command for failures caused by their junior officers. Knowing the weaknesses of his new officer corps, Pershing ruthlessly worked to remove from command any officer not meeting his standard of aggressiveness or sufficiently versed in his expectations for "open warfare." During the Meuse-Argonne offensive, Pershing relieved four brigade and three division commanders. On 12 October 1918, he also removed George Cameron from command of the V Corps. Officers failing to meet, or appearing to fail, the General's standards were sent to the Casual Officers Depot and Reclassification Center in Blois, France, to appear before a reclassification or efficiency board. The depot reclassified 1101 officers considered untrained, unfit or unsuited for their assignments before it ceased operations in February 1919. An additional 270 officers had their competence for command judged by Blois' efficiency board. Of these officers, 39 were returned to combat duty; 48 were discharged; 35 were sent back to the United States; 12 were demoted, and the remainder were assigned to non-combat duty within the Service of Supply.[33] Regardless of the board's findings, for most regular officers being sent to Blois was a career ending experience. While Pershing's actions certainly removed many incompetent officers, they also placed a severe emotional strain on many of the AEF's leaders. Investigators from the AEF Inspector General's office discovered that a number of leaders were afraid of making minor mistakes and that some "officers... exhibit a degree of fear and apprehension lest some unavoidable event, something which they could not control, might operate to ruin their careers."[34] This fear of removal motivated many commanders to keep their subordinates firmly "under thumb" and limit any activities that might reflect badly on the commander. In the II Corps, inspectors discovered that some commanders went as far as limiting the advancement and schooling of their best subordinates "because of the danger to themselves of being relieved from command for some error made by less efficient officers."[35] With the specter of Blois never far from their minds, regimental and higher commanders seldom allowed their subordinates latitude to make, and more importantly, to learn from their mistakes in training and or during operations on the quiet sectors of the front.

While the senior officers often distrusted the abilities of their junior leaders, the AEF's junior leaders frequently held low opinions of their superiors. While recognizing their own limitations, the AEF's captains and lieutenants were quick to discern that the majority of the Army's colonels and generals had no more experience with modern warfare than they did. Prior to America's entry into the war, no serving officer had experience commanding a division or higher unit, and few had commanded anything larger than a company. As with the junior officers, the senior leadership had virtually no experience with massed artillery, machine guns, tanks, trench warfare, gas or air power. The junior leaders chaffed under what they considered hypocritical criticism and shabby treatment at the hands of their superiors. One young officer blasted the "lack of experience and common sense in the handling of large bodies of troops by some higher officers," while another wrote that "the field officers and many general officers did not understand their [the field grade officers'] work."[36] An infantry lieutenant bitingly recalled, "In battle, General and Field Officers remained far to the rear, but after the battle they came and bitterly criticize[d] the work of the combatants, when, if the higher officers had been in their proper places, they could have personally directed the fighting."[37] These charges were not without merit. In a test given by the II Corps Headquarters to a mixed group of field grade officers immediately after the war, only five out of 57 leaders tested could accurately locate map coordinates. The II Corps testing also revealed that "the vast majority of field officers could not read a map, could rarely make a sketch, could not write a clear, concise message, and had small conception of the general tactical principles employed in offensive movements."[38]   Under these conditions, there is little doubt why feelings of contempt, distrust, and resentment were mutual between the senior and junior officers.   At the end of his service, an infantry captain lamented that he and his peers had "been treated more as dishonorable and dishonest men...and not treated as officers should be treated."[39] Dissatisfied with his brigade commander's lack of tact and leadership, one officer in the 82nd Division ruefully noted in the summer of 1918:

> *The General has ridden us so constantly and consis-*
> *tently about picayunish details that he has his entire*
> *staff demoralized.   I appreciate the difference*
> *between disciplinary reprimand and a cursing out.*
> *The General isn't careful [about] which he uses these*
> *days.*[40]

True leadership rests on the subordinates' faith that their leaders are competent and will treat them with due respect and fairness. This level of leadership was seldom attained in the AEF.   The mutual hostility and mistrust that often surrounded the relationship of junior and senior officers in the AEF further hindered the development of tactical competence in the Army's leadership and limited the combat effectiveness of American units in combat. The backbiting attitudes of the officer corps also filtered down through the ranks, weakening the doughboy's faith in his officers and spreading cynicism.

The failings of the AEF's training plan and leadership started to become apparent with the St. Mihiel offensive. The offensive (12-16 September 1918) marked the Americans "coming out" as an independent army with its own sector of the Western Front. Pershing's mission was to reduce a 25-mile-wide and 15-mile-deep salient in the Allied lines that the Germans had held for almost four years. Despite the fact that the Germans were already in the process of pulling out of the salient when the Americans attacked, thus offering a very uneven defense, the shortcomings of the AEF's combat preparations quickly became obvious.   While Pershing intended the AEF to use maneuver to limit American

casualties, the battalion and company grade officers all too frequently lacked the ability to use the terrain to find covered and
concealed routes to the German positions. The junior officers
also lacked the training and confidence to command and control
anything beyond simple and costly frontal attacks. Instead of a
skilled force which used superior firepower and maneuver to
destroy the enemy, the attacking divisions presented the enemy
machine gunners a huddled mass of confused soldiers blindly
stumbling towards their positions.[41]

In the case of the 82nd Division, these failings were very apparent. Though the division had only a minor role in the operation, St.
Mihiel was the first time that all the division's units came under the
operational control of the division commander. The St. Mihiel operation revealed that many of the division's officers were deficient in
the basic skills of map reading and small unit tactics. The confusion caused by these deficiencies is best illustrated by comments
made by the 326th Infantry's Lieutenant Justus Owens in a letter that
he sent to his mother soon after the battle. Owens relates:

> *We left our present positions about 9:00 P.M. ...We
> headed for our objective after cutting thru our own
> wire, but hadn't gone far until we decided we were
> headed in the wrong direction...It afterward turned
> out that we were headed in the right direction at first
> and lost out (and ourselves) by turning right...We
> wandered around in the rain and slush and mire of
> no-mans land for several hours...We finally located
> our woods about 2:15 A.M. It was still so dark that
> we could hardly see anything, so I placed my men in
> one corner of the woods and told them we'd hold
> tight until it got lighter.[42]*

Luckily, Owens' objective had been abandoned by the Germans.
However, his blundering attempts to find the objective and his failure to clear it while he still possessed the cover of darkness put his
soldiers at great risk and gave his men grounds to question his
leadership.[43] Not all of the 82nd Division's soldiers were as lucky

as Owens' command. George Loukides, a private in H Company, 326th Infantry, noted that the officers "were not trained for combat and the privates paid for it." He recalled that during the St. Mihiel battle his company lost "many killed" when their officers attacked across a dangerously open field in broad daylight.[44] Alvin York wrote that during the 328th Infantry's attack on Norroy the regiment's companies "got mussed up right smart," and later his units' inability to cover its flanks allowed the Germans to enfilade the American positions.[45] The officers' tactical incompetence during the St. Mihiel offensive lowered morale and strained the relationship between the leaders and the led. One sergeant bitterly remarked that some of his officers "should have been with the boy scouts."[46] This did not bode well for the division as it moved from the St. Mihiel sector to participate in the Meuse-Argonne campaign. The division itself was still far from being seasoned; one infantry officer who participated in the St. Mihiel battle reported that he did not see his first dead German until weeks later in the Argonne Forest.[47] The battle had been a shock to the division's collective system, but it had been too short, and the division's role too limited, to allow the unit's officers to learn much from their mistakes. Unfortunately, like most AEF units, the 82nd Division had no time to address the training deficiencies of its officers and men or to repair the damage to unit morale cause by the officers' incompetence prior to the unit entering the Meuse-Argonne offensive.

The Meuse-Argonne offensive (26 September - 11 November 1918) was the American army's major military contribution during the First World War. Its purpose was to keep the Germans from reinforcing other areas of the Western Front under attack by the Allies, to destroy German reserves and to penetrate the Hindenberg Line. Though Pershing intended to use the campaign as a vindication of his insistence of an independent American army and his "open warfare" doctrine, the Meuse-Argonne mostly highlighted the lack of American training and the defects of the AEF's command and staff abilities. The AEF's systemic flaws in leadership, training, organization and doctrine hindered the Americans with bloody regularity throughout the army's 47 day ordeal. Well over half of all

American casualties during the war were lost in the seven weeks of fighting in the Meuse-Argonne. These losses are not just attributable to the skillful German defense of the region but also to the incompetence of the American Officer corps. Even with fully and correctly trained officers and soldiers, the Argonne Forrest and the open rolling hills of the Meuse region would have presented a formidable obstacle. Without a clear tactical doctrine or an understanding of the fundamentals of modern combat, such as the employment of supporting fires and the use of terrain, the AEF's leaders usually resorted to frontal assaults that merely sought to smother the defenders under the weight of American numbers. A machine gun officer argued that with these methods, "Too many men were unduly exposed to danger" and blamed the losses on the fact that "officers and men of the American Army had not learned the value of small fighting units in such fighting as we encountered in the Argonne."[48] The 7th Division's Colonel Gordon Johnston noted that the "tendency to belt straight ahead within a given sector was the cause not only of many losses, but of the failure to properly use all the means at hand for overcoming resistance." Brigadier General Malin Craig decried the American habit of going forward "in close masses," thus presenting the Germans an ideal target for artillery and machine gun fire.[49] Given their lack of sound training and experience, battalion and company officers frequently resorted to the easy but costly tactic of moving until you draw fire and then directly attacking its source.

The 82nd Division's experience in the Meuse-Argonne illustrates the systemic failures of the AEF's preparation for combat. The division's first three days of combat in the Argonne shocked the doughboys with its ferocity and deadliness. In the six months that the 82nd Division had served in France prior to the Meuse-Argonne, the division had lost a total of 133 soldiers killed in action, 1244 wounded or gassed and 13 captured. From October 7 to 10, the 327th Infantry alone suffered the loss of 118 soldiers killed, 700 wounded and 96 captured. When the 82nd Division was relieved from the lines on 30 October 1918 after 23 days of continuous fighting, the unit had lost 902 soldiers killed in action, 4897 wounded and 185 taken prisoner.[50]   Many of these losses can be traced to poor decisions made by the division's officers. As the unit's leaders were unable to maintain command and control, the infantry attacks often fragmented into a series of uncoordinated, disorganized and huddled rushes. In one such confused attack, Justus Owens and twelve other soldiers of Company L, 326th Infantry died as they blundered forward in a frontal attack against a dug in machine gun.[51]   Alvin York described the horror he experienced while watching a battalion of the 328th Infantry launch a frontal attack across open terrain:

> *The Germans met our charge across the valley with a regular sleet storm of bullets. I'm a-telling you that there valley was a death trap... I guess our two waves got about half way across and then jes couldn't get no further...They jes stopped us in our tracks... our boys jes done went down like the long grass before a mowing machine. Our attack jes faded out.[52]*

The officers' lack of understanding of modern warfare and leadership are demonstrated by an after action report sent by Captain John K. Taylor to the regimental commander of the 325th Infantry in December 1919.

> *To hasten the movement of the men to the front line positions here, I told them not to mind the bullets, that most of them were from our own machine guns. Upon seeing two men fall dead and another wounded by my side, I overheard a man say "our machine guns are sure hell."[53]*

Whether thoughtlessly charging into machine gun positions or carelessly and unnecessarily exposing their soldiers to fire, the division's officers demonstrated a poor example of combat leadership. Ultimately, the junior officers and their soldiers paid for the convoluted and intertwined problems of the American training program.

Faced with heavy casualties and the realization of their own tactical flaws, American officers fighting in the Meuse-Argonne started to learn the hard lessons of war. Unfortunately, lessons such as the proper use of terrain and supporting weapons, had come at a very high price in terms of losses and morale. As one Captain argued, "It is useless to try to fool the American enlisted man: he soon looses respect for his officers when he observes their lack of experience, gained through the school of hard knocks."[54] This "school of hard knocks" proved exceptionally costly to the junior officer ranks. While the officers lacked experience and "know how," few lacked courage. In terms of percentages, infantry officers (mostly captains and lieutenants) suffered the highest losses of all ranks and branches in the war. Infantry leaders suffered an average of 567 casualties per thousand officers while infantry enlisted men suffered an average of 447 casualties per thousand soldiers.[55] The 325th Infantry provides a striking example of this attrition. When the regiment entered the Meuse-Argonne battle on 8 October 1918, it had a strength of 100 officers; when the unit pulled out of the battle on 31 October 1918, its strength was down to 33 officers.[56] While combat experience increased tactical abilities in some individuals, overall the heavy losses of junior officers tended to off-set these gains and decrease the total level of competence in the AEF. Too many officers like Justus Owens were being killed before they learned the tactical lessons necessary to survive. The officers who replaced these fallen leaders often lacked any experience with soldiers and still possessed the flaws of training that hindered their predecessors. The AEF was never able to break the seemingly endless cycle of half-trained officers being killed or wounded due to their limited competency only to be replaced by other half-trained officers whose limited competency often led them to make the same mistakes. After heavy losses of officers in the summer of 1918 caused a shortage of junior leaders, the AEF scrambled to establish an officer candidate school for commissioning enlisted men. While the school produced 10,976 officers, this move did little to improve the quality or competency of the officer corps. The AEF G-5, Harold Fiske, noted that by September 1918 the candidate school faced the "practical disappearance of suitable officer material from the ranks." He blamed that shortage on the fact that "many organizational commanders bitterly opposed the detachment of their best non-commissioned officers" and that they tended to use the school as a dumping ground for misfits.[57] Given the heavy casualties among junior officers, some enlisted soldiers chose to improve their chances of survival by remaining in the ranks. In a letter home dated 25 October 1918, 82nd Division soldier Benjamin Heath wrote, "I could get an opportunity to go to the infantry training camp, but I would rather come home safe and sound without a commission than perhaps not at all."[59] Given such problems and attitudes, the AEF's officer corps was never able to overcome its problem with tactical competence.

In the end, the officers' lack of tactical expertise and leadership skills greatly affected the lives and attitudes of the average doughboy. In addition to their failure to instill proper technical knowledge, the training schools also failed to teach the officers the fundamental leadership principles necessary to lead and care for their soldiers. An infantry officer admitted and condemned the "tendency of officers to always consider their own comforts and pleasure rather than that of their men."[59] In a survey of officers awaiting demobilization, a number of leaders expressed regret at their own and their peers' failure to better safeguard the welfare and just treatment of their soldiers.[60] Raymond B. Fosdick's April 1919 report to the Secretary of War on the relations of officers and men in the AEF, noted that many officers tended to carry out actions considered "galling to the democratic spirit of the troops." He went on to note that while the intellectual, moral and social distinctions between the two groups was very small, "the difference between officers and men in the point of privileges and social position conferred upon the former has been emphasized to what seems to me a totally unnecessary degree."[61] The AEF felt the results of these failings during the Meuse-Argonne campaign. Lacking the rigid attention to the feeding and health of their soldiers, commanders in the campaign found their ranks decimated by sickness and straggling. Uninformed and apathetic officers did not understand the limitations of their soldiers and often allowed their men to languish for days on end without proper clothing and food. A doughboy in the 82nd Division remembered, "They threw away their raincoats and overcoats when they went over the top, so that later they had nothing at all to protect them from the cold and the wet. They went for days and days, sleeping in shell holes filled with ice-water, living on nothing but bully beef and water."[62] The American rear area was a nightmare, which left the officers at a loss to figure out how to keep the front line units supplied. Under the influence of poor food, clothing and weather, the health and combat efficiency of the units flagged. During October, the 82nd Division's medical staff reported an average of 700 soldiers in their hospitals per day suffering from influenza, diarrhea and exhaustion.[63] Oliver Q. Melton, commander of K Company, 325th Infantry, reported that between 16 and 30 October, "everyone was sick and weak, many of the men were on the verge of a nervous breakdown."[64] Faced with the lack of care, wretched treatment and the tactical incompetence of their officers, over 100,000 American soldiers simply stopped fighting and straggled towards the rear. The AEF Inspector General discovered that one division alone was missing over 6,000 soldiers from its front line units. While the Inspector General blamed straggling on the lack of discipline and personal supervision of the soldiers by their officers, the fact remains that the doughboys had lost confidence in their leaders.[65] In a telling indictment of leadership in the AEF, Major Robert G. Calder wrote, "In this war our men in the ranks have been superior to our officers, that is as soldiers they were better than the officers were as leaders."[66] As their commanders proved unable to competently discharge their responsibilities and duties, many enlisted men in the Meuse-Argonne opted for self-preservation and, following the lead of their officers, abrogated their duties as soldiers.

During the First World War, the United States managed to induct over four million people into the nation's armed forces and ship over two million soldiers to France before the Armistice. However, the nation never learned how to train its officers to lead their soldiers and to fight a modern war. Colonel Fiske, the officer who proclaimed that only an American army could take Berlin, later admitted:

> *....It must be remembered that to the end most of our divisions were lacking in skill. Given plenty of time for preparation, they were capable of powerful blows; but their blows were delivered with an awkwardness and lack of resource that made them unduly costly and rendered it impracticable to reap the full fruits of victory.*[67]

Due to a lack of understanding of modern warfare, mistrust and suspicion between company and field grade officers and the failure to create a realistic doctrine or a meaningful training plan, the AEF's officer corps never reached the level of tactical competence that the United States expects of its military leaders. These failings eroded the mutual trust and respect between officers and soldiers that is so critical to building the cohesion and effectiveness necessary to sustain units in combat and exacted an unnecessary toll of blood from the American soldier. The experience of the American Expeditionary Forces should serve as a warning to those who today would place the demands of technology over those of unit training, leader development, and procurement and retention of quality personnel. As is shown by the example of the 82nd Division, the "school of hard knocks" in warfare often demands a very high tuition.

Chapter Nine

Heroism Under Fire*

by Cole C. Kingseed

In his notes on combat experience during the Tunisian and African campaigns, Major General E.N. Harmon observed that men will follow a good leader practically anywhere and under any conditions of battle. Therefore, placing the right men in positions of leadership is the most important safeguard for success in battle that a commander can have. Addressing the veterans on the 50th anniversary of D-Day, President Clinton expressed similar sentiments while speaking not of Eisenhower, Bradley, Patton or Ridgway, but of men like Len Lomell, Joe Dawson, Lyle Bouck, Jr. and the countless, often nameless, thousands who fought to preserve democracy a half-century ago. Citing an essay by William Brown, the President acknowledged that in their youth, these men and their peers saved the world. They did not fight for glory or for honor, nor for lasting tribute on the printed page, but simply because victory had to be won and there was no one else available to do it. Despite the tremendous sacrifices of the forces arrayed against Nazism, it fell to the American man at arms to save the world from the unspeakable horror of global fascism.

Today, the veterans of World War II are but footnotes in the history of this century's greatest struggle; in a larger sense, however, they represent perhaps the most remarkable generation of fighting men and women this country has ever produced. In many ways, the World War II generation produced the most ordinary of soldiers. Few were professional military soldiers, most were citizen-soldiers who responded because their nation sounded the war tocsin in time of national emergency. Yet their record bespeaks of tales of epic heroism under fire. Before their memory fades from our consciousness, it is fitting to reflect on their achievements. The stories of three soldiers help us remember the patriotism, heroism and sacrifices of the many who answered freedom's call.

Sometimes a single day's combat reveals more about the national character than does an entire campaign. June 6, 1944, the invasion of Europe, was such a day. On D-Day, First Sergeant Len Lomell was the acting platoon leader of D Company, 2nd Ranger Battalion. According to Omar Bradley, the Rangers' mission was the most dangerous and difficult task of D-Day—to land under fire at the face of the 100-foot cliffs of Pointe du Hoc, scale the heights, and destroy a battery of 155-mm coastal guns to prevent the enemy from shelling the invasion beaches and ships at sea.

Born in Brooklyn, N.Y., in 1920, Lomell entered military service on June 13, 1942, at Fort Dix, N.J. Lomell first served with the 76th Infantry Division, rising in rank to platoon sergeant of a regimental intelligence and reconnaissance platoon. Seeking additional adventure, he was one of the first volunteers to join the Rangers since their activation on April 1, 1943. He became a company first sergeant with the Rangers in April, 1943, and later a battalion sergeant major, the highest enlisted rank in each unit. Tough rigorous training prepared the unit for combat and created a mystique that led to a tolerant scorn of any soldier not a Ranger.

Fourteen months later, Lomell was one of nearly 200 men from D, E, and F companies who landed on the ten-meter-wide beach at the base of Pointe du Hoc. No sooner had he landed than Lomell sustained his first wound, a bullet through his right side. Ignoring the pain and grave risk, Lomell quickly led his platoon up the cliff and systematically began destroying German machine-gun nests through fire and maneuver. He continued his courageous assault through two enemy lines of resistance to the rear of the German position. To the Rangers' surprise, the 155-mm battery was nowhere to be seen. The only "guns" that occupied the casemates were telephone poles. Tracks leading inland indicated that the battery had displaced somewhere toward the interior.

Reaching the coastal road, Lomell and his fellow Rangers immediately established roadblocks and began patrolling. Having scaled a 100-foot cliff and fought across 200 meters of heavily defended ground, Lomell's company was reduced to only 22 men from the initial contingent of 70 Rangers. Leaving the survivors of his platoon along the road, Lomell took Staff Sergeant Jack E. Kuhn, acting platoon sergeant, to search for the missing battery. Motivated more from a sense that his unit would fail in its primary mission if his platoon did not destroy the guns, Lomell exercised the personal leadership that characterized most Ranger operations. Front-line leadership was the norm, not the exception, in the 2nd Ranger Battalion.

About 250 meters inland, Lomell and Kuhn discovered the guns hidden in an apple orchard. The battery was set up in firing position with ammunition at the ready. To Lomell's amazement, the closest Germans, approximately 75 men, were 100 yards away, having withdrawn because of the initial bombardment and completely unaware that an enemy patrol had penetrated beyond their second line of defense. It appeared to Lomell and Kuhn that the Germans were checking equipment and preparing to return to the firing position.

Realizing that thousands of American lives were at stake if the battery remained intact, Lomell sensed a fleeting opportunity. Directing Kuhn to cover him, Lomell, armed with two thermite grenades, destroyed the traversing and recoil mechanisms of the two nearest guns. He then bashed the sights of the third gun with the stock of his rifle. Not satisfied with this partial success, Lomell sprinted back to the highway. Collecting all the thermite grenades from his platoon, he returned and disabled the remaining guns. Within 90 minutes of landing, Lomell and his Rangers had accomplished their primary mission. The next days, however, were living hell as repeated German counterattacks attempted to drive the Rangers into the sea. Lomell remained in the thick of the action that resulted in heavy casualties on both sides. The German force withdrew after the third attack, but D Company now numbered a scant 13 men.

For its remarkable achievement on D-Day, the 2nd Ranger Battalion received the Presidential Unit Citation. In addition, First Sergeant Lomell earned the Distinguished Service Cross for his extraordinary heroism. Len Lomell fought throughout Normandy and on October 7, 1944, became the first Ranger from his battalion to receive a battlefield commission. Wounded three times, he was honorably discharged from the Army on the last day of 1945.

Ten kilometers east of Pointe du Hoc, a similar drama was being played out on Omaha Beach. By the time G Company, 16th Infantry Regiment, 1st Infantry Division reached shore, the initial assault waves of the fabled Big Red One had succumbed to the withering fire of German machine guns and indirect fire. G Company was under the command of Captain Joe Dawson, the gangly 31-year-old son of a Baptist preacher from Waco, Tex.

Landing under heavy fire, Dawson found total chaos as men and materiel were literally choking the seawall at the water's edge. He knew that unless he could galvanize his men into action, they would be cut to shreds on the beach. Dawson moved rapidly to the front. Blowing a gap in the concertina wire at the foot of the bluffs, he began the dangerous ascent. Midway up the slope he met Lieutenant John Spaulding and the remnants of his platoon.

Directing Spaulding to cover his advance, Dawson proceeded toward the summit. Nearing the crest, he tossed two grenades and eliminated a German machine-gun position that was creating havoc on the beach below. Without waiting for reinforcements at the top of the bluff, Dawson and his men pressed on until they had silenced the remaining German positions. No one had penetrated the enemy defenses until this moment. Dawson was purportedly the first American officer to gain the summit of the bluffs overlooking "bloody" Omaha. By 1500 in the afternoon, Dawson and his men, joined by the remnants from the initial landings, secured Colleville and quickly established a defensive line.

Dawson attributed his success on D-Day to poor German marksmanship and the fortunate ability to keep his command together, both in the landing and the maneuvering up the bluff, as a fighting unit. Once his men reached the summit, they were able to engage the enemy directly with small-arms fire, which eventually forced the Germans to cease the concentrated small-arms, machine-gun, and mortar fire with which they were sweeping the beach below. General Eisenhower presented Dawson with the Distinguished Service Cross for his dynamic leadership at Omaha Beach.

What G Company accomplished on D-Day, however, was merely one episode in a long war, according to Dawson as he reflected on his career 50 years later. The worst combat he encountered during the war occurred outside Aachen in October 1944. Aachen, the former capital of Charlemagne's empire, was the first German city to be captured by the Allies. As such, it held a special significance for Adolf Hitler that transcended its military value.

In early September, Courtney Hodges' First U.S. Army had penetrated the Siegfried Line, encircled Aachen and prepared to meet the expected German counterattacks. The brunt of numerous counterattacks was borne by G Company, reinforced and still under the command of Joe Dawson. Moving into position, Dawson established his defense east of Aachen along an 838-foot-high ridge running approximately 400 yards.

Two days later, on September 16, the Germans attacked in battalion strength. The intensity of the attack carried the enemy into the American defense, but the GIs held. Following two weeks of intense artillery bombardment, the Germans attacked again on October 4. The result was the same—more than 350 enemy casualties littered the battlefield, "a figure unprecedented in the division's history" according to the 1st Division's operations officer.

For 39 days and nights, Dawson's men held the ridge. At times the front lines were no farther than 50 feet apart. More than once, Dawson called in protective artillery fire within ten yards of his own command post. Often the combat was hand to hand, and at times it seemed that the American defenders could not hold another minute. W. C. Heinz, staff correspondent for the *New York Sun*, noted that Dawson's men stopped the Germans with everything from artillery and rifle-butts to that thing that is still called guts. On October 15, a final regimental attack collapsed in the face of Dawson's artillery and infantry fire.

How did they hold in the face of overwhelming enemy numbers? The answer lies in Dawson's own words — courage and determination. Speaking to war correspondent Gordon Fraser after five weeks in the line, the beleaguered commander reflected on the loneliness of leaders who must make the crucial decisions in war. "How do you think I feel when I tell them there is no coming off the hill? They come in and say . . . 'I can't stand it any longer. I can't. I can't' . . . and I take them by the shirt and say . . . 'you will . . . you will . . . you've got to stand it in spite of yourself,' and what do they do? They go back up there and die." For 39 days in the fall of 1944, the men of G Company fought and died in their foxholes along what entered 1st Infantry Division lore as "Dawson's ridge."

But by battle's end, Aachen remained secure. For its role in the defense of the first German city to be captured, Dawson's G Company, like Lomell's Rangers, earned the Presidential Unit Citation. General Eisenhower also nominated the Big Red One to receive the Distinguished Unit Citation, stating that the fighting around Aachen was the outstanding operation of the 1st Infantry Division in the European Theater. All that had stood against German success was what Dawson termed "just one lousy little old G.I. company" — one lousy company and the indomitable spirit of its commander.

Two months after Dawson's heroic stand, the intelligence and reconnaissance platoon of the 99th Infantry Division's 394th Infantry Regiment moved into a quiet sector of the Ardennes front. The platoon leader was First Lieutenant Lyle J. Bouck Jr., an experienced officer one day shy of his 21st birthday. Bouck had enlisted in the 35th Infantry Division (National Guard) in 1938 at the age of 14 to earn one dollar a day per drill each week and to attend summer camp so he could eat three square meals a day. The division was mobilized and ordered to one year of federal duty on December 23, 1940. Following the attack on Pearl Harbor, Bouck, now 18, applied for the air corps, parachute school, and the Infantry Officer Candidate School. After graduating from OCS fourth in a class of 208, he was assigned to the Infantry school where Bouck taught small unit tactics. This training would later prove critical to his combat success. Having attended the Infantry advanced course, Bouck volunteered for combat duty in 1944, eventually being assigned as the platoon leader for the regiment's intelligence and reconnaissance platoon.

What made the I & R platoon unique was that Bouck and Major Robert Kriz, the regimental S-2, had personally selected every member of the platoon. Kriz and Bouck wanted men who were intelligent, expert riflemen, and comfortable with the outdoor life. Only thirty from the pool of 135 applicants made the cut. Kriz then outlined a strenuous compacted training program and turned Bouck loose. The platoon became competitive within themselves and created a close-knit unit that took immense pride in their achievements and stamina, quite similar to Lomell's Rangers. At 20, Bouck was the second youngest member of the platoon.

On December 10, Kriz briefed Bouck on a new mission. Taking Bouck and his platoon sergeant to a position along the Ardennes front, Kriz ordered Bouck to occupy a prepared defensive position being evacuated by a unit from the 4th Infantry Division. Bouck was then to improve the position, and act as the eyes and ears of the regiment on the adjacent divisional and corps boundary. In addition, Bouck was to maintain contact with a tank destroyer unit located in the small village of Lanzerath barely 100 meters to their front. Bouck's position afforded his platoon a perfect observation post from which to look into German territory.

The platoon was down to 20 members as they moved into a quiet sector of the front lines, but neither Kriz nor Bouck was overly concerned. It seemed to many that the war would soon be over. As American GIs dreamed of returning home, the Germans were planning a massive counterattack to regain the initiative in the West. Unknown to Bouck, Lanzerath lay astride General Sepp Dietrich's Sixth Panzer Army's counterattack axis.

Under Bouck's direct supervision, the platoon hastily improved its position. Classic defensive positions were constructed with overhead cover that all but concealed the unit's forward positions. At the urging of Kriz and with help from a friend at ordnance, Bouck also assembled an array of weapons that included four carbines, one Browning automatic rifle, one light machine gun and a .50-caliber machine gun mounted on a jeep in a dug-in position. The platoon's firepower sounded like a "battalion in the attack demonstration at Fort Benning," noted Bouck a half-century later. Heavy snow fell on December 13 and 15, camouflaging the platoon's extensive defensive network.

On December 16, Hitler unleashed the Ardennes offensive. A tremendous artillery barrage fell on Bouck's forward positions, but the intelligence and reconnaissance platoon suffered no casualties. As the tank destroyer unit evacuated Lanzerath, Bouck and a small reconnaissance team edged forward into a better observation position. What they saw startled them. A German column was assembling for an attack, but they seemed oblivious to the precise location of Bouck's men.

Shortly after dawn, the German infantry approached, having been alerted to Bouck's position by one of the town's inhabitants. Fortunately for the Americans, the German 3rd Parachute Division's 9th Regiment was inexperienced and conducted its assault without supporting fires. Bouck's pleas for artillery support also went unheeded, but within minutes the snow in front of the platoon had turned red with the blood of German dead and dying. Miraculously, not a single American was killed, although several sustained minor wounds.

Reporting the action to regiment, Bouck received the following orders: "Hold at all costs." And hold they did against two more determined enemy attacks. By mid-afternoon, however, Bouck's men were running low on ammunition, and fatigue was setting in. Despite repeated calls for reinforcements, no relief arrived. Bouck estimated that more than 400 enemy lay in the snow before him. The ground was so thick with enemy dead that it was virtually impossible to see the snow beneath them. Still Bouck refused to withdraw, acting on his last orders. As darkness fell, another German attack supported by two assault guns edged forward. This time the enemy was more successful. Infiltrating the American position, the enemy eliminated foxhole after foxhole. Finally, wounded and with his ammunition exhausted, Bouck and the remainder of his platoon were captured. Taken to Lanzerath as darkness descended, Bouck whimsically noted that it was his 21st birthday.

How had a single platoon of American soldiers been able to withstand such vigorous assaults by German paratroopers? The quality of Bouck's men was beyond measure, each being an expert marksman and extraordinarily physically fit. Each was patient and self-disciplined, and each man had a personal desire to maintain his equipment with constant "care and cleaning." Bouck also credited his selection of terrain (an ideal "Benning school solution"), the corresponding inexperience of his German adversaries, and the platoon's constant and intense training on the fundamentals of combat. He might have added his own inspirational leadership.

Of the 18 members of the platoon, two were killed in action and the remainder wounded or captured. Somewhat belatedly, the platoon received a Presidential Unit Citation, and Bouck, like Lomell and Dawson, won the Distinguished Service Cross. In addition to the cross awarded to Bouck, the platoon earned three Distinguished Service Crosses, five Silver Stars and ten Bronze Stars with V devices, thus becoming the most heavily decorated platoon for a single action in World War II. The soldiers had earned the distinction. Bouck and his platoon had inflicted nearly 500 casualties on the enemy and, more important, had impeded the German attack for a full day.

How did the American Army succeed against the Germans? The answer lies, in large measure, in the leadership of junior officers and NCOs, coupled with intense unit loyalty and esprit d' corps. Leon Standifer, a rifleman who fought throughout the campaign in Northwest Europe, noted that despite the rhetoric that accompanies most memoirs and scholarly discourse, he went to war for his country and his community. But going to war and going into combat are two different things, and the motivations behind them differ as well. Standifer fought for his community, but the closer he got to actual combat, that community became less and less the United States of America, and more and more First Squad of First Platoon, flawed but loving and reliable. In truth patriotism did die within several kilometers from the front. Without Standifer's squad and innumerable others, there surely would have been none of the great victories that we typically attribute to our most revered general officers.

Combat always defies description and a leader's job is to make battle "organized chaos, not disorganized mayhem." Lomell, Dawson, and Bouck effectively made that transition. Trusting their instincts, they led disciplined cohesive forces that had trained to a high level of proficiency. Their rigorous training and discipline produced a sense of solidarity that prepared their respective commands for the rigors of combat. Leading by example, these warriors performed extraordinary feats. It was no wonder that Lomell was the noncommissioned officer who consolidated his platoon in a defensive position and then led the reconnaissance party to discover the howitzers, or that Dawson was the first American officer on the bluffs above Omaha, or that Bouck delayed the main effort of the Sixth Panzer Army for a several, critical hours at the outset of the Battle of the Bulge. Dawson, Lomell, and Bouck always led from the front. We still applaud their efforts and marvel in their achievements. Collectively, they answered their country's call not for personal glory, but because there was a war to be won and no one but them to win it. The challenges the Army's small unit leaders faced in World War II were daunting. It was not easy ordering men to scale Pointe du Hoc, fight from a foxhole for 39 days on Dawson's ridge, or face overwhelming odds in the snow above Lanzerath.

In the final analysis it is not so difficult to determine what distinguished Lomell, Dawson and Bouck. In a sense they were representative of the American army that had evolved into a fairly effective military force by the summer of 1944. Why were these three so successful? Again we turn to the first man to reach the summit of the bluffs overlooking Omaha Beach for the answer. When his men looked to him for leadership, Dawson said he "had to answer those guys because I wear the bars. I've got the responsibility." Although Dawson later recalled that he was unsure whether he had what it took to do the job, he, Lomell, and Bouck fulfilled their responsibilities to their country and their soldiers in a most courageous manner.

For this, we take time to cherish their memory.

Chapter Ten

"Culture of Confidence": The Tactical Excellence of the German Army of the Second World War[1]

Kevin W. Farrell

Despite the supposed chronic disunity at the top, disaffection among the officer corps, and disloyalty in the rank and file, despite the acute lack of weapons, ammunition, fuel, transport, and human reserves, the German Army seems to function with its old precision and to overcome what appear to be insuperable difficulties with remarkable speed. Only by patient and incessant hammering from all sides can its collapse be brought about. The cause of this toughness, even in defeat, is not generally appreciated.[2]

Official U.S. War Department
Handbook on German Military Forces,
March 1, 1945

While the cause of that toughness might not have been fully appreciated in 1945, that the toughness itself was *recognized* by their opponents even at this late stage of the war speaks volumes about the high regard the U.S. Army, at least, had for the tactical skill of the German Army. Still, over fifty years later, the source of German excellence is not always fully understood. Most analyses seeking to understand the excellence of the German Army focus on operational art or doctrine, while according little attention to what made the German soldier such a stalwart opponent.[3] This chapter will address how factors such as unit cohesion and leadership enabled the German Army to develop and maintain such recognized (and feared) tactical skill right up to the last days of the war.

The emphasis of the chapter is on regular army units: *Das Heer*. The combat formations of the *Waffen SS* represent a more problematic category regarding unit cohesion in particular — in the most capable *Waffen SS* Divisions (1st *SS Panzerdivision "Leibstandarte Adolf Hitler,"* 2nd *SS Panzerdivision "Das Reich,"* 3rd *SS Panzerdivision "Totenkopf,"* 5th *SS Panzerdivision "Wiking"* and 12th *SS Panzerdivision "Hitler Jugend"*) unit cohesion was even higher than in army units, but the additional cohesion also came with an increased tendency to commit atrocities. Moreover, elite units, whether *Grossdeutschland* of the army, *Hermann Göring* and the parachute regiments of the *Luftwaffe*, as well as the *Waffen SS* units, generally received better equipment and operated from a separate organizational structure. They raise additional questions regarding whether their increased battlefield performance compensated for what they took away from the army (they did not, overall) which are beyond the scope of this paper.[4] Factoring out these elite units allows a more substantive analysis on how ordinary German units forged effective small units.

Most importantly, it is certainly not the intention of this paper to glorify the Third Reich or lessen the magnitude of the crimes committed in its name, but rather to investigate the military performance of regular army units, what factors led to that performance, and their consequences. It is painfully clear that regular army units were complicitous in the war crimes and crimes against humanity committed by Hitler's Third Reich.[5] The German experience serves as an important reminder that combat effectiveness is not the only measure of an army.

OVERVIEW

By late 1944, Adolf Hitler's Germany had suffered 3.9 million men killed, captured, or permanently incapacitated in combat.[6] The dramatic victories of 1939, 1940, and 1941 were distant memories as the war in Europe dragged on into its sixth year. The succession of early triumphs had given way to a series of costly setbacks and outright defeats in 1942 and 1943 at El Alamein, Stalingrad, and Kursk. During the remainder of 1943 and early 1944, the German armed forces continued to be pushed back on every front while the major cities of Germany were steadily pounded into rubble from increasingly severe attacks by allied bombers. The worst was yet to come.

The summer of 1944 witnessed the greatest military defeat in German history as the Soviets launched their offensive, *Bagration*, against Army Group Center, destroying approximately thirty German divisions and killing as many as 300,000 German soldiers.[7] On the western front, the allies broke free from the Normandy *bocage* at the end of July, and by August 19, the U.S. First and Third Armies had eliminated the Falaise-Argentan pocket, capturing some 50,000 German troops after killing at least 10,000.[8] In the Italian theater, the allies had entered Rome on June 4 and by August 26 had crossed the Arno River. As Germany suffered disastrous defeats on the front lines, partisan activity in all of the occupied territories increased dramatically.[9] It seemed clear that Hitler's Germany was on its last legs.

Yet, despite these catastrophic setbacks, the German military did not collapse as hoped and bring an allied victory "before Christmas." On the contrary, the German Army rebounded to an astonishing degree and inflicted a number of serious, albeit temporary, reversals against the allies, especially on the western front. The most noted allied setback in the fall of 1944 was Operation

Market-Garden (September 17-24), the most ambitious airborne operation in the war up to that point. Field Marshall Bernard Law Montgomery intended to end the war in 1944 with an armored thrust through Holland, which would then cross the Rhine after the airborne troops had seized key bridges over the Meuse (Maas), Rhine (Waal), and lower Rhine (Lek) rivers. Instead, the offensive failed to meet its objectives and resulted in 17,000 killed, wounded, and missing allied troops.[10]

Not only did the Germans stabilize the western front and grind the allied advance to a virtual halt, the *Wehrmacht*[11] launched a serious offensive of its own which threatened the entire Anglo-American effort in the west. Hitler believed that if he could split the British and American forces and seize Antwerp, the western allies would be forced to seek a negotiated settlement. Germany could then focus its attention on defeating the Russians. Although the plan was ambitious almost to the point of fantasy, it did achieve some remarkable local success. On December 16, 1944, the Sixth and Fifth Panzer Armies (twenty-four divisions, of which ten were armored) achieved complete tactical and strategic surprise as they slammed into the U.S. VIII Corps. Despite being caught off guard and suffering some serious defeats (the U.S. 106th and 28th Divisions were crushed), the Americans acquitted themselves well overall. By 16 January 1945 the Americans had eliminated the "bulge." The cost was very heavy for both sides — 120,000 German casualties and over 60,000 American casualties[12] — but at this stage of the war, Germany could not hope to replace losses of this magnitude. The Ardennes Offensive was a costly, and ultimately foolish, gamble for the Germans.

This larger perspective, while not the focus of the paper, is important to demonstrate that the *Wehrmacht* displayed extraordinary resiliency when it seemed to many allied observers that its collapse was close at hand. While the relative tactical skill of the combatants has become a matter of recent debate, what is not in doubt is that the German Army sustained a level of excellence at the small-unit level which enabled it to outperform its opponents with alarming frequency for virtually the entire war.[13]

The general issue of German tactical excellence has been examined rather thoroughly by leading military historians, prominent among them Colonel Trevor Dupuy and Martin van Creveld.[14] While these great works tend to focus on the staggering early German victories, the desperate last days of the German Army have largely been examined only from the perspective of the allied victory.[15] While it is certainly worthwhile to study the German victory over France and analyze the Battle of Sedan (May 10-15, 1940), it is equally useful to examine how an understrength panzer division defeated a superior Soviet armored force attacking along the Küstrin-Berlin Highway on March 22, 1945.[16] How was it that despite being faced by 6.1 million Russians, the 2.5 million-man *Wehrmacht* inflicted over 4.5 battlefield casualties for every one suffered?[17] The second half of the war demonstrated the tremendous ability of the German Army to continue to fight on despite overwhelming numerical odds, a shrinking pool of replacements, and constant military setbacks. This suggests that their sustained excellence had an important, lasting, cultural component that merits investigation.

This chapter will demonstrate that the combat excellence of the German Army emanated from the synergy of extraordinary unit cohesion and superb tactical-level leadership.[18] These two factors interacted in a mutually reinforcing manner, thereby enabling a level of performance greater than the sum of each taken individually. German small unit excellence came from a number of interlocking sources. In the case of the *Wehrmacht*, factors such as organization, training, replacement, and unit rotation methods (what I will term "structure"), combined with leader selection and development, when executed effectively, resulted in a superior level of organizational trust. In these units soldiers had tremendous confidence in peers, subordinates and immediate superiors alike, thereby creating a "culture of confidence"[19] at the small unit level. The direct result of this culture was that, despite the strategic and operational shortcomings of the *Wehrmacht*, German tactical units remained, overall, superb until the final months of the war. This synergy of small unit cohesion and leadership contributed greatly to the early victories and was equally important in the ability of the *Wehrmacht* to sustain their effectivenss against overwhelming odds until the very end of the war.

STRUCTURAL FACTORS

Much of the foundation for small unit excellence lay in the structure of the German Army, especially at the tactical level (division and below). This structure, deliberately constructed to develop, support, and maintain the front-line soldiers and the small units they formed, contributed significantly to the German Army's continued effectiveness at a time when most other armies would have long ago succumbed. Despite the often redundant and inefficient nature of the replacement system as a whole and the chaotic and competitive command structure at the national level, the tactical organization worked remarkably well.[20]

One of the principle reasons for the continued cohesion of the German Army was the very method by which units were raised, refitted, and rotated. Central to the raising and refitting of divisions stood the *Wehrkreis* (Military District) system.[21] The goal of the *Wehrkreis* system was to relieve field commanders from as much administrative work as possible while providing a regular flow of trained recruits and supplies to the field army. In this it succeeded to a great extent despite the system's apparent complexity.[22] By 1943 there were a total of 19 *Wehrkreise* in Germany and the occupied territories.[23] Each army division conducted its recruiting, garrisoning, and training within its designated *Wehrkreis* so that a regional association was at the core of each division. All infantry divisions within a *Wehrkreis* constituted an active infantry corps which, in turn, had a corresponding designation with its *Wehrkreis*.[24]

In peace time, the commander of an infantry corps also commanded the Wehrkreis in which it was located. While the corps commander focused his efforts on preparing his unit for combat, administrative matters were assigned to a *General zu besonderer Verwendung* (literally, General on Special Duty), who served as the deputy commander of the *Wehrkreis*. The *General z.b.V.* would be an officer whose age or health prevented him from active field service, but who could provide both expertise and experience.[25] Upon mobilization the infantry corps commander would depart to the field with his command and his deputy would take charge of the *Wehrkreis*. Reserve officers living in the vicinity of the headquarters of the *Wehrkreis* would serve as the staff for the *General z.b.V.* Prior to mobilization, the reserve officers would have extensively studied the mobilization plans and fully prepared themselves to take over the duties of their active counterparts. As the war continued on, these same staff officers assisted in the creation and mobilization of successive divisions. Although the OKW in Berlin retained close control over the entire system and directed such things as when and what types of mobilization orders would be issued, the *Wehrkreise* commanders were allowed great latitude in conducting their mobilization and replacement missions.[26] *Feldheer* (Field Army) and *Ersatzheer* (Replacement Army) commanders were expected to (and did) maintain close contact with their counterparts through correspondence and field visits which facilitated the smooth flow of replacements and convalescents.

In terms of unit cohesion, the divisions benefited from being raised from the same regions because the soldiers already shared basic cultural values and thus felt comfortable with one another. Yet, by drawing soldiers from relatively large geographical areas, Germany avoided the disastrous experience of Britain in the First World War with the "Pal divisions," in which recruits came from such narrow geographical locales that many villages ended up suffering the loss of most of their young men in one fell swoop. Elite units, such as Panzer Division *Grossdeutschland* were drawn from all over Germany, but their elite status helped to compensate for the diverse backgrounds of the members.

Rather surprisingly, the vast majority of recruits were not required to take written or mechanical examinations of any kind. Instead, an initial physical examination classified recruits into one of six categories of fitness.[27] As the medical examination was taking place (in-processing recruits did not go through a series of examinations by specialists at different check points in the

American manner, but were instead examined by a single physician), the *Musterung* (preliminary commander) carried on a conversation with the recruit with the assistance of the examining
physician. This made it possible to immediately weed out those
who had obvious mental deficiencies, while at the same time initi-
ating a personal relationship between leader and soldier.

After the initial screening, the wishes of the recruit, as well as his
physical condition, professional occupation, and previous paramilitary training would be taken into account to determine his place-
ment. [28] In contrast to the practice of the United States Army (transferring the most intelligent recruits into the specialized branches),
the *Heeres Personalamt* (Personnel Section of the Army) ensured
that the vast majority of the most intelligent recruits served as combat troops.[29] The actual decision of what military occupational specialty a soldier would have, i.e. whether he was to become a truck
driver, a tank crew member, or an infantryman, etc., was actually
left to the soldier's regimental commander.[30]

By contemporary American standards, these methods for selecting and assigning enlisted men may seem simplistic, and perhaps
even crude. For the German Army, the aspects of military life that
directly affected the individual soldier — the distribution of recruits
among the various military occupational specialties, regulation of
leave, administration of discipline, and the exchange of personnel
between units — remained the purview of the commander, usually at the regimental level or lower. This extraordinary authority
held by junior officers was designed to "keep awake their sense of
responsibility for the men in their charge and thereby to reinforce
the bonds of mutual confidence between the soldier and his immediate superiors."[31]

One of the more problematic facets of the system was the
German decision to raise entirely new divisions rather than recon-
stitute existing ones. This practice has usually been treated with
scorn by historians, with some justification, on account of its inherent wastefulness. An intended consequence of such a policy, however, was unit cohesion. While late in the war there were exceptions to this policy, the units that deviated from it also demonstrat-

ed high rates of desertion and surrender. Overall, the German Army's system of replacements was designed to reinforce "primary group cohesion."

Rather than having a constant influx of individual replacements, units were raised, trained, committed to battle, and pulled off the line as a whole. After a fierce battle or extended service on the front, units would be pulled off for *Auffrischung* (refitting and retraining), often in the occupied territories. As the situation worsened for Germany, it became more difficult to remove entire divisions, so often only regiments or even just battalions could be spared and sent to *Erholungsheime* (recovery homes).[32] Nonetheless, considering the situation facing Germany, the accomplishments of the system were remarkable. From virtually any perspective, 1944 was a disastrous year for the German Army with the loss of at least 229 regiments comprising some 75 infantry-type divisions (160 regiments/47 divisions on the Eastern Front and 69 regiments/28 divisions in France and Italy). During the same period, however, the German Army's replacement and training system raised 200 regiments totaling 66 divisions.[33] Although the quality of recruits and the amount of training was not generally what it had been during the pre-war and early-war periods, the end result was that German units, especially at battalion level and below, were ones that fought, suffered, played, and died together.

Unit cohesion was further reinforced by versatility at the tactical level. While Germany's strategic organization remained chaotic, at the tactical level the basic configuration present in virtually every division allowed the commanders to construct any type of combat formation needed to accomplish a given mission.[34] Furthermore, although the actual organization, equipment, and even ethnic composition of some individual German divisions varied markedly throughout the war, their staffs shared the same fundamental characteristics. The division staff was divided into three sections: the *Führungsabteilung* (tactical department), the *Quartermeister* (supply department) and the *Adjutantur* (personnel department).[35] The Ia or Chief of Operations (sometimes misleadingly referred to as the operations officer) was in command of the *Führungsabteilung,* the

Ic (Intelligence Officer), and the respective staffs. The Ia, who served as the chief of staff in division-sized units and below, also had combat-oriented subordinates who reported directly to him, such as the Ia for artillery and air liaison. Regarded as the division command post, the *Führungsabteilung* was a compact organization that reflected the German view that the staff should be first and foremost a vehicle "to provide leadership in combat while devoting only the minimum effort possible to all other tasks."[36]

The training of the individual soldiers, noncommissioned officers, and junior officers also played a crucial role in forging such a fierce fighting force. The entire training structure of the German Army — from initial training to daily life in a typical infantry battalion — was dedicated to shaping an environment of mutual trust designed to permeate throughout the rank and file.

Contrary to the stereotyped Prussian soldier, an automaton blindly following orders, the average German soldier was both highly disciplined *and* independent. Well before the turn of the century, German Army leaders believed that the quality of soldiers mattered more than quantity. The *Truppenführung* (Field Regulations) of 1908 emphasized the importance of initiative for the individual soldier and demanded of every one "the total *independent* [my emphasis] commitment of all physical and mental forces."[37]

The loss of the First World War and the Treaty of Versailles had a profound impact on, as well as some unintended consequences for, the development of the post-war army, the *Reichswehr*.[38] The 100,000-man limitation imposed on the German Army resulted in the creation of a small army of dedicated professionals who came to value innovation. The former rigidity of the Imperial Army gave way, to some degree, fostering an atmosphere of experimentation and self-reliance that trickled-down to the lowest levels. As the German Army Training Directions for 1931 stated, "The individual soldier must be educated so that he is able to accomplish his tasks even if left to himself. He must know that he alone is responsible for his acts and failures."[39] The emphasis on quality, independence, and personal responsibility went a long way toward fostering an environment of mutual reliability among officers, NCOs, and soldiers.

Training itself was designed to simulate closely the actual conditions of combat while minimizing as much as possible the demands on the field army. Central to the former objective was the effort to introduce the most recent combat experiences into training. Close interaction between the *Feldheer* (Field Army) and the *Ersatzheer* (Replacement Army), especially between corresponding commanders, ensured that these goals were largely met.[40] The cadre of each division's training battalion was usually staffed with wounded veterans of the division. Regardless of their status, the training battalion staff was expected to know personally the officers of the parent division as well as understand the needs of the division.

The basic training of soldiers, noncommissioned officers, and officers all began in the hands of the Replacement Army with final integration occurring within the Field Replacement Battalion of each division.[40] The training programs fell under the control of the Replacement Army's chief of training who worked in conjunction with the General Staff's training department, the latter of which received regular updates from the front and in turn translated these lessons into regulations governing the training of soldiers. Training focused primarily on the practical rather than the theoretical. The emphasis was on mastery of the individual weapon or weapon system, and a fundamental understanding of tactics gained from frequent field exercises.

The length of basic training varied throughout the war – for infantrymen it had lasted sixteen weeks in 1938, but was reduced to eight in 1940, lengthened to sixteen again in 1943, and it varied from twelve to fourteen weeks in 1944.[42] The basic training of armored crewmen lasted twenty-one weeks for the duration of the war.[43] Basic training was supplemented by additional training at the divisions' field training battalions upon arrival. This further enhanced unit cohesion because new arrivals were trained by their future commanders while benefiting from recent local combat experiences.

In total, these structural factors helped to lay the foundation for an extraordinary level of unit cohesion. The guiding principle behind the way the German Army was organized at the tactical level, from raising units to training them and replacing them, was the creation and support of cohesive platoons and companies, for it is at that level that battles are ultimately won or lost. By consistently emphasizing the personal nature of leadership and selection, from initial assessment, through basic training and ultimate assignment to units, the bonds of mutual trust and responsibility between leaders and led were continually reinforced.

LEADERSHIP

The structure of the German Army was oriented deliberately towards producing combat formations which demonstrated extraordinary cohesion. As such, the German Army placed a primacy on selecting and promoting noncommissioned officers and officers who demonstrated superb combat leadership above all other considerations. The German tactical doctrine, what we now term *Auftragstaktik* (mission-oriented tactics — a post-World War II term), demanded that junior officers and noncommissioned officers be not only disciplined and obedient, but also capable of independent thought. They had to manifest a willingness to seize the initiative in the absence of orders and even to violate orders when they no longer reflected the reality of a changed situation.[44] Selection, training, and promotion of junior leaders were built on the premise that these characteristics were preeminent. A crucial aspect of the selection of future leaders, whether enlisted or officer, was the decentralized nature of the selection process. The same tactical commanders who were held responsible for the lives of their soldiers in battle were also given the authority to select those subordinates who would lead them.

It has long been a cliché, and deservedly so, that the noncommissioned officer is the backbone of an army. It is still the case today that the strength and capability of an army is determined by the caliber of its noncommissioned officers, and it was certainly the case for the German Army of the Second World War. The selection and training of NCO's in the *Wehrmacht* followed a long and proud tradition dating back to the seventeenth century during the reign of Frederick William of Brandenburg, the Great Elector.[45]

The restrictions of the Treaty of Versailles after the loss of the First World War had a profound impact on the development of the noncommissioned officer corps. Because enlistments had to be for a period of twelve years and the army itself was quite small, standards for selection were stringent. The long period of service increased the opportunity for extended training and schooling. It is by no means an exaggeration that a sizable proportion of the noncommissioned officers of the Weimar period were of a caliber quite suitable to receive commissions. And although the Versailles Treaty limited the size of the *Reichswehr*, it did *not* limit the number of noncommissioned officers in the army.

Accordingly, General Hans von Seeckt as *Chef der Heeresleitung* (Chief of Army Leadership) who commanded the 100,000-man *Reichswehr,* intended "to neutralize the poison" of Versailles.[46] His long-range goal was to create an "expansible army" in which every member would be able to serve immediately in at least the next higher grade upon mobilization. As a result, the *Reichswehr* contained over 40,000 sergeants and corporals, or one noncommissioned officer for every two privates, and each infantry company was assigned the name, honors, and banners of a 3,000-man regiment from the old imperial army.[47] The latter practice served not only as a boost for morale, but it created the framework for units to expand to ten times their size with little difficulty. The large proportion of well-trained noncommissioned officers ensured that such an expansion could be accomplished with relative ease.[48] Still, when Hitler came to power, the *Reichsheer* was little more than a small professional army with a light artillery component.[49] The massive expansion under the Third Reich allowed it to come into its own.

Eligibility for selection as a noncommissioned officer came about only after one year's service, at which time company-level commanders would choose the soldiers they believed to be good candidates. The actual training of the noncommissioned officer, which took place in the regimental training battalion, lasted three and one-half years during the Weimar period. It was followed by an additional eight months of regimental duty, then was reduced to two from 1933 to 1939. During the war itself, length of training varied but generally remained between one and two years. Nonetheless, the essential elements remained the same: rather than specialization, the focus of training was first and foremost leadership, then practical knowledge of weapons, and finally sports.[50] While it was impossible to maintain the earlier standards due to the massive expansion of the army beginning in 1936 and the constant demand for replacements during the war, the qualifications still remained high.

Once the war broke out, selection and promotion of NCO's discriminated in favor of those who had seen front-line service. In the Field Army, for instance, promotion to NCO could take place after six months, and in exceptional cases even if the authorized position was not vacant. In the Replacement Army, however, it still took one year of service with two months at the front to be selected, and then only when a position was available.[51] The emphases on performance and decentralized authority for selecting and promoting leaders of these carefully constructed, cohesive small units had, in many cases, a synergistic effect, fostering a superior level of excellence at the tactical level.

The career of Emil Killus illustrates very well the typical path of a successful noncommissioned officer. Although little is known of Emil's education and family background, his promotion and award certificates tell us a great deal about the normal career progression for noncommissioned officers. Born in Wehlawischken on January 10, 1914, he first entered the army for two years of service with the 6th Company of the 512th Infantry Regiment on April 1, 1934. He obligated himself for an additional year of service in the infantry by enrolling in the army flamethrower school in August 1936, by which time he had advanced to the rank of *Gefreiter* (private first class). The following year he advanced to the rank of *OberGefreiter* (senior private first class or acting corporal).   In 1937, he re-enlisted for an additional three years and took part in the Polish campaign, receiving the *Eiserne Kreuz Zweite Klasse* (Iron Cross Second Class) for bravery in action as a newly promoted *Unteroffizier* (corporal).

In April 1940, Emil's Regiment was added to the newly formed 293rd Infantry Division. Still serving in the same company, he was promoted to the rank of *Feldwebel* (staff sergeant) on July 1, 1940, after service in the French campaign. On June 22, 1941, Emil and his unit took part in the invasion of Russia and he received the *Infanterie Sturmabzeichen in Silber* (infantry assault badge in silver) on October 15, 1941. Surviving the brutal winter of 1941/42, Killus was promoted to *Oberfeldwebel* (technical sergeant) on January 18, 1942, and received the *Medaille "Winterschlacht im Osten 1941/42"* (medal for the winter battle in the east, or the so-called "frozen meat award") retroactively on August 25, 1942. Still serving in the same company and regiment, Killus was severely wounded for the first time on October 3 of that same year and received the *Verwundetabzeichen in Schwarz* (wound badge in black) while recuperating in the regimental replacement battalion on February 18, 1943. After taking two weeks of convalescent leave, Killus rejoined his old company and was awarded the *Nahkampfspange in Bronze* (close combat clasp in bronze) for achieving a total of fifteen days of hand-to-hand combat. On the 2nd of March, 1944, the division commander awarded Killus the *Eiserne Kreuz Erste Klasse* (Iron Cross First Class) after three and one-half years of almost continuous combat.[52] Shortly afterwards, the 293rd Infantry Division was disbanded due to heavy casualties; the fate of Emil Killus is unknown.

The career of *Oberfeldwebel* Killus is instructive not only for what it reveals about the military career of a single German soldier, but for what it says about the leadership and cohesion of a typical German infantry regiment. As can be seen by his two voluntary re-enlistments prior to the onset of hostilities, he found the life within the company satisfying. In ten years of service, the soldier remained not only in the same regiment, but in the same company, except for the times he was in a specialty school, such as the flame-thrower school, or when he was recuperating from wounds, but even then he still belonged to the regiment as part of the replacement battalion. Despite his relatively high noncommissioned rank, his personal photographs show a familiar relationship with his soldiers. Furthermore, notwithstanding his obvious and repeated heroism in combat, there is no evidence of awards inflation. In short, Killus was the epitome of those traits the Germany Army sought in its noncommissioned officers: leadership by example, mutual trust, and combat proficiency.

It was not just in the infantry, however, that the noncommissioned officer was expected to be a courageous and innovative leader. All branches, especially the combat arms, emphasized these attributes. A case in point is the example of the highly decorated and successful self-propelled artillery noncommissioned officer — and subsequently officer — Hugo Primozic.[53] Born in Backnang in 1914 and raised to be a locksmith, Primozic decided instead to join the *Reichswehr* and succeeded in passing the rigorous entrance examination on the first try.[54]

Primozic served initially with a horse drawn artillery unit during the invasion of France in 1940. By the conclusion of that campaign he had grown weary of horse-drawn artillery and volunteered for the new, motorized assault artillery. He quickly distinguished himself and became an instructor at the assault gun artillery school.

After repeated requests for duty at the front, he finally received his wish and in July of 1942 he joined the 667th Assault Gun Brigade (*Sturmgeschütz-Abteilung 667*) as a *Wachtmeister* (noncommissioned officer platoon leader) when the unit deployed to the eastern front. There he established a reputation as a calm and capable leader who emphasized initiative and patience, and who recognized that the first shot frequently decided the outcome of armored engagements. He destroyed his first Soviet tank at over 1500 meters.

A typical example of Primozic's coolness under fire is demonstrated by an encounter toward the end of July 1942 for which Primozic received the Iron Cross First Class. Primozic's platoon was supporting an infantry brigade when it came under a strong Soviet armored and infantry attack. When one of his *Sturmgeschützen* (assault guns) had broken down, Primozic personally attached a tow cable to it from his own tank and calmly supervised the recovery operation while at least two dozen Soviet infantrymen surrounded the two vehicles. After the two vehicles were under way, Primozic grabbed hold of an MG34 machine gun and personally drove off the attacking Soviets.

During the battle for Rzhev at the end of August and September 1942, Primozic and his men illustrated with deadly precision the effectiveness small unit cohesion and leadership. By the 15th of September, the Soviets were on the verge of taking Rzhev. In both armor and infantry, the Germans were heavily outnumbered. Primozic's three assault guns went into the line against the Stalin Tank Brigade to defend one of the weakest, but most critical, parts of the German defensive line near the junction of the railway embankment and the river in Rzhev. After dismounting from his vehicle and conducting a quick reconnaissance, Primozic formulated his plan. Aware of the massive armored and infantry attack that was about to take place, he ordered his three vehicles into concealed positions. At the appropriate time, he would then launch a violent assault into the flank of the attacking Soviets. He did just that.

Primozic destroyed his first Soviet tank, a T-34, at 800 meters and quickly destroyed a second as it oriented its gun to engage him. He then switched his ammunition to high explosive and began to cut huge gaps into the advancing waves of Soviet infantry. Throughout the Soviet attack, Primozic directed his three assault guns to reposition themselves to new fighting positions. When Primozic encountered a 52-ton KV-1 heavy tank he scored two direct hits against it before it was destroyed. Incredibly, Primozic's three assault guns not only survived the assault of a reinforced armor brigade, they repulsed the attack. By the end of the first hour of the engagement, *Wachtmeister* Primozic had destroyed seventeen Soviet tanks, and by the end of the day his total had reached twenty-four. The other two assault guns of his platoon each destroyed an impressive number of tanks as well. Primozic's three-gun platoon had literally saved an entire division and proved crucial to the defense of Rzhev by defeating an elite armored brigade. For his heroism he was awarded the *Ritterkreuz* (Knight's Cross of the Iron Cross).[55]

Not surprisingly, Primozic continued to distinguish himself as an extraordinary combat leader. On December 11, 1942, Primozic destroyed another seven Soviet tanks and his individual total rose to 60. On the 25th of January, 1943, he became the 185th recipient of the *Eichenlaub* (Oak Leaves) to the *Ritterkreuz* in recognition for his combat leadership. On the 31st he was promoted to the rank of *Leutnant* (Lieutenant).

Whereas the noncommissioned officers are the backbone of an army, the officers are the critical link in providing leadership and direction at the company level and higher. As such the German Army sought officers who demonstrated character — which they defined as combat leadership potential — rather than just intelligence or specific skills. Leadership ability was the single most important criterion by which junior officers were regarded. It was expected as a matter of course that officers set the example and lead from the front.

Obviously, the selection of future officers is crucial to creating a competent officer corps, and to a large extent the success or failure of an army hinges on this process. The history of officer selection in the Prussian and German Army up to the start of the First World War is likewise intertwined with the larger history of Germany.[56] In the Imperial Army, there were two ways to become an officer: upon graduation from one of the cadet schools or by enlisting into a specific regiment.[57] Officer candidates spent two years with the troops, living in the same barracks as the soldiers, before entering the ten-and-one-half-month officer school. After completion of that school, the candidate then spent another ten and one-half months at a school for his specific branch.[58]

The system remained relatively unchanged through the Weimar years and into the Nazi regime until 1937. While the essentials of the system remained the same, the subject of citizenship was replaced with an hour per week of indoctrination in National Socialist principles. Training also became increasingly practical with the time spent on tactics increased to nine hours of instruction per week. Furthermore, the overall time it took for commissioning was reduced to a little over two years from the previous three and three-quarters. A further change was the addition of time spent with the troops as an officer candidate following the previously existing three periods of training: service with the troops, officer school, and branch-specific schooling.[59]

Although there were variations based upon the demands of the war, the system preserved the basic framework of 1937 and emphasized above all front-line service against the enemy.[60] A training film produced by the *Personalamt* in 1943 entitled *Fahnenjunker* illustrates this very clearly.[61] Furthermore, because of the training it took to become an officer, junior officers were well accustomed to army life and conduct in the field, and had experience serving in leadership positions. Accordingly, jokes making light of the "green" second lieutenant did not occur in the German Army (as they have in the U.S. Army for quite some time). Inexperienced second lieutenants simply did not exist.

The training of officers illustrates the emphasis the army placed on leadership. The 1936 *Truppenführung* (Troop Leadership) regulation of 1936 clearly articulates the German Army's expectation of leaders: • • •

6. Leadership in war demands leaders possessed of judgement, a clear understanding, and foresight. They must be independent and firm in making a decision, determined and energetic while carrying it out, insensible to the changing fortunes of war, and possessed of a strong consciousness of the high responsibility resting on them.

7. The officer is the leader and educator in every field. Besides a knowledge of men and a sense of justice, he must distinguish himself by superior knowledge and experience, moral excellence, self-control and high courage.

8. The example of officers and men in commanding positions has a crucial effect on the troops. The officer who demonstrates cold-bloodedness, determination and courage in front of the enemy pulls the troops along with himself. He must, however, also find his way to his subordinates' hearts and find their confidence by understanding their feelings and

their thoughts. His care for them must never cease. *Mutual confidence is the secure basis for discipline in times of need and danger.* [Emphasis added.]

9. Every commander is to commit his entire personality in any situation without fearing responsibility. A readiness to assume responsibility is the most important of all qualities of leadership. It must not, however, go so far as to lead to headstrong decisions without regard for the whole, or to the imprecise execution of orders, or to an I-know-better-than-you attitude. Independence should not turn into arbitrariness. But independence which knows its limits is the foundation for great success....

12. Commanders are to live with the troops and to share with them danger and deprivation, happiness and suffering. Only thus can they gain real insight into their troops' fighting power (*Kampfkraft*) and requirements. The individual man is responsible for himself but for his comrades also. Whoever possesses more ability, is stronger, must aid and lead the inexperienced and the weak. On such foundations does the feeling of real comradeship grow. Its importance in relations between commanders and men is as great as among the men themselves.

13. ...it is every commander's duty to proceed against breaches of discipline, to prevent excesses, plundering, panic and other harmful effects by using every means at his disposal, including even the most drastic ones. Discipline is the central pillar on which the army is built. Its strict maintenance is a blessing for all.

14. The troops' forces must be conserved so that the highest demands can be made on them at the decisive moment. Whoever demands unnecessary chores sins against the prospect of success. The use of force in combat must be proportionate to the purpose at hand. Demands that are incapable of fulfillment are as harmful to the troops' confidence in their leaders as they are to their morale. • • •

. . .

109. Personal influence by the commanding officer on his troops is of the greatest importance. He must be near the fighting troops.

111. A divisional commander's place is with his troops....During encounters with the enemy seeing for oneself is best.[62]

Overall, these paragraphs speak for themselves and need little elaboration. Although many of the leadership principles expressed are familiar themes even today, what comes across most strongly, and rather surprisingly, is the emphasis on personal leadership, the importance of inculcating unit cohesion through mutual confidence and respect, as well as the expectation of independent thought and action. In sharp contrast to the stereotype of the traditional Prussian Army, and to a large degree the actual experience of the Imperial Army, the officer was expected and encouraged to socialize with his men in order to better assess their capabilities, needs, and concerns. Unit cohesion and effectiveness were recognized as being direct consequences of mutual trust.[63]

An example of the leadership expected of junior officers is the case of a typical infantry officer, Wilhelm Massa, who would subsequently be awarded the Knight's Cross. On 17 September 1943, Massa was a First Lieutenant commanding an infantry company on the Russian Front. Massed Soviet infantry and at least ten T-34 tanks attacked his understrength company, which had no anti-tank assets or armor of its own. Some of the attacking tanks stopped over the fighting positions of Massa's men and pivoted on them, crushing the trapped infantrymen beneath their tracks. Enraged at the horrible fate of his soldiers, Massa grabbed a magnetic anti-tank mine and placed it on the side of the T-34 nearest to him. The tank quickly burst into flames. His example inspired other soldiers in his unit to act accordingly and the Russian attack was thwarted.

On the 13th of October, Massa and his unit were once again faced with a Soviet attack by tanks and infantry. This time the lead Soviet infantry was cleared from the advancing tanks by small arms fire and artillery, but the T-34's and KV-4's continued to move forward. Again, *Leutnant* Massa sprang into action, charging onto the rear of one of the T-34's that had passed him. After climbing onto the rear deck, he jammed a satchel charge of five hand grenades bound together under the turret. The explosion immobilized the turret and ignited the tank. As soon as he was clear from the doomed T-34, he obtained another satchel charge and repeated the procedure with a nearby KV-4.[64]

What is remarkable about the conspicuous daring of a company commander is not the heroism itself, for individual acts of bravery occurred in the armies of all the belligerents in the war, but how heroism such as Massa's was recognized by the leadership of the German Army. Massa's conduct was noted in his *Wehrpass* (military identity and personal record book), maintained in the administrative records section of his battalion, and in his *Soldbuch* (paybook), which was kept in his tunic pocket at all times. His actions meant that he would henceforth be authorized to wear three of the *Sonderabzeichen für das Niederkämpfen von Panzerkampfwagen durch Einzelkampfer* (special badge for the single-handed destruction of a tank). Other than that, his action merited no additional notice. Massa was simply doing what was expected of him as a soldier, officer, and company commander. In other words, Massa was recognized just as were tens of thousands of other German soldiers in the course of the war. Only subsequent, and even more daring, acts of bravery would earn him the highest of all German military awards, the *Ritterkreuz* (Knight's Cross of the Iron Cross).[65]

Guy Sajer, whose autobiography, *The Forgotten Soldier*, is perhaps the best book written from the perspective of the German soldier to come out of the war, captures very well the attitude of many German soldiers towards junior officers:

> *Captain Weisredau often helped us to endure the worst. He was always on good terms with his men, and never was one of those officers who are so impressed by their own rank that they treat ordinary soldiers like valueless pawns to be used without scruple. He stood beside us on countless gray watches, and came into our bunkers to talk with us, and make us forget the howling storm outside... His*

obvious and passionate sincerity affected even the most hesitant... He invited questions, which he answered with intelligence and clarity. He spent his time with us, whenever he was free from other duties. We all loved him, and felt we had a true leader, as well as a friend on whom we could count. Herr Hauptmann Wesreidau was a terror to the enemy and a father to his men. [66]

The words of the highly decorated and successful armor officer, *Ritterkreuz mit Eichenlaub träger* (Knight's Cross with Oak Leaves bearer) Lieutenant Otto Carius, former company commander of the 2nd Company of the elite 502nd Heavy Panzer Battalion, demonstrate as well the essence of what made the German Army so extremely effective at the tactical level:

All military success rests upon good training of the noncommissioned officer while the young lieutenant must serve as a role model in every way. A company is like a family and the commander must know every soldier personally. Success follows when the lieutenant leads from the front. [67]

Even those soldiers captured by the allies in the final weeks, when it was obvious to even the most fanatical types that the war was lost, still expressed great respect for, and confidence in, their noncommissioned officers and junior officers. Interviews with captured German soldiers found that they overwhelmingly viewed their noncommissioned officers and junior officers to be "competent, brave, and efficient."[68]

IMPLICATIONS AND PROBLEMS

The development of capable combat leaders and the construction of lethal, cohesive small units were the key aspects behind the awesome fighting power of the German Army. The methods of producing soldiers, noncommissioned officers, and officers were all drawn from the notion that these elements mattered above all else. In the words of Martin van Creveld:

> *The German Army's system of organization reflected a deliberate choice, a conscious determination to maintain at all costs that which was believed to be decisive to the conduct of war: mutual trust, a willingness to assume responsibility, and the right and the duty of subordinate commanders at all levels to make independent decisions and carry them out.*[69]

To generate such independence, freedom had to be granted. To train men toward responsibility, authority had to be delegated. To create trust, reliability and longstanding acquaintanceships had to be assured. In short, to function as intended, the German Army had to generate an atmosphere of mutual trust in its individual units. The result was a "culture of confidence" in its tactical units.

A notable consequence of the combination of superb cohesion and excellent combat leadership was the ability of small units to remain capable of continued resistance for extended periods of time despite being cut off. Some of the most dogged actions on the eastern front arose from such types of battles — Cholm, Cherkassy, Demyansk, Narwa, and Kurland. The limitation of space prevents even a cursory examination of the many thousands of small unit actions undertaken by the German Army during the Second World War. Nonetheless, it was an environment of mutual trust, forged by cohesive, lethal small units with superb leadership at the tactical level, that undergirded the spectacular victories of 1939 all the way through to the bitter defensive battles in the final years of the war.

It is clear, however, that all units in all theaters throughout the war did not always meet the standards expressed in the 1936 *Truppenführung*. Especially as the war continued and the fortunes for Germany worsened as casualties mounted, it became more difficult to develop an officer and noncommissioned officer corps that met the earlier exacting standards. Furthermore, the whole issue of the impact of National Socialist indoctrination, most strongly felt by junior officers, must be acknowledged in any account of the German Army.[70]

One of the most important considerations for officer candidates was that they be of the right character; that is to say that they demonstrated outstanding combat leadership potential. According to French L. MacLean, the German Army viewed the trait of character as "the ability of an individual to make a difficult decision, often under pressure, and then stick with it and follow it through to its execution."[71] Obviously, such a definition lacks an ethical component. While a good many, especially older, German officers may have been offended if scrutinized on this point, and may have argued that it was a traditional, understood quality in a leader, the absence of an ethical compass in the culture of the Army led to horrible consequences. As the Germans found themselves in the quandary of the Eastern Front, and other fronts as well, too many leaders turned to criminal activity to deal with ethically challenging problems. Many others simply looked the other way. The descent into barbarism, while not confined solely to the Germans, nevertheless can be seen as a logical consequence of an amoral definition of character. Despite the unique tactical ability of the German Army, the absence of an ethical standard along with excellent unit cohesion often fostered a willingness to overlook or actually commit horrendous crimes, crimes which have stained their reputation ever since.

The words of military historian Richard Humble serve as a suitable epitaph, "For having achieved so much, endured so much, and held for so long against such odds, the German Army of the Hitler era stands unique in military history. It lost because it was asked to do the impossible. It should never have been sent to tackle the tasks it did. It is the job of strategists to see that their armies are not asked to do the impossible."[72] It is also the job of leaders at all levels to see that soldiers are not asked to do the immoral as well.

CONCLUSION

The relevance of the lessons learned by the German Army of the Second World War in terms of small unit cohesion and tactical excellence is striking. Clearly, in an era where the constant operating principle is to make do with less, the need for mutual trust in combat formations is as high as ever. The smaller, more deployable armies of the United States and many of her allies do not have the luxury to begin serious training after the fighting has begun. Limited funding and resources will likely remain a constant in the foreseeable future for the armies of the United States and her allies. Such constraints would seem to require a redoubling of efforts — at least at the small unit level — to concentrate ruthlessly on the essentials: preparing for combat.

For the German Army during the Weimar and Nazi years, preparing for combat meant deliberate attention on setting the foundation for confident, effective tactical units in a personalized rather than a de-personalized fashion. Units were raised from the same geographic location and kept together from extended periods of time, some soldiers remaining in the same company or regiment for over a decade. Unit commanders, the ones held responsible for leading their soldiers in combat, were also given the authority to promote and demote their subordinate leaders. This was an authority most of them did not take lightly, for they knew the consequences of placing incompetents in positions in which lives hung in the balance. Moreover, the relationships between leader and soldier rested upon mutual trust and respect, gained through competence and a genuine familiarity and friendship with one another. They understood that developing close, personal bonds were essential toward maintaining a functional discipline, but they also knew that mutual trust and respect meant enforcing high standards of competence as well.

Clearly, the German Army of the Second World War had serious flaws, most obvious among them the fact that it supported one of the most murderous and criminal regimes in the history of the world, and the fact that it willingly committed crimes against humanity. Leaders of today can benefit from understanding the source of the German Army's tactical excellence: small unit cohesion and combat leadership, while remembering as well the consequences of such excellence devoid of an ethical framework.

Chapter Eleven

Leadership, Technology, and the Ethics of Total War: Curtis LeMay and the Fire Bombing of Japan[1]

by Conrad C. Crane

While the recent *Enola Gay* controversy has high-lighted the fiftieth anniversary of Hiroshima and Nagasaki, the same milestone for the raid on Tokyo that inaugurated the deadly incendiary campaign against Japanese cities received little notice. Yet more Japanese died from fire bombs than atomic bombs, and the shift from precision bombing to urban incendiary attacks was a greater leap in the American slide to total war than the subsequent move to nuclear weapons. Secretary of War Henry Stimson, always troubled by civilian casualties, justified his decision to resort to the atomic bomb to some extent because "it stopped the fire raids." One of Army Chief of Staff

George Marshall's arguments to support the use of gas during the invasion of Japan was because that weapon was not as terrible as the "petroleum bomb" that had set so many fires in Japan. Any course of action appeared to be less extreme than the Army Air Forces' commitment to destroy all Japanese cities. The adoption of such tactics is even more surprising when compared with American airpower strategy in Europe. While careful to avoid any public criticism of British allies engaged in nightly area raids to break German civilian morale, General Carl Spaatz and his US Strategic Air Forces consistently resisted similar missions. The more ethical airmen in USSTAF termed such operations "odious" or "baby-killing," while more pragmatic ones just wanted to avoid "being tarred with the aftermath of morale bombing" that would tarnish the AAF image, or believed bombing cities was just plain inefficient. Yet after March 1945, the intensity of the urban area attacks by LeMay's B-29s against Japan matched or exceeded anything Royal Air Force Bomber Command had mounted in Europe.[2]

During the last few years, a number of books dealing with American strategic bombing in World War II have portrayed the total air war against Japan as the inevitable result of a number of forces, including racism, "technological fanaticism," and inconsistent policies aimed at achieving "Victory through Airpower." Racial antagonisms and pressures to end the war quickly were very evident in the Pacific Theater, but a reader can get the impression that the incendiary campaign against Japanese cities was preordained, and was destined to occur as soon as the Army Air Forces could reach these lucrative targets with their heavy bombers. In reality, the course and conduct of the air campaign against Japan were primarily a product of one innovative air commander who took advantage of vague direction and a disjointed chain of command to apply his own solutions to tactical and operational problems, in an aerial onslaught that was a crucial ingredient in the formula that produced the final surrender, yet also set a troubling precedent for nuclear strategies to follow. Even today, viable alternatives to the fire raids seem unclear, and the decision-making process reinforces Michael Howard's observation that when statesmen and their generals deal with the ethical issues of a war threatening their people and nation, "the options open to them are likely to be far more limited than is generally realized."[3]

The war in the Pacific was more intense than that in Europe. More than just distance separated the two theaters of operations. Americans held disparate perceptions of the Japanese and the Germans. Many saw "the Japs" as a primitive, cruel race deserving no quarter or compromise. The Japanese were often portrayed as less than human in the American media, and polls showed that 10 to 13 per cent of the public favored the annihilation of them as a people. President Roosevelt carefully controlled the release of information on Japanese atrocities in order to keep a strong public reaction from threatening the "Germany First" strategy, and to prevent retaliation against American POW's.[4]

Fanatical, savage fighting characterized war in the Pacific Theater. American air commanders like George Kenney of the Fifth Air Force feared that people back home, including the War Department, were underrating the enemy. He wrote AAF Commanding General Henry "Hap" Arnold that those who thought the Japanese would be a "pushover as soon as Germany falls" were due "for a rude awakening." Kenney predicted that it would take a "crusading spirit or religious fervor" to win and there was no time to gradually train up for such an effort. He concluded, "There are no breathers on this schedule. You take on Notre Dame every time you play."[5] And Japanese civilians on the home islands were seen to be just as fanatic as their soldiers. They all supported the war effort. In contrast to commonly held views concerning Nazi Germany, Japanese society was not perceived as a police state or one containing impressed workers.

There were other motivations toward escalation in the Pacific that did not exist to the same degree in Europe. Casualties rose alarmingly as Nimitz's and MacArthur's forces attacked objectives closer to the home islands. American leaders feared that the public could not keep its war fervor up for a long conflict, and became particularly apprehensive as V-E Day approached. Admiral Ernest King typified the attitude of the Joint Chiefs of Staff about civilian war weariness when he told reporters privately that he was afraid "the American people will tire of it quickly, and that pressure at home will force a negotiated peace, before the Japs are really licked." This pressure to do anything to end the war was exacerbated by the confused lines of authority in the theater. In his book *Eagle Against the Sun*, Ronald Spector argues that the two-pronged advance across the Pacific by Nimitz and MacArthur was not the "sensible compromise solution" many claim. Instead it was the result of interservice rivalries that caused much conflict over resources and strategy. The Japanese never did take full advantage of the opportunities this divided command offered.[6] But the AAF did.

When Curtis LeMay took command of the XXI Bomber Command of the Twentieth Air Force he did pretty much as he pleased. Like Spaatz, who commanded all American strategic air forces in Europe, LeMay dealt directly with Arnold and his staff for strategic priorities. Arnold, in fact, retained the position of Twentieth Air Force Commander for himself. Unlike his European contemporary, however, LeMay had no close relationship with any theater commander similar to what Spaatz had with Eisenhower. And while competing British strategies forced the Americans in Europe to unite behind a common course of action, the British played a subordinate role to the US in the Pacific. With the long range of the B-29s, the AAF could focus directly on striking at the fortress of Japan without dealing with the incremental island-hopping Nimitz and MacArthur faced.

It is interesting to speculate what might have happened if LeMay had been controlled by MacArthur. The Southwest Pacific Area commander had the most restrictive bombing policy anywhere concerning civilians. When the Prime Minister of Australia inquired in 1943 as to MacArthur's policies covering the bombing of villages in enemy-occupied Australian territory, the general assured him that missions were limited strictly to military objectives. When punitive bombing was done to insure the safety of coast watchers, only one or two bombs were used, and only with MacArthur's approval. He continued stringent control of air bombardment when he returned to the Philippines. The attack of any target "located within inhabited areas of cities and barrios or sufficiently close thereto to endanger such areas" had to be cleared through MacArthur's headquarters. He sent a message to all air and naval forces under his command explaining his policy, emphasizing that the Filipinos "will not be able to understand liberation if it is accompanied by indiscriminate destruction of their homes, their possessions, their civilization, and their lives." He continued that this position was dictated by "humanity and our moral standing throughout the Far East."[7]

MacArthur maintained his standards even when they hindered his subordinates. He refused General Walter Krueger's request to bomb the Intramuros District during the retaking of Manila, even though such air support "would unquestionably hasten the conclusion of the operation." His rationale was that "the use of air on a part of a city occupied by a friendly and allied population is unthinkable." He also showed concern for the laws of war against Japanese targets. When authorities on Rabaul complained that an air raid had destroyed a hospital there, MacArthur ordered a full investigation revealing that planes were attacking an antiaircraft position right next to the hospital. A detailed report with maps was furnished to the Japanese government through the Spanish Embassy. While it is true that MacArthur did not have to deal directly with the issue of bombing Japanese civilians during his operations, in June 1945 one of his key staff aides called the fire raids on Japan "one of the most ruthless and barbaric killings of non-combatants in all history." This probably represented the ethical views of an old soldier like MacArthur, also, who in his speech at the formal surrender emphasized the "spiritual recrudescence and improvement in human character" necessitated by the development of the atomic bomb.[8]

MacArthur's naval counterpart, Pacific Ocean Areas commander Admiral Chester Nimitz, also demonstrated a more restrained view of the role of strategic bombers. He diverted considerable B-29 assets during April and May 1945 to conduct tactical missions against Japanese airfields and *kamikazes* on Okinawa. When naval and surface forces were in position to attack the enemy homeland in force, Nimitz had his units "attack Japanese naval and air forces, shipping, shipyards and coastal objectives," to include shelling iron works at Kamaishi and bombing military targets in Tokyo.[9]

If LeMay had been under MacArthur's or Nimitz's control, the feisty air commander would have had to work very hard to justify his tactics.   But LeMay was not responsible to anyone except Arnold, and even that long link was tenuous, especially after the AAF chief had his fourth heart attack in January 1945.   The XXI Bomber Command was headquartered on Guam along with the Central Pacific Theater staff, but except for squabbling over resources and the stint supporting the invasion of Okinawa, LeMay and Nimitz rarely communicated.[10]   The Army and the Navy each had their hero, their campaign, and their strategy to pursue the war against Japan.   So did the AAF.

Curtis LeMay was the most innovative air commander of World War II.   His background was considerably different from most AAF leaders.   He was commissioned from Ohio State ROTC and had no previous war or barnstorming background.   He had little interest in theory or strategy, and did not get much from his courses at the Air Corps Tactical School.   He was suspicious of geniuses because they were "inclined to forget about the rest of the team," and instead he preferred "a group of average individuals who were highly motivated."   In addition to flying instruction, LeMay had received special training as a navigator, and he was always looking for a better way to do things.   Like Arnold, he was always willing to try new ideas.   In Europe he had developed staggered formations to increase defensive firepower, designed the non-evasive-action bomb run to improve bombing accuracy, and trained selected lead crews to specialize on important targets.   His own technical expertise was legendary.   On the many missions he led himself, he would often roam around his aircraft demonstrating his skills at every crew position by providing tips and training to the other airmen.   After his battered force landed in North Africa from the first Schweinfurt-Regensburg raid, he supervised the maintenance program to make his aircraft serviceable again, fixing many himself.   Nicknamed "Iron Ass" by his crews in Europe because of his mean and demanding reputation, and known to his men in the Marianas as "The Cigar" because he always seemed to have one clenched in his mouth, LeMay was tough but fair. He had great respect and admiration for his men, and hated to lose them.[11]

Some of his actions in Europe foreshadowed the course he would follow in the Pacific. He pioneered the use of non-visual bombing techniques and became greatly interested in the use of incendiary bombs. In what was probably another of his experiments, in October 1943 he led an area raid targeting the center of the city of Munster that destroyed four hospitals, a church, and a museum along with other targets. His subordinate commanders realized that "the RAF had been doing that sort of thing for a long time." His superiors and the press took little notice of the Munster raid, as it was overshadowed by the epic and costly second attack on ball-bearing plants at Schweinfurt that same week. Whether LeMay was trying to evade effective fighter and antiaircraft defenses that shot down 29 of his 119 bombers, or just trying out a new bombing technique is unclear. He may have been experimenting with tactics used by the British in their devastating bombardment of Hamburg. Such deliberate area attacks were not repeated by the AAF in Europe, but LeMay would make them commonplace in the fire raids against Japan.[12]

The vulnerability of Japan to fire bombing was common knowledge. In 1939 an Air Corps Tactical School course taught, "Large sections of the great Japanese cities are built of flimsy and highly inflammable materials. The earthquake disaster of 1924 bears witness to the fearful destruction that may be inflicted by incendiary bombs."[13] Roosevelt was an enthusiastic supporter of plans advanced by Chiang Kai Shek's adviser General Claire Chennault beginning in late 1940 to furnish the Chinese with American bombers to "burn out the industrial heart of the Empire." Once the United States was drawn into the war, planners in Washington did not take long to focus on inflammable targets in Japan. By February 1942, Arnold's staff had prepared target folders on Japanese objectives that included areas of Tokyo ranked in order of "vulnerability to incendiary attack." Encouraged by FDR, initially the AAF, and eventually the Navy, even pursued Project X-RAY, a plan to saturate Japanese cities with small incendiary bombs carried by Mexican free-tailed bats that was only terminated in February 1944 in favor of the MANHATTAN Project.[14]

Strategic bombing objectives in the Pacific were also being examined by the Committee of Operations Analysts, a group of military and civilian experts on industrial intelligence and target selection that produced special studies for Arnold, as well as by planners involved in the B-29 Very Heavy Bomber program. From these efforts, Arnold prepared "An Air Plan for the Defeat of Japan" that he presented at the Quebec Conference in August 1943. He claimed in a wordy and convoluted passage purposely avoiding any clear reference to killing civilians, that a heavy and sustained bombing of concentrated urban industrial areas would produce "the absorption of man-hours in repair and relief, the dislocation of labor by casualty, the interruption of public services necessary to production, and above all the destruction of factories engaged in war production."[15] Arnold also sent an outline of his views to the President which emphasized that "1700 tons of incendiaries will cause uncontrollable fires in 20 major cities," thus destroying numerous war industries.[16] But it is significant that the AAF Commanding General never revealed these opinions to his field commanders, and the real impetus for the incendiary campaign would not come from Washington.

In December 1944, Chennault, now commanding the Fourteenth Air Force, persuaded General Albert Wedemeyer, in charge of all American forces in the China Theater, to order an incendiary attack by B-29s on supplies in Hankow. LeMay, commander of the XX Bomber Command in India and China since August, reluctantly complied, believing that it was not his mission to attack such a limited objective. The operation was a resounding success, however, and LeMay would not soon forget the results.[17]

The Hankow raid was also notable because it was one of the few successes of early B-29 operations in the Pacific. At the same time that LeMay took over the logistically-constrained XX Bomber Command, Major General Haywood "Possum" Hansell became commander of the XXI Bomber Command in the Marianas. Arnold expected the main attacks on Japan to come from Hansell, long a planner for Arnold and one of the primary architects of precision doctrine. The XXI Bomber Command had better logistics, more secure fields, and was closer to Japan than the XX Bomber Command, and could concentrate its firepower against the heart of the enemy home islands. Arnold had high hopes that Hansell could finally exert decisive airpower against the enemy homeland fortress and prove the worth of an independent air service. Arnold had staked a lot on the Very Heavy Bomber program, and it looked like it was finally going to pay off.

But Hansell faced significant problems. Many of them were due to the haste with which the B-29s had been rushed into combat. Its combination of range, speed, bomb load, pressurization, radar systems, and defensive armament made it a truly revolutionary aircraft, but Arnold fielded it months before final testing was completed. The weapons system still had many bugs to work out, and the engines especially were prone to failure. This resulted in a very high abort rate, and many accidents. Crews were supposedly prepared to bomb primarily at night by radar, but operators had received inadequate training in the United States "due to shortage of equipment and early commitment dates." Hansell planned to get around this shortcoming by bombing visually by day in accordance with precision doctrine and Arnold's directives, but the shift in tactics necessitated that all crews be retrained. And no amount of training could prepare the crews for the weather over Japan, which made high altitude precision bombing almost impossible.[18]

Towering cloud fronts off the Japanese coast broke up formations and increased vulnerability to fighters. Even if planes arrived safely over the target, jetstream winds of more than 230 knots at bombing altitude created conditions that exceeded the capabilities of bombardiers and bombsights. Bombing tables were not designed for the 550 knot ground speeds that tailwinds produced, and B-29s fighting headwinds were sitting ducks for antiaircraft fire. Wind speeds were highest from December to February, but still

excessive in other months. And those periods with the lowest inci-
dence of high winds compensated with increased cloud cover.[19]

As 1945 began, bombing results for the XXI Bomber Command
remained dismal, and abort rates remained high. B-29 crews were
losing faith in their planes and their tactics. Their precision attacks
had little effect on Japanese industry due to the woeful inaccura-
cy of high explosive bombs dropped from high altitude as well as
the dispersion of cottage industries. Hansell seemed unable to
produce timely improvements, and Arnold needed results, not
only to prove the worth of airpower and the B-29s, but also to
keep from losing control of them to MacArthur or Nimitz, or even
to Lord Mountbatten in the China-Burma-India Theater. So in
January, Arnold decided to remove the XX Bomber Command
from China and concentrate all B-29s in the Marianas under one
commander, and as part of the reorganization he relieved Hansell
and replaced him with LeMay. Gen. Lauris Norstad, responsible
for B-29 operations as Twentieth Air Force Chief of Staff under
Arnold, went to Guam to supervise the change of command.
Norstad later said of the changeover, "General Arnold - and all of
us, including, I think, Possum - now know that this LeMay is the
best man for this particular job, the job of carrying out what
Possum and the rest of us started. LeMay is an operator, the rest
of us are planners." It was up to this "operator" to vindicate AAF
planning in the Pacific.[20]

Whenever LeMay took over a new unit, he always seemed to
begin with a low opinion of it. He would make a quick study of
the organization, determine its problems, and develop solutions
that were sometimes drastic but speedily established that a new
commander was in charge. His evaluations were very thorough,
and his conclusions were usually very perceptive and accurate.
LeMay began his tenure at XXI Bomber Command with a total
shakeup of personnel. The staff was "practically worthless" and he
needed to change some group commanders as well, so he brought
over some of his people from China. Incomplete facilities to
include bases were a significant training distracter, and he exerted
pressure to complete them. He set new training programs in

motion, especially concerning radar. For further assistance in operations and training, Norstad also procured some radar lead crews from Europe. LeMay established a better maintenance program that put more planes in the air and lowered the abort rate. He even tried breaking the Russian codes to get their weather information! The staunchly anti-Communist LeMay also delivered medical supplies to Mao Tse-tung in exchange for the right to set up a radio station in Yenan that reported on weather and downed airmen. Crew morale rose and performance improved, but the results of daylight precision attacks remained disappointing. LeMay knew that he could be relieved, too, and began to search for a better way to accomplish his mission.[21]

Many planners on Arnold's staff, wishing to exploit the psychological effects of the loss of the Philippines and further demoralize the Japanese people, recommended that the time was ripe for an incendiary assault on urban industrial centers. But pinpoint attacks on aircraft engine factories retained first priority in Arnold's directives. Neither the AAF Commanding General or any other leader in Washington showed any willingness to order area attacks on enemy cities, especially after the February public relations flap over Dresden that produced accusations in the press that the AAF was now adopting terror attacks. Hansell claims he was unaware of General Arnold's "lively interest" in incendiary raids, and was only prepared to carry out urban area attacks as a last resort. LeMay also believed that the AAF Chief desired continuation of precision bombing methods. LeMay began to query Norstad if Arnold, recuperating from his heart attack, ever went for a gamble. Norstad gave LeMay the feeling that being unorthodox was all right with the AAF chief, but Norstad would not "stick his neck out" with anything more definite. With a sense of uncertainty, LeMay decided to switch his tactics without informing Washington of the details. LeMay claimed that he did not want any of the responsibility for failure laid on Arnold, giving him a free hand to put in a new commander, if necessary, to salvage the B-29 program.[22] There is no evidence that LeMay feared any moral indignation from Washington concerning fire bombing, and he never seemed to worry much about ethical considerations, anyway. He may have been afraid, however, that AAF headquarters would interfere to change his tactics if they found out he was about to risk such valued aircraft in dangerous attacks at low altitude with reduced defensive armament. With the dismal results of the air campaign up to that time, LeMay probably felt he had nothing to lose by trying something new.

There were many tactical reasons for LeMay's adoption of low level night incendiary raids. Planes at lower altitudes normally encountered winds of only 25 to 35 knots and fewer clouds. Scope definition on radar was better, also. Such attacks took advantage of the lack of effective Japanese night fighters or low level antiaircraft fire. These factors all improved bombing accuracy. Additionally, low altitude flying reduced engine strain considerably and required less maintenance while producing fewer aborts. With the elimination of the need to climb to high altitudes or fly in formation, less fuel was needed and a greater bomb load could be carried. To increase it further, LeMay also removed all ammunition from the B-29s except that for the tail guns. Selected urban target areas contained numerous industrial objectives. Mission reports emphasized, "It is noteworthy that the object of these attacks was not to bomb indiscriminately civilian populations. The object was to destroy the industrial and strategic targets concentrated in the urban areas."[23] This wording could have been designed to counter any criticisms of the fire raids, or perhaps to strengthen the resolve or ease the troubled consciences of airmen who may have questioned the value of the missions or felt guilty about the stench of charred flesh that lingered in their bomb bays.

The object of the American bombardment was also not clear to people in Tokyo during that first fire raid, codenamed Operation MEETINGHOUSE, on the night of 9 March 1945. The zone of attack selected included six important industrial targets and numerous smaller factories, railroad yards, home industries and cable plants. But it also included one of the most densely populated areas of the world, Asakusa Ku, with a population of more than 135,000 people per square mile.[23]

Before Operation MEETINGHOUSE was over, between 90,000 and 100,000 people were killed. Most died horribly as intense heat from the firestorm consumed the oxygen from the air, boiled water in canals, and sent liquid glass rolling down the streets. Panicked crowds suffocated in shelters or parks, crushed fallen victims in the streets, or surged toward waterways to escape the flames. B-29 crews fought superheated updrafts that destroyed at least ten aircraft, and wore oxygen masks to avoid vomiting from the stench of burning flesh. By the time the attack had ended, almost sixteen square miles of Tokyo were burned out, and over one million people were homeless. Survivors of the city remembered that terrible night as "The Raid of the Fire Wind."[25]

The resort to fire raids marked another stage in the escalation to total war and represented the culmination of trends started in the air war against Germany. Although target selection, especially of transportation objectives, late in the European campaign showed less effort to avoid civilian casualties, LeMay's planning ignored such considerations even more. His intelligence officers and operations analysts advised him that massive fires were essential in order to jump the fire breaks around factories, and residential tinder fed those conflagrations. Noncombatant deaths were unavoidable in order to destroy Japanese industry and forestall an invasion of Japan, which LeMay feared would cost many American lives. The success of the new tactics at producing obvious results also "salvaged the morale and fighting spirit" of LeMay's crews, and proved to them that the B-29 was "an efficient and reliable combat aircraft." While areas of industrial concentrations remained primary targets, all Japanese were perceived as manufacturing for the war effort, often in their homes. LeMay defended burning Tokyo by writing, "We were going after military targets. No point in slaughtering civilians for the mere sake of slaughter. . . The entire population got into the act and worked to make those airplanes or munitions of war . . . We knew we were going to kill a lot of women and kids when we burned that town. Had to be done."[26]

LeMay also emphasized that, whenever possible, populations were warned to evacuate. His intent was to capitalize on the fear generated by his fire bombing to disrupt industry and the social infrastructure without killing everyone. Refugees clogged the roads and caused the Japanese government immense relocation problems. Leaflets depicted a B-29 dropping incendiaries, with the names of eleven cities printed around the plane. The text emphasized that air attacks were only aimed at military installations, "to destroy all the tools of the military clique which they are using to prolong this useless war." It continued, "But, unfortunately, bombs have no eyes. So, in accordance with America's well-known humanitarian principles, the American Air Force, which does not wish to injure innocent people, now gives you warning to evacuate the cities named and save your lives." It concluded with the promise that at least four of the named cities would be attacked, but also noted that unnamed others could be hit as well. This psychological warfare campaign was very successful, and at its height, more than six and a half million Japanese were involved in leaving their cities. The government had been trying to get people to disperse from the hard-to-defend cities, but the fire raids are what actually convinced one-seventh of the Japanese population to eventually flee to the country.[27]

This campaign to exploit civilian morale incorporated a plan that had been proposed and rejected as "too terroristic" in Europe, another sign of the intensification of the war in the Pacific. Though LeMay sincerely believed that the leaflet warnings would "convince the Japanese people and certain articulate minority groups of our own people that our Air Force policy is aimed at destruction of the war-making industrial capacity of Japan and not at the Japanese people," this use of psychological warfare really made the generation of terror a formal objective of the fire raids.[28] Though no American leader would publicly admit it, the AAF was now engaged in area attacks against Japan similar to those that RAF Bomber Command conducted against Germany. And LeMay's XXI Bomber Command was more efficient than the RAF, and Japanese cities were much more vulnerable than German ones.

LeMay wrote in April 1945 that he believed that he had the resources to destroy the enemy's ability to wage war within six months. When Arnold visited Guam in June, on one of a series of trips to help recuperate from his illness, LeMay's staff presented a briefing describing how their bombers could bring Japan to the brink of defeat by destroying all industrial facilities by October 1. Arnold was skeptical, but mused in his journal, "We did it in Germany with much more difficult targets and much more intense antiaircraft. Why not in Japan? We will see." Arnold had already received a message that President Truman wanted to meet with the JCS to discuss the invasion of Japan and whether the AAF could really win the war by bombing, and the AAF chief decided to send LeMay back to Washington to assist General Ira Eaker, Arnold's deputy, in presenting the air force position. Arnold saw this effort as "another opportunity to make military history." LeMay's staff went with their commander, and repeated the briefing to the JCS that they had just given Arnold. General Marshall slept through most of the presentation, and LeMay came away convinced that leaders in Washington were fully committed to invading Japan just as they had invaded Europe.[29]

During June and July, Norstad chaired meetings in Washington between the Joint Target Group and the United States Strategic Bombing Survey staff which had studied bombing results in Europe. In final reports to the Secretary of War, both the USSBS and the JTG agreed there was a large gap between the most important target system, Japanese transportation, and any other objective. Second in priority for the USSBS was ammunition reserves, followed by precision industrial targets and attacks on rice production. Attacks on urban industrial targets were last priority, and they were only to be hit if there was a less than one-third chance of hitting more precise objectives. The JTG was in general agreement, except they placed no emphasis on most precision targets or the rice crop, and more on incendiary attacks on cities. Both groups briefed General Spaatz, newly-designated commander of the newly-created US Army Strategic Air Forces, which included the Eighth and Twentieth Air Forces. He was being sent to the Pacific to take over the direction of most strategic air operations there. Typical of the convoluted command structure in the theater, MacArthur and Kenney retained control over their own heavy bombers. In accordance with his record of adherence to precision bombing, Spaatz agreed with the USSBS recommendations for his forces. He went to Guam with a directive from Eaker to concentrate on, in order of priority, Japanese railway targets, aircraft production, ammunition supplies, and only then industrial concentrations and stores.[30]

However, there was little Spaatz could do to change the course of the air war in the Pacific. There was too much momentum behind the fire raids. Ammunition dumps were filled with incendiary clusters, and aircrew training and operations were geared for the night, low level attacks. Statistics covering the amount of bombs dropped and number of factories destroyed were being used to demonstrate the power of the AAF, while data on civilian bombing casualties was ignored. Much attention was paid to predictions of potential losses of American lives, however, and the devastating raids were tied into preparations for the impending invasion. The Twentieth Air Force was fully committed to the fire bombing of Japanese cities.

So was General Arnold. At the same time Spaatz was trying to reshuffle priorities, the AAF Commanding General was telling his staff at the Potsdam Conference, "The war with Japan is over as far as creative work is concerned. The die is cast. There is very little we can do other than see the planes and personnel with supplies get over there." Arnold passed out books of photographs showing the destruction of Japanese cities, and when Stalin made a toast to a meeting in Tokyo, Arnold bragged, "If our B-29s continue their present tempo there would be nothing left of Tokyo in which to have a meeting." His attitude was well received by those assembled, since hatred for the Japanese was very evident. Arnold was optimistic about his air forces' ability to end the war, betting British colleagues that it would be over "nearer Christmas 1945 than Valentine's Day 1946."[31]

Arnold would win his bet handily. When Spaatz arrived in the Pacific, an examination of the situation convinced him "that unless Japan desires to commit national suicide, they should quit immediately." Continued fire raids and the dropping of the atomic bombs helped bring some Japanese leaders to the same conclusion. Appalled by the destruction being wrought on Japan, Spaatz wrote in his diary about the new weapon and the fire raids, "When the atomic bomb was first discussed with me in Washington I was not in favor of it just as I have never favored the destruction of cities as such with all inhabitants being killed." According to Spaatz family recollections, he had been reluctant to take the USASTAF command because of the revulsion he felt about the destruction dealt German cities, and expectations about doing worse to the Japanese. Directed to continue bombing until surrender arrangements were completed, Spaatz canceled one raid due to weather, and tried to limit other attacks to military targets. When the press interpreted Spaatz's cancellation as a cease-fire, Truman ordered him to halt bombing to avoid a misperception that the resumption of bombing indicated a breakdown in negotiations. When the Japanese delayed, Truman ordered more strategic attacks, and Arnold demanded a peak effort to show the importance and power of the AAF. Despite Spaatz's anxious queries, no cancellation was ordered, and more than a thousand planes hit Japan on August 14, some even after Japanese radio announced acceptance of the surrender terms.[32]

While AAF officers quibbled over the number of American lives saved by bombing, all agreed with Prince Konoye's claim, "Fundamentally, the thing that brought about the determination to make peace was the prolonged fire bombing by the B-29s." LeMay's air campaign had burned out 180 square miles of 67 cities, killed at least 300,000 people, and wounded another 400,000.[33] Hansell, who remains remarkably objective in his memoirs, makes a case that precision attacks on the Japanese electrical industry, utilizing low altitude attacks at night with new radars and tactics, would have destroyed Japan's ability to make war and brought it to the peace table "at less cost with fewer undesirable side effects." This alternative strategy would have taken fewer sorties and saved many civilian lives, though it would have taken more time (and perhaps cost more American lives) because of the need to await the arrival of new equipment. Hansell's clean and rational strategy also assumed that the Japanese would realize that they logically could not continue the war without electricity, and it would have lacked the strong component of psychological shock produced by the incendiary conflagrations. Yet one can only wonder what would have happened if another leader, like Spaatz, had commanded the B-29s, someone more committed to precision doctrine, and perhaps more experienced and secure in his position. Would he have been more likely to take more time and effort to explore other alternatives before resorting to the extreme of the fire raids? Such a course would have been difficult, especially after Hansell's experience, and might have risked the loss of AAF operational control of the B-29s. Even Hansell concedes that after his relief from command, the chosen strategy of the fire raids was "decisively effective" and a "sound military decision," because of the time pressures that existed in the Pacific.[34]

Another possibility was the transportation targeting proposed by the United States Strategic Bombing Survey. The Japanese rail network was especially vulnerable, with many critical bottlenecks at bridges and tunnels. The most promising commodities to target were "food and fuel," and combined with the destruction of Japanese shipping, some analysts claimed that such a campaign would have forced Japanese surrender by itself. As Barton Bernstein has shown in a recent article in The Journal of Strategic Studies however, there are many reasons to question the USSBS data and conclusions, and the actual results of such a campaign are hard to predict. And while such a blockade would not have had the terrifying psychological impact of the incendiary campaign, it would not necessarily have been more humane. Just as many German civilians died from the hardships of the British naval blockade in World War I as were killed by the bombs of the Allied air offensive in World War II.[35]

Spaatz was not the only leader troubled by the urban area attacks. Old and ill, poorly informed by his military subordinates, and preoccupied with logistical and personnel problems, Stimson appears to have only realized the severity of the fire raids in May.

He was probably alerted by news coverage of a 30 May press conference by LeMay where he showed photographs of the destruction of Tokyo and generated headlines that trumpeted "1,000,000 Japanese Are Believed to Have Perished in Fires," the first time civilian casualties were explicitly mentioned. Stimson complained that he had been misled by Robert Lovett, Assistant Secretary of War for Air, and other AAF leaders who had promised to restrict operations against Japan to "the precision bombing which [the AAF] has done so well in Europe." In his diary he wrote, "I am told it is possible and adequate. The reputation of the United States for fair play and humanitarianism is the world's biggest asset for peace in the coming decades." Discussing the topic later with President Truman, Stimson realized the validity of Air Force arguments for area bombing, but "did not want to have the United States get the reputation of outdoing Hitler in atrocities." He often agonized over sanctioning bombing raids and wondered about the lack of public protest. Robert Oppenheimer recalled that Stimson thought it was "appalling" that no one protested the heavy loss of life caused by the air raids against Japan. "He didn't say that the air strikes shouldn't be carried on, but he did think there was something wrong with a country where no one questioned that." As troubled as he was by bombing results, however, Stimson justified Hiroshima and Nagasaki with the same "Airpower Ethic" espoused by the most zealous airmen, claiming that in the long run the air attacks that ended the war saved more lives than they cost.[36]

In his exemplary study of the escalating air war between Germany and Great Britain in 1940, F. M. Sallagar notes that "changes crept in as solutions to operational problems rather than as the consequences of considered policy decisions. In fact, they occurred almost independently of the formal decision making process." The political and strategic desires of leaders in Washington had much less impact on bombing policy against Japan than did the advice of the Operations Analysis Section of XXI Bomber Command. Those experts focused on technical problems without giving much, if any, consideration to nonquantifiable ethical or human factors. For Curtis LeMay, the "operator," the fire raids seemed to be the only way with the combat conditions and available resources in the Pacific that he could destroy the ability of Japan to wage war in a timely and efficient manner. The operational analysis approach favored by the Army Air Forces soon influenced the other services as well. In the postwar period, American military doctrine as a whole began to shift its focus to quantifiable firepower formulas at the expense of more subjective maneuver considerations. The characteristics of atomic warfare also influenced this trend.[37]

As destructive as the incendiary campaign was, the course of the Pacific War may very well have been even more terrible without it. LeMay's urban area attacks hit their crescendo shortly before the dropping of the atomic bombs, and were an important component of the series of shocks that brought about the surrender. The accumulated destruction of the incendiary assault did much to destroy the Japanese infrastructure and economy, and to degrade the will of leaders and the populace to continue the war. The lengthy attrition of the air and submarine campaigns combined with the dual August blows of Russian entry into the war and the atomic bombs were probably all necessary to finally end the war. If Hansell, or some other commander, had been allowed to pursue precision tactics, even if he had perfected them, the delayed and different effects of the air campaign might not have been terrible enough to be an important factor in the Japanese decision to surrender. If they had not capitulated, proposed Allied plans to support the invasion included using gas against defenders, destroying the Japanese rice crop with chemicals, and dropping as many as nine tactical nuclear weapons to protect the landings in Kyushu. If Prince Konoye is correct, then without conflagrations like Operation MEETINGHOUSE, and leaders like Curtis LeMay, the war in the Pacific might have been even longer and even bloodier. LeMay's experience with the possibilities, and temptations, of new technology highlights the challenge for future leaders that Bill Moyers has called "the great unresolved dilemma of our age: Will we go on doing what our weapons make possible?"[38]

Chapter Twelve

Soviet Operational Art: The Theory and Practice of Initiative 1917-1945

by Frederick Kagan

The First World War posed fundamental challenges to the major armies of the world which they each met differently. The two losing major powers, Russia and Germany, responded with revolutionary new doctrines and organizations that were to prove their worth in the Second World War. The three victorious major powers, England, the United States, and France, responded in fundamentally conservative manners, retaining with relatively little change the doctrines, organizations, and attitudes that they felt had won the Great War. This conservatism would almost prove their undoing. It is almost a commonplace that the Germans led the way both in the revolutionary nature of their new doctrine and in its success.   Quite the contrary, the most revolutionary – and most accurate – perception of the revolution in military affairs that occurred in the 1920s and 1930s was reflected in the development of Russian operational art between 1919 and 1937.

One of the most important factors that distinguishes the doctrines of the major powers is the view that each took of the importance of the initiative.   The concept of "initiative" is really two ideas.   In military operations "initiative" has a doctrinal definition: "Setting or changing the terms of battle by action."   Within a chain of command, initiative can also refer to the willingness of commanders to encourage their subordinates to undertake actions of their own, depart from the plan, and be creative - what is called "subordinate initiative."

Throughout the interwar years, the French steadfastly adhered to a doctrine that discouraged subordinate initiative and, although they did not think so, continually ceded initiative on the battlefield to the enemy.   The British and the Americans were not especially concerned with either aspect of the concept, and their doctrines were superior to the French with respect to both.   The German army is, of course, well-known for the pervasiveness of subordinate initiative at the tactical level, but the prevalence of subordinate initiative at the operational and strategic levels is much more questionable.   Similarly, at the tactical level German military thought encouraged seizing and holding the initiative against the enemy, but the methods for doing so which later came to be called "blitzkrieg" practically ensured the loss of the initiative at higher levels in long campaigns, as happened in Russia.   Only the Soviet Union developed a doctrine that had as its primary focus the seizure and maintenance of the initiative at the operational and strategic levels, and that combined that emphasis with a determination to encourage subordinate initiative at those levels as well.   It is in part for this reason that Soviet military theory of the interwar period was far superior to all others', including the Germans'.

Part of the reason for the fundamental differences in the military doctrines of the great powers during the interwar years is that each power saw as fundamental a different part of the problem posed by the First World War and each designed a unique doctrine to solve that problem.   The French saw the problem as breaking through the enemy's trench line, and developed a technique of "methodical battle" to solve it.   Methodical battle was almost a pure firepower doctrine, with the catchwords "artillery conquers, infantry occupies."   It relied upon extreme centralization to ensure the proper massing of fires and the proper coordination of infantry and armored units with that fire.   Surprise and initiative of both kinds at all levels were lacking and, in fact discouraged.   Subordinate initiative entails deviating from the plan, but for the French, the plan was predominently a firepower concentration plan that hinged on very careful timing.   Deviations from that plan could not help at all, but ran serious risks either of fratricide or of sending infantry charging into defensive positions that had not been suppressed.   Centralization was, therefore, absolutely essential to success, and centralization is the mortal enemy of subordinate initiative.

Since the French saw their firepower coming from artillery, moreover, and since they did not motorize the majority of their artillery in the interwar period, they necessarily saw war proceeding in a series of staccato attacks punctuated by pauses in which the artillery would be brought forward.   Each of these pauses would present the enemy with an opportunity to regroup and reform for an attack - in other words, offered the enemy the chance to regain the initiative.   This problem did not concern the French, who believed that their massive firepower concentrations would continually blow through enemy lines, but it ensured that the maintenance of the initiative at all levels of war was not a priority.[1]

The British, on the other hand, divided roughly into two camps.   One, by far the larger, saw the basic problem in Britain's willingness to involve herself in a continental war at all.   Members of this group, such as B. H. Liddell Hart, would argue that Britain should simply stay out of future European wars and thus avoid the problems posed by World War I entirely.   If, against their wishes, Britain were to enter a European war with a ground force, most of the members of this group felt that the war would go pretty much as it had gone before. One notable exception was Liddell Hart himself, who simultaneously saw a revolution in warfare in the tank. Together with the leader of the other group, J. F. C. Fuller, Liddell Hart would argue vociferously that the tank had rendered trench warfare obsolete and irrelevant and had restored maneuver to battle. The focus of the "revolutionaries" was on the massing of tanks and their pure use as an arm of decision. Almost completely lacking was any notion of combined arms operations or any concept of how trenches were to be defeated if they were once set up. Similarly, the simplistic nature of Fuller's and Liddell Hart's writing allowed them to ignore the issue of initiative almost completely. They focused so intently on what the new technologies would allow them to do that they tended to ignore what the enemy might do to unhinge their attacks - in other words, to regain the initiative.

The Germans, on the other hand, focused less on the emergence of new technologies than on the need to solve the fundamental problems of World War I. They saw as the most fundamental problem not so much the initiative, but the complete loss of surprise required by the attacker's need to "prepare the battlefield" with artillery barrages lasting for days or even weeks. In the face of such forewarning, even the most dimwitted adversary could be relied upon to bring to the point of the attack sufficient reinforcements to stall or defeat the pending assault. The Germans sought to deal with this problem by revising their offensive technique. The critical points of *blitzkrieg* warfare[2] were encapsulated nicely by General Heinz Guderian as "surprise, deployment *en masse,* and suitable terrain."[3] Armored forces must be gathered together into *panzer* divisions, corps, and, ultimately, groups, together with mechanized or motorized infantry, and must strike with no warning to achieve maximum surprise at every level of war.

It is generally thought that this view of modern maneuver warfare is the correct one – it is even intimated that the Soviets "stole" it from the Germans during the period of German-Soviet cooperation in the 1920s. On the contrary, the Soviet concept of operational art for maneuver warfare is fundamentally different from the German, and was far more carefully developed theoretically long before *blitzkrieg*.

The Soviets saw the fundamental problem of warfare in the interwar years not in accomplishing the breakthrough, as the French did, nor in the maintenance of surprise, as the Germans did, but in the seizure and permanent maintenance of the initiative. The Soviets recognized, as the French apparently did not, that the problem of attaining a breakthrough had been solved many times: "Now, thanks to masses of artillery of various calibers, tanks, gas, aviation, mines, and specially trained troops, the frontal assault has become easily accomplishable."[4] The problem, the Soviets saw, arose once the breakthrough had been accomplished.

The Germans, to be sure, recognized the same problem, and they proposed to solve it with a combination of speed and mass that would overpower their enemy. But the Soviets had a more complicated picture of war than that. In the first place, they pointed out that, although the problem of accomplishing the breakthrough had been solved in many ways in the First World War, the problem of sealing off such a breakthrough, even achieved with surprise, had also been solved by the use of the elastic defense.[5]

The elastic defense concentrated the bulk of the defender's combat power not at the initial line of resistance, but much further to the rear. Pickets posted to the front of the main line of resistance – during World War I the main trenchline – delayed the attacker's advance and disrupted his movement. By the time he had reached the main trenchline, the attacker's forces would already be in disarray – if he took the main trenchline, his destruction, ironically, would be complete. For, in advancing so rapidly so quickly, the attacker would have quite outrun his artillery support, whereas he would be continually advancing toward the defender's artillery, placed deep in the rear, and the defender's reserves, rushed up by railroad from the operational depths.

The Soviets' proposed solution to this problem was a doctrine that came to be known as "Deep Battle"[7] and that was encapsulated authoritatively in the 1936 Field Regulations. Marshal M. N.

Tukhachevksii, one of the principal authors of Deep Battle, defined it as "the simultaneous disruption of the enemy's tactical layout over its entire depth."[7]   The idea was that long-range attacks striking enemy troop concentrations, communications nodes, roads, and rail junctions would paralyze the enemy and prevent him from concentrating overwhelming reserves against threatened sectors.   Continuing these long range attacks throughout the fight even as Soviet ground forces advanced deep into the enemy rear would ensure that the defender would never be able to respond; the exploitation of the breakthrough would proceed unhindered.   The Soviets envisioned Deep Battle as a way of seizing and holding the initiative.

When the need for Deep Battle as a solution to the dilemmas of the First World War first became clear to the Soviets in the 1920s, the technology did not exist to implement such a doctrine.   The Soviets, therefore, set out both to perfect the doctrine and to develop the technology.   From the outset Deep Battle was a combined-arms doctrine, like *blitzkrieg,* and most emphatically not like Fuller's conceptions.   The Soviets went the Germans one better, however, for aviation was always a prominent part of the Soviet concept of Deep Battle, whereas the *Luftwaffe* was not figured into German ground warfare until shortly before the attack on Poland.

By 1936 Deep Battle had crystallized into an accurate image of modern mechanized warfare.   Field Regulation 1936 stated:

> With all arms and forms of support acting in concert, an offensive operation should be based on simultaneous neutralisation of the entire depth of the enemy defence.   This is achieved by:
>
> a) air action against reserves and rear areas
>
> b) artillery fire on the entire depth of the enemy tactical layout
>
> c) deep penetration of the enemy tactical layout by long-range tanks

d) incursions into the enemy tactical layout by infantry and infantry support tanks

e) sweeps far into the enemy's rear by mechanised and cavalry formations

f) extensive use of smoke, both to cover manoeuvres by friendly forces and, on secondary sectors, to deceive the enemy.

In this way the enemy should be pinned down over the entire depth of his dispositions, encircled and destroyed.[8]

This injunction proved to be an extremely accurate description not only of Soviet offensive operations against the *Wehrmacht* after Stalingrad, but also of Operation COBRA, the break-out from the Normandy beachhead in 1944. With some modification, this passage is also an accurate description of Desert Storm.

Most students of mechanized warfare in the West are familiar with the Soviet concepts of Deep Battle, but Deep Battle was only one component of the theory of Soviet operational art in the interwar years. The most important difference between *blitzkrieg* and Soviet operational art was that whereas *blitzkrieg* was a technique in search of the same sort of quick, decisive victories that Napoleon sought and sometimes obtained, the Soviets rejected the notion that modern wars could be decided in a single battle or campaign. Whereas the Germans focused their theoretical efforts on the tactical level of war within the context of a single operation, trying to find the best way to achieve immediate and decisive victory on the battlefield, the Soviets emphasized the need to plan for multiple successive operations.

The basis for the Soviet belief in the need to plan for successive operations was the rise of the modern mass army. One Soviet military theorist wrote in 1922, "The general engagement, that is one in which one of the warring sides wins the entire campaign, has been transformed in the struggle of mass armies into an entire period of battles..."[9] The destruction of even a substantial portion of a front would not in itself win the war, for a fully mobilized modern state has the manpower and industrial resources rapidly to bring reserves to bear to plug the hole, and the speed with which troops can move on railways ensures that even the most successful initial attack can be brought to a halt eventually.

The Soviets argued that, in consequence of the impossibility of winning the war in a single battle or campaign, the question of linking operations together became paramount. This question was the more important because a defender given an operational pause could reconstruct a solid defensive line based on the principles of the elastic defense and undertake to regain the initiative. If the pause was long enough, the defender might decisively seize the initiative by launching attacks of his own, unhinging the further advance of Soviet forces. Even if the pause were only long enough for the defender to reestablish his lines, however, the success of further attacks would be very much in question. Although the Soviets felt that the problem of breaching such a line had been solved, they also recognized that such breaches inevitably required profligate expenditures of manpower and materiel. Moreover, it is always possible to lose a set-piece battle.

The Soviets turned instead to a belief in the need to plan for successive operations that followed one another without pause. Tukhachevskii wrote,

> One must bear in mind here that as a rule operations executed consecutively amount to extensions of one and the same operation, though widely dispersed in space as called for by the enemy's retreat....One must remember that, even if he has only routed the enemy in the initial operation rather than destroyed him, the attacker is in an extremely favourable position vis-à-vis the defeated side. He has control of the situation, provided only that he denies the enemy freedom of action by continuous pursuit and that he maintains unrelenting pressure in striving for the final destruction of all the forces opposing him. In general, operations conducted in

*succession offer the penetration force the same
degree of initiative that it enjoys directly after the
breakthrough. If the enemy holds firm on other axes
after the heavy break-in battle, he can be [destroyed]
with a single offensive. If he starts to withdraw he
will be dealt with by a series of operations, until he
is forced back against some kind of obstacle or into
an area which he cannot abandon.*[10]

The key to victory, the Soviets argued, was in holding the initiative. Having once seized it by breaking through the defensive line, it was critical never to relinquish it. Subsequent operations must follow on the breakthrough operation with no pauses until the enemy had been completely destroyed.

It is one thing to assert that the key to victory lies in seizing and permanently holding the initiative, but it is another thing entirely to design an army and a doctrine that make that possible. The Soviets saw the solution to this challenge in encouraging subordinate initiative and in careful long-range planning that is, paradoxically, essential to that subordinate initiative. When subordinates take action on their own that was not foreseen by the superior commander, the results are likely to be positive only when those subordinates have a solid understanding of the plans and intentions of their superiors. Moreover, subordinate initiative can only be meaningful if the subordinate commanders have the force and materiel at their disposal with which to implement their creativity. To ensure that such force and materiel is present requires skilful planning at all levels, which also makes possible the transmission to subordinates of senior commanders' intentions.

Thus, Tukhachevskii argued, "To win the day in a manoeuvre operation one has to envisage the subsequent development of the action."[11] In particular, "in mounting a penetration operation, the transition from break-in battle to turning movement must be carefully thought out and adequately planned. These offensive phases must follow one another without any gap in time, let-up in intensity, or hiatus in communications and resupply.... A well conceived operation must be planned and backed up with materiel over its whole course, right up to the destruction of the enemy..."[12]   Another Soviet military theorist, V. K. Triandafillov, also emphasized the need to plan for and resource operations to their ultimate conclusions:

> *...an army intended for action in the sectors of the main blow, must be organized so that it will be capable with its own forces of conducting a series of successive operations from start to finish. It must have the resources that will allow it to surmount any enemy resistance, both at the outset and during operations....*[13]

In other words, commanders and staffs contemplating maneuver operations must consider the ultimate development of those operations and must ensure that supply, command and control, and reinforcement can continue without interruption. The alternative is enforced pauses to recover communications, reestablish supply, and bring up reserves. The Soviets found this alternative completely unacceptable:

> *A pause faces [the attacker] with the need to fight a new battle, in which the chances of success are more or less equal for both sides, just as they are in the initial operation.*[14]

The need to surmount this planning challenge was very great.

Although careful planning is essential to the maintenance of the initiative against the enemy, it can easily become the death of subordinate initiative. The French reliance on detailed and invariable firepower concentration plans, for instance, required that they virtually outlaw subordinate initiative lest their firepower destroy their own forces. Stalin's Russia, moreover, was not the place one would expect to find an officer corps which excelled in taking risks and deviating from the plan.

Yet Soviet doctrine explicitly recognized the critical importance of encouraging the development of subordinate initiative at all levels. In a passage which seems surprisingly modern and un-Soviet, Field Regulation 1936 described some aspects of this strain. On the one hand, the regulation recognized that centralization was critical to success in modern war:

> *The diversity of modern materiel and the complexity of co-ordinating its employment impose exceptionally severe demands on command and control. Systematic reconnaissance and uninterrupted maintenance of physical security are prerequisites for success in battle. Above all, clarity and precision in the allocation of tasks will ensure co-ordination of the actions of subordinate units and of all arms. Once taken, decisions must be put into effect resolutely and with the utmost energy, regardless of the fickle influence of chance on the tactical situation. Unforeseen circumstances and unexpected difficulties are bound to arise in the course of battle. The overall commander must evaluate all new information on the situation judiciously and take appropriate action forthwith. Command must be uninterrupted, with the commander keeping a firm grip on the battle throughout.*

On the other hand, the Soviets stressed that the overall commander must clearly communicate both the situation and his vision and intent to his subordinates, and that he must encourage them to take initiative on their own:

> *[The overall commander] must see to it that all his subordinates know and understand his manoeuvre, and know where the enemy are and what they are doing. The exercise of individual initiative by subordinates confronted with a sudden change in the situation is of enormous importance. The commander should encourage every sensible initiative taken by his subordinates in all possible ways, exploiting it in*

furtherance of the overall aim of the battle. Sensible initiative is based on an understanding of the superior commander's intention, on striving to find the best means of furthering this intention, likewise on exploiting every favourable turn of the rapidly changing situation.[15]

The resolution to the tension between centralization and subordinate initiative is not simple and the Soviets did not attempt to find simple solutions to it. It is possible, however, to identify key points in a battle or a campaign when centralization is critical, and to note other points when subordinate initiative is paramount. The emphasis in the Soviet doctrinal description of the planning process, therefore, is on distinguishing in advance what the critical decision points will be, so that subordinate commanders can have an understanding beforehand of when best to take the initiative and when to await orders.

It is commonplace in the West to imagine that the Soviets actively cultivated an atmosphere of docility and subservience on the part of subordinate commanders. NATO forces tended to see in Soviet command and control hierarchies inflexibility and pure top-down command structures that are the death of subordinate initiative. It may be that this was so for the Cold War army, although evidence from Afghanistan suggests that, as in most modern armies, the situation was more complicated.[16] Part of this Western conviction, however, results from the different viewpoints of Western and Soviet thinkers and the fact that an army that encourages initiative at the tactical level can discourage it at higher levels, or vice-versa.

The American Army today, like the German army of the interwar period, is fundamentally a tactical army. The backbone of both has been the talented and professional NCO corps and the motivated and skilled junior officer corps. Although there have been talented American and German generals, most victories for both armies have been won primarily by their incredible tactical superiority over their foes.[17] The Soviet NCO corps has always been made up largely of glorified privates, while Soviet junior officers are notoriously unprofessional and incompetent, performing tasks that in the West are performed by privates and corporals – and performing them rather less well.

Soviet doctrinal writers and military thinkers, however, have never been particularly interested in the tactical skills of their forces, focusing instead on the operational employment of those troops. Soviet soldiers fought valiantly in World War II, but were outmatched in almost every tactical engagement by their German adversaries. But Soviet operational art carried the day for the Red Army, by allowing the Soviets to concentrate overwhelming forces against particular points and then exploiting the penetrations thus made to the fullest. All of which is to say that when Soviet regulations talk of "subordinate commander initiative," they do not mean what we do.

American generals command armies and think in terms of brigades, or, sometimes, divisions. Soviet generals command fronts, and think in terms of armies and corps. American "subordinate commanders" are, therefore, colonels, brigadiers, and, possibly major-generals. The "subordinate commanders" the Soviets were concerned with were the lieutenant-generals and colonel-generals commanding corps and armies.[18] During the Second World War, those "subordinate commanders" did indeed exercise a great deal of initiative!

If the Soviets did, in fact, encourage initiative on the part of *operational* subordinate commanders, they also recognized the limitations of their tactical units and exhorted operational commanders to reckon with those limitations. Tukhachevskii argued,

> *One must not count on the heroism of one's troops. The strategy must ensure that the tactical task is a readily feasible one. It does this first and foremost by concentrating at the point of the main offensive a force many times superior to the enemy not only in infantry but in artillery, aviation, and other technical forces too.... Over and above this, the tactical task must be made as easy as possible by the mainte-*

nance of surprise, by setting up a good signals net-
work and good physical communications, and so
on....In sum, to be confident of accomplishing the
allotted tasks, one must assign to individuals and
units alike tasks which will call for a minimum
expenditure of strength and energy. One must thus
work out and mount the operation in such a way
that, on the main axis, each detailed task within it
will be simple and easy to execute.[19]

The massive concentrations of forces and artillery barrages the
Soviets employed before each of their major breakthroughs in
World War II were testimony to their determination to follow this
advice: strategy must make tactical tasks not merely attainable, but
easy. The reason for this requirement is that "if individual phases
of these actions are soundly organized and do not depend for their
success on contributions from 'great heroism,' one can often predict
the course of the operation right through to its conclusion."[20]

It is this ability to predict the course of the operation that is key.
Heroism is a fleeting quality, and even patriotic Soviet marshals
realized that they could not rely upon the inherent heroism of their
troops. They might have hoped, moreover, that their troops would
show tactical initiative in place of heroism in accomplishing their
assigned tasks, but they were probably resigned to the fact that subordinate initiative in the attack did not, on the whole, penetrate the
lowest levels of the Red Army. Yet they had to be able to ensure
that the tactical tasks associated with making and holding a breach
in the enemy's lines would be accomplished by the forces assigned
to them. To commit forces allocated to the breakthrough force to
making or holding the penetration would unhinge the main effort.
The solution they found was to emphasize ensuring the presence
of overwhelming firepower and surprise at all levels.

The reliance of the Red Army on overwhelming firepower is
notorious. It is usually ascribed to the Soviets' need to cover other
weaknesses in their force with fire. Although there is some truth
to that assertion, the real cause for the development of the "red

god of war" before and during World War II lies in the imperative that Deep Battle creates of *ensuring* that front-line tactical tasks will be accomplished. Soviet operational art is not a firepower doctrine; it is a doctrine in which overwhelming firepower is employed at critical points to make absolutely certain that key tasks are accomplished.

This distinction is critical for, unlike the French army before 1940, the Soviets specifically instructed their commanders *not* to hold up operations until the guns could be brought up. The emphasis, once the breach had been made, was not on firepower, but on speed:

> *Every breach opened in the enemy defence should be exploited forthwith for the development of the offensive in depth. Commanders at all levels21 must hurl themselves into any breach, even though this means a switch of thrust line not covered by their existing orders. An attack launched even with weak forces against the flank and rear of enemy elements already engaged may prove decisive.* When operating in depth, any delay, such as waiting for orders or for flanking units to catch up, is extremely dangerous. *Audacity and dash disorganise the defence and break the enemy's resistance. Higher commanders must do all they can to support and develop successful breakthroughs by individual sub-units.*[22]

The belief that even a weak attack is better than no attack is based on the fundamental principle of Soviet operational art: once the breach has been made, exploitation should proceed uninterrupted until the enemy has been completely destroyed. If this is done, each battle will be a meeting engagement in which the exploiting forces are prepared and the defenders are not; pausing creates the conditions for a set-piece battle in which a new breach must be made against a prepared defense. Reliance on firepower leads to pauses; to eliminate pauses, the army must rely on speed.

*The Soviets addressed still another problem that tends
to slow down forces – and that has become the subject of much discussion today: maneuver in the
absence of perfect intelligence. Field Regulations
1936 argued: In launching an encounter battle,
nobody must wait for the situation to become completely clear. Information from long-range reconnaissance will never be exhaustive and is soon outdated when the enemy is mobile. In the encounter
battle, inadequate information on the enemy will be
the norm. Anybody who dallies or marks time while
waiting for the situation to clear up will himself be
scouted out by the enemy and will lose the initiative.[23]*

The bottom line of Soviet operational art as it developed in the
interwar years was that all efforts were devoted to ensuring a continuous advance at the highest possible speed in order to retain permanent control of the initiative. The Soviets recognized that this
doctrine would place a great deal of strain upon their command
and control systems, and upon commanders at all levels. They also
recognized that it could only work if subordinate commanders were
allowed to and encouraged to take the initiative themselves. They
developed a doctrine codified in the 1936 Field Regulations that
could serve as the departure point for an intelligent U.S. Army Field
Manual today. What went wrong in 1941?

Two fundamental problems hindered the implementation of
Soviet interwar doctrine in wartime: the innate conservatism of military organizations and Stalin. The execution in 1937 of Marshal
Tukhachevskii, along with most of the other talented senior officers
in the Red Army, dealt a great blow to the prospects for intelligent
military thought in the Soviet Union. Among other things, it led to
the reintroduction of large horse-cavalry organizations under the
sponsorship of the incompetent Marshal Budyennyi, Stalin's favorite
and a cavalryman from way back. But there is reason to believe
that even had Tukhachevskii survived, the Red Army would not
have fared much better in 1941.

The Soviets explicitly recognized in the interwar years that a revolution in military affairs (an RMA) was underway. One author wrote in 1932, "we are at the beginning of a new epoch of the military art and must transition from a linear strategy to a deep strategy."[24] Such transitions are not easily made. It was one thing to draw up the blueprint for a new-style army in Field Regulation 1936 – it was another thing entirely to create it, even starting almost from scratch as the Soviets were. For one thing, although Soviet military writers frequently emphasized the critical need for radios in every tank and airplane, Soviet industry simply was not up to the task of supplying them. Coordination remained a problem throughout the war. Likewise, although Tukhachevskii constantly insisted that tanks and infantry must always work closely together, Soviet industry could not supply enough trucks to motorize the infantry.

On an organizational level, although Stalin did allow his operational commanders surprising leeway during the war, he did not do so in peacetime. Training inevitably discouraged initiative and encouraged conformity, as it usually does in peacetime armies. Many of the fundamental organizational and leadership problems inherent in Soviet operational art, finally, did not become apparent until the Soviets tried to execute it.

It is clear from a cursory look at Soviet operational theory that the command and control problem is severe. A deeply echeloned offensive line accomplishes tactical breakthroughs at several points. Exploitation forces of tanks, infantry, and artillery, supported by aviation, drive through the breaches and deep into the enemy rear. Who commands them? Who coordinates their operations with those of the rest of the front? The easy answer is that the front commander should, but he will have remained far in the rear coordinating the operations of the front as a whole – he will be completely out of touch with exploitation forces which have outraced their signals capabilities. They will be effectively on their own. The Soviets sought and found answers to these problems in the course of the Second World War when, beginning with the encirclement of Stalingrad, they relearned the lessons of operational art.

During the Battle of Stalingrad, the Soviets came to appreciate what Tukhachevskii and others had preached before the war, especially the essential need to hold the mobile force in reserve until the breach has been made completely. The Soviet General Staff Study of the battle spelled out the problem clearly:

> *One of the most responsible moments is the selection of the time of the beginning of the movement of the mobile group into the breach. If the mobile group begins the movement into the breach before the enemy defenses have been completely broken through, it may be drawn out into a combat of combined arms, or it may be obliged to wait for the execution of the breakthrough, and during this time it could be under the action of the fire of aviation and long-range artillery. When the mobile group goes into battle, it can, of course, ensure a great tactical victory and hasten the breakthrough. However, what actually results in nearly all cases is that the mobile group suffers such heavy losses that it is weakened for the execution of its basic mission.[25]*

The study goes on to point out:

> *These theoretical statements pertaining to the employment of mobile groups verified by the experience of the Great Patriotic War are known to the commanding personnel of the Red Army. It would not be necessary to disseminate them if in combat practice there had not been cases when large tank or mechanized units, intended for the exploitation of successes, were used for effecting a breakthrough jointly with the infantry and even independently of it, as a result of which they were exhausted prematurely and could not exploit the successes.[26]*

As a direct result of these failures, the report concluded, the timetable for the Soviet advance was set back: "Hence the three-day mission by the 5th Tank Army for the defeat of the 3rd Rumanian Army and the encirclement of the Stalingrad group was carried out in a period of five days."[27]

This failure was not critical at Stalingrad, for the Soviets caught the Germans napping, but it reflected one of the fundamental difficulties in developing a mobile breakthrough doctrine. It is one thing to write theoretical treatises about when to commit the exploitation force, but quite another actually to do it. The tendency on the part of Soviet commanders at Stalingrad was to be over-eager: having assigned inadequate forces to assure a breakthrough, they were then too quick to commit the exploitation forces, first to finishing opening the hole, then to exploiting it. The Soviets found the solution to this command and control problem through experience; we would do well to study it carefully and game it thoroughly, for it is an enormous challenge.

In the battles that followed the encirclement of Stalingrad against von Manstein's relief forces and through the Battle of Kursk, the Soviets encountered the most difficult leadership challenge posed by exploitation operations: determining the proper size, organization, and command and control of the exploitation forces. In solving this problem, however, the Soviets were handicapped by organizational defects that were not easy to fix.

In the first major operation after the encirclement of Stalingrad, Operation LITTLE SATURN, Soviet penetration forces once again stalled, and the exploitation forces were once again drawn into the penetration battle, delaying and weakening the exploitation of the hole opened in the German lines. Worse still, the exploitation forces were two mechanized corps, and when they did break through, they attacked along diverging axes. Infantry that was supposed to support them could not keep up; the exploitation forces were out of communication with each other and with *front* headquarters for much of the battle. They took heavy casualties and ran low on supplies. One of the corps was surrounded and virtually destroyed; neither achieved its objectives.[28]

The Soviet general staff study of this battle identified the serious command and control problems that led to these misfortunes. On the one hand, the exploitation forces had been too small and had not coordinated their efforts:

> *...in order to intensify and assure the continuous effectiveness of a thrust throughout the entire depth of the operation, it is necessary to merge tank and mechanized corps into one mobile group, consisting of several corps (not less than two) and to commit this group to breakthrough by echelons – in two or even three echelons – in any one direction.*

On the other hand, the Soviets concluded that leadership and command and control failures which contributed materially to the disaster had resulted from inadequate organizational structures:

> *It is considerably more difficult than in the case of infantry to form and to weld together an improvised HQ team and the command of a mobile group of this kind directly before an operation. Hence, while they are in the process of being formed and welded together, formations and their commanders should receive their control organs, and go through their battle training as component parts of large mobile groups.... The experience has shown that an operation of this kind can be accomplished only by a group of corps placed under a unified command or merged into one tank army.*[29]

The Soviets took these lessons to heart and established new tables of organization for tank armies, but reorganizations of this variety cannot be instantly implemented during wartime.[30]

It is important to note that these operations saw a high level of initiative among Soviet operational commanders, particularly the daring tank commanders who charged heedlessly, and sometimes recklessly, into the rear of the German army. Nor were they punished: the commander of the mechanized corps that was surrounded during LITTLE SATURN received command of that *front*'s operational mobile group upon his return. Initiative at the operational level was, on the whole, present among Soviet operational commanders. The trouble was that seizing and holding the initiative against a determined and competent force such as the German army is inherently difficult and aggressiveness alone is not enough.

By August 1943 the Soviets had largely solved the organizational and theoretical problems of their doctrine. Operation COMMANDER RUMIANTSEV, the pre-planned counterattack following the failed German attack against the Kursk salient, used tank armies as *front* exploitation forces operating in pairs along parallel axes. The tanks were held away from penetration battles and so were not exhausted when they drove through the German operational depths.[31] By mid-1944 the Soviets had perfected their techniques even more:

> *In executing the breakthroughs, the Russians showed elegance in their tactical conceptions, economy of force, and control that did not fall short of the Germans' own performance in the early war years. They used tightly concentrated infantry and artillery to breach the front on, by their previous standards, narrow sectors. The tanks stayed out of sight until an opening was ready, they went straight through without bothering about their flanks.*[32]

By attacking over a broad front with many smaller and mutually-supporting breakthroughs, Operation BAGRATION, 22 June - 18 July 1944, advanced over 300 miles in less than a month and utterly destroyed the German Army Group Center. This operation was the climax of the development of Soviet operational art.

The Soviets continued to improve and continued to make mistakes throughout the war. They succeeded because they were willing to take a sophisticated look at the theoretical leadership and command and control challenges posed by operational-level exploitations and to try honestly to develop and implement solutions to those problems. Their experiences have important lessons for us today.

All of the other solutions to the problem of World War I resolved the leadership problem by simplifying it: the French eliminated initiative and centralized control; the British and the Americans posited armored forces operating independently in the enemy's rear not needing to coordinate with other arms; the Germans relied on large armored formations to make their own penetrations and then exploit them with foot-bound infantry panting along behind. Only the Soviets seriously examined the question of making breakthroughs, exploiting them, and maintaining proper command and control over the exploitation forces before, during, and after the breakthrough. Their experience shows that this question is not easily resolved.

The problem breaks down into three major parts: doctrinal, organizational, and leadership. The Soviet experience makes it quite clear that the problem of conducting breakthrough-exploitation operations against a skilled and determined foe cannot be resolved on the spot. It must be solved theoretically in advance of the battle and codified in doctrine that all commanders understand and implement both in training and in combat. To conduct a breakthrough-exploitation operation successfully, planning has to be conducted in such a way as to consider the development of the operation from inception to conclusion. Resources must be allocated and then brought forward continually as operations progress. Above all, the critical decision points of the operation must be pinpointed in advance.

Even with the right doctrine and proper planning, however, the correct organization of the force is critical to ensuring success in such operations. As the Soviets learned so painfully, it is difficult to mesh the staffs of heavy units together on the spot so well that they work as a single unit. The overall commanders and staffs, moreover, must understand and be comfortable with coordinating the actions of exploitation forces with the rest of the line and with other exploitation forces. *Ad hoc* command arrangements are not likely to work well, for they do not allow commanders to be comfortable with their roles and, most of all, they do not allow those commanders to train and war-game scenarios in the situations they will likely encounter in battle.

Exploitation operations, finally, place a great deal of strain on the entire chain of command and create leadership challenges that must be resolved. Subordinate initiative is absolutely critical, yet coordination is also essential. During the breakthrough phase, moreover, centralization is key because of the need to concentrate overwhelming force on a small sector. The transition from breakthrough to exploitation, then, places enormous strains on senior commanders who, having fought a relatively centralized battle of breakthrough, must now give free reign to the subordinate commanders of the exploitation forces. This is a problem that must be addressed through doctrine, training, and education.

The Soviet experience shows that it is very easy to theorize and write about seizing and holding the initiative or encouraging subordinate initiative, but it is a very difficult thing to do in practice. The failures of 1941 help to show how hard it is to work on the practical aspects of these problems in peacetime. In order to take their own initiative, commanders at all levels have to be comfortable with their units. They have to be familiar not only with the individuals who comprise those units, but with the capabilities and limitations of their forces. Soviet commanders, unable to train adequately with the hastily reformed mechanized corps in 1941, were therefore unable to command them under pressure. Repeatedly throughout the war both the high command and subordinate commanders had unrealistic expectations of what their units could accomplish and at what rate—with the result that many units were destroyed by the excessive demands placed upon them. This was a learning process not only for the corps, army, and *front* commanders, but for the high command as well—it was at least as important that Stalin understand the capabilities and limitations of his units as for the unit commanders themselves to do so.

It is impossible to judge with certainty from the Soviet case how to inculcate the requisite qualities of intellectual creativity, intellectual courage, and boldness in an officer corps in peacetime, for the

Soviets did not succeed in doing that. Their success in World War II resulted from their ability to locate and rapidly advance those officers who demonstrated the necessary traits in combat. At the same time, the Soviet officer culture was far from "anti-intellectual" for most of the interwar period. On the contrary, most of the senior commanders of the Red Army in World War II had grown up in an officer culture steeped in theorizing and debate. The key to developing officers who can take the initiative successfully obviously cannot be found in theorizing. Neither is it wise to rely on wartime experience to mark out the leaders with the appropriate traits by a sort of combat Darwinism.

An army operates in its first battles with the same habits it developed in peace. Rigid, centralized habits that result from routine micro-management and fear of failure have resulted historically in rigidity and inertia in combat. Subordinate leaders are either untrained to recognize opportunities or lack the authority and confidence to act independently when the need arises, or both. The results have often been disastrous.

To promote an officer corps with the right combat leadership qualities, an army must implement a developmental system that bridges the gap between theory and practice. Leaders who wish to develop independence and initiative as well as intellectual creativity and courage in subordinates must have the patience to train these qualities and the fortitude to accept the associated risks as junior leaders mature. Implementing the right habits in peacetime, training independent tactical decision-making in challenging exercises, and educating leaders *how* to think through complex problems represent some ways ahead. An army must develop a training and promotion system that ties advancement to the demonstration of the positive traits of initiative. There is no real model for such a system—it has never really existed in peacetime. But the army that finds and implements it will have found, without doubt, one of the keys to future victories.

Section III

Contemporary
Experiences and
Reflections on Leadership

Chapter Thirteen

21st Century Leadership: The Broadened Attributes of a Soldier

by Daniel W. Christman

Great leaders make the difference between winning and losing. In the 21st century, the broadened mission of the armed forces which includes *Operations other than war* (peacekeeping, peace-enforcing, disaster relief, among others) has sparked thoughtful debate on which core principles the Army must develop in its leaders to continue to make that difference. Clearly, we must always inculcate in our leaders the "warrior spirit" which is the foundation for military credibility and success on the battlefield. But exactly what does this concept entail? Does the "warrior spirit" also involve the notions of sensitivity to and compassion for the needs of noncombatants —

civilians, non-governmental actors, as well as enemy soldiers who no longer have the will or means to resist? Is it possible that the qualities needed for a warrior in direct combat are consistent with those for the warrior in other roles? The questions are not new — Plato contemplated very similar problems in his *Republic*. The notion that there exists a dichotomy between the "warrior spirit" and the qualities that a soldier needs to be effective in roles beyond those involving direct combat is incorrect. The same respect for the dignity of others[1] which has enabled warrior-leaders to forge effective organizations in the past will continue to be the cornerstone of success in future missions that involve the armed forces, whether in direct combat roles or in support and stability operations within and outside of our borders.

While respect for the dignity of others has been a principle of good leadership at least since ancient Greece,[2] a number of instances in our own history indicate that leaders have often had difficulty internalizing this principle. In August 1943, Lieutenant General George S. Patton was at the zenith of his career. Acclaimed as the conqueror of Sicily, he was seemingly assured of the key American ground command in the forthcoming cross-channel invasion. Then, in two separate incidents in American hospitals, he slapped soldiers suffering from combat stress, in one case even waving his pistol in the terrified private's face. In the words of his biographer, Carlo D'Este, those incidents of abuse "not only ruined him professionally but were indirectly to change the course of history."

Patton, at that time, lost the confidence of his superiors, peers, and subordinates. General Dwight Eisenhower issued Patton the most severe censure given to any senior American officer in World War II, writing that nothing could excuse the "brutality, abuse of the sick, nor exhibition of uncontrollable temper in front of subordinates . . . I must so seriously question your good judgment and your self-discipline, as to raise serious doubt in my mind as to your future usefulness." Congressmen and senators demanded Patton's dismissal, and he was booed by soldiers during the series of apologies that he made to the units under his command. The slapping incidents ended Patton's long friendship with John J. Pershing, who became one of Patton's most severe critics; Pershing himself had told the USMA graduating Class of 1924, "Leadership requires human sympathy first of all." Patton admitted later that "in both cases, the action was inexcusable on my part." Though Eisenhower managed to retain Patton for later, and brilliant, use in the European campaign, the dynamic general lost influence in the planning and conduct of the invasion.[3]

Unfortunately, examples of American military leaders mistreating subordinates can be found in any era.[4] While formal leadership training in the U.S. Army and at the United States Military Academy is a fairly recent development, there were some institutional efforts after the Civil War to eliminate abusive leadership practices. At West Point, a series of Superintendents battled the evils of hazing. General John M. Schofield, for instance condemned abusive behavior in his address to the Corps of Cadets in 1879:

> *The discipline which makes the soldiers of a free country reliable in battle is not to be gained by harsh or tyrannical treatment. On the contrary, such treatment is far more likely to destroy than to make an Army. . . He who feels the respect which is due to others cannot fail to inspire in them regard for himself, while he who feels and hence manifests disrespect toward others . . . cannot fail to inspire hatred against himself.[5]*

Cadets today still memorize Schofield's "Definition of Discipline." *Respect for others* and *Honor* remain two essential values.

Demeaning treatment of plebes at the Academy nonetheless continued into the twentieth century, even though hazing was banned by Congress in 1901. A victim of severe treatment during this era was Cadet Douglas MacArthur, who, when he returned to West Point as Superintendent in 1919, was determined to stamp it out. Inspired by his experiences in World War I, MacArthur argued that warfare and armies had changed, and that the leadership practices in the U.S. Army had to be reformed. While previous conflicts had usually been fought with professional armies who utilized rigid methods of training and severe forms of discipline, MacArthur contended that "war had become a phenomenon that truly involved the nation in arms...[and] discipline no longer required extreme methods. Men generally needed only to be told what to do, rather than to be forced by the fear of consequence[s]." To MacArthur, officers must demonstrate "all of the cardinal military virtues as of yore, but [possess] an intimate understanding of the mechanics of human feelings, a comprehensive grasp of world and national affairs, and a liberalization of concept which amounts to a change in [the] psychology of command."[6]

Although MacArthur did make changes in the West Point curriculum to broaden the educational base for future officers, efforts to formalize leadership training in the Army were rebuffed by some generals who believed that it could only be learned by experience in a unit.[7] However, widespread complaints about incompetent and abusive leadership during World War II led to the establishment of the controversial Board on Officer/Enlisted Relationships under General Jimmy Doolittle in 1946. At about the same time, Army Chief of Staff Dwight Eisenhower directed that ROTC and USMA cadets be given instruction in psychology and leadership. Eisenhower abhorred abusive behavior such as Patton exhibited in the slapping incidents, stating, "In war and in peace I've no respect for the desk-pounder."[8] In a letter to USMA Superintendent, Major General Maxwell Taylor in 1946, Ike explained:

> *Too frequently we see young officers trying to use empirical and ritualistic methods in the handling of individuals — I think that both theoretical and practical instruction along this line could, at the very least, awaken the majority of cadets to the necessity for handling human problems on a human basis and do much to improve leadership and personnel handling in the Army at large.*[9]

Accordingly, West Point established the Department of Military Psychology and Leadership along with formal courses in those fields. By the early 1960s the responsibility for leadership training had passed from individual units to Army institutions such as USMA and the Infantry School at Fort Benning.[10]

The real revolution in Army leadership training and philosophy came out of the tumultuous 1960s and 1970s. Books with titles like *Self Destruction* and *Crisis in Command*, along with various self-studies, decried the failure of leadership in the Vietnam-era Army. At the same time, leaders realized that the move to an All-Volunteer Force would bring even more stress to an organization that was facing problems with race relations, drug abuse, and absences without leave. New human resources programs focused on solving those problems while leadership manuals emphasized that "the concept of leadership for the United States Army is based on accomplishing the organizational mission while preserving the dignity of the soldier."[11]

At West Point, the battle to eliminate upperclass abuse and harassment of plebes continued even as the approach to leadership in the Army evolved. Despite the efforts of Schofield in the 1870s and MacArthur in the 1920s, there was little change in cadet behavior. A 1969 study commissioned by Brigadier General Bernard Rogers, then Commandant of Cadets, concluded that, "Unfortunately, both cadets and officers at West Point have historically equated challenge with a negative and punitive style of leadership."[12]

Following the 1969 study, the Military Academy made a concerted effort to correct the deficiencies by attempting to institute "positive leadership" — emphasizing leadership that was inspirational and demanding, rather than intimidating and demeaning. Leaders were to use both encouragement and criticism when appropriate, and always with recognition for the dignity and worth of the individual. It was not, however, until 1990, with the creation of the current Cadet Leader Development System (CLDS), that the Academy witnessed a more complete "paradigm shift." What changed? Instead of focusing on the subordinate, CLDS sought to develop the skills, maturity, judgment, values, and character of the *leader*. At long last, the Academy was fulfilling MacArthur's call for "a progressive increase of cadet responsibility tending to develop initiative and force of character rather than automatic performance of stereotyped functions."[13] The CLDS challenges all cadets, not with negative or punitive methods, but by inspiring them to accomplish a stressful and progressive series of developmental tasks success- fully. Most importantly, CLDS challenges cadets to develop as suc- cessful leaders of character who respect the dignity of their subor- dinates. Cadets of all classes must now practice leadership in a manner that is congruent with the values and ideals that shape our democracy and the Constitution we are sworn to defend. In essence, cadets must lead at West Point as they will be expected to in the Army.

In today's Army, as in the past, there is no place for humilia- tion, derision, or scorn of our soldiers or civilians. Respect for others is a combat-readiness imperative, because it forms a critical foundation for establishing an effective organizational culture. The importance of this principle to success on the battlefield is reflect- ed in the Army's formal introduction of "Respect" as one of its seven core values. Those who respect the dignity and worth of others will receive that same respect in turn, thereby forming the bonds of cohesion and teamwork among subordinates, peers, and leaders that will enable a unit to function effectively under the stress of combat.

Respect provides a framework for how soldiers should treat other soldiers, as well as civilians and noncombatants, regardless of environment. According to the soldiers of the U.S. 10th Mountain Division who were in Haiti, or the soldiers of the 1st Armored Division in Bosnia, peace operations are *impossible* with- out this fundamental soldier attribute. There must always be the capability and willingness to use deadly force, when necessary, but this must exist in a complementary relationship with respect for the dignity of others.

Future military operations will almost invariably be "multination- al." Thus, our Army will require leaders who can achieve consen- sus, promote cooperation, and build teams in partnerships with people of widely differing views and traditions. In this regard, Chairman of the Joint Chiefs of Staff General John Shalikashvilli declared in *Joint Vision 2010,* "Our leaders must demonstrate the very highest levels of skill and versatility in ever more complex joint and multinational operations."[14] Bosnia brings the problem into sharp focus — more than thirty nations have joined the United States in efforts to bring peace and stability to this troubled region. Few of these nations consider English their first language or embrace Western culture. In these circumstances our actions and our words can do much good if "Respect" is stressed, or much harm if it is ignored.

The formal introduction of "Respect" as a core value for warriors does not constitute a "clash of cultures." The fact that abusive leadership practices have, in our own history, often come under strict censure indicates the enduring importance of this principle to the Army. Enlightened leaders and philosophers have long recognized that a code of civil and dignified behavior is an absolutely essential moral and ethical counterpoise within a profession whose competence is armed conflict.[15] In the original edition (1950) of the Department of Defense pamphlet, *The Armed Forces Officer,* written by Brigadier General S.L.A. Marshall, the connection between the warrior and respect for others was clear, "The military officer is considered a gentleman, not because Congress wills it,. . . but specifically because nothing less than a gentleman is truly suited for his particular set of responsibilities."[16]

Society has entrusted military officers with an awesome capacity for violence and the equally awesome responsibility to employ it to preserve or restore peace in a civilized manner. Competent leaders who possess the strength of character to respect the dignity of others are absolutely essential to success in any mission.[17] Any soldier who does not possess all of these critical attributes is simply *unfit* to lead.

The world will turn to America for leadership in the 21st century because it believes we can meet the challenges of the future as well as we have in the past. It is not only because of our military prowess and our economy — which has increasingly become the model for the world — but also because of our commitment to government by democracy, individual rights, and justice.

These values, won in our fight for independence, excite the imagination. They bring hope and confidence for a better future and a world where disputes are resolved peacefully. We, as a society, are the most diversified in the world. Yet, we have demonstrated that people of different backgrounds can live together in relative peace and harmony. We show this every time our Army deploys with its men and women, soldiers and civilians, all of diverse races and religions.

It is my belief that our leadership characteristics, including respect for others, enable us to be an example of selfless service for the world. The same principles that compel us to treat the diverse members of our Department of Defense community with dignity apply with equal force to operations and people outside our borders.

Leadership, today and tomorrow, is the art of influencing others in a manner that earns their respect, their confidence, and their whole-hearted cooperation. It is developed through education, training, and experience. In this way, the leader learns to inspire others to do their best in order for the team to accomplish the mission. Leaders also know that at times they will have to issue unpleasant orders and demand obedience, with life or death implications hanging in the balance. Soldiers respond in these times of crisis only when the foundations of mutual trust and respect have been clearly established between the leader and led.

The officer professional development that we provide today must prepare our future leaders to build and inspire cohesive units that can win in environments of enormous complexity and stress. These leaders must be courageous and competent, but they must treat soldiers and noncombatants with respect. This is the message for the 21st Century warrior from Schofield, MacArthur, Eisenhower, Doolittle, and Rogers. This is how the "soldiers of a free country" fight and win our wars. And, it is also an enduring guide for those American warriors who are given the awesome privilege to lead them.

Chapter Fourteen

Charisma

by John C. "Doc" Bahnsen

DEFINING CHARISMA

Charisma: some leaders have it, some leaders don't. The very best leaders have it in abundance. Deep down, every leader wants it. With a determined effort any leader can develop some degree of charisma. Like good leadership, charisma starts with an enthusiastic, positive, joyful approach to life in general. This inner strength, when properly cultivated and expressed, strikes a chord in others, enabling a leader to bring out the best in them. Charisma, however, until very recently has been an almost completely ignored or misunderstood facet of leadership.

Some have seen charisma as merely a set of behavioral tricks, while others have derided it as a form of demagoguery that ultimately undermines the effectiveness of an organization.[1]

Some contemporary analyses have added considerably to our understanding of this subject. Bernard Bass, for instance, argues that charisma is an integral part of "transformational" leadership. Charisma, he asserts, comes from behaviors that enable leaders to be role models for their followers. Such leaders are admired, respected, and trusted because of their extraordinary capabilities, persistence, and determination. They are willing to take risks, they are consistent rather than arbitrary, and they maintain high standards of moral and ethical conduct.[2] Jay Conger and Rabindra Kanungo likewise view charisma as a set of behaviors. They argue that charismatic leaders are 1) sensitive to environmental constraints and have the ability to identify poorly exploited opportunities in the status quo, 2) can formulate and articulate an idealized future vision in a manner that separates them from the norm, and 3) employ innovative and unconventional means to achieve their vision.[3] In essence, the arguments in both studies condense charisma into a set of behaviors exhibited by leaders that make them admired for their exceptional competencies and their abilities to favorably alter the status quo in a meaningful and important direction.

While many of the charismatic leaders I have known have exhibited the qualities mentioned above, plenty of "charismatically challenged" leaders have possessed them as well. The latter were effective leaders to be sure, but they were not charismatic — at least not in the Weberian sense. What separates the charismatic leaders from others is not the authoritative set of behaviors, but their profound understanding of and genuine regard for others. Charismatic leaders have a special insight into the human condition. They know what makes people tick both on a general level and on the level specific to each individual. This understanding, when combined with a sincere desire to touch people in a very personal and meaningful way, impacts people in a very positive and lasting manner. Charismatic leaders, especially the most effective ones, do exhibit many of the behavioral components listed above, but it is the charisma that animates the behaviors. Merely copying the behaviors will not produce charisma, for charisma comes from the inside — from the heart, the mind, and the soul of the leader. The external behaviors are merely manifestations of it.

Charisma, according to Max Weber, derives from early Christianity. Meaning "the gift of grace," charisma gains its legitimacy from "devotion to the specific and exceptional sanctity, heroism or exemplary character of an individual person."[4] Charisma, then, signifies that special quality which gives an individual extraordinary influence over a large number of people. This force of personality, however, can have a curious paradoxical quality. On one hand this sense of devotion has the potential to motivate people to achieve incredible levels of performance. On the other, it has similar potential to foster a sense of dependency: the people need the charismatic figure for energy, enthusiasm, guidance and direction. Without this figure, the organization falls apart; a particularly dangerous proposition in contemporary society as leaders rarely remain in the same position for extended periods of time. In the military this can be especially troubling given the truncated life-expectancy of leaders in combat. The key, then, is to cultivate leaders who can motivate others, while simultaneously fostering the independence, initiative and development of their subordinates so these people can continue to achieve these levels of performance when the leader departs.

Generally, those exercising this influence fall into one of two camps: the demagogue or the leader. The demagogue is a person who, for purposes of self-aggrandizement, inflames or arouses people by tapping into their fears and prejudices. As a person solely driven by notions of personal power, the demagogue seeks to gain support by negative integration — in other words, rallying people against a perceived threat or enemy while simultaneously offering nothing positive of any substance to unify them. This form of influence naturally encourages reciprocal dependency. People need the demagogue to remind them of the constant threat, while the demagogue needs to continuously conjure up new enemies in order to maintain that influence. The process is a charade, however. Once the threat is gone or people see through the deception, the demagogue is gone as is the sense of unity.

The charismatic *leader*, on the other hand, is a force of *positive* integration — a person who inspires a sense of belonging and unity for positive reasons. The charismatic leader knows and cares about people, about what they feel is important and about the positive forces that motivate them to excel. In doing so, a charismatic leader appears to have a divinely conferred gift or power; a natural charm or appeal, a magnetism that attracts the attention and regard of others. When this quality is combined with professional competence and character, we usually find an outstanding leader — a person who can touch the souls of others, bringing out their best qualities and challenging them to overcome their limitations. By taking an active interest in developing the character and competence of others, the leader makes a lasting impact that naturally fosters independence, initiative, and the ability to excel in the leader's absence.

The US Army as an institution, however, has a real problem with such leaders. Charisma by definition exceeds the formal organization's legal and rational authority. Not surprisingly, there are very few charismatic leaders in the higher ranks of the army. Formal organizations like the army, which control soldiers by means of a bureaucracy and the law, want nonetheless to instill loyalty and affection toward certain values, the nation, and the constitution. When charismatic army leaders develop a powerful control over subordinates because of their personal traits, it scares the hell out of the system. The institution fears a cult of personality — loyalty to a person more than to the system itself. Such fears are justifiable in the case of the *demagogue*. The charismatic *leader* is, however, an asset to any organization, the army in particular.

William Wallace, the Scottish leader as portrayed in the movie, *Braveheart*, provides one of the most compelling examples of charismatic leadership. His extraordinary ability to rally the Scots against a numerically and technologically superior foe and win, exemplifies charisma of the highest order. His strong, positive character and purity of purpose, combined with his intellectual and martial prowess make the film's Wallace a source of strength and affection to those he led.   In a similar vein, English King Henry V demonstrated his charismatic leadership before and during the Battle of Agincourt in 1415.[5]   Through his speech to his knights and soldiers before that battle on St. Crispin's Day and by his personal example on the field, Henry was the catalyst in motivating his subordinates to achieve a new level of battlefield performance.   The legacies of Wallace and Henry V indicate the long-term, positive impact they had both on their followers and on subsequent generations.

Since charismatic leadership is so valued, many great leaders have sought ways to foster it and enhance the effectiveness of other already capable leaders.   I will discuss a few of those exceptional people who have been instrumental in my development as a leader and analyze why they were so effective. While each of them employed different techniques and behaviors on account of their personality and their specific context, behind those behaviors were the genuine and sincere understanding of and regard for others.   In other words, it was their charisma that made the techniques they employed so successful.   It is useful to study and use the techniques, if appropriate, but it is more important to understand the force that makes them meaningful.

MY MENTORS

In the summer of 1952, Lieutenant Colonel Jim Hollingsworth made a lasting impression on me.   He looked and talked like an outstanding soldier who had been to war and had proven his abilities in combat. His military appearance was striking and unusual. He wore tanker boots, the first I had seen.   He wore a different type of overseas cap than other officers.   The only ribbons he wore set him apart from the rest of our superb tactical officers — a Distinguished Service Cross, Silver Stars, and a Purple Heart with 5 oak-leaf clusters.   He had a direct manner of speaking to you that you never forgot.   He looked right at you and talked native Texan. He used a fair amount of profanity, colorful but not vulgar.   Best of all, Lieutenant Colonel Hollingsworth had a tremendous sense of humor.   He laughed easily and he saw the funny side of most things.   You got the feeling that he was not afraid of anything.

As I got to know this tremendous soldier over the years, I found him to be one of the most competent, most daring, most self confident leaders I could imagine.   He told stories about his experiences in action against the Germans — stories we always remembered.   He went to war as a lieutenant cavalry leader after graduating from Texas A&M in the early '40s.   He found his niche as a tank leader in an Armored Division in Europe in '44 and '45. He was wounded several times because he moved to the front and led by example until the war was over.   Later in his career he did the same thing in Vietnam when he lead soldiers against the Viet Cong and the North Vietnamese Army as a general officer.   While colorful in language, distinctive in dress, aggressive in spirit, and fun to be around, Jim Hollingsworth also delivered when it counted the most — in combat.   He possessed that magic spark of charisma.

So did Captain Hank Emerson, later Lieutenant General Emerson. Hank was a unique West Point company tactical officer.   He stood out as a successful infantry company commander in the Korean War, earning a Silver Star, two Bronze Stars, and a Purple Heart. What most impressed the cadets was Captain Emerson's unparalleled, infectious enthusiasm and his will to win.   Tall and slender with a hawk-like nose, he exuded energy and enthusiasm in whatever he was involved, especially cadet athletics.   He was able to infuse this spirit into his cadet companies, and in later years, into any organization in which he served.

During his first year as a tactical officer his cadet company won the Banker's Trophy (the Cadet Intramural Brigade Sports award). His Regimental Commander rewarded him for his outstanding performance by transferring him to the last place company in the regiment the next year.   Hank Emerson did not flinch, he did not slow down, and his second cadet company excelled and nearly won the same trophy the next year.

Hank Emerson lived for competition.   He intended to win everything — a point you needed to understand at the beginning.   He was especially gifted in talking with younger leaders. He remembered your name and made it his business to know people he considered winners. He remembered me because I led a company lacrosse team to the brigade championship and beat his team. He made it a point to always speak to me and remembered me as a hard competitor and a winner. He was a fiery orator and gave the first "jeep-top talk" I ever heard, a technique I used throughout my career. He used the phrase "get up close so I can look you in the eye" when he talked. I embellished that phrase and added some other pithy sayings to my own talks with great success.

He was a brilliant battalion and brigade commander in combat in Vietnam, a superb division commander in Korea, and an enthusiastic leader wherever he was assigned. He was decorated with two Distinguished Service Crosses, 4 Silver Stars, 3 Bronze Stars for Valor, and many other decorations during his two combat tours in Vietnam. He armed all the men in his Airborne Infantry Battalion with hatchets (modern day tomahawks) and had the radio call sign of "Gunfighter 6." This call sign stuck with him for the rest of his career. Soldiers who served with him never forgot him or his great sense of humor. From his days as a Captain through his command of an Airborne Corps as a Lieutenant General, Hank Emerson never lost his charismatic qualities.

Nor did Captain George S. Patton, son of the famous World War II general. He was my Camp Buckner cadet tactical officer and later my Regimental Commander in Vietnam. He exuded a natural charm which he expressed in a unique mixture of profane language that stuck in the minds of his soldiers. He is my most vivid combat memory. Our 11th Armored Cavalry's Regimental motto was "Find the Bastards and Then Pile On!" and George Patton enjoyed every minute of finding and destroying the bastards. From this superb soldier I learned some exceedingly colorful expressions, profanity that at times relieved the stress of combat and made you chuckle.

Soldiers and leaders of every rank loved being around George Patton, especially in combat. He made you feel good about yourself and confident that you would always beat the enemy. Most of all his profane sense of humor relaxed you and made you comfortable in a situation where killing was the rule of the day. He was also a genuinely emotional man and cried at memorial services and funerals, something many senior soldiers are not able to do.

Like his father, he cared about his soldiers and did everything he could to take care of them — and *every* soldier knew it! His lifetime of study of the profession of arms was evident in combat in particular. He knew the staff functions almost intuitively and made his staff support the soldiers on the firing line. He smoked cigars in combat, making it a trademark. He would ask you your opinion on things happening in combat and respected an honest answer. He has always had a wonderful sense of humor in all circumstances, a warm, fun-loving personality, and natural charm and charisma!

Those qualities were shared by Norm Schwarzkopf whom I have known for over 45 years, ever since our plebe year at West Point in 1952. He was as personable when I first knew him as he is today. Norm has charisma that stems from a boyish-like enthusiasm for being a soldier. His enthusiasm has been his most important professional trait among a number of other extremely important and unique qualities. Norm loves soldiers and he loves soldiering, and it shows in everything he does and says. His outgoing personality has made him internationally popular. His sincerity is genuine. What you see is what you get. He has walked the walk of a soldier all his life and he can talk the talk of a soldier based on solid credentials and impressive performance in peacetime as well as in war.

Brilliant intellect and rock solid integrity have been key factors in Norm Schwarzkopf's development as a charismatic leader. Being a big man makes him stand out in a crowd, but what makes people remember him is his bright, infectious, enthusiastic conversation. You remember talking to Norm, you remember him looking directly at you, and you remember his thoughtful and colorful comments. His sense of humor is well developed and although he is not overly profane, he can cuss colorfully if the occasion so dictates.

I did not know General Bill DePuy until he was a Four Star General, but his reputation in the army preceded him in my imagination. He was a small wiry man with a twinkle in his eye who made an instant hit with me the first time I met him because of his professional aura and naturally charming manner. This emanated from the feeling I got from him that he considered me to be a professionally competent, albeit outspoken, soldier. He made me feel good about myself when I was around him.

General Bill DePuy had a distinguished career, beginning in World War II where he soon witnessed the results of poor leadership in combat operations. He served in the infamous, later highly decorated, 90th Division. Because of his professional competence, he rose rapidly in rank during combat in 1944 and 1945 and ended the war commanding an infantry battalion. He never forgot the lessons he learned early in his career and was a tough task master as a division commander in combat in Vietnam twenty years later.

Bill DePuy had an outstanding personality and he liked good soldiers, especially bright, hard charging officers who had ideas on how to improve the Army. He surrounded himself with smart people and did not tolerate incompetence for a second. He was direct in his language and was a careful listener. He respected his subordinates and always listened to their views, especially if they disagreed with him. He was a superb dancer and charmed the ladies as easily as he charmed his soldiers. He also had an extraordinary sense of humor and could relax and have fun. He had charisma of the highest order.

General Dick Cavazos is another truly charismatic soldier who was highly decorated for his brilliant combat service in both Korea and Vietnam, having been awarded the Distinguished Service Cross and numerous other awards. Among many other things, he made a point of checking to see if his newly assigned soldiers were issued a pillow when they arrived in his corps. Pillows do not seem that important, yet many supply sergeants do not have enough of them on hand for newly assigned soldiers. Within 48 hours of arriving on post, General Cavazos's Sergeant Major would see the newly assigned soldier and one of the questions he asked was whether or not the soldier had been issued a pillow. Negative answers were followed by a phone call from Lieutenant General Cavazos to the first general officer in the chain of command.

I had to take two of those phone calls. Dick Cavazos did not chew me out, but his friendly admonishment made me feel terrible. Soldiers ought to have a pillow; it's "fundamental taking care of soldiers 101!" His concern for what many people might consider minor issues illustrates why he is one of the most caring officers I have ever known. His moving speaking style and his sincere concern for soldiers always made a positive impression on those serving under him. He exuded charismatic leadership qualities in everything he did and said.

Charisma is such a part of some leaders' natural character that it seems as if they are born with it. These six leaders all have some things in common, such as a keen sense of humor and an enthusiasm for soldiering and being a soldier. But they also have a natural way with their fellow soldiers and their subordinates which springs from a genuine regard for their well-being, and an uncanny ability to develop the very best qualities in others. While the magic "spark" of charisma may indeed be an innate quality in these leaders, the genuineness and sincerity of their regard for others suggests that charisma has an important developmental component as well.

APPLYING THE LESSONS

What are the lessons I learned from all these distinguished leaders? Charisma can and must be developed. The first requirement is self-assurance. By this I do not mean becoming a narcissist, but developing as a person who is comfortable with his or her appearance, physical strengths, and mental abilities. In other words, a person with solid self-confidence but without arrogance or false humility. When a leader combines this positive attitude with a genuine regard for others, we have a prime candidate for charisma.

Charismatic leadership really starts with the right positive attitude. I always think of Lieutenant General Hank Emerson when this comes to mind. He felt that "winning is the only thing" long before Vince Lombardi coined the phrase. You must project an attitude that is both positive and realistic. Any discouragement that a leader feels must be held within. Bubbling enthusiasm *a la* Schwarzkopf, Hollingsworth, Cavazos, and Emerson must always be the order of the day, even in combat.

Personal appearance is a small but significant factor in developing a charismatic personality, although not everyone will agree with my views on this subject. For instance, we only have to look at a few photos of General George S. Patton in World War II to see that different dress causes a leader to stand out from the group. Soldiers notice this and generally admire the nonconformity of their officers. There are any number of other examples of unique dress and accouterments that have caused distinguished leaders in history to stand out.

In combat, I folded an Olive Drab triangle bandage into a neck scarf and wore it. It caught on with many of my officers and soldiers. We simply rolled it and tied it loosely with a square knot. Some of my officers used OD handkerchiefs for the same purpose. In addition to being distinctive, it had practical use in the Vietnamese climate. I also carried a sack of grenades around my neck for use in ground actions, and rode a motorcycle with a radio on my back when dismounted during my time as an Air Cavalry Troop Commander. This captured motorcycle was carried in the back of my command helicopter for use when needed. Its utility was not nearly as great as the image it projected of a dashing cavalryman jump-starting it when he landed, speeding off to a meeting with other commanders or staff officers.

Having a sense of humor is another common feature of the charismatic leader. J.F.C. Fuller, for instance, believed that a sense of humor was the lubricant of a good unit. Soldiering is tedious, difficult, often unappreciated work that requires sacrifice and often loss of life of soldiers under your command. If you can make soldiers feel good about themselves and about their situation no matter how difficult it appears by using humor as your medium, then you are on the way to developing charisma. Humor, however, is only truly effective when it touches someone. You need to know about people, their needs, their feelings and what is important and meaningful to them in order to have a positive, genuine sense of humor. People like to laugh, yet we do not do enough of it in our day-to-day life. I have never found situations where a little of the right humor did not make others feel good about having me around them. This is true even at a funeral when the deceased was a close friend who had served with me or shared time with me.

From Patton and Cavazos I learned to know when to let my emotions flow. I recommend it to everyone who suffers the loss of soldiers and loved ones. It shows your human side that people around you may not think you have.

Individual traits, however, are not enough. These attributes must resonate with soldiers in a substantive manner to be effective. True caring about soldiers is the critical element that translates the personality of a leader into the catalyst that results in charismatic leadership.[6] Caring consists of a genuine understanding for the needs and aspirations of others and a demonstrated willingness to *act* on their behalf. Mere words are not enough. Caring starts by looking soldiers in the eye when you talk to them and listening to them when they talk to you. There is an art to listening that requires undivided attention and study. Very few people have mastered the art. Charismatic leaders are the ones who know how to talk to and listen to soldiers of all ranks; to make the soldier feel and believe that their seniors, by virtue of their actions, are listening and sincerely care about their concerns and needs.

The ability to remember names is another key example of caring. This is an art that must be continually practiced. I have never known a truly charismatic leader who was not especially good at remembering names and people. Being able to recall events where a soldier has excelled and associating his name with that accomplishment is elementary. Hank Emerson remembered people who won in sports contests and other competitions. George Patton remembered the soldiers who were especially heroic on the battlefield and those he called "*bona fide* killers!" Charismatic leaders remember names.

There is an art in talking to soldiers that almost always starts with "Where are you from"? "Are you married?" "How many kids?" "What's your job in this outfit?" The litany of questions is worthless unless you listen and remember what the soldier tells you. Every leader must establish a technique for dealing with and talking to soldiers. Sincerity and working to remember who told you what are key ingredients. Another important factor in talking to soldiers is an understanding of their concerns and interests versus one's own concerns.

When soldiers were deploying to Germany or going to be in the field in cold weather I always made walk-through inspections in ranks before they departed. My concern was about what they were wearing. I would often look to see how many layers they had on, looking under the coat and scarf for the appropriate layers. Asking was never enough for me, I wanted to see the layers. It told the soldiers that a senior officer cared enough about them to inspect their clothing in detail. Words are not enough. Leaders must act on those words before soldiers know that the caring is genuine. Many lieutenant colonels and captains in my units learned that to ask a soldier what he had on was one thing, to inspect that clothing was another matter. Wearing of gloves and scarves was mandatory in cold weather wherever I soldiered. Keeping soldiers in gloves was a constant problem, but making sure that they did demonstrates genuine caring. Soldiers remember you being tough on things like that.

Giving soldiers an opportunity to be winners and then recognizing their achievements is another technique utilized by charismatic leaders. For instance, the use of flags, medals and guidons for military units goes back to the beginning of our army. There are a lot of official devices including medals, streamers, and other accouterments than you can use to recognize soldiers. You can also design and present your own awards. Several of the things that I used for motivational purposes were especially well received.

The "Gunga Din" certificate was an award I gave to officers who could beat me in a designated competition. The idea sprang from a technique that a fellow tank battalion commander used during tank gunnery.   The specific name, of course, comes from the Rudyard Kipling poem "Gunga Din" — "Though I've belted you and flayed you, by the livin' Gawd that made you, you're a better man than I am, Gunga Din!" The "Gunga Din" challenge was a competition in events like shooting, swimming, and running, using a scale similar to the Army's Physical Fitness Test based on age for athletic events. For the "Old Man" this was not an easy chore! The best of these events were two triathlons I sponsored as an Assistant Division Commander, changing only the weapon we shot in the second competition. In the first triathlon only 13 officers were able to beat my total score. Motivated by this, the second competition was much tougher and 40 officers beat my score. The secret was that they trained twice as hard for the second go round, having been motivated by a poor showing the first time.

The result of this competition was a lot of talk about physical training, including swimming and weapons skills. It also gained respect for genuine, up-front leadership. My camaraderie with the officers of the division grew and I was able to commend in public those who beat me. Winning a "Gunga Din" certificate became a special event in the Division.

During my brigade command I designed and had made a company guidon called the "Colonel's Own." It was a simple design with an golden eagle embroidered on a blue field and "Colonel's Own," and "1st Aviation Brigade" above and below the eagle.

Every Monday morning I presented this mounted guidon to a different company for their outstanding performance the previous week. This was done at company formation where I gave a jeep-top talk to the unit about why they had won the guidon and how proud I was of their performance. The reasons for presenting the guidon varied, but I always got a good reaction from the soldiers receiving it no matter what the accomplishment. Invariably, I always had something good to say about the unit and its performance, often summarizing their hard work since I last talked to them. The purpose of this award was to motivate and to thank a company of soldiers for their hard work every week. It also started my week off on the right foot by being genuinely complimentary to a group of soldiers, letting them know they were special in my book and that I wanted them to carry my personal guidon. This caught on with the lieutenant colonels and they would make their nominations at the end of every week for my selection. Since many of the units would excel on a weekly basis, I would spread the award around purposely so it was many weeks before a company won it a second time. The key point is that the award was for a real achievement; I did not give it out just to give it out — awards given on that basis quickly lose their meaning in the eyes of soldiers. As a result, over a period of two years I was able talk to and motivate every company several times. I continued to use this award when I was an Assistant Division Commander, substituting instead a "General's Own" guidon made with a white star in the center of a red flag with the Second Armored Division's "Hell on Wheels" embroidered on the bottom.

Talking to soldiers and commending them for superior performance on a consistent and measured basis is an extremely important lesson that I learned from all of my mentors over the years. Soldiers get to know you and they tend to like you if they hear a consistent flow of sincere and deserved praise. Soldiers want straight talk not phony flattery, so you must get your facts right and learn to praise with honesty. Sometimes it requires you to give serious thought to what you say to a unit not quite up to standards.

Charismatic leaders are also outstanding mentors and developers of their subordinates. This ability springs from a corresponding desire to have successful, highly motivated winners working for you. Charismatic leaders routinely and faithfully develop and train their immediate subordinates (also knowing full well that these officers, as a group, will add luster to their own performance). What really distinguishes the leaders I have mentioned above was their devotion to developing leaders for the future of our army. They all spent an incredible amount of time mentoring.

Mentoring by charismatic leaders involves a higher level of personal involvement with subordinates that goes far and above the job. It goes into deep and personal concern for the subordinate as a person. I know that my best leaders cared about me personally and I know that I cared very much for those leaders I have mentored over the years. The only legacy, if any, that a good leader leaves to the army is the number of quality subordinates they develop— a truism that I am fond of quoting now that I am retired from the army.

CONCLUSION

All of the most charismatic leaders I have known have been unique in personality, speech, and appearance. They were intentionally different and admired their subordinates who were as well. Soldiers want to be led by leaders who they think are special people. An "aura" is the desired effect, combined with absolute professional competence and character. The most salient characteristic they exhibit, however, is their sincere and genuine regard for and interest in others. Charismatic leaders know what is important to others and thus can strike positive chords that resonate with them. Knowing their subordinates and their context also enables the leader to know when certain behaviors are appropriate and when they are not. In this way charisma becomes a lasting rather than a fleeting quality.

Charismatic leaders are also entirely predictable even though they are unique in many ways. Subordinates enjoy watching them because they know exactly what the charismatic leaders are going to do. Furthermore, their mere presence symbolizes a coherent set of values and a recognizable philosophy of leadership. Charismatic leaders empower subordinates because they clearly articulate their standards and expectations, and then give their well-trained subordinates the freedom to exercise initiative and imagination to accomplish the mission.

Charisma is the warrior's basis of authority. In trying times, people naturally look to and rally around the spirit of the charismatic leader for inner strength. The warrior spirit, embodied in the charismatic leader, is the quality we must encourage in our leaders.[7] We must, however, cultivate this quality in peacetime so that it is there in war. Whether the leader is present or not, the positive legacy that leader has imparted to others will help sustain them in the most difficult circumstances.

Serious students of leadership know that our understanding of charisma needs further development. My hope is that these thoughts and reflections will stimulate discussion on this subject, and will also help to add luster to the leaders of the next century. Our soldiers deserve the very best leadership with a "touch of class" that our nation can provide. Charismatic leaders can make the tough job of soldiering and fighting more enjoyable and more meaningful, especially in a society that so quickly forgets the sacrifice of its young men and women.

Chapter Fifteen

Looking Up:
Leadership from A
Follower's Perspective

by Douglas E. Lute

INTRODUCTION

Much has been written on the theory of leadership. Many of the classics in this field relate to military and political leadership, and in recent years the topic has received expanded treatment in the business world. Today, bookstores feature a formidable array of works covering every perspective of leadership from the battlefield to the boardroom. Related topics such as organizational theory, historical analyses of leaders, motivational techniques, and improving human efficiency add weight to this collection.

The U.S. Army has its own doctrinal framework for senior leadership that includes three attributes, three perspectives, three imperatives, fourteen skills, and eleven principles, illustrated with examples from the rich experience of military history.[1] While this framework is comprehensive, the vast array of elements begs the question as to which of them are *most important* in practice.

When considering the complex blend of art and science that comprises leadership, one might conclude simply that while it is difficult to describe, you recognize good leadership when you see it. In practice, therefore, perhaps the best authority on leadership rests with the led. This chapter takes the perspective of one follower and offers a simple framework to help bridge the gap between theory and practice by identifying which leadership attributes seem to have the highest payoff. The framework — founded on my personal observation of leaders, both military and civilian, in times of routine activity and crisis — is descriptive, not prescriptive. From this follower's perspective, the most effective leaders seem to combine three attributes:

- they provide vision and a plan;
- they vote with their time; and
- they are who they are.

LEADERS PROVIDE VISION AND A PLAN

"If you don't know where you want to go, you're not likely to get there."[2] As if in response to this saying, many leaders today spend considerable time thinking about the future of their organization. This effort takes various forms depending on the leader's position. Lower-level leaders tend to focus on tangible results in the short term; they set objectives, sometimes even day to day. More senior leaders take broader, longer term perspectives; they set strategic goals and craft "vision" statements.

Effective leaders at all levels guide their organizations by looking forward, but this is not enough. The most effective leaders provide vision <u>and</u> a plan of action — a set of synchronized programs — to attain the vision. This combination of vision and planning is what sets apart the most effective leaders.

The leader's vision is the general target for the organization — where we are going; the plan is the road map with specific milestones — how we will get there. A plan coordinates specific programs that move the organization along a general azimuth toward the vision. Programs speak louder than vision alone: they demonstrate to the organization and others the leader's commitment to his view of the future. A leader who links vision to a set of programs provides a plan of action that is meaningful to subordinate leaders and thereby magnifies the impact of the vision.

Too often leaders provide either vision or a set of programs, but not both. Some leaders know where they want to go but do not have a plan for getting there; their organizations tend to wander without focus. In the absence of implementing programs, a vision becomes vague or even meaningless. Other leaders have pet programs but no overarching concept for the future; their organizations tend to focus on the near-term without a sense of where they are headed. The programs become ends unto themselves instead of contributing toward a goal. Still other leaders who do provide both vision and programs fail to link the two explicitly, leaving their organizations confused over which — the vision or the programs — the leader really wants. Here again the various programs tend to take on lives of their own, and grow independently of one another and the vision to which they should contribute. All of these shortcomings lead to organizations hampered by incoherence, confusion, and ultimately chaos. Only the most effective leaders avoid these debilitating problems by combining coherent vision and programs.

One technique for linking vision and programs begins with a comprehensive assessment of the organization by the leader. This is similar to the commander's estimate conducted as part of the Army's tactical planning process.[3] The commander begins by assessing the mission, the situation, and the assets available. The result of the process — with staff input — is a plan that assigns specific tasks to specific units over time to accomplish the mission.[4]

The key point here is that the process that links mission to tasks — i.e., vision to programs — begins with the commander's assessment. In short, a leader who begins with a careful assessment of the organization, a vision for the future and the assets required to attain it, is well along the way to developing meaningful programs.

Several examples drawn from observations of actual Army units show how to link vision to programs. After assessing his unit, one commander of a combat unit stationed in the United States established a three-part vision: trained to fight, prepared to deploy, caring for soldiers and their families. Focusing first on the "trained to fight" element, he employed Army training doctrine: he established the essential tasks required for his wartime mission, set realistic goals, assessed his unit's proficiency in these tasks, and developed a training program that moved the unit toward his goals.[5] He reviewed training progress periodically and adjusted his training programs as necessary through written guidance to his subordinates. By implementing the Army's doctrine for training, he combined a vision for the unit with specific programs that moved the unit along his azimuth. This commander did what the Army expected and was very effective in training his unit; victories at the National Training Center documented his success.

What set this commander apart, however, was that he realized this same process of linking vision and programs in the training arena could pay dividends for the unit in other dimensions. For example, as he assessed the essential elements of being "prepared to deploy," he recognized that tasks such as maintaining operational readiness standards for combat vehicles could be addressed more effectively by treating them like training tasks. The same proved true for tasks having to do with caring for soldiers and their families. In these two key non-training dimensions of his unit's life, he established goals, assessed his unit's status, and developed specific programs to move the unit forward. Each quarter, as part of his written guidance to subordinate commanders, he covered not only conventional training programs as prescribed by doctrine, but deployment and soldier and family-care programs as well.

With this approach, he began to address routinely the <u>full</u> scope of his vision. Conducting periodic maintenance services on tanks in the motor pool and bolstering the unit's family support group took their place alongside traditional training tasks such as tank gunnery and platoon battle drills. In this way, he linked everything he expected of his unit with specific programs, thereby bridging the gap for his subordinates between his long-range vision and their quarterly work-plan. This approach to developing and implementing an integrated plan of action marks the most effective leaders. They know where they want to go and how to get there.

Of course, a leader must be versatile enough to attend to both the long-term and more immediate requirements of the organization. The most effective leaders are able to shift their attention from their long-range objectives to the enabling programs and back again to ensure consistency. They scan the horizon one minute and focus intently the next. They suffer neither from near sightedness nor farsightedness. In times of crisis, they block out everything but the problem at hand, then once the situation is stable they are again thinking ahead in time, anticipating what may come next. Over time, they compile a "rolling assessment" that measures progress of day-to-day programs toward their objectives. They are able to strike an effective balance between providing so little program guidance that their organization operates without central purpose and so much guidance that there remains no room for initiative among subordinate leaders. This flexibility and sophistication does not come quickly for most; it is the product of training and experience that reflects a habit of matching vision to programs, and programs to vision. It marks the most effective leaders.

LEADERS VOTE WITH THEIR TIME

Army leaders at all levels are familiar with the maxim: "Units do well those things the boss checks."[6] Few contest its validity, but most come to recognize that it has an absolute limit: the leader's time. The most effective leaders I have observed understand that time is their most important — and most constrained — personal resource. The key point here is that a leader's time is a personal resource, one that may be controlled to a greater extent than many other resources such as budget, materiel and personnel. As such, how a leader chooses to spend his time is one of the most important factors in determining his effectiveness.

The most effective leaders "vote" by spending their time on the programs that matter most. They understand that they are leading every day by means of what appears on their schedule and what they actually do. Subordinates assess where the leader spends time and they draw conclusions about the leader's priorities. Most important, this occurs whether or not the leader intends it to be so. In practice, the leader's schedule becomes one of the most revealing documents for an organization: there is no clearer statement of what is important and what is not. For example, one senior combat arms leader emphasized the importance of routine "command maintenance" periods each week as a way to improve the operational readiness status of his unit's fleet of vehicles and aircraft. The program lagged until he began to show up at these maintenance sessions and to engage his subordinate commanders on maintenance issues. He voted with his time; his subordinates got the message, and the unit's readiness posture improved significantly.

Given the importance of a leader's time, what factors influence when and where the leader commits his vote? The most effective leaders select carefully the events to which they commit their time — they cast their vote with great discretion. These leaders may not be as attracted to a "great event" as they are to preliminary, more routine, less sensational events. They understand that their time may be as well, and perhaps even better, spent during the mundane preparatory phases of a program as compared to the high visibility grand finale. During a three-month tank gunnery program, for example, one leader devoted as much of his time to early preparatory training as he did to the final live-fire qualification events, the gunnery equivalent of the Olympics. This leader understood that the foundation of successful gunnery lay in the fundamentals that are drilled repeatedly at the lowest levels, so he voted by visiting and even participating in low-level gunnery classes and in early training sessions in crew gunnery simulators.

He knew that showing up for the final qualifications was important, but he also knew that by then his vote would not have the same weight as it did earlier.

In other words, when final qualification was at hand, the die already had been cast. This leader understood that in the case of the gunnery program his ability to influence the outcome with his presence had diminished over time. He chose to vote early, when it mattered most.

As a leader, your time is constrained. You only have a limited number of votes, and not everything can require your vote all the time. The most effective leaders make sure that their organizations do routine things to a satisfactory standard routinely. The result is an organization that operates at an efficient, sustainable pace, which then allows the leader to spend time with discretion on high-payoff activities. Establishing an organization's routine can dominate the leader's time initially, but, once set, routine activities need only be sustained with occasional leader involvement. One technique for sustaining routine activities is to delegate responsibility to key subordinates such as a deputy, command sergeant major or chief of staff. Essentially this means the leader votes by proxy; subordinate leaders demonstrate the leader's interest in the routine activity. Occasionally, the leader may find the need to "refresh" a proxy by spending time directly on a routine activity — ideally with the proxy present — to remind the organization of the importance of the activity and the role of the proxy.

In deciding where to spend time, a leader constantly faces the choice between accepting a new activity as a priority to which he will commit his vote, rejecting it outright, or perhaps adding it to the routine category and designating a proxy. My observation is that leaders tend to accept new activities and seldom reject any. Leaders tend to be activists. One way that a leader can expand the number of activities attended to personally is by increasing those handled concurrently while decreasing those handled sequentially. This increase in concurrent activity is more typical the higher the level of leader. Senior leaders tend to handle many priorities concurrently; indeed, they usually cannot afford to act sequentially.

At face value, increasing the leader's own ability to influence the organization with concurrent activity makes sense. It seems like a sure way to enhance the leader's effectiveness, in effect granting him additional votes. A pattern of increasing concurrent activity can, however, prove a hazard to the entire organization. A shift to concurrent activities allows the leader to influence more actions, but also increases demands throughout the organization. As concurrent activity replaces sequential, pace and complexity increase. This demands increased capacity, endurance and synchronization from the organization. Taken too far, the result can be that the organization feels as though it is drinking from a fire hose; it is doing a great many things, but not to a very high standard and with little satisfaction. This may be caused by a leader equating his own capabilities to those of the organization. While these capacities may be close at lower echelons, they can differ markedly at higher levels of command. Effective leaders monitor the pulse of their organizations. They do not allow the concept of voting with their time to create hyperactivity within their units.

An example from a combat action in Vietnam summarizes well this point about how a leader spends his time. Lieutenant Colonel Hal Moore noted after heavy fighting in the Ia Drang valley in November 1965 that throughout the three-day operation he found himself repeatedly considering three questions: what is happening, what is not happening, and what can I do to influence the situation?[7] Even in the stress of prolonged combat and heavy casualties, he was considering how he could contribute to focusing the energy of his command toward a common end. He was assessing constantly where he should vote with his precious little time.

LEADERS ARE WHO THEY ARE

From this follower's perspective, the single characteristic that most distinguishes effective leaders is that they are genuine: they are who they are. Effective leaders typically combine many of the personal characteristics cited in books on leadership. For example, the Army lists 11 principles for leaders — including the need to make sound and timely decisions, set the example, and build the team — and effective leaders seem to employ most if not all of these. While these principles might be considered as baseline attributes, they are necessary but not sufficient for the *most* effective leaders. In my experience the best leaders are those who *genuinely* possess the required attributes of competence and character. In short, they are authentic. Being a leader is not merely a role that they are playing; it is who they are.

Genuine leaders are most effective for several reasons. First, they know themselves. They appreciate their own strengths and weaknesses and can take these into account when assessing their role in the organization. Honest self-assessment leads to self-confidence, humility, and respect for the contributions of others; it is the foundation of character and a prerequisite for self-improvement. Genuine leaders recognize their own passions, their sources of energy and enthusiasm. This is the first step in translating their own personal enthusiasm into energy for the entire organization.

Second, genuine leaders demonstrate a continuity between what they say, what they do, and who they are. Their followers know that what they see is what they get. Further, there exists a continuity between what genuine leaders ask of others and what they require of themselves. They share the hardships of their subordinates. Leaders who have this quality of internal consistency are credible to their subordinates. This credibility between leaders and followers is a key ingredient in building teams founded on mutual respect and trust.

Again, the best example of this kind of genuine leadership that I know of is Hal Moore and the Seventh Cavalry. General Moore trained the unit, deployed it to Vietnam, and fought with it in fierce combat against North Vietnamese regulars in the Ia Drang valley in 1965.[8] Ever since then and for over 30 years now, Hal Moore has displayed genuine concern for the men of his battalion and their families. He serves as the honorary colonel of the regiment, participates in veterans' association events around the country, has dedicated years of research and writing to commemorate his men's valor in battle, and even sponsors a scholarship for their family members. He loves his men, and they and their families love him.

Why? Because he is genuine. Over many years, he has been consistent in his care for their well-being — before, during and long after their combat actions in Vietnam. They trust him.

CONCLUSION

In conclusion, I offer two final observations. First, the three attributes highlighted here are all at the discretion of the individual leader. These leader characteristics are not dependent upon the hand the leader is dealt; they are largely independent of circumstances. These attributes are a matter of personal choice; it is up to the individual leader to develop them. Second, taken one at a time, the three attributes may seem obvious and unimpressive. When considered as a whole, however, they are much more powerful and illuminate the essence of effective leadership. In my experience, it is rare indeed to find leaders who provide both vision and a plan, who vote effectively with their time, and who are who they are. These distinguished few feature continuity between what they say (their vision and plan), what they do (how they vote with their time), and who they are. If one dimension is neglected or inconsistent with the others, the leader's impact is diminished greatly. When these three dimensions of leadership are consistent — when they are synchronized — the leader's effectiveness is magnified. From a follower's vantage point, the difference is all too clear.

Chapter Sixteen

The Battle of Oom Chalouba, 17 June 2008:
The Leader's Role in Preparing Units for the Physical Demands of Combat

By Mark P. Hertling

1537 HRS. SOMEWHERE BETWEEN N'DJAMENA AND CHALOUBA.

"Well, guess it's time to see how tough we really are," LTC Steve Cash thought as he gazed at the IVIS-2A in the console of his M17 Battle Command Vehicle (BCV). All the soldiers, vehicles, and aircraft of his small Strike Force — the first organization of the Army's new structure to be deployed in harm's way — were moving toward Chalouba. The display showed his unit spread on a frontage of over 30 kilometers and a depth nearing 50 kilometers.

He held his anxiety in check and decided he needed to again show outwardly the confidence he had in his soldiers as they headed toward their first battle. "Never ceases to amaze me," Cash said aloud and vibrantly to his crew over the intercom. "When I was a young buck, we did a lot of things differently than we're doing now.   Our Task Force moved in a desert wedge, we used radios incessantly, and we certainly weren't as physically prepared and well trained as all of you. I'm tellin' ya, I almost feel sorry for those guys were about to face...we've got the most advanced equipment, the best training, and the toughest soldiers that ever came together on the field."

"Sure you're right, sir," interrupted 1LT Jim Ross, the Enemy Operations Officer seated next to Cash in the BCV, sensing his commander's intent to reinforce the crew's already high confidence level. "This is gonna be a walk in the park."

Doctrine, tactics, leader development and unit organizations had all changed in the late 1990s because myriad visionaries had efficiently coordinated emerging technologies with new ways of applying force on the battlefield. While exotic alloys, more powerful engines, unique weapon systems and the computer chip had all contributed to many of these changes, all of the new technologies were synchronized through digitization. This form of burst communication had revolutionized the way combat systems were controlled and the way soldiers were commanded. The centerpiece to digitization was IVIS. The early version of the inter-vehicular information system had undergone numerous product improvements and had since become the user-friendly computer officially known as the IVIS-2A, to which LTC Cash now devoted his attention while mentally checking off the other readiness indicators which were drawing his interest.

The IVIS-2A, the centerpiece of the console inside the BCV, represented a quantum leap in tactical communications. A decade before, the Army's ability to produce and disseminate operations orders had advanced little from the Napoleonic era. Staffs spent hours writing or typing and then reproducing orders that were disseminated either by courier or by subordinate leaders driving to the command post to get the document and receive a briefing. Satellites and the microchip changed all of that. The database inside the computer contained precise topographical information of the entire world. By inputting a few coordinates, a map would appear on the screen. The commander could modify the scale of the map to meet his needs, draw graphical control measures to orient his forces, and input suspected enemy positions. In addition, he had a "text box" in which he could write a brief operations order. Once complete, he could send the information to his unit with a simple keystroke, bring his subordinates into a video-teleconference, and issue his guidance. What used to consume 6-12 hours in developing a plan, and then typing, reproducing, and disseminating it, was reduced to about two. As the speed of information flow rippled throughout the echelons of the organization, the pace of military operations increased by an order of magnitude.

Since each vehicle and dismounted soldier had a tracking device linked to a satellite, the IVIS-2A also showed the location of friendly units on the screen, as well as their supply and maintenance status. In addition, once enemy vehicles and soldiers were acquired by the many sensors in the unit, such as Unmanned Aerial Vehicles (UAV) and sensors on-board vehicles and aircraft, their type and location went into the database and appeared on the screen as well. As a result, each vehicle had a clear picture of friendly and enemy locations that greatly improved the awareness of each leader and crewmember. With data-links to fire support units, the commander could "click" on an enemy unit or location and bring indirect fires quickly and accurately to bear. Furthermore, the command vehicles also had a "stealth" device linked to the database that enabled the commander to observe terrain and both friendly and enemy vehicles cybernetically.   The ability to transmit orders and graphics rapidly and to visualize the battlefield more clearly gave leaders tremendous capabilities.

But Cash knew there was more to applying force on the battlefield than just making use of new technologies. So while he was known as one of the new generation of leaders who many said had helped usher in the tactical application of the so-called "revolution in military affairs," Cash saw himself as a pragmatist who had tempered the new technologies and vision for improved combat maneuver with the way he knew great soldiers had always been trained and led. Cash knew combat as a life and death struggle, and only the best trained and the most fit would survive. He had found that out up close as a brand new second lieutenant.

Eighteen years earlier, Cash had reported to his first unit straight out of the Armor Officer Basic Course. He was cocky, anxious to taste some of the famous German beer he had heard so much about, and he was ready to learn. Exactly three weeks after reporting, his learning curve became very steep, indeed. His cavalry squadron would deploy from the rolling hills of Bavaria to the flat desert of Southwest Asia.

Cash did well as a young cavalry platoon leader. In his two months in theater prior to the initiation of combat, he developed a strong sense of teamwork in his scout platoon. His soldiers saw him as a strict but fair leader and a hard trainer. His noncommissioned officers (NCOs) willingly taught him all they could in the short period they had before crossing the berm into Iraq. His superiors saw in him a tactical and leadership savvy that few of the more experienced lieutenants had. In battle he performed well. He kept his cool on the radio and even personally knocked off two T-72s and a BMP during one of the night engagements. He wound up doing more in his first three months of active duty than many officers do in a lifetime.

But a few things bothered him as he reviewed his unit's battle-field performance after their redeployment. They were good, but they could have been better. His peers chided him for finding fault with what they all saw as the best force ever to face combat, but Cash knew that even the most brilliant diamond could always use some polishing; the best teams can always find ways to improve.

He had learned this many years earlier. Cash had been an extremely competitive and gifted athlete throughout high school and college; he had been to, and won, many championships. He had been shown how to train and compete, and he had been taught that the best prepared — physically and mentally — would always come out on top.

He had some great coaches who knew techniques that made individuals and teams winners: ensuring no lulls in practice, mak-ing the drills tough, preparing for the unexpected, analyzing what they wanted to do and tailoring their practices to address every aspect of their game plan, determining the specifics of each indi-vidual's strengths and finding a way those strengths would con-tribute to the team's performance, conditioning the mental respons-es. As he saw it, he was still a competitor, but now he was also assuming the role of the "coach" for whatever organization he found himself leading. While the competitive struggles he had been through in his past athletic career had been important, he knew there was no more important contest than the life and death struggle of combat. Cash came to the realization that the lives of his soldiers would depend on how he could emulate the methods that all his great teachers and coaches had shown him. He vowed he would never allow any soldier in his unit to be physically, men-tally or emotionally unprepared for struggles of combat as long as he held the mantel of leadership.

In the summer of 1994, Cash headed to the Armor Officer Advance Course with a newfound sobriety concerning his respon-sibilities. He knew the profession of arms was for him, and he knew he wanted to continue preparing to be the best company commander in the Army...the advance course would help him with that. But he also reported with a strong bias about training, organizing for combat and training soldiers for the modern battlefield, and he wanted to spend some time further examining the issues he had begun to focus on in the desert of Southwest Asia.

As part of an Advance Course assignment, Cash used his combat experiences and his knowledge of high performing "teams" to put together a thought piece. In that paper, Cash used three battles — Hastings, Gettysburg and 73 Easting — as a means of developing a hypothesis that there were three key areas which successful leaders, throughout history, focused upon when preparing their forces for combat. He argued that leaders must train themselves how to properly maneuver compact forces on the battlefield, they must train their soldiers to engage and destroy the enemy efficiently with the weapons at their disposal, and they must determine the best ways to protect their soldiers before and during the battle. While the historical portion of the study was interesting, it was the conclusions about the leadership demands of the future that were most striking.

The article posited that in information age warfare, leaders would be faced with a new style of warfare for which they might not be ready. Using football as an analogy, Cash suggested that forces on future battlefields would no longer remain fixed in rigid formations; rather, individual vehicles and individual soldiers would be dispersed throughout the battlefield, like players being placed at different locations all over the field. Each would then be required to act independently to execute precise maneuvers and actions that would contribute to the success of the entire force. While technology would contribute — the control of the force might be easier and weapon probabilities of target hits would continue to improve due to emerging technologies — the preparation of the force, and specifically the preparation of individual soldiers, would be much more challenging. Teamwork would be required as never before, and all members of the team would be required to perform as world-class athletes. In smaller, more independent forces roaming the new digitized battlefield, the physical and mental capabilities and the skill competencies of the individual soldier would be paramount.

Many others who made predictions about the information age battlefield suggested these new forms of maneuver would require a bevy of button-pushing soldiers who performed their duties in near-sanitized conditions. But CPT Cash knew better. The precocious young officer knew that the information age would be much more physically and mentally taxing on the soldiers who bore the brunt of combat. There would need to be monumental changes in the training and leader development realms before the advantages of the information age were fully incorporated into the fighting force.

But how best to prepare himself as a leader and to train his soldiers who would be, by necessity, comparable to the world class athletes he had once seen rising to the top of their sports? How did leaders in the past best train their units for the demands of combat, and how could he improve on that training?

Cash searched for answers to his first question. He found an historical study conducted at the US Military Academy which showed a high correlation between success in combat and the physical conditioning and health of combat leaders.[1] Successful leaders, firmly in control of their units and recognized as such, were more often than not physically fit themselves. Their positive self-image, which researchers had repeatedly found went hand-in-hand with fitness and physical readiness, was successfully transmitted to their soldiers. In tough, rugged and physically prepared units, soldiers were more capable of overcoming minor illnesses, the stress of long periods in the line, and battle fatigue than most other units in a theater of war.

While the West Point study stressed the importance of fitness in successful combat units, Cash found it frustrating that it gave few examples of commanders relating their physical readiness goals to soldiers through specific training programs. He knew he had a correlation, but felt he must search further to find *how* the most effective leaders had prepared their soldiers for the demands of combat in the past, so he could apply it to his hypothesis about the future. It did not take him long to discover numerous examples in history which would help him refine his style.

He found his first example in an 18th century Russian infantryman who also was adapting to the changing nature of warfare in his time. After taking command of the Suzdal Regiment in 1762, Alexander Suvorov began developing new tactical methods based on the prevailing consideration of speed and surprise.[2] While many of his contemporaries believed speed to be correlated with disorder and a lack of adequate support, Suvorov felt that controlling the tempo of operations — especially unexpected quickness — would multiply the effectiveness of any tactical maneuver. He soon realized that he could not expect agility until his men were adequately conditioned through training.

In all types of weather and conditions, Suvorov would march his men repeatedly over prohibitive terrain to areas where they would conduct maneuvers. Where there were no obstacles, the Russian commander created them. Suvorov believed it critical to instill a high degree of self-confidence in his soldiers, and found he could accomplish that by ensuring they knew they were undertaking physical demands that were different and tougher from every other army in the world. Even after being chastised by Catherine the Great for suddenly storming a hilltop monastery in his training, Suvorov explained that soldiers loved to be trained hard if they understood what they were being trained for; upcoming battles in the Swiss campaign would necessitate storming impregnable heights. Catherine relented.[3]

Cash was fascinated by the accounts of Suvorov's training and battles. Just as this Russian found it critical to gear his training for all the unexpectedness of war, so was Cash convinced that he had to incorporate tough conditions in his training regimen. Historical works describing other commanders — Mikail Dragomirov, Stonewall Jackson, Terry Allen, Lucian Truscott — men who trained their charges for the physical demands of combat, confirmed Cash's primary principle: Soldiers and leaders who train for the specific physical activity and demands expected of them will perform exceedingly well in battle. Demanding physical training based on what soldiers can expect to experience in combat prepares them and their leaders to overcome much of the physical stress related to combat.

In researching the physical stresses of combat and the way historical figures had sought to overcome those pressures through demanding training, Cash stumbled upon other historical figures who had addressed other aspects of combat — that of overcoming fear on the battlefield. Theorists like Clausewitz, Ardant Du Picq and S.L.A. Marshall were among some of the first to notice and then address a distinct physical relationship between fear and the ever-present fatigue found in soldiers facing combat.

From his days as an athlete, Cash was very familiar with the concept of fatigue; his inability to push himself further had made a "coward" of him more than once on the fields of friendly strife. But he did not know much about how fear affected the soldier on the battlefield. He was amazed at the physiological reactions caused by both fatigue and fear.

Physiologists know what happens in the body to cause fatigue: junctions between nerves and muscles fail due to the depletion of various chemical transmitters. Lack of oxygen and an inadequate blood flow cause the contractile mechanisms of the muscles to fail, and the central nervous system's sensory nerves send inhibitory signals to the nerve cells in the body's motor system.[4]

The individual can prepare to overcome all those effects with specific, intense and increasingly demanding training that prepares the body for the exertion that causes fatigue. For Cash, it was simple: Exacting, unrelenting and proper physical training will prepare soldiers for the fatigue experienced in combat.

With fear, an increased heart rate, increased muscular tension, increased blood sugar level, and increased number of reactionary signals from the brain cause a massive dumping of damaging hormones within the body.[5] While the Army had sometimes conducted such training they called "battle inoculation" in an attempt to help give soldiers a degree of mental toughness, they had never really addressed the issue of how to overcome fear in combat. Additionally, sports psychologists had found that even highly trained athletes, at the peak of conditioning, were still affected negatively by pre-competition stress anxiety, or fear. No amount of physical conditioning could diminish the effects of fear. However, some experiments involving mental relaxation training and progressive imagery techniques with athletes had, in fact, helped them to overcome the impact of pre-race jitters.[6] Could we utilize similar techniques for preparing soldiers for both the physical and psychological demands of the battlefield?

As early as his advance course years, Cash began developing these theories and began incorporating them into his training concepts, his leadership style and his command philosophy. They would contribute to victory on this hot, African day.

1615 HRS. THE BATTLESPACE CONTROL CENTER (BCC).

Major Mike Lloyd watched from the steps of the C4V (Command, Control, Communications, and Computers Vehicle) as SGT Leon Moss brought the Pegasus back behind his head, then threw it forward like a child throwing a paper airplane. When it was eight feet above the ground, the engine of the Unmanned Aerial Vehicle

(UAV) kicked in and a small red light appeared behind the tail, indicating the daylight TV camera was on. It headed northeast toward the objective.

"That's one small launch for me, one giant launch for the Strike Force," SGT Moss said with a smile as he gave the thumbs up sign to his Deputy Commander. Lloyd grinned as he remembered Moss the first day he reported to the unit.

Entering the service, Leon Moss was a product of his society. Soft from too many video games and too little physical activity, he had enlisted in the Army for challenges he knew he would never find in civilian life. During his one-station unit training, he performed exceedingly well in the classroom learning the skills requisite to his desired military specialty of "information analyst" (IA), but he barely met the physical standards associated with basic soldier qualifications. The rifle qualification ranges and forced marches were tough, but passing that damned PT test was nearly impossible. During the last week of basic training, however, he eked out a passing grade and thought he had seen the last of such physical demands. He was wrong. He was going to LTC Steve Cash's unit.

Moss was the only IA the unit had, and LTC Steve Cash had given MAJ Mike Lloyd the mission of ensuring this new asset to the small staff was combat tough and mentally ready. Within six months of reporting to his new unit, then-PFC Moss knew that constant training — in his staff skill and the related physical skills needed by every soldier — would make him the professional that he now knew he wanted to become. Within two years, SGT Moss was one of the most competent and ready leaders in the small task force. He got that way through a lot of hard work, the charismatic leaders that he had as supervisors, and some tough, combat-related training.

Each generation of leaders believes the soldiers they are asked to lead come from a "soft" society. Additionally, many leaders believe that the training new soldiers undergo prior to reaching their first unit of assignment is never demanding enough and falls short of producing the tough, combat-ready soldier that every organization desires.

LTC Steve Cash had heard both of those opinions from his seniors as he progressed through the ranks, but his time spent as a major in a training unit — and, as always, some additional study — showed him a different side to the story.

During one of his many trips to the library while a student at the Command and General Staff College, Cash stumbled upon an interesting study commissioned by the federal government but completed by a civilian academician from the University of Pittsburgh.[7]

In 1945, the federal government found that 45% of all selective service registrants at the outbreak of World War II did not possess the physical or mental health qualities necessary for armed service. The professor charged with conducting the study quickly found and revealed that after every major war in our nation's history — dating from the Revolution — lawmakers in both Houses of Congress sought appropriations for physical and military training for the youth. In every instance, these bills were initiated because of inadequate fitness levels shown by those conscripted at the start of the wars.

Rather than attacking the civilian sector for a lack of preparation for combat, the University of Pittsburgh monograph suggested that the military relook their own physical readiness programs. After all, soldiers had only a short time in initiation training to prepare for the demands which would be placed on them during their careers as soldiers in combat ready units. The Army took the recommendations and rewrote the physical training manual.[8]

Cash searched for both the 1941 and 1946 version of the physical training manual in the bowels of the Leavenworth library. He was amazed to find the 1946 version, which incorporated many of the lessons learned in combat concerning the physical *readiness* of soldiers, was much different from the 1941 version that only emphasized physical fitness. Most of the 1941 manual focused on physical fitness testing, while the 1946 version emphasized drills, exercises and training that prepared soldiers for the physical and emotional demands of combat. He made another note in his soldier's notebook to ensure that he supplemented those things found in doctrinal manuals with a healthy dose of common sense.

Like any good leader, Cash was interested in all of his soldiers receiving passing scores on the physical fitness tests. But he was more interested in preparing his soldiers for combat. Meeting the demands of the battlefield required strength, cardiovascular conditioning, neuromuscular and motor learning skill. All of his soldiers would be trained as world class athletes in their specific "event" and they would all be preparing for the competition of their lives as a part of a bigger "team." After all, medics who might be required to carry a wounded comrade over a difficult battlefield needed different physical skills than a truck driver delivering supplies or a tanker slamming rounds into a gun tube. Each would need different kinds of physical and mental training, just like any group of athletes performing different events on the same team. Training them in all the same techniques would be like requiring a javelin thrower to run repetitive 400-meter intervals. Yeah, it was great that they passed the PT test, but all soldiers in Cash's unit — like SGT Moss — knew the real question centered on the ultimate demand: Could that soldier do his or her job, without failure or fatigue, when the bullets started flying.

As he helped his subordinate leaders plan their specific training programs in the first few months after he took command, LTC Cash made sure each leader considered the specific physical and emotional stresses that their soldiers would experience in combat. He wanted his subordinate leaders to determine the toughest conditions in which the soldiers might be asked to do their job, and then to prepare physically and emotionally for that occasion. This became an ever-present drill in weekly training discussions, and it paid off. SGT Leon Moss was now one of the many individual success stories, as he had become one of the "world class athletes" in his particular event that would contribute to the Strike Force "team's" upcoming victory.

And while undergoing all the tough physical and mental preparation for combat, SGT Moss actually maxed his PT Test as well.

1727 HRS. IN THE CAB OF L-21 (A FUEL-PALLETIZED LOAD SYSTEM HEMMT)

SPC Kellie Reese was daydreaming as she rolled across the grassy plain. She was remembering her father's visit back before the deployment. CSM (retired) Daniel Reese had always been very proud of his daughter, but he seemed especially so as she showed him around and introduced him to all her friends on his first weekend at the post. Then, during the week, Kellie was able to get special permission for the old Sergeant Major to view some of the unit's daily training. He had to admit they were treating him like a VIP. It might have had something to do with the fact that he had been the post Command Sergeant Major right before he retired.

He also had to admit he was very proud of his youngest daughter. She was in a high-speed, high-tech unit — no volleyball and grabass in this organization — and the old Sergeant Major was duly impressed. Things weren't quite the way he had left them. Many of the predictions about the "information age" army were obviously coming to fruition, but there were some interesting side effects as well.

"I can't believe how much electronic gear is in a fuel truck," CSM Reese had commented the day SPC Reese had snuck him into the motor pool and showed him the HEMMT, her name proudly stenciled on the windshield. Then he was amazed even more as he watched her speed her huge rig through the unit's weekly driver's rodeo, which took place on a mounted obstacle course. He watched

her control her equipment on the back deck of the huge truck —
which took a great deal of physical strength — and he drove with
her as she conducted something she called an individual resupply
action. It was obvious that she was part of a tough team, and she
had the skill competencies to outperform many of her comrades.

"You take care of this stuff, Kellie," her father advised, "and you
keep training the way your NCOs are teaching you. This equipment,
and this tough training, just might save your ass some day."

The "electronic gear," as her father had called the tactical displays and the telepresence package in the cab of her vehicle, had
already done just that on several occasions in this conflict. During
one episode, Reese was on her way to deliver fuel to a Comanche
in Strike Team Bravo when she received a warning from the Strike
Force's BCC. The "Alert" message across the bottom of her IVIS-
2A screen indicated the presence of land mines and a suspected
enemy rocket team along the path she was taking to the helicopter. On the map above the message, the Support Cell in the BCC
had conveniently plotted a new route for her to follow so she could
accomplish her mission. As she drove along the new route she saw
friendly artillery striking, eliminating the hazards identified just a
few minutes earlier.

The incorporation of all this advanced technology in support
vehicles had occurred as a matter of necessity over the previous
decade. In the evolving operational doctrine — the latest version
of FM 3.0 was published in 2005 — combat service and service supporters were told they needed to operate as independently and
with as much agility as their sister combat forces. Long, lumbering
fuel convoys and time-consuming resupply operations were not
tolerated in the high- tempo operations of the information age.

So emerging technologies were fielded in service and service
support units, and supporters became an integral part of the combat arms strike force. The Army leadership had discovered
economies and efficiencies in all this new technology and true combined arms warfare. For example, by knowing the maintenance

and supply status of each vehicle, the Support Cell could send direct data-burst messages to independent logistical vehicles that carried the needed items. The Army thus eliminated excessive stockage of various classes of supply once thought necessary to sustain extended combat operations, and exponentially increased the speed and effectiveness of logistical operations.

But with all these changes in technology came challenges in training and preparing support soldiers for independent operations. For example, women — who, because of societal and armed forces demographics, still made up a large percentage of support units — had once been excluded from service in Infantry, Armor and Cavalry units. But now women were integral team members in the new combined arms Strike Force. Additionally, because of the increased premium placed on independence, those who performed these occupational specialties needed requisite improvements in their skill competencies, mental endurance and physical strength.

Title IX — that 1970-vintage federal regulation which mandated equal female participation in sport — resulted in prolific research on the true physical and mental capability of women athletes. Army senior leaders used results from this research to overcome previously held biases on the integration of women into combat units. Using correct and challenging training techniques, leaders were capable of more effectively training female soldiers to execute all the demanding requirements associated with the improved technologies and new operational doctrine. It became apparent in this transfer of Title IX lessons that rugged, tough, well-conditioned, physically and mentally prepared soldiers — male or female — just like rugged, tough, well-conditioned, physically and mentally prepared world-class athletes, had a better chance of reaching their full potential and winning when put to the test.

1855 HRS. THE TURRET OF A-23
(AN M17 FIGHTING VEHICLE-HYPER GUN (FV-HG)
IN THE NORTHWESTERN SECTOR)

Irredentism. SFC Terry Brailsford had looked up the word in the dictionary right after he first saw it on a presentation at PLDC in 1999. The instructor had predicted it would be one of the many types of conflicts facing the Army in the 21st Century. Brailsford didn't know what it meant at the time, but now his force was deeply involved in that type of conflict. The current situation was somewhat confusing but for him and his platoon it all seemed to come down to helping a democratic nation retain newly found freedom against a group of thugs.

The battle that was raging less than twenty kilometers from his location was the result of these irredentist conflicts. Brailsford watched it evolve on the small screen mounted in his cupola. He closely followed the artillery crosshair as it centered on each of the enemy vehicle icons that appeared on his screen. That UAV that was new to the Strike Force — did the ole man call it Pegasus? — was probably seeing the enemy and reporting pin-point location to the BCV. He wasn't sure which Strike Force element was acquiring the targets — the robotic rovers from the scouts or the UAV — but one thing was certain: since he and his crew were close to the battle, they were going to be sent forward by their commander. With his Non-Line-of-Sight (NLOS) Hyper-Gun, he could engage targets fifteen kilometers away. It would be their first fight, but he knew they were ready.

The ability to "see" the enemy prior to an engagement was probably the most interesting aspect on the 21st Century battlefield. Determining and then confirming where an enemy was and what he was doing — sometimes with video images transferred into icons, other times with virtual reality displays — was the primary advantage of information age technology.

Battles fought in this manner did not last long. Once the enemy was found, it became a matter of bringing a variety of lethal platforms into weapons range and then presenting the enemy with a multitude of distasteful options. NLOS Hyper-Gun systems increased engagement ranges up to fifteen kilometers and afforded protection to the lightly armored FV-series vehicles. Instead of standing toe-to-toe with the enemy in a direct-fire fight, the FVs armed with a Hyper-Gun could remain masked behind terrain outside of the direct-fire range of an enemy tank. Gaining sensor contact at long range with UAVs, Air Cavalry, ground Scouts, and robots generated options for the commander to position forces and mass lethal fires. This had quickly become the hallmark maneuver of the U.S. Army and it was a new twist on the old targeting methodology: *detect, then decide, then deliver, then assess.* The switch was more than just a change in procedure; it was a difference in how leaders prepared for the demands of the battlefield.

Soldiers in his platoon had many more demands on their abilities than Terry Brailsford had when he was a young soldier. While there were still the requirements for mental alertness and the need to be in great physical shape (after all, Hyper-Gun rounds still weighed upwards of 60 pounds, maintenance on vehicles was still formidable and arduous physical labor, and there were still just as many — if not more — obstacles on the battlefield as ever), Brailsford knew his soldiers had more stresses than he ever had. But their leaders had also developed better ways to train them.

LTC Cash had addressed these issues many times in his leader "huddles." He had ingrained in his subordinate leaders the responsibility to provide their "world class athletes" (Brailsford always smiled when the Colonel used that phrase) with tough, demanding training. One of the things he said made particular sense: "You don't train 2008 Olympic athletes by using 1980 training methods."

Brailsford used the best training methods of the day. The charismatic sergeant had used every bit of his physical training periods to make his soldiers stronger and tougher. He always ensured his soldiers had partners that would push them to the limit of their abilities while he made mental note of the strengths and weaknesses of each member of his team. He approached every training event with a zeal that many of his peers soon emulated. For him, every opportunity to train was a chance to try something new that would relate to how his team could approach the fight when, not if, they were called.

Not surprisingly, he was the first in the Strike Force to try new training techniques that the Colonel had recommended.

LTC Cash had read about situational awareness training that NFL quarterbacks were using;[9] Brailsford started using those drills in the conduct of fire trainers and the platoon tactical trainers to help his gunners and vehicle commanders ignore cues that did not impact on their required actions.

The Strike Force Commander had also mentioned mental imagery and progressive relaxation skills that were used by most college athletic teams, and which had once been used by tankers preparing for international shooting competition in the 1980s.[10] He had seen the results of sensory overload and combat noise interference training in a conduct of fire (UCOFT) trainer when he was at the Armor Advanced Course. Brailsford pressed the commander for more details, and the young sergeant was soon incorporating training techniques that had his soldiers eliminating crew drill mistakes by visualizing successful gunnery runs.

His crews liked one particular technique, sensory overload training, and the best. In these drills, multiple sensory impulses (combat noise and excessive radio traffic, smoke, and light flashes) were fed into some of the advanced technology training devices they were using. The expected result was for the soldiers to ignore these impulses. At first the impulses worked as distracters, but his soldiers soon learned to ignore the disturbances and work through the sensory interference. His soldiers always had fun in these demanding training sessions, but more importantly they were being stressed beyond the level they would experience in combat. Brailsford did not understand his commander when he once mumbled "just like Suvorov" after viewing one of his training sessions, but it must have been good because the "old man" was smiling.

LTC Cash had passed these training suggestions — and more — to all the leaders in the Strike Force, and Brailsford had seen to it that these methods were incorporated into his crew training at every opportunity.   After all, the platoon sergeant would often think, that is what good leaders do who really care for their soldiers: ensure they always have an edge over any potential enemy. In just three minutes, SFC Brailsford was about to find out how much of an edge he had given his charges.

2231 HRS.   ON THE OBJECTIVE, NEAR THE TOWN OF CHALOUBA

LTC Steve Cash leaned against the front slope of his vehicle as he talked on the cellular to Major Mike Lloyd at the Battlespace Control Center. They had already discussed the success of the Strike Force and the potential follow-on missions. But Cash was still concerned about the western passages into their area of operations. If more of the enemy was foolish enough to enter the area across the plains, he wanted to be ready for them. The Commander and his Deputy chatted for a few more minutes about the maneuver, and then Cash touched the "off" key and put the phone in its holder on his web vest.

In the fifteen years since his attendance at the advance course, Cash had seen the Army go through incredible change. Many of the old black-boot soldiers would even say it was a greater change than that which had transpired between the Vietnam War and Operation Desert Storm. Cash didn't know about all that. He was just thankful there had been some leaders in this great Army who were visionaries and forward thinkers, and some leaders who could temper the vision with pragmatic training programs. Without them, the members of his small force would certainly not have had the decisive battlefield victory on this hot, African day. All his soldiers were alive and well, and they were probably talking in hushed tones — as all soldiers flush with combat victories always had — about those things they had accomplished. That was what being a disciplined, winning team was all about.

The impact of the information age was not just the technology. The microchip had influenced everything that was a part of this army. Doctrine, training, leader development, organization, and the way soldiers approached each battlefield task were all altered by the power of the small post-industrial miracle. It had even begun to influence age-old warfighting theory. The smart guys were now looking out over the next fifteen years to determine what to call the blend of offensive and defensive operations that this information age had allowed them to create. Yes, it certainly was a revolution in tactics and lethality, and in the ways battles were fought — but the smart guys would have to figure all that out for the Army of 2020. He would continue to concern himself with training the force.

Cash looked up at the darkening sky, and then pulled out his cellular to make another call to one of his subordinate leaders. He just wanted to tell him to be prepared for the upcoming fight. World-class soldiers always liked to have as much warning as possible before their next event.

Chapter Seventeen

Battle Focused Training

by Robert W. Cone

INTRODUCTION

Command of a battalion sized unit in the United States Army is an awesome responsibility. The serious burden of command lies ultimately in ensuring that the soldiers under one's care are prepared to perform their jobs in combat without needless loss of life. Fortunately, this is a burden that a vast majority of commanders escape simply because the call to arms will not come during their time at the helm. However, tested or untested, today's soldiers from the greenest scout to the most senior non-commissioned officer know whether or not they and their unit are tactically and technically proficient. A unit's true level of training readiness may be misunderstood by senior leaders, the Army system, or the commander himself — but rarely the soldier. The purpose of this chapter is to describe a system for generating small-unit excellence that places combat readiness and training as the driving force, the engine, of all activities in the unit. If we make focused, demanding, and realistic training our top priority, and invest our personal time and energy accordingly, the competencies generated will carry over into all aspects of our units. The bottom line in this process is to keep the system simple, tell people what you expect, trust them to do what is right, and focus on mastery of the basics.

DEFINING THE TRAINING CHALLENGE

The concept of "Battle Focus" as described in the Army's training doctrine means the process of directing training energies to accomplishing specific wartime missions. Leaders must establish with great precision the fundamental critical tasks that will enable the unit to perform its role in combat. "Focus" is the key: establishing a deliberate training program centered on mastery of core competencies.

Units cannot do everything well. Leaders who believe that they can are destined to delude themselves into thinking their units are better than they really are. Resources to train units are finite. We are limited by money, repair parts, facilities, and most importantly soldier training time. If we try to perform every conceivable task to standard, we are likely to be proficient at none. A leader's role lies in picking the right things in which to invest precious resources and focusing on training the tasks with the highest payoff.

What is success for a small unit? If we define tactical success in terms other than defeating an uncooperative enemy, we are taking the easy way out. While the US Army field manuals and training plans provide Training and Evaluation Outlines (T&EOs) that list the sub-tasks for a given mission, these are only a means to an end. They provide rigor and standardization in accomplishing a training task. They do not define success. In order to accomplish our mission successfully, we must accomplish training tasks against resistance provided by a living, breathing, and thinking Opposing Force (OPFOR) or enemy. Simply stated, in order to win you have to be able to beat somebody.

So how do we go about training units that are capable of winning against resistance? We must discipline ourselves to focus tactical training on complete mastery of a relatively small number of training tasks. Our ability to execute these critical tasks violently and aggressively at the section and platoon level provides the foundation for mission success. These tasks equate to a football team's ability to block, tackle, pass, and kick. No team is capable of winning regardless of the brilliance of the offensive and defensive schemes unless players are capable of executing the fundamentals. Yet, teams have been successful by executing very basic plays with superior performance at the player level. My premise then is that our focus for training at the battalion level should be on training platoons and sections that have mastered a handful of critical tasks that will always keep us in the game.

This would seem like a blinding flash of the obvious. Unfortunately, as simple as the concept may seem, it has proven incredibly difficult to execute. For some unknown reason, we are rarely content to demonstrate the commitment necessary to achieve actual mastery at the section and platoon level. Whenever we get close to proficiency at one level, we seem to want to move on to the next higher level of training. The reasoning behind this impatience is not at all clear. Whether leaders at the battalion level do not really understand what mastery looks like, or surrender to the pressures of limited resources and time, is irrelevant. The consequences of moving on so quickly is that we do not achieve the confidence necessary to execute with the precision, violence, and aggressiveness required to win against a determined enemy. We do relatively well at demonstrating proficiency against the checklists, but often come up significantly short in achieving the level of training required to accomplish our ultimate mission — winning on the battlefield.

ACHIEVING A TRAINING FOCUS

The thrust of battle-focused training is that we "cannot achieve and sustain proficiency on every possible training task. Therefore, commanders must selectively identify those tasks that accomplish the organization's wartime mission."[1] Given the demands created by the current world situation, there are an increased number of potential wartime and operations other than war (OOTW) missions spread across a decreasing number of available units. It is the commander's responsibility to "recognize the peacetime training limitations faced by subordinates and tailor wartime missions within these practical constraints."[2] At the same time, it is the subordinate commander's responsibility to notify the higher commander if he cannot accomplish all of the mission essential tasks to standard and request modification of mission requirements.[3]

The process for achieving Battle Focus is clear. However, the realities that commanders face in dealing with increasing possible contingencies and potential missions can be daunting. The key to maintaining Battle Focus in the face of these new realities is found in the Mission Essential Task List (METL) development process. The thought process behind selection of METL tasks includes a variety of important factors. The unit's role in specified war plans should clearly establish priorities for task selection. Again, the problem lies in the sheer number and variety of war plans in which a unit might be committed. In the absence of a clear contingency, a commander might select missions that highlight the unique features of a specific unit.

For instance, a Heavy Armored Cavalry Regiment or Divisional Cavalry Squadron would select tasks that relate to their unique capabilities in conducting reconnaissance and security rather than emphasizing missions that could be performed by an armored or mechanized infantry brigade or battalion. Ultimately, the commander is responsible for ensuring that wartime missions and related METL tasks are both consistent and achievable. We are far better off frequently changing our METL in the face of new world contingencies than providing a laundry list of tasks and letting our subordinates decide what is really important.

The problem with a METL that is too large at the brigade/regiment level is that it generates a pyramid effect at the battalion/squadron and company/troop level. Each subordinate level must identify supporting collective tasks that can rapidly become unmanageable unless we exercise discipline at the higher levels. Careful analysis of wartime missions and selection of truly essential tasks is the first step to achieving training focus at the battalion and company levels. Next we must focus our training energy at the platoon level on certain critical tasks that bring us to the highest level of proficiency for the overall training effort.

THE CRITICAL TASK APPROACH

Regardless of how difficult and complex we senior officers sometimes make the business of warfighting, reality at the platoon level must be quite different in order to be successful on the battlefield. Even the most difficult missions at the battalion/squadron level must be broken down in simple and achievable tasks at the platoon level. We don't need tank or scout platoon leaders who can impress their battalion commander with their ability to make things complex. We need platoon leaders who can make complex tasks simple for their soldiers.

Think about it. The most complex task in an armored cavalry squadron's METL is probably the Moving Flank Guard, in which the squadron must move at the same pace as the force it is protecting while orienting its attention perpendicular to its direction of movement. I could go into great detail about the complexity of maintaining contact with the main body, occupying battle positions on battalion sized avenues of approach, conducting reconnaissance forward of lead ground elements, moving units alternately or successively to battle positions, positioning fire support for a moving force, and all the logistics issues related to moving in a very restricted area. This is all very impressive and the principal reason commanders have two field grade officers and a staff to help think this through. But what does this mean to a tank platoon sergeant? I would submit it means little or nothing in terms of his success.

The business of winning at the platoon level means lethal execution of a handful of critical tasks. In general terms, the tasks that will guarantee success in this mission – moving, defending, and attacking – are the same tasks that provide success in a number or other, less complex missions. Battles are won at the platoon level. Our job in training is to focus the energies of platoons on mastering a set of simple, critical tasks which will lead to success in a variety of missions.

As a cavalry squadron commander, I experimented extensively with achieving a training focus. After a session in establishing my troop and company METLs, I called all my tank, scout, mortar, and battery leadership together. We reviewed the unit METLs and then asked them to identify a total of five or six platoon-type critical tasks that supported the unit METLs. In other words, what five or six tasks when performed to standard would ensure mission success? After about six hours of work, each group by platoon type made a presentation of critical tasks. Each task was presented in specific doctrinal terms tied to a specific set of tasks, conditions, and standards. For example, the tank platoon critical tasks were: Actions on Contact, Conduct Tactical Movement, Defend a Battle Position, Conduct an Attack by Fire, and Assault an Enemy Position.

By mastering these critical tasks we believed that our units could achieve success in all our specified METL tasks. I add special emphasis to the word "mastery." It was not just enough to meet standards marginally; rather, we wanted to be able to confidently, aggressively, and violently achieve these tasks against a competitive OPFOR. Mastery of these tasks would make us lethal enough to win.

THE SEQUENCE OF TRAINING PROFICIENCY

Once we had identified the appropriate critical tasks, we developed a training strategy to achieve proficiency. We believed a lane training methodology best suited our requirements for task mastery. Lane training focuses an organization's training activities on a limited number of training tasks conducted on a specific piece of terrain usually for a relatively short duration. OPFOR activities and conditions on the simulated battlefield are very tightly controlled by the commander conducting the training to bring out specific learning outcomes. Lane training provides a redundant methodology of task execution, assessment, remediation, and re-execution. The fundamental feature of this training approach is the ability to repeat lane iterations in order to truly master the training task.

The lane training methodology has some unique features that merit discussion. In addition to mastering a specific critical task, each lane must have a set of very specific training objectives. Stated another way, what specific learning outcomes do we want to see as the result of executing a lane? An understanding of these objectives, coupled with application of the critical training task, drives the commander's decisions regarding OPFOR play and lane conditions.

A lane focused on the critical task of "Actions on Contact" in which the unit commander adds OPFOR or directs OPFOR actions based upon the specific learning outcomes desired illustrates this concept. For instance, while the platoon is in contact with an enemy observation post, an anti-tank weapon would be used off a flank to emphasize the importance of disciplined scanning techniques or reconnaissance in depth. Key terrain can also be used to reward units for conducting proper movement and reconnaissance techniques. Platoons that find enemy observation posts or anti-tank positions first due to good reconnaissance, or minimize losses due to good movement and scanning techniques, and quickly return accurate and lethal fires, are rewarded by being able to move rapidly and seize key terrain before the enemy. Units that fail in these tasks receive high losses and ultimately must transition to defense before reaching key terrain and then face an enemy under more adverse circumstances.

The key to this training technique is to control the training variables in the lane so that you can make the platoon in training pay dearly for its mistakes and reap the rewards of meeting standards. Control of the OPFOR and the conditions of the battlefield are indispensable variables in this regard. The After Action Review

(AAR) is the vehicle used to draw out the lessons learned from the exercise. Blinking Multiple Integrated Laser Engagement System (MILES) lights, indicating a vehicle kill, and control of key terrain are the inherent punishments or rewards.

Most importantly, the lane provides the opportunity to do it all again correctly. Following the AAR, the training unit goes back to the drawing board for a quick rehearsal and a few modifications to the plan. The controlling commander resets the OPFOR and battlefield conditions with some minor modifications to the learning objectives. The lane is repeated again under the same tight control. With sufficient repetition and learning, the platoon departs the lane having achieved mastery of the task and the specified learning objectives.

My unit's experience with this training methodology has been rewarding. The first time we used this technique each platoon was required to spend an entire day on the initial task of Actions on Contact. My subordinates' initial response was not positive. They implied that I was perhaps a little simplistic in my overall approach to training. I resisted and demanded that each platoon find and kill the enemy in its lane without loss of a friendly vehicle. After four days of training, we had mastered our Actions on Contact drills at least in regard to several of the forms of direct contact. We did not know or understand it at the time, but we had begun to unleash the lethality that task mastery can create.

The squadron continued the exercise for the remainder of the month achieving mastery of each of the specified critical platoon tasks. Some platoons obviously did better than others but all demonstrated great progress. In retrospect, many of the non-commissioned officers in the platoons commented that this was the first time in their careers they had ever successfully conducted a Movement to Contact or Hasty Attack. By success, they meant more than getting lucky and achieving the objective, but actually getting the task correct with minimal casualties. Others, commented that most of their training events in the past had ended with a grueling "checklist" After Action Review after a 72 hour External Evaluation. They knew exactly what they had done wrong, but since there was never time to do it again, they had no earthly idea how to do it correctly.

GAINING THE COMPETITIVE DIMENSION — WINNING

At a certain point in this training process, the length of time varying with the maturity of the individual unit, the soldiers in the platoons develop a competitive dimension. They begin to project a sense of lethality beyond their physical presence on the battlefield. As the platoon matures in training, the leader can begin to focus more on enhancing the effects of platoon's weapon systems than on drilling their movement techniques. The platoon gains the ability to cast a shadow forward at the maximum extent of its weapon systems. Mastery of fundamental skills leads to lethal projection of combat power.

I would liken this process to watching the development of a high school football team as it evolves from pre-season workouts to post-season form. Initially, the team spends an incredible amount of time in getting its basic formations straight. The team's focus is more on getting everyone in the right place and looking good than on facing an opposing team. As time progresses, the team begins to attempt to run the same plays against resistance offered by an opposing defense or offense. The team struggles at first, but then begins to reap the benefits of disciplined execution. Ultimately, precise execution of the plays becomes second nature and the team's focus turns to exploiting the opposing team's weakness.

The development process in both organizations is remarkably similar. Both organizations must learn to execute processes with discipline and precision while ultimately dealing with an uncooperative opponent. The critical transformation occurs as the focus shifts from internal procedures to competing against a thinking and reacting enemy. Football teams achieve this proficiency through the redundancy of mastering plays in scrimmage. Tactical units achieve this level of proficiency through the redundancy found in mastery of critical tasks in the lane training methodology.

It is important to emphasize the distinction between using a live competitive OPFOR for the sake of competition versus using competition to reinforce standards of performance. Clearly, the intent is to use the challenge and excitement generated by competition to reinforce rigorous adherence to training standards. The intended lesson for soldiers and leaders is that the ability to perform critical tasks correctly — almost instinctively – while under pressure leads to success on the battlefield. Occasionally, units are successful against their opponent without performing to standard. In my experience, this probably reflects a failure in the design of the training event. The key point to remember is that nothing provides your soldiers more intrinsic reward and excitement than reaching their tactical objective against a tough opponent because their unit performed to standard!

The ramifications of a platoon achieving this level of proficiency are truly remarkable in terms of leadership and morale. Much like the outlook of a winning football team, soldiers believe they are capable of performing the most difficult aspect of their profession. All other activities begin to take on new meaning in light of their contribution to the platoon's warfighting capabilities. Home station maintenance and vehicle readiness are improved because we must have the combat power necessary to take the objective. Soldiers are less tolerant of malingering peers because every person is needed in the field to win. Sergeant's Time[4] is much more clearly focused because we now know which individual tasks provide the highest payoff toward the platoon's success. The ability to win on the battlefield becomes the central feature of the unit's existence. Battle focused training has become the driving philosophy of the organization — a philosophy of leadership.

No one feels worse than the soldier who is not confident in his unit's ability to conduct its wartime mission. Task mastery is so powerful because a vast majority of our soldiers are learning what "right looks like" in terms of skill proficiency for the first time. We are capable of achieving this end simply by focusing our training approach and doing it until we get it right. The violence, aggressiveness, and lethality generated in these platoons can lead to success in even the weakest squadron/battalion plan.

TRAINING MANAGEMENT

We have now talked about basic assumptions, establishing unit priorities, and a training methodology that focuses proficiency on mastery of critical tasks, the emphasis now is on describing how the overall system fits together. At the battalion/squadron level, the system that makes sense of it all is the training management system, specifically the conduct of a unit assessment and development of a quarterly training plan and training guidance. Effectiveness at keeping battle-focused training as the top priority is a direct reflection of the leader's ability to plan, synchronize, coordinate, and anticipate competing requirements.

First, the training management process must begin with a detailed, specific unit training assessment. A training plan will only be as good as the level of involvement and participation that the subordinates provide. Although evaluations of the company, battalion, and battle staff METLs are good yardsticks to use as a starting point, the real thrust of the battalion's analysis must be at the section and platoon levels. The technique I normally used was to analyze performance on a major exercise such as a National Training Center rotation and examine the unit's effectiveness in performing its critical tasks. I would normally learn a great deal in these sessions about which tasks needed to be emphasized, added, or changed in future training events. Generally speaking, the assessment process strongly reinforced the importance of Battle Focus and the "critical task" methodology. The real payoff from this process came from subordinate ownership in the training plan. Many senior non-commissioned officers reacted very positively when their ideas were captured in my training intent and objectives for the future quarter.

Second, in order to be effective training management cannot be limited only to training. The quarterly training plan development process contains all the mechanisms necessary to plan, synchronize, coordinate and resource all of a unit's activities for the upcoming quarter. The quarterly training plan must include every activity that involves the unit or has the potential to expend the organization's energy. As a commander, you must work extremely hard to reach out to every organization or activity that might place demands on your unit's time or resources. Getting this right is the most difficult aspect of the entire process. Many of the activities and functions that place requirements on a unit's time do not operate on the same planning cycle as tactical units. But often times asking agencies such as the Director of Community Activities, Officer Wives Club, Enlisted Wives Club, Red Cross, local school, etc. to specify dates of events and make their requirements known in your planning cycle allows you to coordinate more effectively and provide better support of worthwhile activities. In the end, your plan is only as good as your ability to anticipate and identify all possible demands.

Central to my argument is recognition that unit resources are finite. This point is particularly relevant as we move ahead with initiatives to increase predictability in our soldier's lives and reduce overall personnel tempo. What this means is that a commander had better know exactly how much time things will take because the training schedule must be something a soldier can rely on. It also means that leaders must avoid the practice of working late or on weekends to get the job done if they failed to plan properly. We should no longer rely on an ability to surge by working extended hours. Another key realization is that we will always have more things to do than we have time to accomplish them. In every quarter I planned as a squadron commander, I never had a "reserve" of time. I committed every available moment, frequently going back to my higher commander to take things off my plate. When you plan a quarter this full, it means that for every event added, something must be removed.

DEVELOPING A PLAN

The development of the commander's intent for the quarter and specific training objectives come next. This is where the commander makes sense of all the competing activities and develops significant themes for the quarter based upon the results of the training assessment. A good technique in developing the commander's intent is to focus on the quarter's end-state. Typically, the commander might state that the battalion will have a successful quarter if the unit safely achieves the following conditions by the end date. The criteria of success would normally focus on a mark-on-the-wall for major training events, safety, command inspections, or other significant unit activities. In a typical quarter, my desired end-state would generally focus on about 70% warfighting and 30% soldier care, administration, inspections, etc. The real test for an effective intent is the ability of any leader in the organization to articulate the unit's focus for expending energy in the coming quarter.

The commander then develops specific objectives based upon the training assessment for each event and activity occurring in the quarter. This is very serious business, and the commander needs to craft each objective personally. Remember, soldiers will do what you ask them, if you make what you want clear. Objectives are specific, measurable achievements that tell the your subordinates exactly what you expect of them. If your unit is going to spend time doing something, you need to take the time to tell them what you expect.

This is incredibly hard work. We are asking a commander to think through an entire 90 day period almost 60 days from its start and describe exactly what he wants. The very best commanders I have ever worked for had an uncanny ability to look at the upcoming quarter and lay out their precise expectations for every aspect of their unit's performance. These expectations empowered everyone in the organization to get on board and develop a plan to meet them.

Conversely, I have worked for commanders who could never be nailed down on what they really wanted. Despite my best efforts, I could not get them to focus on upcoming events and specify their expectations. They seemed to reserve the right to change their minds just prior to the execution of an event. This process wreaks havoc on well meaning subordinates who have spent countless hours writing memoranda of instruction and developing subordinate unit plans. While war is indeed the province of chaos and unpredictability, the proper place to train for this is in a well-designed exercise with a competitive adversary, not through poor planning and incompetence rationalized by "flexibility." A commander's failure to articulate expectations clearly indicates a lack of either self-discipline or of knowledge of the profession.

TRAINING EVENT DEVELOPMENT

The next major step in the process is designing training events and activities based upon objectives. Again, the commander must describe his vision for each specific training event or activity. The best technique is to begin with the high payoff, major muscle movement training events. The focus of every training event should be linked to the results of the training assessment and identified platoon "critical tasks" whenever possible. There must be a consistent application of your training methodology in every training event. Every staff section must be involved in this process as the end result of each of these discussions is a written order for training event execution. Numerous In Progress Reviews (IPRs) are normally required as the commander's guidance and intent is translated into a specific plan by the staff. The hardest part of this process is in designing a plan to meet the specified objectives given the constraints of time and resources.

As we move from major training event to more minor activities, the cast of characters involved becomes more diverse. The unit chaplain, physician's assistant, Family Support Group leadership, representatives from the Education Center, and Army Family Team Building are typical players in this process. Everyone involved has great intentions. The key to success lies in developing the organizational discipline to produce good ideas at the appropriate point required in the training process. This is difficult at first, but once institutionalized, fosters real enthusiasm for the planning process.

SYNCHRONIZATION AND SCHEDULING

The next major challenge is trying to fit all these events and activities onto the training calendar. A great technique is to use a synchronization matrix. Units from the battalion headquarters down to platoon level are listed on the vertical axis and dates are specified on the horizontal axis. Major training events and directed events from higher headquarters are addressed first. These are normally followed by routine events like command maintenance or Sergeant's Time training. Other events are then added as they best fit subordinate unit calendars. Scheduled services, inventories, and command inspections offer some degree of flexibility in scheduling. The synchronization matrix format provides immediate visibility of every activity in the battalion or squadron and makes obvious the best time to schedule key events like officer/non-commissioned officer professional development sessions, hail and farewells, or other unit-wide events.

The remarkable thing about this methodology is the recognition of how busy we really are. A typical quarter consists of thirteen weeks with 91 total days. Subtracting weekends and normally at least one long weekend, we are looking at an average of about 63 training days per quarter. If we assume one major field exercise or gunnery practice of four weeks duration, we are down to 43 days. Proper preparation and normal recovery take another 15 days. We are now left with a total of 28 days. We must also make allowances for other activities such as deployment readiness checks (1), scheduled services (10), red cycle commitments (a period mandated for external taskings) (5), drivers training (2), command maintenance (5), small arms qualification (2), and Sergeant's Time Training (5). We can quickly find ourselves over committed. The synchronization matrix technique allows us to immediately determine when we are over committed as well as when we have available time and units.

TRAINING AND LEADERSHIP OUTCOMES

The critical element in this approach to training management lies in the commander's responsibility for specifying training outcomes and managing time. Going back to our basic assumptions, we are holding commanders responsible for telling their subordinates what they want and allocating resources to accomplish these tasks. We take nothing for granted. Our subordinates will do exactly what we want if we clearly state our expectations. Each quarter of training has a major theme, specific expectations for performance, criteria for success, and a detailed allocation of resources and unit time. All of these products are specifically tied to our philosophy of small unit proficiency and the justification of the expenditure of time and energy toward that end. The quarterly training brief and synchronization matrix should be sufficiently detailed that a company/troop/battery commander could write training schedules for the entire quarter from the end product.

Dissemination of this product becomes the critical link in achieving predictability and establishing Battle Focused Training as a leadership philosophy. Every soldier in the unit must view this process, related objectives, and schedules as the driver of virtually everything that occurs in the unit. Once the contract is approved in the quarterly training brief at the battalion/squadron level, the process is repeated at the company/troop/battery level. This process, coupled with a series of briefings to non-commissioned officers, officers, and key Family Support Group members explaining the coming quarter's intent, objectives, and schedule, becomes the centerpiece of all unit activity.

The success of this approach can be measured by talking to the soldiers and family members in the unit. The most junior member of the unit should be able to discuss the major events of the upcoming quarter, why these events are important, the goals for each of them, and deployment and redeployment dates. Family members should be able to make reference to deployment dates, pre-deployment briefing dates, and understand in general terms why upcoming training events are important to their spouse's level of proficiency. Soldiers and family members who are fully onboard with the training plan are quick to pull out unit calendars from wallets or post quarterly calendars on refrigerators in the home.

This approach to training management differs in principal from what I will describe as the "weekly routine" approach. In our attempts to achieve greater predictability in soldiers' lives we have established a set of weekly or routine activities. For example, a unit does command maintenance on Tuesday mornings, Sergeant's Time on Thursdays, physical fitness training four days per week, inventories Monday afternoons, etc. Doing the same activity each day of the week can lead to greater predictability in a soldier's life, but it is only the start. The problem with this approach occurs when units fall into a thoughtless pattern of expenditure of unit energy and resources. In my experience, too many soldiers are marching to the motor pool on Tuesday simply because it is Tuesday, but without a plan or set of objectives. Too many soldiers go through the motions of routine Sergeant's Time training on Thursday mornings without seizing the opportunity to link into building proficiency in a "critical platoon task." Worse yet, many commanders are sitting in their offices thinking up "good ideas" while their greatest opportunity for conducting purposeful activity and mission essential training slips away in the execution of a routine.

The commander's purpose and objectives need to drive even the most routine events. When a soldier gets out of bed on Tuesday morning he should think "Command maintenance — Let's see, we are working on air induction system checks today because that will be critical to putting all four tanks on the objective in our upcoming NTC rotation." Routine is just one technique to help achieve greater predictability. Real predictability in units stems from understanding the purpose and objective of events and following a training schedule derived from a well-known training calendar. Planning focuses the energy of the organization in a purposeful direction.

CONCLUSION

Nothing in this chapter is new, revolutionary, or even original. Life in a unit makes a great deal more sense when it is driven by a common purpose instead of an unrelated series of processes, demands, and activities. Soldiers perform better when they understand what they are doing, why they are doing it, and how it will ultimately allow them to perform their key functions – functions that may ensure their survival in combat. Our training doctrine does a remarkable job of providing us with the framework, mechanisms, and processes to make this kind of focus and leadership a reality for our soldiers. This approach is based on understanding our purpose, mastery of platoon "critical tasks," and management of our expectations, energy and resources in order to achieve our organization's full potential.

As commanders, we need to demonstrate the self-discipline and commitment to our profession to put first things first. There is no doubt that a combat unit is endowed with incredible capabilities and resources. We can accomplish a great many things other than proficiency for our wartime mission with those resources. This is acceptable as long as it is built upon a base of proficiency in our unit's METL. Units which train well, understand how it all fits together on the battlefield, and are confident in their ability to win will generate the pride, morale, and esprit necessary to excel in all tasks. Conversely, units which divert essential resources and energy away from their primary mission to "look good" in a series of unrelated activities are playing a high stakes shell game. While few may get caught short by real world deployment or actual combat, the soldiers in the unit will always know if they were really ready. The soldier will always know the truth.

Chapter Eighteen

The Renaissance Force: Selecting Soldiers and Forging Teams for Special Operations

by Richard W. Potter and Kalev I. Sepp

Militaries need elite forces. Almost all successful armies have had some sort of select body of troops, or special units, that set a standard of martial excellence, gave the commander an extra measure of capability, and served both as vanguard and final reserve. From Alexander's Companions, to the Japanese Samurai, to the hand-picked light infantry companies of the imperial-era British Army, elite forces have often made the difference between victory and defeat in battle. Even the egalitarian "people's armies" of Revolutionary-era France eventually produced Napoleon's Old Guard. Today the US Army contains a formidable array of Special Operations Forces.

These include the Special Forces themselves, known as the "Green Berets," the Ranger Regiment, the 160th Special Operations Aviation Regiment (SOAR), and Army Special Mission Units

Elite military formations have long been the focus of popular and professional fascination.   The members of elite forces, to paraphrase Jean Lartéguy's description in *The Centurions*, are dedicated warriors to whom impossible tasks are given — and they are determined to succeed. Elite forces are innately synergistic: their commitment to military prowess builds on itself.   There is another dynamic to this cycle of excellence — a constant self-evaluation that drives a process of self-testing which leads to self-improvement, and in turn produces an internal re-generation of each discrete unit.   Elite forces, when properly motivated and led, are physically and intellectually at the edge of established operational domains.   They are the most likely to cross, then extend, the bounds of conventional wisdom.

One of the enduring challenges throughout my service in the United States Army was leading the supremely professional soldiers of special operations units.   They are self-motivated, keenly intelligent, and multi-talented.   Their tremendous personal confidence lends itself to strongly-held opinions, often very individual in nature.   Naturally, the potential exists for teams of this nature to suffer a fate similar to many athletic "all-star" teams — great individual performance within a disjointed team effort.   The 1998 U.S. Olympic Hockey Team, for example, fielded twenty-three of the very best professional hockey players in America, but could not win a single game at Nagano.   The stakes in the military profession, however, are much higher.   The consequences of poor team performance or destructive individualism are often both immediately and deadly.

If there is a short answer to the question, "How can these independent strong-willed personalities be made to work together as a team?" — the response is "Leadership."   If the question follows, as it should, "What skills and experiences do leaders need to find, select, train, and command special operations soldiers?" — the answer is longer.   I feel that for leaders of elite organizations, the necessary professional competence is gained only by a thorough understanding in the organization and functions of the larger institution. For the US Army Special Operations Forces, that is the United States Army.

My own career began as a draftee in 1960, and proceeded through the Fort Benning Infantry Officer Candidate School, to duty in a mechanized infantry battalion in Germany when the Berlin Crisis roiled up. Inspired by President John F. Kennedy's call to "bear any burden" and "oppose any foe" in the defense of liberty, I volunteered for the U.S. Army Special Forces. I was soon in Vietnam, leading an "A-Team" of twelve Americans as the cadre for a full battalion of Khmer Serai Cambodians. My later tour as an instructor at the U.S. Army Ranger School, while recuperating from wounds, qualified me to return as the senior advisor to the Vietnamese 35th Ranger Battalion, and subsequently serve in a light infantry battalion in the U.S. 25th Infantry Division.

Following two years of company command in the British Parachute Regiment, and two years auditing every training installation in the United States as a general staff officer, I commanded a mechanized infantry battalion at Fort Hood, Texas. After helping establish an Army special mission unit, and advising the Pennsylvania National Guard, I led the 10th Special Forces Group for nearly three years, overseeing missions to the Middle East, Europe, and Africa. Working as Director of Operations Group for the Army War College prepared me for duty as the Deputy Commandant of the U.S. Army John F. Kennedy Special Warfare Center and School. There I supported the implementation of a personnel selection and assessment process, which drew in part on my experiences in the British "Paras," the Ranger school, and the Army's special mission unit.

As the brigadier general heading Special Operations Command-Europe, I led a Joint Special Operations Task Force during Operation "Desert Storm," Task Force Alpha for Operation "Provide Comfort" (the relief effort in northern Iraq following "Desert Storm"), the Joint Task Forces supporting the evacuation of American citizens from Sierra Leone and Zaire (now Congo), and the security augmentation for the Barcelona Olympics. My final mission for the Army came when I was extended past my scheduled retirement date to command Task Force "Raleigh" during Operation "Restore Democracy" in Haiti.

These thirty-four plus years of service, much of it in active combat and on operational missions, has shaped my opinion about how to find, select, organize, and train elite soldiers for special units. While elite formations are often characterized by distinctive missions and attire that set them apart from their conventional counterparts, the true "magic" of an elite force is grounded in something much less glamorous: mastery and maturity. Elite soldiers and units are masters of the fundamentals of their trade, and they possess a maturity that is developed through training that emphasizes stress, uncertainty, and cohesion.

Mastery and maturity make the US special operations units a "Renaissance Force" — thoroughly grounded in the competencies and values of their profession while adaptable enough to thrive and excel in dangerous, chaotic, and often politically sensitive situations. This chapter focuses on the "Green Beret" component of the Special Operations Forces as a case study, but the principles for creating and sustaining an elite unit have relevance for virtually any kind of organization that wishes to maximize its own performance.

CREATING THE FORCE

Recruiting is necessary to find the right people for special operations; volunteerism by itself is insufficient. The Special Forces model is a total package, from initial individual accession to long-term unit sustainment. When the Army's Special Forces were modernized during President Ronald Reagan's military build-up program, which included Army Chief of Staff Shy Meyer's SOF Enhancement Program, four major changes were implemented to achieve a high-quality force. First, recruiting standards were formalized, setting objective measures of fitness, intelligence, proven performance and discipline, linguistic aptitude, *et al*. Recruiting was limited to within the Army, and only soldiers and officers with three years' service were eligible to volunteer. To ensure the search for talent was properly and aggressively conducted, the Special Warfare Center's recruiting office was completely overhauled. Four sergeants on temporary duty were replaced by ten professional "Gold Badge" recruiters, and the office's annual budget was raised from $20,000 to one million dollars.

Second, the three-week-long Special Forces Assessment and Selection process (originally called Special Forces Orientation Training) was designed, validated, and put in place. Third, the six-month-long Qualification Course was restructured; notably, the training standards for officers were raised.   Fourth, the Army markedly increased the "Operating and Maintenance" funds for special operations units, in order to sustain and enhance the level of training of the successfully selected and schooled officers and soldiers.   Understanding recruiting as an integral and extended procedure is essential to building and employing a world-class elite force.

Selecting leaders for special forces is both an art and a science. The U.S. Army's Special Forces Assessment and Selection (SFAS) and subsequent Qualification Course (the "Q") and language training, the Ranger Regiment's Ranger Indoctrination Program (RIP) and Ranger Assessment and Selection Program (RASP), and the 160th Special Operations Aviation Regiment's "Green Platoon" training are prime examples.   But an assembly-line "cookie-cutter" product is not the desired result.   Individuality must be maintained so the selected officer can exercise command in the context of his own personality.   This aspect of leadership development is an art, and cannot be prescribed by checklists and standardized testing.

An officer in Special Forces requires a deep educational background and sense of cultural perspective.   In general, it has been my experience that the best Army officers, whatever their formal academic training, have a strong liberal arts background — they may be engineers or economists, but they know history, literature, music, and art.   They can read, write, and speak the "King's English" proficiently.   They possess a thirst for knowledge, and they understand the mores, languages and perspectives of other cultures.   This broad education best prepares officers for the kind of challenges that are continuously presented to the "A-Team" leader, whether working as a liaison between the French Foreign Legion and U.S. Marines in Somalia, advising counter-narcotics operations in the Upper Huayaga Valley in Peru, or hunting for Scud missiles deep behind Iraqi lines. The Special Forces officer must know *how* to think rather than merely *what* to think; he must be able to think through the complexity of a unique and ambiguous situation, make the right decision, and implement it through personal leadership.

Absolute personal integrity, strength of character, and self-confidence are essential. These leaders must be able to operate independently at the cutting edge of U.S. policy while building bridges to other peoples and nations. The extended operating distances from headquarters, the infrequent contact with superiors, the sensitive missions that blur the distinction between soldier and diplomat are manageable only if the officer has engendered a sense of complete trust in his soldiers and in his chain of command.

During the Vietnam War, an "A-Team" leader commanding one of the border camps built to interdict communist supplies and soldiers faced a exceptional task. Besides commanding his team, he was typically in charge of a 600-man Montagnard battalion, which likely included some 1,800 family members. He and his NCOs had to lead, train, pay, and discipline their soldiers, organize their logistics, call for artillery fire and air strikes, and plan and coordinate operations with adjacent American and South Vietnamese units. They also ministered to their sick and wounded troops, delivered the wives' babies, presided over the burial ceremonies of the fallen soldiers, and paid restitution to their grieving kin.

His American company commander, a major in charge of a "B-Team," was usually based a hundred kilometers away, and tried hard to visit and inspect once a week. The lieutenant colonel leading the "C-Team" and commanding the US battalion often had his headquarters three hundred kilometers distant, and if the tempo of combat permitted, could see the captain face-to-face about once a month. The colonel commanding 5th Special Forces Group might see each of his captains two or three times in a year.

The recent and highly successful work of the Special Forces "A-Teams" scattered across Haiti in Operation "Restore Democracy" recalls this situation a generation later. In conventional unit operations, company, battalion, and brigade commanders often operate within a few dozen kilometers of each other. The dispersion and isolation that is so much a part of non-linear warfare and the special operations suited to it, calls for independent and self-reliant leaders: those who combine courage of conviction with an appreciation for the context in which they are operating.

The key to the career and combat success of elite-unit officers in the US Army is an attitude: to recognize themselves as Army officers, first and foremost, and to lead by personal example with confidence and courage. As possessors of the unique set of skills required for the difficult brand of missions they are expected to accomplish, they must also know that they will be held to a higher standard. It might seem to an outsider that officers commanding elite forces, comprised of highly intelligent, talented, and self-motivated soldiers, organized in smaller, more intimate groupings, should find the burden of command lighter than their conventional counterparts. In fact, just the opposite may be true. In the US Army's Special Operations Forces, the sergeants, by virtue of their superior quality, push their officers to higher levels of performance. When I was a young Special Forces captain with the Khmer Serai project in the III Corps area of Vietnam, I learned immediately that the NCOs expected of their officers not only professional competence, but the ability to move faster, farther, and with a heavier load. Mental and physical toughness are essential for officers to establish and maintain their credibility as leaders.

Leading Special Forces NCOs is certainly not easier than leading conventional troops, and it is decidedly different. It is different because of the higher proportion of NCOs in Special Forces and their exceptional professionalism and capabilities. Today, a "typical" Special Forces NCO is a Sergeant First Class and combat veteran, about 31 years old, conversant in a foreign language, with 12 to 14 years of Army service. He also has 13 to 14 years of formal education (about 40% have either an Associate's or Bachelor's degree), and a standard Army intelligence test score of around 127 (100 points is the Army mean; 110 is needed to enter West Point). Contrary to the popular "bachelors-only" myth, he is also married with two children.

The relationship of the officer to the NCO in Special Forces is analogous to the association among senior and junior officers in a conventional unit: there is mutual esteem and camaraderie, but the ranking officer must constantly re-validate his worthiness to command. The apparent informality associated with small units has no impact on the officer's authority, precisely because he and his soldiers are organized as per their designation: a "team." The very name implies the necessity of a leader, and underscores the importance of the leader's orders to accomplish the team's mission. It is often said, "Every Special Forces soldier (like every Ranger) is a leader." This is true, but only one leads the team. The officer's mastery of fundamental individual and collective skills is essential, and these core skills must be continually re-addressed. This aspect of trustworthiness is particularly crucial because a captain in his first command finds himself in charge of a team of very experienced, professional NCOs who in many regards know the captain's job as well or better than he does, at least initially. The officer must very quickly earn the trust and respect of these NCOs. When the bullets start flying, they look to the officer for leadership and decision-making and must have complete confidence in his competence, character, and judgment.

While maintaining the Special Forces as both a separate branch of the Army (like the Infantry or Transportation) and a distinct regiment is crucial to sustaining its competence and sense of purpose, an operational perspective alone is not enough. Leaders must comprehend the complete environment where Special Forces soldiers and units operate and work — and this requires involvement in the greater Army to grasp its mechanisms, its missions, and its ethos. A Special Forces officer would do well to follow a pattern of assignments from a common basic training, to general-purpose units, to special operations duty, to schools (as student and instructor), to high-level staffs, periodically and alternately returning to conventional and special units for command and staff postings. This is the surest way to cultivate the leaders for elite units that both the Army and the special operations soldiers need and deserve.

For officers whose assigned missions often have strategic consequences, the ability to comprehend their strategic circumstances is critical. The other skills they are selected for — high intelligence, initiative, languages — make them natural choices to serve on U.S. ambassadors' "Country Teams" as staff officers, or to run training programs for allied military personnel. The more responsibility placed on newly-selected officers to see beyond their duties as small-unit leaders and assess their roles in a broader context, the higher the dividends when they mature into senior leaders assigned as battalion and group commanders, overseas advisors, defense attachés, and military assistants to U.S. ambassadors.

In the same way as the officers, the soldiers of elite forces must be carefully chosen. Physical toughness and endurance are clearly important, but the need to cope with the academic and operational requirements call for abilities in mathematics, linguistics, and deductive reasoning. There is a direct correlation between individual intelligence as measured in written tests, and performance in SFAS and follow-on training. Similarly, psychological testing tuned to the requirements of the force helps find the best person for the special operations environment.

Maturity cannot be overstated, and is not an ill-defined benchmark. The existing Army SFAS pre-requisites allow only older soldiers who have completed their first term of enlistment to volunteer, when they are 22 to 24 years old. After the initial two years of SFAS, the basic Q-Course, advanced training and language schooling, they arrive at their team around their 25th birthday. It is my experience that there is a threshold at around 26 or 27 years of age, when the "kid" is excised from the Special Forces soldier, with a commensurate gain in individual reliability and judgment. He will have volunteered for two Army enlistments, parachute training, and Special Forces. Tacitly, he has also volunteered to leave his original branch and build a new reputation in a different regiment. At this point in his professional life, he has accepted the military lifestyle and is fully assimilated into the military culture.

Maturity is also essential to steel the newly-selected leader for the occasional rude shock of rejection by elements of the parent organization which had once embraced him. I recall two of my own experiences in Vietnam as a study in contrasts. During operations in the northern III Corps area, I brought my six hundred Vietnamese Rangers to a 1st Cavalry Division base for food, ammunition, and rest. We looked like "Terry and the Pirates," but the commanding general greeted me as one of his own battalion commanders, even though I was only a major. He ensured that my force was properly provisioned. Later, at another firebase, I could not even get water for my troops, because the American commander did not want Special Forces and their "dinks" inside his defensive perimeter. Nothing I could do or say would overcome his prejudice. This sort of experience sorely tests a Special Forces officer's love for the Army, but must not diminish it.

While the accession system is designed as much to discover the right candidate as to uncover the wrong one, the process does not brand non-selectees as failures. The system recognizes that Special Forces duty is not for everyone. Accordingly, unsuccessful volunteers are congratulated for their effort, and their commanders are sent a written commendation to present to the returning soldier for participating in the assessment. They are counseled on how to improve their performance, and often invited to try again. Those who make a second effort have almost double the success rate of "first-timers."

The quality of NCOs presents the corollary to the officers' question: is the smarter, better soldier less reliant on leaders to accomplish his mission? The answer is that soldiers in battle will always look to their leaders. In the case of elite soldiers, there is less blind obedience and more "why" questions either stated or implied. The officers have to explain their rationale and justify their intent more often — but in my thirty-four-plus years of service as an Army officer, I never had a Special Forces NCO tell me, "No, I won't." Because of their competence, and their confidence in that competency, these soldiers are fully cognizant of their professional obligation to obey. Sustaining this professionalism requires that their officers lead by establishing a bond of trust.

CULTIVATING THE ETHOS

Once the leader and soldiers are selected, the process of imbedding the elite ethos begins. A part of the ethos is achieved by the symbols of the organization's elite status. These are not simply cosmetic, and the power of these totems, badges, and uniforms has been recognized as essential to the martial spirit for centuries. Remarking on the inspirational value of medals for valor, Napoleon claimed, "If I had enough ribbon, I could conquer the world." In the same way, when President Kennedy personally authorized the green beret as the headgear for the U.S. Army Special Forces, he explained its importance in a memorandum to the entire Army, calling the beret "a symbol of excellence, a badge of courage, a mark of distinction in the fight for freedom." It is essential to the reputation of any elite unit recognized by a visible emblem, be it a shoulder tab, a jacket pin, or a hat or badge, that the high standards of performance that garnered its "mark of distinction" be maintained.

Likewise, the value of tradition cannot be overestimated. Traditions of academic excellence in great universities and of corporate excellence in leading businesses and firms directly contribute to continuing superior performance by revealing to an institution's members not merely what is expected, but what is possible to achieve on a sustained basis. In the same way, newly-formed elite forces draw on the traditions of their parent service to provide a similar foundation for martial excellence. The precedents and paragons of courage, loyalty, and sacrifice in war extend to modern American elite forces of the Army that have been serving the nation for over two hundred years.

Building on the symbols and traditions of the force, the Regular Army inculcates its ethos into recruits during basic training. A "boot camp" certainly challenges men and women fresh from high school or college, and brings them, firmly and quickly, into the military culture. The objective of the training is to transform the recruits into capable, disciplined soldiers. To that end, the tasks, conditions, and standards they must accomplish each hour and each day are clearly established and are attainable with time and practice. It is a tribute to the US Army's basic training centers that almost all inductees who respond to sound leadership and motivation, regardless of their educational background, can graduate from their courses.

Inculcating an ethos of excellence in potential officers and soldiers of elite forces requires an experience beyond and apart from the demands of basic military training. The approach taken by the Army SFAS course is thus fundamentally different from the Regular Army. The central components of SFAS may seem similar to other tough training courses, especially in physical exertion and both sleep and food deprivation. These thoroughly fatigue a candidate, and help the evaluators see what the individual is "really made of."

However, a fourth element — induced stress — is added. This stress is achieved by not revealing to the candidate what standard he must achieve to pass a given test. With a rifle and heavily-loaded rucksack, the candidate must find a rendezvous point a dozen kilometers distant across broken terrain. But how much time does he have? He does not know. When he finds the point, he is not told how well he did, but simply receives his next task. The Army aviators who volunteer for duty with the 160th SOAR find their flying skills tested in the cockpit of a small helicopter that has been out of the Army inventory for over a decade. To execute aerial navigation, the electronic beacons and satellite positioning systems are turned off, and the "legs" of their route must be calculated with a paper map and a stopwatch. Can the pilot adapt to new demands quickly and effectively? Can these volunteers deal with ambiguity?

Forging these exceptional officers and NCOs into high-performance teams is a process that stems from the selection and training of the volunteers for Special Forces. Given their immediate comprehension of the advantages of group efforts to attain goals, experienced soldiers tend to coalesce into functional units more readily. But this is aided by the assessment process itself, which tests and selects not just for individual attributes, but for "team-player" abilities as well.

The SFAS process has been tuned to American soldiers coming from the American culture, after extended dialogue and specific advice of elite force leaders from Britain's SAS, Germany's GSG-9, Israel's Commandos, France's GIGN, and the Dutch Marines. Each country must have its own selection process adjusted to the nature of its population, for it would be unwise to simply copy such a culturally-based system from another nation's army. Inherent to the American character is a genuine acceptance of most other cultures and peoples at face value, and a readily apparent sense of fairness. As citizens of a "nation of nations," American Special Forces soldiers can immerse themselves in another culture without being co-opted or "going native," while building mutual respect and rapport. During a combat operation in Vietnam, a hasty attack went wrong, and in the ensuing fight my left leg was shattered and my left bicep shot off by enemy fire. It was three Khmer Serai who dragged me to safety. This is the level of camaraderie that elite forces personnel must be able to engender in whatever organization they join.

Members of elite units are comfortable with ambiguity; they enjoy the latitude uncertainty provides, and exploit it to achieve success. The Special Forces advisers in the Salvadoran Civil War, usually operating alone in provinces as large as Rhode Island, had orders to "Do what you think best to support U.S. policy objectives in your area of responsibility." As their individual situations permitted, they trained soldiers and staffs, built bridges and schools, vaccinated people and livestock, organized refugee camps, curbed human rights violations by government forces, and directly helped end the war. After "Desert Storm," the 10th Special Forces Group was sent into the trackless, barren mountains of northern Iraq to "Provide Comfort" (the operation's code name) to impoverished Kurd refugees numbering in the hundreds of thousands. No one knew for certain how many. In the dead of winter, the Special

Forces soldiers had to furnish them food, water, shelter, and "stop the dying; especially among the children." They did.

During Operation "Restore Democracy," eighty percent of the population of Haiti and ninety percent of its land area was effectively controlled by only 1,500 Special Forces soldiers. As a Task Force commander in Haiti, I was very aware that our doctrinal manuals did not prescribe that a 12-man "A-Team" be prepared to establish and maintain civil order in a town with some 40,000 frightened inhabitants. Nonetheless, it was done in town after town, and the intelligence, maturity, and adaptability of the individual Special Forces soldier and his officer were the keys. Colonels Bill Tangney and Mark Boyatt, commanding 10th and 3rd Special Forces Groups in northern Iraq and Haiti, respectively, masterfully transitioned their units from combat operations to humanitarian assistance. They turned seemingly hopeless situations into success stories. This is the acme of Special Forces leadership.

SUSTAINING THE TEAM

While developing an ethos is critical to building the force, the core value that will hold a team together through the hardest trials is trust. Trust has several components: honesty, integrity, high personal and professional standards, family-like concern for fellow team members, and doing what is right for its own sake. The sort of team training that builds and enhances this trust is fairly obvious, and extends from standard Army combat training, increasing stress and risk as appropriate to the capabilities of the team. Tactical drills with live ammunition, three-person party climbs up vertical cliff faces, night parachute jumps onto unmarked drop zones, and over-the-horizon maritime infiltrations from submarines are typical of the kind of exercises that strengthen the team and its members. But day-to-day trust is just as critical — keeping promises, not revealing confidences about a teammate's personal difficulties to the whole team, and doing all one can for one's comrades, even in seemingly trivial administrative matters.

Trust is tempered in combat, and can provide salvation from mistakes in battle. In 1966 in a hard-fought action on Nui Ba Dien

Mountain, my Khmer Serai unit was running out of ammunition and giving way under heavy enemy attack. I told the team sergeant to withdraw, while I called in artillery fire to break contact with the enemy. After the fight, however, he confronted me: "Sir, why didn't you call for smoke shells along with the HE (high explosive) to cover our withdrawal? We took a lot of unnecessary casualties." I had made a terrible mistake, and I might have lost the moral authority to command at that point. Fortunately, I had been team leader for ten months before that battle and had demonstrated the confidence to accept criticism from my subordinates and learn from my mistakes. The bonds of trust we had built allowed me to recover, and the team to keep going.

Even if training is made as rigorous and realistic as possible, it is insufficient to travel only to "Range 34" or "Training Area G" at home base. Since the nature of special operations is global, and is keyed to interacting with foreign cultures on a face-to-face basis, there is no substitute for team deployments to foreign countries. The team, and hence its officer, must be sent out on their own. On these demanding training missions, the inexperienced leaders must be protected, as appropriate, from casual accusations and arbitrary authoritarianism that may come from some party in the host nation, or occasionally the team's own sponsoring embassy. This should not deter senior commanders from sending their soldiers overseas instead of to safer local training sites. Think in terms of not just mountains, but the Urals; not just swamps, but the Amazon Basin; not just towns, but an Indonesian village. These are the best proving grounds for teams and team leaders, short of actual combat.

Discipline is another critical component of trust, and its primacy is certainly appreciated by elite soldiers. Given the difficult situations they are often thrust into, elite soldiers must be able to rely implicitly upon each other's character and competence, and this requires the ability to enforce standards outside the formal purview of the leader. Long-term service together does not "breed contempt" or undermine discipline; rather, it builds mutual trust, loyalty, and reinforces high individual and team standards. Discipline in elite units may have some different features and priorities from that of conventional forces, for it is a quality that must be tailored to the needs of the unit and serve a specific, functional purpose. As such, discipline forms a central pillar to the sustained effectiveness of elite units.

To maintain discipline in special units, I set broad (but clear) limits of action, and presented a few well-chosen and well-articulated central rules. This provided room for initiative and creative solutions, while reminding officers and soldiers alike that they are bound by laws and that they serve a higher cause. Over the years, I developed and refined my own set ("Potter's Rules") for my troops: Adhere to the rules, regulations, customs and mores of our Service; Keep your word and don't compromise your signature; Be personally responsible for the skills and knowledge expected of your pay grade; Don't get involved with drugs or become dependent on alcohol; and Remember that you've taken an oath to your country and your family — keep them both. Longs lists of decrees and orders do not serve the purposes of Special Forces, or their personnel. The broad left and right limits open the door to creativity, initiative, and high performance. The strict definition of those limits also defines a set of boundaries that if crossed require immediate and certain consequences.

Some soldiers, no matter how carefully selected, never fully integrate into the organization. There are very few cases of indiscipline in most elite units. In Special Forces, for example, there are only about 900 officers and 5,500 NCOs in the entire regiment, and "peer pressure" serves to keep almost everyone in line. And by definition, Special Forces are voluntary. Individuals select themselves in, and when they do not meet their own expectations, they select themselves out. Some, though, "lose the fire." They cease performing as good soldiers but cannot bring themselves to leave, so the chain of command has to make the decision for them. It is contingent on the leaders to anticipate this, and re-assign the "at-risk" soldiers to new units in other environments where they can rejuvenate themselves. Officers are a different matter — the higher standard expected of them means they cannot flag in their daily efforts and still prove their worth as leaders. The officer's personal efficiency report is the commander's proscriptive tool in this regard. Such failures are fortunately rare, and these small numbers validate the trying selection and training process and affirm that officers recognize that their NCOs deserve the best support and leadership possible.

CONCLUSION

The return for the investment necessary to create and maintain elite units cannot be calculated in dollars. The end of the Cold War precipitated a radical reduction of conventional US military strength because the threat of conventional war sharply diminished. Those forces, exemplified by armored divisions, fighter wings, and battle fleets, are designed solely for that specific kind of warfare. However, the global political turbulence that has followed the dissolution of the Soviet empire has spawned an unexpected array of threats to American national interests. No one predicted the missions of world-wide de-mining, counter-proliferation of nuclear weapons, or global peacekeeping. However, the "Thin Green Line" of US Special Operations Forces — purposefully selected and trained to cope with ambiguity, experienced in cross-cultural communications, aware of their political context — readily adapted to the new world environment. Their ultimate utility may be in their universal adaptability and high assurance of mission accomplishment in high-risk scenarios when success must often be defined by their actions.

Creating and sustaining such a force requires the development of mastery and maturity in its leaders and soldiers. While the difficult missions and distinctive emblems clearly set them off from their conventional counterparts, these alone are not sufficient to maintain the level of excellence expected of elite units. Absolute mastery of the fundamentals in terms of competence and character are the true foundations of the force, building the bonds of trust between mature leaders and soldiers. When the maturity of the team is developed through arduous training, fostering the resilience and fiber to excel in ambiguous and uncertain situations, it possesses the substance of an elite force.

Mastery and maturity, however, are not confined to specially designated elite units. Leaders who desire to maximize the performance of their organizations, and have an impact beyond their mod-
est size, need to start with a focus on the fundamentals of their
trade: the development and inculcation of core skills proficiency
and the values that embody the organization's ethos. Leaders then
need to develop the maturity of their teams by thrusting them into
stressful, ambiguous situations in which they must rely on their
own intellectual capital, character, and judgment to solve complex
problems. Since people are likely to make honest mistakes during
this process, it takes an enlightened leader with personal confidence and courage of conviction to underwrite training errors in
pursuit of developing a high-performing team. When this level of
excellence is achieved, however, the payoff for the leader and the
organization is their transformation into a true "Renaissance Force."

Chapter Nineteen

Unleashing Human Potential: The Leader's Role in Creating the Climate for High Performing Organizations

by John W. Woodmansee, Jr.

THE ORGANIZATIONAL CHALLENGE

The legendary Israeli armor commander and tank designer, General Israel Tal, when asked which was the best of the advanced tanks in the world: the Israeli Merkava, the US Abrams, the German Leopard, or the British Centurion, replied: "The best tank is the one with the best crew." While enhanced technology and optimized processes can create the opportunities for dramatic success in warfare and business, both these enterprises remain, essentially, human endeavors. It is the human element that must turn these opportunities into successes or failures. It is to this fundamental, but extremely complex, issue that we focus our attention. How, in the midst of rapid change and adaptation to new technologies and restructured processes, can leaders create the conditions that release the full potential of the members of their teams to dominate their competition? There may be many leaders who understand the potential of the technology, and of that group, a large number who also grasp the requirement for new processes to exploit that technology. The ability to dominate the battlefield and the market place, however, will reside with the few leaders and institutions who, in addition, can best accomplish the difficult task of organizing and motivating the human element to achieve consistent high performance. First prize will go only to those institutions which are successful at the business of creating "the best crew."

Creating these high performing teams that dominate their competition rests on several key ingredients. First, the teams need to know what is expected of them and how their work fits into the organizational objectives. They must, with their leaders, share a "vision" for the organization, and they must feel the freedom, indeed the expectation, that they can use their initiative and creativity to achieve the vision. To succeed over an extended period of time, it is necessary that this vision, or purpose, be based on higher order social and human values, not just "return to the shareholders." Finally, leaders must establish a culture of trust within the organization, built upon proper recognition and reward of achievement while simultaneously providing objective feedback loops at all levels to know "ground truth," as we call it in analyzing a tactical exercise, whether it be to measure the effectiveness of our gunnery or the confidence in our leaders. Taken together, vision, enhanced with a value-based purpose and a climate of trust that emphasizes a performance-based culture can create the framework for organizations to unleash human potential to achieve, as General Bill Depuy used to describe it, "effortless superiority."[1]

VISION: CONTINUITY AND CHANGE

Leaders in all organizations have prime responsibility for understanding the new realities facing them and for recognizing emerging opportunities to meet these challenges. To adapt rapidly without jeopardizing the core values of their organizations requires both a clear understanding and commitment by all members of the organization to these objectives. Vision is the formulation of an end-state that acts as the beacon to guide an organization through the uncertainty of change. As such, vision provides a context for change while allowing the organization to stay firmly rooted in its core values.

In July 1996, the Chairman of the Joint Chiefs of Staff, General John Shalikashvili, published the vision statement, "Joint Vision 2010," that guides the formulation of our national "Concept for Future Joint Operations." This vision statement was endorsed by Secretary Cohen in the Quadrennial Defense Review:

> *The information revolution is creating a Revolution in Military Affairs that will fundamentally change the way US forces fight. We must exploit these and other technologies to dominate in battle. Our template for seizing on these technologies and ensuring military dominance is Joint Vision 2010. . .* [2]

Just as Secretary Cohen is relying on the "Joint Vision" statement to guide the Department of Defense, the commercial world also endorses the importance of having a powerful vision to guide organizations through the crucible of change. The CEO of Bell Atlantic has proclaimed that "with a clear vision, alignment is inevitable."[3] Although I find his assertion somewhat overstated, I would certainly argue that without a clear vision, alignment is impossible. Another senior business leader has even defined leadership as "the fulfillment of a vision through others."[4]

While managing change has become something of a mantra with the evolution and expansion of Information Technology (IT), John Gardner, discussing the need for renewal of all mature organizations, offers a much needed caution: "Leaders must understand the interweaving of continuity and change."[5] In other words, it is just as important that leaders, in managing change, appreciate what things should not be changed. In their book, *Built To Last*, Jerry Porras and James Collins reinforce Gardner's insight by pointing out that successful, "visionary," companies, which have endured for at least 50 years, seldom, if ever, change their core values. These values, they assert, are the bedrock on which these successful companies "display a powerful drive for progress that enables them to change and adapt without compromising their cherished core ideals." [6]

But we must recognize that vision alone, though essential, is insufficient. Vision is only a means to an end. The payoff does not come until the organization can actualize the vision and do it better than those against whom they are competing. The ability to differentiate the organization, whether it be military or commercial, from their competition (or their potential enemies), and to dominate them in the marketplace (or on the battlefield) is, of course, the real goal. As John Gardner reminds us, "The consideration leaders must never forget is that the key to renewal is the release of human energy and talent."[7] Professor Warren Bennis echoes Gardner's point, "To survive in the 21st Century, we will need leaders who can conquer the volatile, turbulent times we face by learning to unleash the full potential in others."[8] I would only add to Professor Bennis' observation that the same was true in the twentieth and earlier centuries.

ORGANIZATIONAL CLIMATE

The key to unleashing the potential in others to actualize the vision rests in large part on creating the right climate in the organization. People who are uninspired by the nature of their work, lack confidence in their skills, are uncertain about their responsibilities, are concerned with being criticized for making mistakes, and who rarely get feedback on their performance are unlikely to surprise you with high performance or innovation. Members of an organization need to believe that the work they are asked to do is important. They must, as a *sine qua non*, be competent. They must understand, very clearly, what is expected of them, how their work fits into the overall plan, and how their performance will be evaluated. Within certain controls and boundaries, they must feel the freedom to try new ways to improve performance. High performing organizations try new ways; they "play with" ideas. Their teams are very cohesive in the workplace and often off duty. This is the climate that leaders must create throughout their organizations. It is not a byproduct of a strategy or vision statement, or a streamlined process, or even profitable operations.

While each leader has his or her own unique style, there are elements that seem to be essential for leading complex organizations through dramatic change, especially where the critical advantage must be achieved by smaller teams working in concert throughout the organization. Leaders must understand that their role is primarily that of a facilitator rather than a director; they influence how their organization thinks more than they command its working details. They tell it where to go, but not how to get there. They ensure that feedback is provided throughout the organization, and that performance, both good and bad, is recognized appropriately. They must be comfortable knowing that their success will be determined by the collective success of those under them. Intel's Vice President for Business Development recently described the challenge facing his company:

> *We deal with exponential change. . . .We build factories that cost $2 billion andtake three or four years to build. We build them for products we haven't designed for markets that don't exist. . . .The people working on (this problem) are a team. They have to learn to trust each other—and we have to let them do it. The biggest challenge is to give up the notion of control, because we can't control this kind of project.*

This is a scary thought for many leaders, especially those who are confined to very centralized organizations, to those organizations that have no appetite for mistakes, or those in which goals are too short-sighted to be focused on long-term health. Commercial companies that kneel solely at the alter of quarterly results fit that category. Military organizations that stress "no mistakes" for leaders in their short tours as unit commanders also fall into these endangered categories. It is in this kind of restrictive, centralized climate that the most talented members in the organization tend to vote with their feet when the opportunity presents itself.

While it is the role of the senior leader to facilitate and communicate the vision and to guide the resource allocation to support the organization goals, it remains the job of the rank and file to outperform the competition. It was Earle Dixon, a company employee at Johnson and Johnson who came up with the idea of Band Aids,[9] and it was the persistent advocates of "Post-it" adhesive notes team at 3M who would not let their idea be dismissed.[10] It was a spotter plane pilot, a courageous company commander, Lieutenant Karl Timmerman, and the brigade commander of the lead elements of the US 9th Armored Division who seized the bridge over the Rhine River at Remagen in World War II before the Germans could destroy it.[11] These were all unexpected opportunities that the chief executive officers, corporate presidents, and generals had not imagined, but that their subordinates created and capitalized upon.

Rather than having our leaders feel that they must exercise their authority and "get their arms around their organizations," we must teach them to appreciate that their role as leader is to "turn it loose" and let it achieve its collective potential. Of course there will be times when "the boss" has to bite the bullet and make a decision, perhaps an unpopular one, which only he or she can make. But most of the time a leader will really be ratifying a decision that he or she has guided through the process of formulation and acceptance by the key subordinate leaders who must implement the decision. There are very few organizations in which things get done well simply because the boss says so. Essentially, leaders of organizations have only the "authority" that the members of an organization give to them. Chester Barnard was the first in his 1938 classic, *The Functions of an Executive*, to define authority as "the character of a communication by which it is accepted by a member of the organization."[12] Ronald Heifetz, in his current book, *Leadership Without Easy Answers*, which questions how leaders and those in authority really contribute to their organizations, ratifies Barnard by defining authority as "power conferred to perform a service."[13] The message has now been clear for 60 years, leaders must not confuse "leadership" with the exercise of "authority."

I grew up in the Army and experienced "authority" as the senior leader of groups of soldiers from platoon level (20 soldiers) to Corps (62,000 soldiers). From this experience, I can attest that the authority one may think he has by virtue of rank or position is not nearly as important as the authority subordinate leaders and teams give him. The operative word here is trust. If the people in an organization trust a leader's motives, if they trust his integrity, if they trust his competence, they will accord him great authority. If they don't, they won't. It is amazing how little authority some leaders really have, and it does not matter what rank they are.

In 1970, as a lieutenant colonel on my second tour in Vietnam, I commanded the 7th Squadron, 1st (Air) Cavalry Regiment, which consisted of 1200 soldiers with 200 rated aviators flying 116 helicopters. We operated by sending out our air cavalry troops on separate missions throughout the Vietnam Delta. After I assumed command, I grew concerned about one particular troop, and, based primarily on a "gut" feel, denied a request for extension by the commander. Flying on a mission with the troop after it had changed commanders, I learned during one of the refueling stops that the platoon leaders used to maintain another radio frequency for themselves. When the previous troop commander told them to do something that was not sound and was likely to get someone hurt, they would confer on the other channel among themselves and decide what part of his order they were going to obey. I learned that the new troop commander, though junior to all other troop commanders in the squadron, was seen by the other leaders in the troop as an exceptional leader and pilot. They told me that they did not need an alternate command channel anymore. They had given their new leader authority. They trusted me enough to share that information with me. They told me things about the previous leader that confirmed my uneasy feelings, and they thanked me for making the change.

General Fred Franks, who lost a leg in Vietnam, commanded the VII Corps in Desert Storm. In his book, *Into the Storm*, authored with Tom Clancy, he wrote about a conversation with one of his soldiers just before the initiation of the ground attack. The soldier said to Franks, "Don't worry, General, we trust you."[14] Fred reflected later: "If generals can remember [that], and do their best to fulfill that trust, they will have done their duty." Leaders, on occasion, may have to move their organizations against the grain of consensus, but they need to rely on a storehouse of trust and respect. Authority in the military, especially in matters of life and death in combat, is largely given from the led to the leader. I have not found it any different in my commercial experience (except that sometimes the enemy is a bit more difficult to identify).

Any time I read scholars describing the need for "new flat, self-governing organizations" to replace the "old hierarchical military methods," I interpret that to be a description of the assumed basis of authority versus leadership within the two organizations. Actually, it has nothing to do with civilian versus military. The "old hierarchical military method" equates to a lack of caring leaders capable of empowering and developing others. That method rarely worked in either the military or civilian sector.

Leaders who understand this philosophy operate in a consistent manner. They are inclusive in decision making. They do not promulgate policy decisions that surprise their subordinates, and they make sure that their subordinates have been given a reasonable time to comment on policies being developed or revised. They encourage input from the organization and respect it. They are careful to encourage debate and even argument. Critical to fostering creativity and accountability, leaders avoid making decisions that can (and usually should) be made lower in the organization. To their subordinates, these leaders are predictable. There is no lost energy in the organization worrying about whether they are acting as their leaders want them to. These leaders influence their direct subordinates with ample two-way communications. There were times when I realized that I had not reached some of my subordinates and sold them on certain policies that I felt strongly about. Unfortunately, I discovered this only after the fact. As I grew older, I reached the conclusion that my ability to influence my subordinates was directly proportional to the amount of time I was willing to listen to them.

VALUE BASED PURPOSE

In commercial organizations, profits are necessary to stay in business. They are necessary, but insufficient, to motivate the high performance necessary to build and sustain a great company. Those companies which succeed and remain at the top of their industry adopt, as their corporate compass, a purpose for the organization that goes beyond making profits. This purpose is value based, and describes the contribution that the organization wishes to make to society.[15] For example, Merck, the pharmaceutical company, says it is in the business of "preserving and improving human life."[16] Marriott wants to "make people away from home feel that they are among friends and really wanted."[17] In a recent article, author Jim Collins reported that Nike's expressed purpose is "To experience the emotion of competition, winning, and crushing competitors."[18] It will be interesting to see if that is the kind of statement that will carry them well into the 21st Century. It certainly does not lack enthusiasm and clarity.

As a former Chairman of Johnson and Johnson asserts, "The reason we were so successful at Johnson & Johnson was our reputation of trust that went back 100 years. All previous managers had acted in a way that created a feeling in the minds of virtually everybody that you could trust us." [19] Founded in 1886, the company adopted the aim of "alleviating pain and disease," and placed service to customers and concern for employees ahead of returns to shareholders. The Johnson & Johnson credo, originally published in 1943, is a one page expression of the values of the company.[20] In the early 1980s, the CEO indicated that he spent 40 percent of his time communicating the credo throughout the company. A company not committed to its creed might have foundered in the poisoning crisis the company faced in 1982 when someone tampered with bottles of Tylenol in Chicago, injecting cyanide into them, resulting in the death of seven people.[21]

In the military, readiness to produce victory in combat is the *raison d'être* of armed forces, and the goal to which combat units concentrate virtually all of their daily energy in peacetime. But a lifetime commitment of servicemen and women to the uniform may require a broader expression of values. West Point speaks of "Duty, Honor, Country." It is a creed that graduates have held very dear now for over 100 years, and one that seems even more important than it was in 1898 as our society's mores today seem to diverge from the concept of duty and service to others and move toward the expression of individualism. Perhaps no clearer value statement is found than the oath all soldiers take upon joining the Army, and which is repeated with each officer's promotion: "to defend the Constitution of the United States against all enemies, foreign and domestic."

I commanded the US Army's V Corps from 1987-1989, a time when one might take for granted that the defense of the Central Region of Germany was a mission with an obvious purpose of immense value. In the Cold War the threat of the Soviet Union was believed to be serious, and the US Army units in Germany were on "freedom's frontier." The border, with its fences, mine fields, and watch towers installed by the communists, were testimony to the reality of the mission. It was not difficult for our soldiers to understand that the Free World's "line in the sand" was drawn along the Iron Curtain.

While the military mission was preeminent and clear, the establishment of a broadly based purpose for the Corps was not so simple. In addition to the 62,000 soldiers stationed in Germany, there were almost 100,000 family members living there. Over 52 per cent of our soldiers were married. We had over 24,000 school aged children in Department of Defense schools. Over one thousand soldiers were single parents, and we had day care centers with over

12,000 children. Living in a foreign country, a long way from home, without speaking the language, and at a time when the dollar to deutsch mark conversion rate was not attractive was a daunting experience for most of our military families, especially the junior enlisted ones. If one lives near Fort Hood, Texas, and has an exceptional child, there are state and county mechanisms to provide assistance. There are no comparable state and county agencies in Germany to assist these parents. If a dependent was a standout football player on the US Frankfurt High School football team, or an all-star on the Hanau girl's soccer team, it was far more difficult to get recruited by US colleges than if he or she attended Killeen High School, a perennial sports powerhouse outside of Fort Hood. For many, and perhaps most, families the opportunity to learn a foreign culture and language, to meet German families and make lifelong friends, and to travel throughout Europe was the opportunity of a lifetime. But a large number of families had difficulty coping with the challenge of living in Europe.

There were also strains associated with being a foreign army stationed in West Germany. Imagine having several German armored divisions training in the Boston-Washington DC corridor, or in the Seattle-Tacoma region, with huge barracks complexes in the middle of the cities. It is not surprising that German youth would prefer to have the US youth in uniform return to the US. Back when everyone remembered the Marshall Plan's contribution to the reconstruction of Germany, I imagine this was not a problem. But in the 1980s, especially with some of our junior families so poorly paid as to be eligible for food stamps, personal economics affected the morale of our soldiers and the harmony of our Alliance. Issues such as these impacted on the readiness of the command. All the senior US leaders understood that we could not achieve success in battle if our soldiers were alienated from the communities they were expected to defend and if their families were not properly cared for.

I chose to resolve these matters by meeting with the top 50 uniformed and civilian leaders in the Corps and their spouses. We defined our most important goals in an effort to ensure that the priorities of the leaders throughout the Corps were properly aligned. The meetings took place three times a year at a German convention site. These were working sessions with very little transmitting from the headquarters. Part of the conference was split into separate military member and spouse agendas. Part consisted of joint sessions. We brought in distinguished military and civilian leaders to speak to us. Our dinner entertainment was based on the talent within our American communities, which boasted many gifted artists, and a thriving arts and theater program. In the final meeting of each session, decisions were made. Assignments and suspenses were listed. As a result of the work done at the initial meeting and subsequent contributions from committees formed at the site, we were able to agree on a set of five goals. The goals were distributed throughout the Corps, and a large framed version hung in the Corps' main conference room was signed by all the top leaders of the command. The five goals that we chose were:

READINESS: A Corps capable of executing its wartime mission.

QUALITY OF LIFE: A Corps where soldiers and their families enjoy a safe, supportive, stimulating, and friendly community.

PARTNERSHIP: A Corps that lives and works in partnership with our host nation and successfully fights in wartime as a member of the NATO Alliance.

HEALTH AND FITNESS: A Corps which fosters holistic well-being for all soldiers, civilians, and family members.

CLIMATE OF COMMAND: A Corps in which every member can achieve personal and unit excellence within a cohesive organization.

Each of these goals had a set of objectives that helped to establish measurable results, and which could be used as input to our annual budget submission. For example, under the Quality of Life goal, there were three objectives: quality soldier and family support, quality school support, and quality working and living conditions. We created a position on the staff to coordinate with the Department of Defense Dependent Schools (DODDS) European office. We assisted DODDS by conducting an engineer survey of our facilities, cataloging the deficiencies against the DODDS standards and helping the schools establish a five year improvement budget to bring their facilities up to standard. We created video walking tours of our worst facilities and provided them to officials at the Department of Defense to gain their support for construction projects that our schools needed badly. And we argued, albeit unsuccessfully, that the shortage of over 100 classrooms should not have to be provided from our constrained corps and community budgets.

During one of our leaders' conferences, we created a volunteer position of V Corps Consumer Advocate. This position was elected during the meeting by the senior spouses within the Corps, who were the backbone of our ten communities. The Consumer Advocate was my personal representative to our European Post Exchange system, our European Commissary system, from which our families purchased groceries, and to our Medical Command, which ran the hospitals within the V Corps. We established consumer advocate kiosks in each community, usually near the post exchanges, manned by volunteers, where family and service members could bring their concerns. The problems they tackled ranged from difficulty in getting dental appointments, to choices of products in the PX, to requests that the commissaries stock "I Can't Believe It's Not Butter." In all cases, the supporting agencies appreciated the presence of community interest.

During one of our off-site conferences, from a presentation by the team working the Quality of Life Goal, we came to realize that we had not done very much, as an institution, for our teenagers. We created advisory councils of high school students in each of our ten community areas. The councils were the voices of our teens and helped us select facilities, teen clubs, and sports activities that could meet their needs. One summer we created a European equivalent of the Boys and Girls State conference. The experience was very helpful in building leadership skills among our rising seniors.

Almost none of this energy and activity created within the corps was "directed" by the corps commander. After the Goals and Objectives were agreed upon among the top 100 leaders of our communities, the ideas and energy came from talented and concerned members. And when the obstacle to progress turned out to be inadequacy of funding, I could show our community advocates what resources we had, where we had assigned priorities, and ask for their opinions of the prioritization of community issues. So, not only had we released the creative energies of our families for making their lives better, we had also increased their participation in our decisions for the distribution of budgetary shortfalls, and gained their understanding of those areas where we were resource constrained.

Providing attention to matters other than training for war might seem a far cry from what people expect of their military leaders, but sustaining a volunteer, and predominately married, force today requires leaders to be as concerned about the quality of life for families as well as soldiers. By empowering families to improve their communities, leaders can achieve the goal of a highly trained, lethal force whose members have a strong commitment to their profession and peace of mind by knowing their families are properly cared for. It would be impossible to quantify the increase in combat readiness achieved during the period of time I served the soldiers and families of V Corps. But I know that our "Quality of Life" was improved for the 160,000 service and family members and civilians in the corps, and that their commitment to our Army was stronger as a result.

CREATING A PERFORMANCE-BASED CULTURE

When the leaders of an organization have done a good job communicating the purpose and clarifying the goals so that all the teams understand what they are to contribute, they have laid the necessary foundation to create high performing organizations. If the governance is designed so that the subordinates have latitude to contribute to that process and also have reasonable authority to make decisions on how best to accomplish their assigned goals, the leadership has created the proper framework. But, it is only through the establishment and maintenance of a performance-based culture, with objective feedback systems, that the energy of a competent organization will be released in a manner to dominate the competition. If the indifferent or incompetent are allowed to impede the progress of the unit, or if initiative of the dedicated is wrongfully criticized, then the contributors will lose trust in their leaders, and it is unlikely that they will operate as a high performing team. Those doing the work must trust that their leaders will act as they advertise, and that they will recognize individual and team performance appropriately, whether good or bad. In this way, each member with skill and the motivation has an opportunity to be recognized individually and to become a member of a great team.

The Army's creation of the National Training Center (NTC) and the institutional use of After Action Reviews (AAR) to examine, in exhaustive, objective detail, the performance of each small unit under simulated combat conditions at the center is an example of "breakthrough" thinking in how to place institutional emphasis on creating a performance-based culture. During the AAR, there is no debate about what happened in the fight. There is adequate data to show where each participant was throughout the battle, and who shot whom. This revelation of "ground truth," where everyone on the ground really was, is a compelling learning experience in preparation for combat the next day, especially for those who lost. Some senior management consultants have used the NTC and the AAR as examples that industry should look to. Richard Pascale calls it "the world's most powerful laboratory for leadership development and organizational change."[22] A generation of leaders had "passed through the fire" at the National Training Center when the US went to war against Iraq. Those veterans led a volunteer army of intelligent soldiers, equipped with superb technology, and who had trained realistically in simulated warfare more than any other force on the planet. The result of that war, as is widely known, was a demonstration of dominance over an enemy that has few precedents in the history of warfare.

In V Corps, under the Climate of Command goal, we specified an objective of creating "Institutional feedback loops that provide commanders at all levels a clear view of the climate from the bot-

tom up." The mechanisms we put in place to do that were organizational surveys and subordinate assessments. Responsibility for
the administration of these instruments was assigned to the office
of the Inspector General (IG). With the assistance of the Center
for Creative Leadership, we developed a series of surveys that
could be administered to individuals based on their leadership
level, down to junior non-commissioned officers. Subordinate
surveys were required for all commanders at the lieutenant
colonel level and up (including the Corps Commander), with a
personal debrief by the Inspector General himself, keeping the
input data anonymous.

We modified a standard Army Unit Climate Survey for administration to our junior enlisted members to highlight some of the special concerns we had due to our being stationed in Germany. The
climate survey was controlled by the IG, and the results could be
known only by the leader of the surveyed unit and the officer who
requested the survey. If the company commander requested the
survey, he was the only one who might see the data. Aggregate
data, which protected the identity of the units, was shared throughout the command. For example, if a tank company commander
wanted to run a survey on his company, he could have the results
back from the IG with the average scores of all other company units
in the Corps and with all other tank companies in the Corps.

Keeping a corporate data-base allowed all commanders to com-
pare their data with the aggregate data of all units in the corps or
with specific sections, such as "all other combat support units." The
data from the surveys was excellent material for use at commanders' conferences. As far as our subordinates were concerned, they
found us, collectively, highly competent in technical and tactical
areas, but needing improvement in communication, feedback, and
empowering skills. The data was there. Like our tactical leaders at
the NTC, we could not hide from "ground truth."

The subordinate survey must be used as a tool to help train leaders, not as an evaluation of their performance. It is the most powerful method for individual leader development that I have seen.
Like many others, I am convinced that the most effective place for

leadership development is in the unit, not in the classroom. One can read about it, be lectured about it, and can watch those around him and learn a lot about leadership. But, as Norman Douglas reminds us, "there are some things you can't learn from others, you have to pass through the fire."[23] These surveys acted as feedback mechanisms to make sure leaders understood what was happening while they were passing through the fire.

I had tried similar surveys, using my Organizational Effectiveness Staff Officer (OESO) at Fort Hood, Texas, when I commanded the 2d Armored Division. It was in a discussion with the Corps Commander, Lieutenant General Walter F. Ulmer, Jr., that I was persuaded to treat all these evaluations as the property of the person being evaluated. The only personal evaluations I ever saw in the 2d Armored Division or V Corps were the ones that the individuals shared with me. At V Corps, instead of using the OESO, I chose to have my Inspector General, who had previously proved himself as a commander and was regarded highly by his peers, administer these surveys and debrief the officers. The most frequent question he was asked by the commanders receiving the subordinate survey was "Who is going to see the results?" And the answer by the IG was an unequivocal, "Only you and I."

I recall vividly the experience of one of my subordinate generals in V Corps bringing me his evaluation and dropping it on my desk. I reminded him that this was his evaluation and that he did not have to show it to me. He confirmed that he wanted me to see it. The report was devastating to him. I recall a question in which 30 subordinates were asked, on a scale of 1-5, if they would emulate their leader's personal and professional conduct. All 30 had responded with 1s, "absolutely not." I asked him what he was going to do about it. He told me that he had called his subordinates and staff together and thanked them for their honesty, and indicated to them that he was going to try to change his behavior. He said that he had come to ask me to give him another survey in six months. The results of the second survey revealed dramatic improvement. The counseling the general got from those under him was far more effective in modifying his behavior than any he could have received from me. Later, his wife confided to me privately that he was also a better husband.

I had "directed" that these surveys begin, but after we were about one-third through the corps, I had breakfast with six colonels, all brigade commanders, who had completed their surveys. I knew them well and had a high regard for their leadership. I started the breakfast with the announcement that I would continue the program or terminate the program based upon their recommendations to me that morning. Their response was unanimous: continue the surveys.

The colonels were quite open about the process. One artillery brigade commander said that he had been disappointed in his results, and had wrestled with the criticism of some of his battery commanders. They complained, he told us, that he did not know them and that he had spent very little time with them. They were uncomfortable that he, as their "senior rater," would be the person most responsible for their selection as battalion commanders or not. He told us that he finally realized that with many of his battery commanders stationed in distant locations, he had not done a good job of spending enough time with them. He had, since the survey, scheduled an off site conference with all his battery commanders and their wives, and promised them all that he would have a monthly breakfast with them. He said that he also wanted the survey to be repeated in six months.

In the hands of these dedicated commanders, with the provision that the surveys were "their" instruments not any one else's, they were a powerful leadership training tool. And because I kept my nose out of them, the surveys created a great deal of trust between the senior leaders and their Corps Commander. Had I injected myself in the process, I am convinced that it would have corrupted the data as well as the climate I was trying to create.

The unit climate surveys served the same purpose for company-level commanders. Creating the proper awareness in company commanders of their impact on their subordinates is necessary to transform average units into a high performing ones. Company commanders are usually limited to 12 to 18 months in command

and rarely get the opportunity to command more than one company. So the learning curve is steep, and the experience level of officers in this position is relatively limited. Anything that can be done to accelerate the leadership development of the new company commander pays great dividends throughout the whole organization. I directed that these surveys be done for me at the time of the Annual General Inspection.

In a conversation with the top company commander in V Corps, and my nominee for the prestigious MacArthur Award, he indicated that he had learned from the survey that there were complaints from women in the second platoon of sexual harassment by the departing platoon sergeant. The captain had investigated and confirmed these complaints and had taken proper disciplinary action. He had also found out that his third platoon was complaining of the lack of a certain tool for changing large tires safely, although it was present in the supply room. That, he said, was an easy one to fix. Further, the survey was quite critical of the First Sergeant's behavior, complaining that he was very abusive. The commander told me that he had felt that the First Sergeant was overly harsh, but because of the sergeant's greater experience and of his overall effectiveness, he had not felt comfortable counseling him until he saw the results of the survey.[24]

The big risk in the unit climate survey is that when one asks soldiers to tell what they think about the unit, they will. If the commander refuses to address the concerns raised, the morale of the unit will be worse than before. Once leaders start this process, responsiveness is critical.

I recall reviewing the climate survey of one of my tank companies in the 2d Armored Division. It was taken as part of the Annual General Inspection for then Captain Bob Cone (author of Chapter 17 in this collection). I knew Bob was one of the top company commanders in the 2d Armored Division, but the results of the survey exceeded even my high expectations. The troops held their officers and their First Sergeant in the highest regard that I had ever seen. They believed, without question, that they were ready for combat. The scores were literally pegged at the

top.   That was until I got to the part of the survey about the dining facility.   There I found the harshest criticism I have ever read.
Several soldiers added written comments about the sad state of
their dining facility.   One said, "Every time I eat there I [defecate]
green."   We changed mess stewards in the facility that afternoon.
The survey is a double edged sword.   When the troopers point out
a valid problem to their leaders, they need to see an effort to fix
it.   The bank account on vertical trust in the organization is then
adjusted accordingly.

After we had established a large data base of unit climate surveys, we searched to see if there was a question or set of questions,
the score to which correlated very highly with the overall score of
the 96 question survey.   In a data base of over 360 unit surveys,
question 23 had the highest correlation with the overall score of the
survey: "In your unit are corrections for careless or intentionally
poor performance made fairly?"   Question 21 was not too far
behind: "Do soldiers in your unit who perform well on the job
receive praise, recognition, or reward?"   The last question, number
96, also had a very positive correlation: "Do you think your unit
commander will use the information from this survey to improve
the unit?"   Units that had scored very low on performance-based
culture, specifically units in which the soldiers were not recognized
properly, either for good work or poor work, had correspondingly
low climate and cohesion results.   When the performance-based
culture was evident in the minds of the soldiers, the overall climate
and cohesion results were high.

In V Corps, I also required that each unit administer a Health
Risk Appraisal Program (HRAP) for all our service members and for
family members who volunteered to do so.   The HRAP program
was administered by the medical staff and was treated with doctor-
patient confidentiality, but the aggregate data was provided to each
battalion commander and put in the corporate data-base for use
throughout the Corps. Support for this program was not unanimous
among my leaders.   I borrowed from my "authority" bank and
directed it to be done. One colonel, commanding an armored
brigade, told me that it was a distraction to his training program,

and that he did not have time to do it. I told him to find the time. Two months later he sent me a note saying that one of his young soldiers had performed a testicular self-exam, as described by the battalion surgeon in the HRAP session, and found a suspicious lump. Immediate evacuation to the 97th General Hospital in Frankfurt confirmed evidence of cancer, which was treated aggressively while the soldier remained on active duty. The commander, in a personal note to me said, "HRAP has saved the first soldier's life in our brigade, and I am now, belatedly, it's most zealous advocate." The self-appraisals provided us a significant data base and shocked us with disturbing degrees of stress levels, alcohol consumption by males 25 years of age or less, and the suicide proclivities of the female soldiers.[25] During my breakfasts with groups of battalion commanders, I could tell from the discussion whether or not a commander had already taken his unit through the program. After the commanders had gone through the experience and had seen the "ground truth" aggregate results of their soldiers and family members, their whole notion about "taking care of soldiers" reached a higher level. All the senior leaders of the Corps, including myself, were surprised by the impact of the program on the climate within our units. As more families participated in HRAP, demand for alcohol counseling, weight reduction, and domestic violence counseling programs soared. It was an experience that marked us all.

In 1997 I was invited to Ft Carson, Colorado, to give a talk to the officers. The Commanding General at Ft Carson, then MG John Pickler, had been a colonel commanding the division artillery of the 8th Mechanized Division for me in V Corps. Before the presentation, John showed me through their new inprocessing center, where every new soldier on the post must report. As we walked through, he drew my attention to one group who was doing a Health Risk Appraisal survey. John smiled and said to me, "Don't think that we've forgotten what we learned."

There were two other programs unique to the corps that were important in nurturing both leader development and high performing units. These were the institution of Squad Olympics and a program for designating Distinguished Units and Distinguished Leaders. The Olympics program was meant to emphasize excellence at the lowest tactical level. The goal was to standardize procedures and to focus attention on excellence at the cutting edge. Since the combat arms had ample tactical evaluations at the crew and platoon level, we emphasized the supporting arms. In 1989 we designed and implemented an excellent aviation olympics, an engineer ("sapper") stakes that met the NATO competition standards, a medical stakes, and a military police squad stakes. It was an important contribution to the business of clarifying standards, encouraging excellence, and (hopefully!) objectively measuring the competition and designating the best. The process was all about creating high performing units.

The Distinguished Unit program set forth conditions within which a unit might apply for distinguished status. There were very demanding standards for marksmanship, physical fitness, and tactical skills. All members had to have passed their individual Department of the Army Skill Qualification Test scores, with a unit average 5 percent higher than the DA average. There could be no safety or disciplinary incidents. One of the tougher standards, especially for the senior non-commissioned officers, was a requirement that 75 percent of the unit be non-tobacco users.

A key here was that to start the process, all the members of the aspiring organization, generally a platoon-sized unit 8-40 people, had to sign a request to their chain of command asking that they be evaluated over the next few months for selection as a Distinguished Unit. If one person did not want to sign up, then the unit could not apply. If during the trial, any member of the unit had a disciplinary problem, failed a drug test, or had a reportable accident, the trial period ended. For those units who won the award, they kept it for a year. Since new members who joined the unit were authorized to wear the award, the members of the distinguished unit made sure that the new person did not go out drinking, get arrested, and take them all off distinguished status. In those outfits, "socializing" new members into the organization reached an art form. Our Unit Climate Surveys of the

Distinguished Units confirmed that these were the most cohesive units in the Corps.

The Distinguished Leaders program was to foster professionalism and encourage excellence in our junior officers and non-commissioned officers. Sergeants (E-5, 6, and 7), warrant officers (WO1 and WO2), and company grade officers (lieutenants and captains) were eligible to apply. There were high personal standards of physical fitness, marksmanship, and professional skills. The culminating trial was a grueling "night ride" in which the officer had to navigate to hidden positions in the field and perform a set of tests to satisfactory standards. The rating was conferred on them by the Division Commander. As with the Distinguished Units, Distinguished Leaders awards, a distinctive metallic insignia on a leather fob, were authorized for wear on the uniform breast pocket. When I was the 2d Armored Division commander, the final test, after the night ride, was a meeting with me and a discussion of a designated portion of the Army's governing field manual on Operations, FM 100-5. When Distinguished Leaders left the division, and later the corps, I forwarded a letter to the gaining commander informing him that he was receiving one of our Distinguished Leaders.

In my final months with the V Corps, we were putting together a large field exercise. It attempted to orchestrate, for the first time in the Army, a combination of actual units in the field, cadre units in the field (for example, with one artillery piece representing the whole battery of eight guns), and other units playing in the exercise at their home station or in field locations from their command posts using computer simulation to drive their part of the battle. As I dropped in to get an update from then Colonel Pat Barrett's exercise planners, one of his briefers said to me, "This next item is another simulation area we have added to the exercise. We have not had the opportunity until now to talk to you about it." After the briefing I applauded their initiative and told them that I was very pleased with the addition. He looked around to his colleagues and back to me with a big grin said, "we knew you'd love it."

It was clear to me that this team knew what was being asked of them and that they felt like they had the authority to be very creative in adding improvements and ideas far beyond any guidance that they had been given. It was also quite clear that the group was able to predict, confidently, that I would be pleased with their work. In that one part of a very large organization, there was a very dedicated group whose energies had been released to create a product better than any of their leaders had conceived. They helped to produce a training event that became the model for all future major training exercises for the US Army in Europe.

The culture in a high performing unit is organic. It must be nurtured on a daily basis. It grows, and it can be easily damaged. It is virtually impossible to be universally high in all parts of a complex organization. Because of the turbulence of leaders and members changing the composition of the team, the culture cannot even remain static in one piece of the organization for long periods. But when you can sense the special relationship among the members of a particular team, and when they surprise you by exceeding your expectations, you know that they are operating at a special level and that the organizational and individual goals are aligned and well served. If a leader can do that in numerous parts of a military unit or commercial company, that organization, based on superior performance and execution, will dominate any enemy or competitor they face.

CONCLUSION

The challenge facing the leaders in the Department of Defense today is the same as it is at Intel, Federal Express, General Foods and other great commercial companies. Can they lead their organizations in the face of accelerating technological change to dominate their competition? While mastering the improvements in technology is important and process reengineering will obviously be necessary, the true test will be their ability to develop "the best crews," point them toward their objectives, and turn them loose.

Creating a performance-based culture within the organization, after establishing and communicating a value-based purpose, are the keys to building these high performing organizations called "best crews." Both of those conditions are much easier to talk about than to create. The purpose has to be "lived" on a daily basis by the members of the organization, especially the leadership. A corrupt leader, or even an "unconvinced" one, will be watched by the members to see if the organization is committed to living its values. Creating and maintaining a culture that honors productivity, recognizes "ground truth," learns from setbacks, and adapts to take advantage of opportunities is a daily challenge at all levels of the organization.

The climate to encourage this process can only be created by a team of leaders whose sensitivity to the internal needs of the organization matches their sensitivity in understanding the external market forces and accelerating technology changes taking place, especially in distributing information. But when these leaders are successful and the organizations are up and running, it's a beautiful thing to see!

Biographies of
Contributing Authors

THE EDITOR

Christopher D. Kolenda is the Operations Officer of the Second Armored Cavalry Regiment at Fort Polk, Louisiana, after serving as the Operations Officer of 3rd Squadron, Second ACR. Major Kolenda was previously assigned to the First Cavalry Division at Fort Hood, Texas, where he commanded an armored cavalry troop for two years. He has served in the 11th Armored Cavalry Regiment in the Federal Republic of Germany and has attended U.S. Army Airborne, Air Assault, and Ranger Schools. Major Kolenda is a 1987 graduate of the Military Academy and holds a Master's degree in modern European History from the University of Wisconsin-Madison. As an Assistant Professor of History at the United States Military Academy he taught a variety of history courses including ones in Diplomacy and Classical History.

THE AUTHORS

John C. "Doc" Bahnsen is a retired U.S. Army Brigadier General who currently serves as a consultant to several defense companies, a motivational public speaker and a writer for military publications. Prior to his retirement in 1986, General Bahnsen served two tours in Vietnam commanding at the platoon, troop and squadron levels, earning (among others) the Distinguished Service Cross, 5 Silver Stars, 3 Distinguished Flying Crosses, 4 Bronze Stars (3 for Valor), 51 Air Medals and 2 Purple Hearts. He has commanded a tank battalion in Germany and the 1st Aviation Brigade at Fort Rucker, Alabama. After selection to Brigadier General, "Doc" Bahnsen served as the Assistant Division Commander, 2nd Armored Division at Fort Hood, Texas, then as Chief of Staff for both the Combined Field Army (US/ROK) in Korea and III Corps at Fort Hood. A 1956 graduate of the Military Academy, General Bahnsen holds a master's degree in Public Administration from Shippensburg State University and has published seventeen articles since his retirement.

Charles F. Brower IV, is the Professor and Head of the Department of Behavioral Sciences and Leadership at the United States Military Academy. Colonel Brower has served in a variety of Armor and Cavalry assignments in the United States, Germany, and Vietnam, and was the Army Aide to President Reagan from 1982 to 1984. He holds a Ph.D. in History from the University of Pennsylvanvia. He is the author of articles on strategy in World War Two and Vietnam, and the editor and co-author of *World War II in Europe: The Final Year.*

Daniel W. Christman is the Superintendent of the United States Military Academy. After graduating first in his class from the Military Academy in 1965, Lieutenant General Christman served in a variety of demanding command and staff assignments, including serving as the nineteenth U.S. Representative to the NATO Military Committee in Brussels, Belgium; the Commanding General, U.S. Army Engineer School at Fort Leonard Wood, Missouri; and the Commander of the Savannah District, U.S. Army Corps of Engineers in Savannah, Georgia. General Christman holds master's degrees in civil engineering and public affairs from Princeton University and a law degree from George Washington University.

Robert W. Cone commands Second Brigade in the 4th Infantry Division at Fort Hood, Texas. Previously he commanded 1st Squadron, 3rd Armored Cavalry Regiment at Fort Carson, Colorado. A 1979 graduate of the Military Academy, Colonel Cone earned a master's degree from the University of Texas at Austin in preparation for assignment as an Instructor and Assistant Professor in the Behavioral Sciences and Leadership Department at West Point. He has published several articles in *Parameters* and *Armor Magazine*, and is a graduate of the U.S. Army Command and General Staff College and the Naval War College.

Conrad C. Crane is a career Air Defense Artillery officer who has written and lectured extensively on airpower issues. He holds a doctoral degree from Stanford University and is a 1974 graduate of the United States Military Academy. His professional education includes completion of the Command and General Staff College and Army War College. His most recent book, *Bombs, Cities, and Civilians: American Airpower Strategy in World War II*, was published by the University of Kansas. He has given presentations at the Naval War College, the National War College, and at numerous universities across the country. Lieutenant Colonel Crane currently serves as an Academy Professor at the United States Military Academy, where he teaches a variety of military history courses to include one on Generalship and the Art of Command.

Gregory Dardis, a U.S. Army Lieutenant Colonel, is an Associate Professor in the Behavioral Science and Leadership Department at the United States Military Academy. An Infantry Officer, Lieutenant Colonel Dardis holds a Ph.D. in Behavioral Science from the University of North Carolina. He currently teaches courses on leadership theory and combat leadership.

Kevin W. Farrell is currently an Armor Battalion Operations Officer in the 1st Infantry Division in Germany. Major Farrell has led soldiers at the platoon and company levels at the 1st Cavalry

Division at Fort Hood, Texas, and the 4th Infantry Division at Fort Carson, Colorado. A 1986 graduate of the Military Academy, Major Farrell has earned a Ph.D. in history from Columbia University. As an Assistant Professor of History at the United States Military Academy, he has served as an editor to the West Point Series Atlas of Military History, and taught a course on the History of Imperial and Nazi Germany.

Richard S. Faulkner is an operations officer in the 16th Cavalry Regiment at Fort Knox, Kentucky after serving as an Assistant Professor of American History at the United States Military Academy. A graduate of Kennesaw College in 1985, Major Faulkner has commanded two companies, one of which was during the Gulf War in which he earned the Bronze Star for Valor during combat actions in Operation Desert Storm. He holds a master's degree in American History from the University of Georgia. His articles have been published in *Armor, Georgia Historical Quarterly*, and *Military Images*.

Mark P. Hertling is the Commander of Operations Group at the National Training Center in Fort Irwin, California, after previously commanding 3rd Brigade, 2nd Infantry Division at Fort Lewis, Washington. A 1975 graduate of the Military Academy, Colonel Hertling has also commanded at the platoon, company and battalion levels in a variety of stateside and overseas assignments. During the Gulf War, he served as the operations officer for the 1st Squadron, 1st U.S. Cavalry, 1st Armored Division, where he earned the Bronze Star, Army Commendation Medal with V device (Valor) and the Purple Heart. Colonel Hertling holds a master's degree in Exercise Physiology from Indiana University and was formerly an instructor in the Department of Physical Education at the Military Academy.

Fred Kagan currently serves as an Assistant Professor of Military History at the United States Military Academy. Professor Kagan earned his doctoral degree in history from Yale University, and has written extensively on Russian and Soviet Military History. His book, *The Military Reforms of Nicholas I: The Birth of the Modern*

Russian Army, is under consideration for publication. A prolific writer, Professor Kagan has recently published articles in *Parameters, Commentary*, and *The Wall Street Journal*, and provides important input on the formation of U.S. Operational Doctrine as a member of the Future of Warfare Committee at the Military Academy.

Cole C. Kingseed is an Associate Professor of History at the United States Military Academy. An infantry officer, Colonel Kingseed has commanded at the platoon, company, and battalion levels. A graduate of Dayton University, Colonel Kingseed holds master's and doctoral degrees in History from The Ohio State University and a master's degree in National Security and Strategic Studies from the U.S. Naval War College. He has been published extensively in a variety of military journals, including a number of articles in the recent series on leadership in *Army* magazine. One hundred seventeen of his book reviews have been published. His own book, *Eisenhower and the Suez Crisis of 1956*, was published by Louisiana State University Press in 1995.

Douglas E. Lute currently serves as the Executive Assistant to the Chairman of the Joint Chiefs of Staff, after commanding the Second Armored Cavalry Regiment at Fort Polk, Louisiana. Colonel Lute graduated from the U.S. Military Academy at West Point and was commissioned as a second lieutenant of cavalry in 1975. He then served in various command and staff positions in the Second Armored Cavalry Regiment stationed in Germany. He received an M.A. from Harvard University and taught international relations for three years in the Social Sciences Department at West Point. He served as special assistant to the Chief of Staff of the Army, then returned to the Second Cavalry as operations officer during Operation Desert Storm. He commanded 1st Squadron, Seventh U.S. Cavalry, at Fort Hood, Texas, followed by service in the Joint Staff's Directorate for Strategic Plans and Policy (J-5), where he specialized in U.S. military operations in Haiti and Bosnia.

Robert W. Madden is a Garrison Commander in the Republic of Korea. He has served as the Tactical Officer for the Fourth

Regiment, United States Corps of Cadets at the United States Military Academy. A field artillery officer, Lieutenant Colonel Madden has commanded at the platoon, battery and battalion levels in a variety of assignments in the United States and overseas. A 1978 graduate of the Military Academy, Lieutenant Colonel Madden holds a master's degree in Military Art and Science (Theater Operations) from the School of Advanced Military Studies at Fort Leavenworth, Kansas, and is a graduate of the US Army War College. He has published articles in *Army* and *Field Artillery* magazines.

Richard W. Potter is a retired Brigadier General who has commanded Infantry and Special Forces units from platoon to brigade level. During his thirty-five years of service, General Potter has played a critical role in assessing, selecting and training elite forces to accomplish national objectives. He has coordinated and led these teams in combat operations in Laos, Cambodia, Vietnam, Iran, Iraq and Haiti, and in noncombatant evacuations in Liberia, Zaire and Sierra Leone. In addition, he has trained or led indigenous forces in Laos, Cambodia, Vietnam, Lebanon, Ethiopia and Great Britain, and lived with Kurds in Northern Iraq while directing the humanitarian relief and assistance program following the Gulf War. General Potter holds a Master of Arts in History from Shippensburg State University

Kalev I. Sepp has served as a Field Artillery and Special Forces officer in the 82d Airborne Division, the 2d Ranger Battalion, the 2d Infantry Division in Korea, the 11th Armored Cavalry Regiment in Germany, and the 7th Special Forces Group in Latin America. He was a brigade advisor in the Salvadoran Civil War, and an assistant professor at the United States Military Academy at West Point. In his current duty as a general staff officer, Lieutenant Colonel Sepp designs strategic political-military wargames to explore future technologies and organizations. He holds the degrees of Master of Military Art and Science from the U.S. Army Command and General Staff College, and Master of Arts in history from Harvard University, where he continues as a Ph.D. candidate.

Dennis Showalter is professor of history at Colorado College and current president of the Society for Military history. In 1997-98 he was Visiting Professor of Military History at the U.S. Military Academy. His recent publications include *The Wars of Frederick the Great* and "German Grand Strategy: A Contradiction in Terms?" He has written or edited eleven books on German and military history and has four additional volumes forthcoming.

Gordon Sullivan, author of the critically acclaimed book *Hope is Not a Method*, was the 32nd Chief of Staff of the United States Army. During his thirty-six years of active service, General Sullivan, an Armor officer, served in the United States, Vietnam, Korea and Germany. He commanded the First Infantry Division, was the Assistant Commandant of the Armor School, Deputy Commandant of the Command and General Staff College, and served as the Operations Deputy and Vice Chief before becoming Chief of Staff in 1991. Today, General Sullivan brings his considerable leadership skills to bear as the President of Coleman Federal, Coleman Research Corporation; Chair of the Boston University CEO Leadership Forum; and Director of the Shell Oil Company, Rubbermaid Corporation, General Dynamics Corporation, and the Armed Forces Bank. He also serves as a consultant to corporate leaders and is a member of several charitable organizations. A graduate of Norwich University, General Sullivan holds a Master of Arts in Political Science from the University of New Hampshire as well as honorary degrees from several colleges and universities.

John W. Woodmansee is currently responsible for Perot Systems' North American sales and operations. Prior to Perot Systems, Lieutenant General Woodmansee served 33 years in the United States Army, including two tours in Vietnam where he earned the Silver Star, 5 Distinguished Flying Crosses and 39 Air Medals. After rising to the rank of Lieutenant General, he commanded the 62,000 soldiers of the V United States Corps in Europe where he initiated innovative programs for training, leadership development, health and fitness and community development. A former White House

Fellow, he was assistant to the Secretaries of State Dean Rusk and William Rogers. He also served as a National Security Fellow at the Hoover Institution of War, Revolution and Peace at Stanford University. General Woodmansee is a 1956 graduate of the Military Academy and holds master's degrees in public administration from George Washington University and political science from Stanford University. He was an Assistant Professor of History at the United States Military Academy and wrote and appeared in a CBS television documentary on the history of revolutionary warfare.

Endnotes

Chapter One

1 Xenophon, *Oeconomicus*, XXI. 4ff (I have used the Penguin Classics edition: Xenophon, "Estate Manager," in *Conversations of Socrates*, translated by Hugh Tredennick and Robin Waterfield (London: Penguin Books, 1990)). All classical citations are by the original book and paragraph numbers.

2 Neal Wood, "Xenophon's Theory of Leadership," *Classica et Mediaevalia*, (XXV, 1964), 33. Colonel J. M. Scammell asserts, "He [Xenophon] proved himself a great soldier and consummate leader. He was the pupil of a great philosopher and the master who taught our forefathers the Art of War." See J.M. Scammell, "The Art of Command according to Xenophon," *The Army Quarterly*, IX (January, 1925), 365.

3 Xenophon, *Oeconomicus,* III. 18ff; see also IV. 18-19; XX. 1, 7.

4 Wood, 52.

5 Lord Moran, *The Anatomy of Courage* (Garden City Park, New York: Avery Publishers, 1987), 180.

6 Ibid., 194.

7 James MacGregor Burns, *Leadership* (New York: Harper and Row, 1978), 19.

8 Xenophon, *Memorabilia*, I. ii. 8ff. See also I.ii. 36ff; III.ix.7ff; IV. vi. 11ff (I have used the Penguin Classics edition, "Memoirs of Socrates" in *Conversations of Socrates* above).

9 Plato, *Republic*. For "persuasion" see: 432c, 445c, 474b-c, 517a, 529a, 548b, 565d-569c; for "force" see: Book I (Thrasymachus' arguments concerning justice), 411e, 444b, 492d, 517a, 548b, 565d-569c, 574b, 580c. (I have used Allan Bloom's translation, *The Republic of Plato* (New York: Harper Collins, 1991)).

10 Plato, *Statesman*, translated by Harold N. Fowler (Cambridge: Harvard University Press, Loeb Classical Library, 1925), 276e. see also Aristotle, *Politics*, translated by T. A. Sinclair and Trevor J. Saunders (London: Penguin Books, 1981), 1325a16: "But not all rule is rule by a master, and those who think it is are mistaken. The difference between ruling over free men and ruling over slaves is as great as the difference between the naturally free and the natural slave." See also 1284a17, 1295a17, 1295b13, 1310b40, 1315a40, 1312b38, 1313a18-1315b10. See also Aristotle, *Politics*, 1285a16.

11 Cicero, *De Re Publica* (Republic), translated by Clinton Walker Keyes (Cambridge: Harvard University Press, Loeb Classical Library, 1988), II.51. For Cicero, the State is an association of justice. Once the king ceases to be just, he is no longer a king but a tyrant. Once a tyrant rules the result is not a bad form of commonwealth, but the destruction of the commonwealth itself (I. 49, I. 65, III.43). For the use of persuasion over force see Cicero, *De Officiis* (On Duties, or On Moral Obligations), translated by Walter Miller (Cambridge: Harvard University Press, Loeb Classical Library, 1990), I. 34-5; I. 64; I. 77; II. 24.

12 This does not imply that the ruler should never punish citizens who commit crimes or fail in their duty; they also had a responsibility to the good citizens to punish the bad and enforce standards of justice. The difference is in the approach to leadership. The statesman would treat those who would act without reason as exceptions, harmonizing, as Plato suggests, persuasion and compulsion to correct the behavior. The tyrant would treat all as if they were without reason, i.e. beasts. The subject of discipline will be addressed in Chapter 5.

13 Aristotle, *Politics*, 1277b7, 1277b16, 1255b20.

14 Aristotle, *Nicomachean Ethics*, translated by Martin Oswald (New York: Macmillan Publishing Company, 1986), 1103a. See also Lord Moran, "Character. . . is a habit, the daily choice of right instead of wrong; it is a moral quality which grows to maturity in peace and is not suddenly developed in war" (160). Similarly, Howard D. Graves, former Superintendent of the United States Military Academy, defines character as "the ability to understand right from wrong, the courage to choose the right, and the toughness to follow that decision through." Interview with LTG Howard Graves, *Army Times* (20 November 1995), 16.

15 Cicero, *De Re Publica*, I. 41.

16 Cicero, *De Officiis*, I. 107-9, 115-118.

17 Ibid., I. 118.

18 Aristotle, *Rhetoric*, translated by J. H. Freese (Cambridge: Harvard University Press, Loeb Classical Library, 1959), 1356a13, 1377b20, 1378a6.

19 Xenophon, *Memorabilia*, I. i. 17ff.

20 Plato, *Republic*, 505a.

21 John W. Brinsfield ("Army Values and Ethics: A Search for Consistency and Relevance," Parameters (Autumn, 1998), 79) makes this mistake when he argues that the "virtue ethics" of the ancient Greeks (he mentions only Aristotle) are an incomplete guide for soldiers because such ethics center only on living well and doing well and carry with them no obligation to defend the state and its constitution. The so-called "virtue ethics" may be incomplete, but certainly not for the reason he mentions.

22 Plato, *Republic*, 534b-c.

23 Plato, *Republic*, 592b.

24 Aristotle, *Politics*, 1331b24.

25 Cicero, *De Re Publica*. III. 33.

26 See especially Book VI of *De Re Publica*, "The Dream of Scipio," and *De Legibus* (Laws), I. 23-4.

27 Plato, *Republic*, 383c.

28 The Stoic concept of *oikeiosis* (to be well-disposed toward) best expressed the system the Stoics advocated for resolving dilemmas involving conflicting loyalties. In essence, people developed "circles of attachement" to families, friends, community, state, and humanity. Naturally, such loyalties could conflict so the Stoics argued that loyalty to the cardinal virtues was the only way to resolve the problem of conflicting loyalties in the appropriate manner while still remaining devoted and true to one's family, friends, community, state, and humanity. For further development see S.G. Pembroke, "Oikeiosis," in A.A. Long (ed.), *Problems in Stoicism* (London: Althone Press, 1971). Also Cicero's *De Officiis* centers on the premise that one should make decisions based upon the cardinal virtues in order to lead a dignified and consistent life.

29 Cicero, *De Officiis*, I. 13; II. 17, 42; Xenophon, *Memorabilia*, I. vii.

30 Cicero, *De Officiis*, I. 142. Cicero believed that the easiest way to gain the good-will of others was through self-restraint and self-denial (*De Officiis*, II. 77).

31 Wood, 60.

32 Xenophon, *Memorabilia*, IV. v. 1ff.

33 Cicero, *De Officiis*, I. 72.

34 See Xenophon, *Memorabilia*, III. iii. 2-11. See also *Oeconomicus*, "The gods have ruled out success for people who do not know either what they ought to do or what steps they should take to achieve what they ought to do" (II. 7ff).

35 Aristotle, *Politics*, 1314b18. See also Xenophon, *Hiero*, I. 33; III.

36 Cicero, *De Officiis*, I. 41; I. 50; I. 91; I. 98; I. 149; II. 41; *De Legibus* I. 23-30; *De Amicitia* (On Friendship), XIV. 50.

37 Plato, *Republic*, 342e, 345d, 347d; *Statesman*, 275b, 276b. See also Aristotle, *Politics*, 1333b37.

38 Xenophon, *Cyropaedia* (Education of Cyrus), translated by Walter Miller (Cambridge: Harvard University Press, Loeb Classical Library, 1914), VIII. ii. 2; *Hipparchicus* (Cavalry Commander), VI. 3; *Memorabilia*, III. ii; *Oeconomicus* VII. 36ff; Wood, 53.

39 Xenophon, *Oeconomicus*, VIII. 37; IX. 13-5; *Hipparchicus*, VI. 3; *Cyropaedia*, I. vi. 15; VI. I. 23-5; VIII. ii. 7-23, 24-5, 27; *Hiero*, XI. for a further discussion of Xenophon's theory of discipline see Chapter 5.

40 Cicero, *De Re Publica*, I. 27, 53-4, II. 47; *De Officiis*, I. 20, 85; II. 16-7.

41 Plato, *Statesman*, 311b-c.

42 Xenophon, *Cyropaideia*, I. i. 2,3.

43 Ibid.

44 Ibid., I. i. 6.

45 Garrett Mattingly, however, makes an interesting argument that The Prince was intended by Machiavelli as political satire rather than political science in "Machiavelli's Prince: Political Science or Political Satire," *The American Scholar* (Volume 27, Number 4, Autumn 1958), 482-491.

Chapter Two

1 S.L.A. Marshall, *Men Against Fire: The Problem of Battle Command in Future War* (Gloucester, MA: Peter Smith, 1978), 27.

2 Anthony Kellett, *Combat Motivation* (Ottawa, Canada: Department of National Defence, 1980) and Richard Holmes, *Acts of War: The Behavior of Men in Battle* (New York: The Free Press, 1985).

3 Gerald F. Linderman, *The World Within War: America's Combat Experience in World War II* (New York: The Free Press, 1997); Stephen Ambrose, *Band of Brothers: E Company, 506th Regiment, 101st Airborne Division from Normandy to Hitler's Eagle's Nest* (New York: Touchstone Books, 1993); Lord Moran, *The Anatomy of Courage* (Garden City, New York: Avery Publishing, 1987), John Dower, *War Without Mercy: Race and Power in the Pacific War* (New York: Pantheon Books, 1986); Dave Grossman, *On Killing: The Psychological Cost of Learning to Kill in War and Society* (Boston: Little, Brown and Company, 1995).

4 Harold G. Moore and Joseph Galloway, *We Were Soldiers Once...and Young* (New York: Random House, 1992);   Charles B. MacDonald, *Company Commander.* Third Printing. (New York: Bantam Books, 1982): Mark Boden, *Blackhawk Down: A Story of Modern War (New York: Atlantic Monthly Press;* 1999); Rhonda Cornum (as told to Peter Copeland), *She Went to War* (Novato, CA: Presidio Press, 1992); John S. McCain (with Mark Salter), *Faith of My Fathers: A Family Memoir* (New York: Random House, 1999).

5 Linderman, 25.

6 Kellett, 309.

7 Moran, 13.

8 Ibid., 314.

9 Another equally powerful example is that of Captain Ramon A. Nadal's audacious bayonet attack out of the dry creek bed on LZ X-Ray in his effort to break through the NVA ring and to rescue a lost American platoon. Nadal's motivation of his soldiers after a long, confusing and bloody day of combat, inspirational from-the-front leadership, and calmness and competence in extremely hazardous and ambiguous circumstances is a case study in combat leadership. Throughout that desperate fight, his pervasive commitment to his soldiers bound his troopers together and sustained them. For the details, see Moore and Galloway, 140-151.

10 Ambrose, 77-78.

11 Ibid., 77-83. The quotation is on 79.

12 Ibid., 84.

13 Ibid., 21.

14 General George S. Patton, *War As I Knew It* (Boston: Houghton Mifflin Company, 1947), 336.

15 Marshall, 44, 154.

16 The expression is, of course, that of Richard Holmes, 74ff.

17 Cited in Grossman, 43.

18 Ambrose, 13.

19 Marshall, 56.

20 The argument in this and the following paragraphs is derived from Grossman, 249-295.

21 Dower, 77-93, 118-146, 242. Gerald Linderman's chapters "Fighting the Germans: The War of Rules" and Fighting the Japanese: War Unrestrained" in *The World Within War* are also very useful resources for stimulating discussion on this topic. See Linderman, 90-184.

22 Sledge cited in ibid., 63. Sledge was a young Marine rifleman who participated in two of the fiercest battles of the Pacific war, Peleliu and Okinawa.
His *With the Old Breed at Peleliu and Okinawa* (Novato, CA: Presidio Press,
1981) remains one of the very best memoirs of that war.

23 Colonel Ramon A. Nadal, "Small Unit Leadership in Combat," Lecture to
PL470, Leadership in Combat, West Point, New York, 10 November 1998.

Chapter Three

1   The original version of this essay was originally published by *Military Review*
(August 1994). They have granted permission for publication in this volume.

2   U.S., Department of the Army, FM 100-5 *Operations* (Washington D.C.: U.S.
Government Printing Office, 14 June 1993), 2-9.

3   Clay Blair, *Ridgway's Paratroopers* (Garden City, NY: The Dial Press, 1985), 4.

4   George T. Simon et al., *The Best of the Music Makers* (Garden City, NY:
Doubleday and Company Inc., 1979), 91-92.

5   General Matthew B. Ridgway, USA (Ret.), with Harold H. Martin, *Soldier*
(New York: Harper and Brothers, 1956), 35-38.

6   Stanley Sadie (ed.), *The New Grove Dictionary of Music and Musicians*
(London: Macmillan Press, Ltd., 1980), 20 vols., Volume 3: *Bollioud-Mermet to
Castro*, 349; Volume 12: *Meares to Mutis*, 305-6; Volume 16: *Riegel to
Schusterfleck*, 701-6, cover Brubeck, Milhaud and Schoenberg, respectively.

7   Blair, 5.

8   Gunther Schuller, *Early Jazz* (Oxford: Oxford University Press, 1968), 134-5.

9   Blair, 6.

10 T. R. Fehrenbach, *This Kind of War* (New York: Macmillan Co., 1963), 419.
On p. 439 Fehrenbach pays this tribute: "No man who saw Lieutenant
General Matt Ridgway in operation doubts the sometime greatness of men."

11 Hitchcock and Sadie, *The New Grove Dictionary of American Music*, Volume
1: A-D, 313-4.

12 Ibid,. 313.

13 Margaret J. Wheatley, "Can the U.S. Army Become a Learning Organization?"
Journal for Quality and Participation (March 1994), 3.

Chapter Four

1   Reuven Gal, "Unit Morale: From a Theoretical Puzzle to an Empirical Illustration — An Israeli Example," *Journal of Applied Social Psychology*, (Volume 16, No. 6, 1986), 551.

2   William L. Hauser, "The Will to Fight," in *Combat Effectiveness: Cohesion, Stress, and the Volunteer Military*,   Sam C. Sarkesian, ed. (London, Sage Publications, 1980), 187.

3   Carl von Clausewitz, *On War*, Michael Howard and Peter Paret, eds., (Princeton, N.J.: Princeton University Press), 185.

4   FM 100-5, *Operations* (Washington, D.C.: HQ, Department of the Army, Jun 93), 1-2. Hereafter referred to as FM 100-5 (1993). In a review of the Final Draft FM 3-0 (previously 100-5) dated 21 April 2000, the Army continues to emphasize the force projection and contingency nature of future operations. However, acknowledgement of the human dimension does get slighted. FM 22-100 (June 1999 version) increases emphasis on team-building and cohesion over previous versions. There are no direct quotes from FM3-0 because it is not yet approved doctrine.

5   A.J. Bacevich, "Old Myths: Renewing American Military Thought," *Parameters* (Mar 1988), 20.

6   FM 100-5, *Operations* (Washington, D.C.: HQ Department of the Army, May 1986), 26. Hereafter referred to as FM 100-5 (1986).

7   Casualty data is obtained from the preface to DA PAM 350-2, *Developing and Maintaining Unit Cohesion* (Washington, D.C.: U.S. Government Printing Office).

8   In a larger perspective, while the Army put over 8 million Americans under arms during WWII, it also discharged 332,000 men for psychiatric reasons. See Roger J. Spiller, "The Thousand Yard Stare: Psychodynamics of Combat in World War II," 3. An unpublished copy of this article was provided to me directly from the author.

9   Gregory Belenky, Shabtai Noy, and Zahava Solomon, "Battle Stress: The Israeli Experience," *Military Review* (July 1985), 29.

10   Anthony Kellett, "Combat Motivation," in *Contemporary Studies in Combat Psychology*, Gregory Belenky, ed. (New York: Greenwood Press, 1987), 278-279.

11   FM 22-100, *Military Leadership* (Washington, D.C.: HQ, Department of the Army), June 1983), 156.

12   DA PAM 350-2, Intro., Para 2.

13   Flavius Vegetius Renatus, *The Military Institutions of the Romans*, in *Roots of*

Strategy, BG Thomas R. Phillips, ed. (Harrisburg, PA: Stackpole Books, March 1985), 75. Hereafter referred to as Vegetius.

14 Ibid., 75-76.

15 Statement made by the editor, BG Phillips, in Vegetius, 67.

16 Antoine Henri Jomini, *A Summary of the Art of War*, in Roots of Strategy, Book II, BG J. D. Hittle, ed. (Harrisburg, PA: Stackpole Books, 1987), 554. *Hereafter referred to as Jomini.* Jomini's influence was so profound in that it has been said that many a Civil War General went into battle with a sword in one hand and a copy of Jomini's *Summary of the Art of War* in the other. His ideas became accepted and applied as military doctrine in the French, British and American Armies.

17 Ibid., 458-459.

18 Clausewitz, 187-188. Whereas Jomini's writings were influential in the military doctrine of France, England, and the United States; Prussian General Carl von Clausewitz' theories began to shape the doctrinal concepts of the expanding Prussian Army under Helmut von Moltke (the Elder). The philosophical seeds sown by Clausewitz were manifested in the conduct of the Franco-Prussian War (1870-71) and WWI.

19 Ibid., 189.

20 Ibid., 189.

21 Ibid., 122.

22 Ibid., 189.

23 Ibid., 101.

24 Ibid., 122.

25 Ibid., 187.

26 Ardant du Picq, *Battle Studies: Ancient and Modern Battle*, in *Roots of Strategy, Book 2*, trans. John N. Greely and Robert C. Cotton (Harrisburg, PA: Stackpole Books, 1987), 141-142. Hereafter referred to as Du Picq.

27 Ibid., 136.

28 Ibid., 122.

29 Ibid., 252.

30 Ibid., 137.

31 Ibid., 255.

32 Ibid., 48.

33 SLA Marshall, *Men Against Fire: The Problem of Battle Command in the Future War* (Gloucester, MA: Peter Smith, 1978), 170.

34 Samuel A. Stouffer, et al, *The American Soldier: Combat and Its Aftermath, Vol II* (Princeton, NJ: Princeton University Press, 1949), 130-131. This study confirmed SLA Marshall's well-known conclusion that, "I hold it to be one of the simplest truths of war that the thing which enables an infantry soldier to keep going with his weapons, if any, is the presence or presumed presence of a comrade." (Marshall, p. 42)

35 FM 100-5 (1993), 14-3.

36 FM 100-5, (1986) 5.

37 The concept of these doctrinal assumptions comes from Michael L. Combest, "Building the Will To Fight — Prerequisite to Winning the AirLand Battle," *AMSP Monograph* (1 December 1986), 3-5.

38 Kellett, *Combat Motivation: The Behavior of Soldiers in Battle* (Boston, MA: Kluwer Boston, Inc., 1982), 136.

39 Lord Moran, *The Anatomy of Courage* (Garden City Park, NY: The Avery Publishing Company, 1987), 166.

40 Marshall, 78.

41 Sun Tzu, *The Art of War*, trans. Samuel B. Griffith (London: Oxford University Press), 84.

42 George C. Wilson, *Mud Soldiers* (New York: Charles Scribner's Sons, 1989), 63. This profile is a survey of infantry recruits at Fort Benning and is offered as a representative sample of recruits throughout the Army and their demographics.

43 Ibid., 64. George Wilson's survey was conducted on a select population of infantry soldiers as they began basic training at Ft..Benning, Georgia.

44 Email from LTC Denise Dailey, Department of the Army, Office of the Deputy Chief of Staff for Personnel, 20 August which contained the results of the 1997 New Recruit Survey asking those who enlisted why they enlisted during reception station processing.

45 Ibid., 64.

46 Doonesbury© Gary Trudeau, *I'd Take the Helmet, Ray* (Kansas City, MO: Andrews and McMeel, a Universal Press Syndicate Company, 1991), 75. Used with permission. All rights reserved.

47 Bacevich, 24.

48 Kellett, in *Contemporary Studies*, 220.

49 Summarized from Jesse J. Harris, "Soldier Stress and Operation Urgent Fury," in Consultation Report #85-002, *Proceedings Fourth User's Workshop on Combat Stress: Lessons Learned in Recent Operational Experiences* (United

States Army Health Care Studies and Clinical Investigation Activity, January 1985), 167-168.

50 Diana R. Haslan and Peter Abraham, "Sleep Loss and Military Performance," in *Contemporary Studies in Combat Psychiatry*, 175

51 Interview with MAJ Charles Jacoby, Commander of A Company, 2-235 Inf., 82d Airborne Division during the invasion of Grenada.

52 Roger J. Spiller, "Isen's Run: Human Dimensions of Warfare in the 20th Century," *Military Review* (May 1988), 18.

53 Napoleonic maxim quoted in du Picq, 147.

54 Du Picq, 142.

55 Kellett, in *Contemporary Studies* ... , 101.

56 FM 100-5 (1993), 2-11.

57 FM 100-1, *The Army* (Washington, D.C.:   HQ, Department of the Army, August 1986), 22-23.

58 The elements of spirit is an idea obtained from an oral briefing delivered by LTC James D. Channon, "Cohesion Technology," presented to the Commanding General, MG Robert Elton, 9th Infantry Division , March 1982.

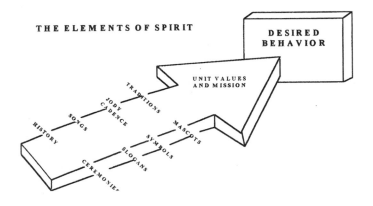

The elements of spirit in many Army units today exist simply because of inertia—they have always been there. But they must mean something to the soldier or they become nothing more than excess baggage. Norman F. Dixon, in his work *On the Psychology of Military Incompetence*, refers to the elements of spirit as "bull." Although he recognizes the purpose of bull is to allay anxiety, he warns that such indoctrination can lead to rigidity, conformity, traditionalism, over-obedience, and aversion to progress. Such can be the case if spirit is developed without regard to the realities of the modern battlefield.

59 The employment of a bonding cycle is an idea obtained from an oral brief-ing delivered by LTC Channon.

60 DA PAM 600-65, *Leadership Statements and Quotes* (Washington, D.C.: HQ, Department of the Army, November 1985), 21.

61 FM 22-100, 157.

62 The ideas of the married Army come from Larry H. Ingram and Frederick J. Manning, "Cohesion: Who Needs It, What Is It, and How Do We Get It to Them?" in *Military Review* (June 1981), 5. Statistics for the marital state of the military are from an email to the author from Timothy Whyte, U.S. Army Community and Family Support Center, 17 May 2000.

63 Interview with MAJ Jacoby.

64 Stouffer, 124-125.

65 Spiller, 22-23.

66 FM 22-100, 157.

67 Clausewitz, 189.

68 Guy Sajer, *The Forgotten Soldier* (London: Sphere Books Limited, 1971), 208.

69 The "Ten Foot Tall" experience is an idea obtained from an oral briefing delivered by Lieutenant Colonel Channon. Examples include a 100 mile road march (spread over several days) and adventure training such as rappelling, confidence courses, etc.

70 Clausewitz, 153.

71 Stouffer, 222-223.

72 Ibid., 230.

73 Nora Kinzer Stewart, Research Report 1469, South Atlantic Conflict of 1982: A Case Study in Military Cohesion (US Army Research Institute for the Behavioral and Social Sciences, April 1988), xi.

74 Stouffer, 234-235.

75 Terry Fullerton, Consultation Report #85-002, 147.

76 Moran, 160.

77 Du Picq, 258.

Chapter Five

1 The notion of "right" is problematic. For the purposes of this essay "doing what is right" entails performing job-related skills to a defined standard and conducting behavior in accordance with established organizational values.

2 These methods of control will be further developed in Section II.

3 Michel Foucault, *Discipline and Punish: The Birth of the Prison*; translated by Alan Sheridan (New York: Vintage Books, 1979), 135-7.

4 Mature military organizations can take a variety of forms from guerrilla units to regulars to elite special operations forces. Examples of such organizations include many partisan units on the eastern front and in the occupied territories during World War Two, the German Storm-Troop units in the First World War, many regular German divisions at the outset of World War Two as well as several seasoned US and British divisions later in the war, and US Army Rangers and Special Operations Forces.

5 Lord Moran, *Anatomy of Courage* (Garden City Park, N.Y.: Avery Publishing Group, 1987), 166.

6 Ibid., 173.

7 Ibid., 162-3.

8 As Ardant du Picq suggests, "Today, why should not the men in our companies watch discipline and punish themselves. They alone know each other, and the maintenance of discipline is so much to their interest as to encourage them to stop skulking." See Ardant du Picq, "Battle Studies," in John N. Greeley and Robert C. Cotton (eds.), *Roots of Strategy, Book II* (Harrisburg, Pa.: Stackpole Books, 1987), 255.

9 Confucius, *Analects*, translated by D. C. Lau (London: Penguin Books, 1979), II. 20.

10 Aristotle, *Nichomanchean Ethics*, translated by Martin Ostwald (New York: Macmillan Publishing Co., 1986), 1103a15 ff.

11 As Plato asserts, education is the true guardian of the guardians. See the discussion in Plato, *Republic*, 374a - 383c.

12 The classicist Neal Wood, who studied Xenophon's theory of leadership, in an otherwise insightful essay on Xenophon's theory of leadership, suggests that the ancient Greek philosopher considered the foundations of obedience to be compulsion, self-interest, and rational organization. The leader exacts obedience, Wood explains, by instilling in his followers the fear of punishment for incompetent or disloyal service and the promise of reward for good behavior. Coercion, according to Wood, forms the foundation of Xenophon's theory of discipline. This argument, however, is difficult to reconcile with one of the core principles underlying Xenophon's philosophical framework: that persuasion, not force of coercion, is the proper way to wield authority. See Neal Wood, "Xenophon's Theory of Leadership," *Classica et Mediaevalia* (XXV, 1964), 49-51.

13 Xenophon, *Oeconomicus*, III. 18ff; IV. 18-19; XX. 1, 7.

14 Xenophon, *Oeconomicus*, III. 5-13; *Memorabilia* (Memoirs of Socrates), III. iii. 2-11 (in *Xenophon: Conversations of Socrates*).

15 Xenophon, *Oeconomicus* (Estate Manager), in *Xenophon: Conversations of Socrates*, translated by Hugh Tredennick and Robin Waterfield (London: Penguin Books, 1990), XII.9.

16 Xenophon, a friend of Cyrus, was asked by the latter to accompany him on an expedition with Greek mercenaries to the heart of the Persian Empire to dethrone Xerxes, the brother of Cyrus. While Cyrus' force emerged victorious from the ensuing battle, Cyrus was killed and Xerxes remained alive. When the Greeks asked Xerxes for safe passage back to Greece, the latter had the Greek military leaders executed after summoning them to a conference. Xenophon, the only Athenian in the expedition, volunteered to lead the Greeks back. He recounts his dangerous retreat of the "Ten Thousand" in the *Anabasis*.

17 Xenophon, *Anabasis*, II. vi. 9-14, 20.

18 Xenophon, *Oeconomicus*, XIII. 10ff. See also V. 5-19; *Memorabilia*, III. iv. 8. See also Cicero, *De Officiis* (On Duties, or On Moral Obligations), translated by Walter Miller (Cambridge: Harvard University Press, Loeb Classical Library, 1990), I. 88-9. Punishment, according to Cicero, the Stoic philosopher and Roman politician, must be for the benefit of the organization as well as for the offending person and must be recognized as such. It need not be insulting, nor applied merely for the personal satisfaction of the one administering the punishment. Above all, it must not be out of proportion to the offense and must be applied consistently — some should not be chastised for a fault to which others are not called to account if the standards are to be taken seriously.

19 Xenophon, *Hipparchicus*, VI. 1. See also Sun-Tzu, "If commands are consistently enforced in the training of the men, they will obey; if commands are not consistently enforced in their training, they will not obey. The consistent enforcement of commands promotes a complementary relationship between the commander and his men." *The Art of War*, 144

20 John M. Schofield, quoted in *Bugle Notes*, vol. 42 (West Point, N.Y.: United States Military Academy, 1950-1), 206.

21 Command climate is the atmosphere in an organization that results from the interaction between performance results and shared values. In an organization that gains good performance results within the context of healthy, shared values, a positive command climate is the result. This climate creates a cohesive organization because the members believe in each other, what they are doing and how they do it. For further discussion, see section III.

22 Xenophon, *Cyropaedia* (Education of Cyrus), translated by Walter Miller (Cambridge: Harvard University Press, Loeb Classical Library, 1914), I. vi. 21.

23 Aristotle, *Politics*, translated by T. A. Sinclair and Trevor J. Saunders (London: Penguin Books, 1981), 1261a22, 1261b16; *Nichomachean Ethics*, V. v. 1132b21 ff.

24 Anthony Kellet, "Combat Motivation," in Gregory Belenky (ed.), *Contemporary Studies in Combat Psychology* (New York: Greenwood Press, 1987), 278-9.

25 Modern industry, in fact, has experienced the same diffusion of direct supervision, presaging that of the armed forces. Gone are the antiquated days when employees always worked in close proximity with the owners and managers. Sometimes connected only by a telephone or computer-network link, managers must rely upon the discipline of their subordinates to accomplish their tasks in the absence of direct and constant guidance.

26 Initiative, in the context of this essay, relates to the level of independence and decision-making authority given to subordinate leaders. Initiative in the sense of making decisions and implementing them faster than one's enemy is possible in a highly centralized organization. Soviet doctrine, in fact, was based upon that premise. For further study see the provocative essay "World War III, Soviet Style" by E.B. Atkeson in his book, *The Final Argument of Kings: Reflections on the Art of War* (Fairfax, Va.: Hero Books, 1988), pp 183-189.

27 The following discussion is based on my argument in Christopher D. Kolenda, "Navigating the Fog of Technological Change," *Military Review* (November-December 1996), 37-40. For further discussion, see also Robert R. Leonhard, *The Art of Maneuver: Maneuver Warfare Theory and Air-Land Battle* (Novato, Ca.: Presidio Press, 1991), 48-58.

28 For further discussion see, William S. Lind, *Maneuver Warfare Handbook* (Boulder, Colorado: Westview Press, 1985), 5-6. As Colonel John Boyd, a former Air Force fighter pilot, argues, conflict can be seen as time-competitive observation-orientation-decision-action cycles. A combatant observes the situation. Based on the observation, the combatant orients, making a mental snap-shot of the situation. On the basis of the orientation, the combatant makes a decision, then acts on that decision. Since the situation has now changed, the combatant observed again, and the cycle repeats itself. The side that consistently goes through the "Boyd-cycle" faster enjoys a tremendous advantage, because that side can dictate a new reality while the other is reacting to an older one. Eventually, the slower side's decisions become more and more inappropriate to the changing reality and ultimately ceases to be effective, resulting in physical and/or psychological dislocation and

destruction. Boyd developed his theory after studying aerial combat in Korea between the U.S. F-86 and the Soviet-style MiG-15 aircraft, in which the F-86, despite some technical shortcomings, enjoyed a 10:1 advantage in kill ratio over the MiG.

29 The German Army cultural doctrine, argues Trevor N. DuPuy (A Genius for War: The german Army and the general Staff, 1807-1945 (Englewood Cliffs, NJ: Prentice-Hall, 1977), was based upon the values of discipline, obedience, independence and initiative. Together, these would form the basis of trust in the organization.

30 Daniel J. Hughes (ed.), *Moltke on the Art of War: Selected Writings* (Novato, CA: Presidio Press, 1993), 184. For an insightful discussion of the dysfunctional ramifications of the "pathology of information" on the U.S. Army in Viet Nam, see Martin van Creveld, *Command in War* (Cambridge, MA: Harvard University Press, 1985), 258-60.

31 Varro was the Roman commander whose force was annihilated by Hannibal in the battle of Cannae (216 BC) during the Second Punic War.

Chapter Six

1 C.B. Welles, "There Have Been Many Alexanders," in Eugene N. Borza (ed.), *The Impact of Alexander the Great* (Hinsdale, Ill: Dryden Press, 1974), 9.

2 Sir William Woodthorpe Tarn, *Alexander the Great*, Vol II. (Cambridge: Cambridge University Press, 1948), 399-400.

3 Ernst Badian, "The Struggle for Independence," in Borza (ed.), 111.

4 N.G.L. Hammond, *Alexander the Great: King, Commander and Statesman* (Park Ridge, New Jersey: Noyes Press, 1980), 248.

5 J.F.C. Fuller, *The Generalship of Alexander the Great* (Westport, Conn: Greenwood Press, 1960), 303.

6 John Keegan, *The Mask of Command* (London: Penguin Books, 1987), 77.

7 Ibid., p. 35.

8 Ibid., p. 89. The three plots Keegan refers to are the Philotas plot in 330, the "Old" Companions in 328 which ended with the murder of Cleitus, and the Pages' revolt in 327.

9 While the dialogues reported in the primary sources (Arrian, Quintus Curtius, Diodorus, and Plutarch) are certainly invented by the author, they nevertheless are representative of the cultural context to which Alexander and his soldiers belonged.

10 Fuller, 285. Justin, XI, vi. This same advice was allegedly given to Alexander by Parmenion as the former considered burning Persepolis to avenge the

burning of Athens by Xerxes. See Arrian, *Anabasis Alexandri*, translated by P. A. Brunt (Cambridge: Harvard University Press, Loeb Classical Library, 1976), III. xviii. 11-12.

11 For an outstanding discussion of Alexander's great battles, see Fuller, 147-199. Fuller analyzes the battles at Granicus (334 BC), Issus (333 BC), Arbela (Gaugamela) (331 BC), and Hydaspes (326 BC).

12 See the diagrams in Fuller, 165, 171.

13 This confusing part of the battle is neatly reconstructed in Fuller (173-180), who sorts through the accounts of Arrian III. xv; and Quintus Curtius, *History of Alexander*, translated by John C. Rolfe (Cambridge: Harvard University Press, Loeb Classical Edition, 1992), IV. xv.

14 Fuller, 226-234; Arrian, III. xviii. 1-9; Curtius, V. iii. 17 ff.

15 This force was commanded by Ariobarzanes. Arrian gives him 40,000 foot and 700 horse (III. xviii. 2); Curtius' figures are 25,000 foot (V. iii. 17); Diodorus' are 25,000 foot and 300 horse (Diodorus Siculus, *VIII.*, translated by C. Bradford Welles (Cambridge: Harvard University Press, Loeb Classical Library, 1983) XVII. 68. 1).

16 Arrian, III. xviii. 8-9. Curtius (V. iv. 33-4) claims Ariobarzanes was escaped with 5000 foot and 40 horse to Persepolis but were shut out of the city by its garrison, and then killed by the pursuing Macedonians.

17 A.B. Bosworth, *Conquest and Empire: The Reign of Alexander the Great* (Cambridge: Cambridge University Press, 1988), 91.

18 Another striking example of Alexander's genius for maneuver was his campaign against Porus on the Hydaspes in "India" (326 BC). See Fuller,180-199.

19 Hammond, 255.

20 For a full account of the siege see Fuller, 206-216.

21 Arrian, II. 23. 4.

22 Curtius reports that the Macedonians seemed struck with fear at the prospect of having to fight the "most warlike nations of India" as they moved South towards the Indian Ocean (IX. iv. 16-18).

23 Arrian, VI. viii. 3.

24 Ibid., VI. ix-x.

25 Ibid., II. iv. 11. See also Curtius III, vi. This trust and loyalty is in striking contrast to his actions over the alleged Philotas conspiracy in 330 BC and the purges of his satraps and governors in 324 BC over alleged corruption and mistreatment of their populations.

26 Ernst Badian argues that the march through the Gedrosian desert in order supply the fleet was merely a pretext for a more mystical motive. Shaken by his "defeat" at the Hyphasis, Alexander needed to reassert his "supernatural standing" among the men and saw the desert march as a means to achieve a "countervailing triumph to erase the memory" (Ernst Badian, "Alexander in Iran," in I. Gershevitch (ed.), *Cambridge History of Iran II* (Cambridge: Cambridge University Press, 1985), 472-3; see also John Maxwell O'Brien, *Alexander the Great: The Invisible Enemy; A Biography* (London and New York: Routledge, 1992), 179-184.).

27 See Bosworth, 143; Arrian, VI. xxiv. 2-3.

28 The march certainly cost many civilians their lives. The soldiers made it through in better shape, but the death toll must have been significant. See Bosworth, p. 145.

29 Arrian, VI. xxvi. 1-3. Plutarch, *Alexander*, 42. 7, claims this occurred during the pursuit of Darius in the summer of 330 BC; Curtius (VII. v. 10) has it occur in Sogdiana near the River Oxus in the summer of 329.

30 Alexander was especially generous in bestowing wealth on his soldiers. They were always paid promptly and generously. He even assumed his soldiers' considerable debts in 324 BC. See Bosworth, 158; Arrian VII. v. 1-3.

31 Keegan argues that the Macedonian officers never struck or belittled their soldiers, equality of respect was the ethos of this army of warriors. "To such men a blow from a superior was a deadly insult, a denial of manhood, which could be expunged only by violence in return" (45).

32 Arrian, I. xvi. 5-6.

33 Ibid., I. xxiv. 1.

34 Ibid., II. vii. 7. See also Curtius, III. ix. 4.

35 Arrian, II. xii. 1.

36 The definition of "cosmopolitan" is elusive. For the Stoics, cosmopolitanism referred to the notion that all human beings were members of the "Cosmopolis," the divine city ruled by God through Natural Law, and hence were equally entitled to Justice regardless of race, tribe, etc. Stoicism was founded after Alexander's time, but the argument here is concerned with whether Alexander entertained a notion of the "unity of mankind" in which all members of the species were "equal" or whether he viewed the Macedonians and Greeks as superior to the "barbarians."

37 Tarn, *Alexander the Great*, Vol 2, 399. According to Tarn, "Zeno's great city of the world took up and was founded on Alexander's idea of human brotherhood" (448).

38 Ibid., 400. Hammond makes a similar argument, claiming that Alexander "set himself an unparalleled task when he decided in advance not to make the Macedonians and Greeks the masters of the conquered peoples but to create a self-sustaining kingdom of Asia" (258).

39 Ulrich Wilcken, *Alexander the Great* (New York: Norton Library, 1967), 207-8.

40 Ernst Badian, "Alexander the Great and the Unity of Mankind," *Historia* 7 (1958), 443-444.

41 Badian's argument seems to have the most currency at present. See Bosworth, 161.

42 Diodorus, XIII. 26. 3. Quoted in W.K.C. Guthrie, *The Sophists* (London: Cambridge University Press, 1971), 84.

43 Isocrates, *Panegyricus*, 39-40. Quoted in Ibid., 83-4.

44 R.G.A. Buxton, *Persuasion in Greek Tragedy: A Study of Peitho* (Cambridge: Cambridge University Press, 1982), 62. For further development on the relationship between persuasion and force in ancient ideas of leadership see chapter 1.

45 See Aristotle, *Politics*, translated by T.A. Sinclair (London: Penguin Books, 1981), 1253a7-18.

46 Buxton, p. 58.

47 The Corintian League, established in 337, was an association of Greek city-states that Philip constructed after the Battle of Chaeronea in 338. Sparta refused to join it. One of the first acts of the League, tightly controlled by Philip, was a declaration of war against Persia.

48 Bosworth, p. 38.

49 Arrian, II, vii, 4-5. Emphasis added.

50 Aeschylus, *Persians*, 242.

51 Bosworth, 96-7.

52 Arrian, III. xxix. 5. C.A. Robinson ("Extraordinary Ideas of Alexander the Great," *American Historical Review*, 62 (no 2), January 1957, 335, note 59) makes the argument that the Thessalians had revolted near the Oxus River, thus forcing Alexander's hand to send home those allies who opted not to remain in the army (a number of them volunteered to continue their service with Alexander). Robinson cites Arrian (V. xxvii. 5) as evidence when Coenus reminded Alexander that he sent the Thessalians home because they no longer were eager to undergo labors. For a different view see Tarn, II, p. 290 who regarded this a partial proof against the genuiness of Coenus' speech. A further problem for Alexander was the alleged plot of Philotas, the com-

mander of the Companion Cavalry, in October 330 B.C. Philotas was convicted in a trial before the army and was executed. Alexander also had Philotas' father, Parmenion—Alexander's second in command, executed as well. For further development of this subject see Ernst Badian, "The Death of Parmenio," *Transactions of the American Philological Association*, 91 (1960), 324-38.

53 Ibid.

54 Arrian, IV, vii, 4.

55 J.P.V.D. Balsdon, "The 'Divinity' of Alexander," *Historia*, I (1950), 373. See also Arrian, IV. viii. 6. Curtius, VIII. i. 27 and 30.

56 Arrian, IV. viii. 4. See also Bosworth, 114. Cleitus had saved Alexander's life at Granicus.

57 Balsdon, 372.

58 Arrian, IV. ix. 7.

59 Arrian, IV. ix. 7-9. See also Badian, "The Struggle for Personal Independence," in Borza (ed.), 107. Callisthenes, Alexander's court historian had spread the story that Alexander was greeted as the Son of Ammon (Zeus) when the king visited the oracle at Siwah in February 331 BC. (Arrian, III. iii. 1-2; III, iv, 5; Curtius, IV. vii. 6-8 and 25-32). Whether Alexander regarded himself as such is a matter of considerable debate. For arguments concerning Alexander's divinity see Balsdon, p. 373ff; and D.G. Hogarth, "The Deification of Alexander the Great," *English Historical Review*, 1887, 318-329, both of whom discount Alexander's aspirations for divinity. Tarn (II, 350ff) believes Alexander sought divinity for political reasons. See also Bosworth, 278-290.

60 Aristotle, *Rhetoric*, 1361a36, regards it as a specifically barbarian mark of honor. In Greek popular perception, the Persians regarded their king as a peer of the gods.

61 Bosworth, 284.

62 Hogarth, 319.

63 Aeschylus, *Persians*, 827-8. Callisthenes, in arguing against the introduction of *proskynesis*, reportedly gave Alexander a litany of examples of Persian kings who, consumed by the same hubris, were all "brought to their senses" by "poor people but free." Darius, too, was brought to his senses by Alexander, "who does not receive obeisance" (Arrian, IV. xi. 9). Hammond, 198, doubts the veracity of Arrian's account of this speech.

64 Badian, "The Struggle for Personal Independence," in Borza (ed.), 107.

65 Balsdon, 372.

66 While the exact role of Philotas in the affair is uncertain, the conspiracy was a serious attempt on Alexander's life. Philotas was apparently informed of the plot but did not alert the king, perhaps because he believed it fictitious, perhaps because he had some sympathy for the conspirators. Nevertheless, Philotas had many enemies in the court, and this was a convenient opportunity to discredit or get rid of him. As for Parmenion, his policy disagreements had become frustrating to Alexander, so the latter had sent him to Ecbatana in an administrative role. While there was no way to implicate Parmenion in the plot, the increasingly autocratic Alexander was not about to let an aggrieved father survive his son. Alexander sent a letter with Cleander, the mercenary commander in Ecbatana and one of the accusers of Philotas, to Parmenion. As the old general read it, Cleander and his men struck him down. Bosworth, 101-104.

67 Arrian, III. xxvii. 4. The command was split between Hephaestion, Alexander's life-long friend and Cleitus the Black who Alexander murdered in Bactra.

68 Bosworth, 88, 104.

69 Arrian, IV. xiii. 2.

70 Arrian, IV. xiv. 2-3. See also Curtius VIII. vii. Hermolaus and the other conspirators were stoned to death.

71 Bosworth argues that the growing despotism of the court may have alienated the younger members of the nobility as much as it did their seniors, and the recent attempt to introduce *proskynesis* could have served as a catalyst to their disaffection (p. 118).Callisthenes was also implicated in the plot but was not executed immediately. The circumstances surrounding his death are uncertain in the sources.

72 Victor Ehrenberg, *Alexander and the Greeks* (Oxford: Basil Blackwell, 1938), 52-61.

73 Bosworth, 133.

74 Arrian, V. xxvi. 1-4. See also Curtius IX. ii. 25-6.

75 Arrian, V. xxvii. 2. Emphasis added. Coenus makes another interesting argument towards the end of his dialogue: "Nothing, Sire, is so unquestionably good as a sound mind in good fortune and. . .the strokes of divine power are beyond the foresight and therefore beyond the precautions of human beings" (V. xxvii. 9). Coenus is clearly making a case for moderation (*sophrosyne*) and setting limits. To exceed those limits is hubris or *pleonexia* (wanting too much) and not befitting a sound mind. Ruin is inevitable, beyond the precautions of human beings, for one puffed up with hubris.

76 Curtius' account is similar, "Therefore, if you *persist*, we, even unarmed, naked, and worn out, follow wherever you desire. . .Clad in Persian dress. . .we have *degenerated* into foreign ways. Victors over all, we lack everything" (IX. iii. 5, 10-11. Emphasis added.).

77 Arrian, V. xxviii. 1, "Alexander resented the freedom which Coenus had spoken and the poor spirit shown by the other officers, and dismissed the conference."

78 Arrian, V. xxviii. 4-5.

79 Bosworth, 164. Alexander had in the meantime resolved to pay off all of his soldiers' debts. This laudable gesture was met with suspicion because the soldiers felt Alexander was trying to use the record of payments as a basis for punishment sometime in the future. Alexander then dropped the requirement for the soldiers to register their names prior to receiving payment. Arrian, VII. v; Curtius, X. ii. 9-11; Diodorus, XVII. 109. 1-2; Plutarch, *Alexander*, 70. 3. Alexander had also punished several satraps for alleged corruption and maltreatment of the people. According to Arrian, "Alexander himself is said to have grown quicker to give credit to accusations, as if they were reliable in all circumstances" (VII. iv. 3).

80 Arrian, VII. vi. Alexander had also arranged marriages between Macedonian officers and Persian women, himself taking a Persian wife as well.

81 Arrian, VII. vi. 5. Hammond (p. 244) argues that the Macedonians felt insulted at being declared unfit for war. Hogarth (p. 322) believes the mutiny arose not among those ordered home, but among those detained who equally wished for discharge.

82 Arrian, VII. viii. 3.

83 Ibid., VII. ix. 2.

84 Ibid., VII. ix. 8.

85 Ibid., VII. x. 7.

86 Hammond, 260. Tarn arrives at the same conclusion, citing the fact that Macedonians and Persians were seated together at the banquet and interpreting Alexander's prayer for unity and harmony in the empire (Arrian, VII. xi. 8) as an example of Alexander's "cosmopolitanism" (II, p. 448-9).

87 Arrian, VII. xi. 8.

88 See Bosworth, 161; Badian, "Alexander the Great and the Unity of Mankind," *Historia* 7 (1958), 442-4.

89 Alexander's marriage to the Bactrian princess Roxane did produce Alexander IV, but the child was born after the death of Alexander. Roxane, Alexander

IV, and Heracles (an illegitimate son of Alexander) all perished during the wars of succession (O'Brien, 59, 141.).

90 Tarn, I, 141.

91 F.W. Walbank's account of the wars of succession is revealing on this issue. The history of the fifty years after Alexander's death (323-276) was one of struggle between Alexander's generals and their sons and successors to take what they could for themselves. They eventually divided the empire into separate dynasties: Egypt (Ptolemy), Babylonia and northern Syria (Seleucus), and northern Anatolia and Thrace (Lysimachus). Macedonia was eventually ruled by Antigonus Gonatus, the son of Demetrius. According to Walbank, the Greeks and Macedonians formed the ruling classes of the dynasties. "The creation of this ruling class was the direct outcome of the decisions taken by the armies and generals of Alexander, who after his death decisively rejected his policy of racial fusion and very soon expelled all Medes and Persians from positions of authority" (F. W. Walbank, *The Hellenistic World* (Cambridge: Harvard University Press, 1993), 46-7, 65).

92 Aeschylus, *Prometheus Bound*, §506.

93 Ibid., §393.

94 Curtius, IX. iii. 11.

95 Arrian, VII. ii. 2. See also Hammond, 254.

Chapter Seven

1 This concept is developed in Marc Raeff, *The Well-Ordered Police State: Social and Institutional Change through Law in the Germanies and Russia, 1600-1800* (New Haven, CT.,1983).

2 Cf. Gerhard Ritter, *Frederick the Great: A Historical Profile*, Tr. P. Paret (Berkeley, CA., 1968); or Christopher Duffy, *The Army of Frederick the Great* (Newton Abbot. 1974).

3 Reinhard Koser's *Geschichte Friedrichs des Grossen*, 4 vols. (Stuttgart, 1921), remains the most detailed account of the King's life. The most perceptive modern interpretation is Theodore Schieder, *Friedrich der Grosse: Ein Koenigtum der Widersprueche* (Stuttgart, 1983).

4 Cf. Frederick to K.D. von Natzmer, Feb., 1731, in *Die Werke Friedrichs des Grossen*, ed. G.B.Volz, 10 vols. (Berlin, 1912-1914), VII, 197 ff., and *L' Antimachaviel, ou Examen du prince de Machaviel*, in *Oeuvres de Frederic le Grand*, ed. J.D.E. Preuss, 30 vols., (Berlin, 1846-56), VIII, 55ff.

5 Theodor Schieder, "Friedrich der Grosse und Machiavelli-das Dilemma von Machtpolitik und Aufklaerung," *Historische Zeitschrift* 234 (1982), 265-294.

6 "Considerations sur l'etat present du corps politique de l' europe" in *Ouevres*, VIII, 3ff.

7 Peter Burke, *The Fabrication of Louis XIV* (New Haven, CT., 1992), is an excellent case study of the process at work.

8 See.Peter Smith, *War, State, and Society in Wuerttemberg*, 1677-1793 (Cambridge, 1995), for an example of this paradigm shift.

9 John Keegan, *The Mask of Command* (New York, 1987), pp. 92 ff. For his context see above all Linda Colley, *Britain: Forging the Nation, 1707-1837* (New Haven, CT., 1992).

10 These points are developed in the author's *The Wars of Frederick the Great* (London, 1996).

11 D.de T., *Tactique et manoeuvres des prussiens. Piece posthume* (n.p., 1767), is an eyewitness summary of the prewar maneuvers.

12 Cf. R.L. Gawthrop, *Pietism and the Rise of Eighteenth Century Prussia* (Cambridge, 1993); and for a comparative dimension Mary Fulbrook, *Piety and Politics: Religion and the Rise of Absolutism in England, Wuerttemberg, and Prussia* (Cambridge, 1983).

13 Klaus Epstein, *The Genesis of German Conservatism* (Princeton, 1966), pp. 65 ff.

14 Paul Muench, *Lebensformen in der fruehen Neuzeit, 1500 bis 1800* (Frankfurt, 1982), is a German-focused overview developing this point among others.

15 Cf. Hartmut Harnisch, "Preussische Kantonsystem und Laendliche esellschaft: Das Beispiel des mittleren Kammerdepartements," in *Krieg und Frieden: Militaer und Gesellschaft in der fruehen Neuzeit*, ed. B.Kroener, R. Proeve (Paderborn, 1996), pp. 137-165.

16 Thomas Ricks, *Making the Corps* (New York, 1997), is a convincing contemporary case study based on a recruit platoon of the U.S. Marine Corps.

17 F.K.Tharau, *Die Geistige Kultur des preussischen Offiziers von 1640 bis 1806* (Mainz, 1968), is a useful overview.

18 Willerd r.Fann, "Foreigners in the Prussian Army, 1713-56: Somwe Statistical and Interpretive Problems," *Central European History* 23 (1990), 76-84.

19 J.D.Dreyer, *Leben und Thaten eines preussischen Regiments-Tambours* (Breslau, 1870).

20 Michael Sikoora, Verzweiflung oder "Leictsinn"? Militaerstand und Desertion im 18. Jahrhundert," in *Krieg und Frieden*, 237-264.

21 See John Lynn, *Giant of the Grand Siecle: The French Army, 1610-1715* (Cambridge, 1997), pp. 419ff.

22 L.V.Smith,   *Between Mutiny and Obedience: The Fifth French Infantry Division during World War I* (Princeton, 1994).

23 On the latter point see Edgar Melton, "The Decline of Prussian *Gutsherrschaft* and the Rise of the Junker as Rural Patron, 1750-1806" *German History* 12 (1994), 334-350.

24 J.W. Archenholtz, *Geschichte des siebenjaehrigen Krieges in Deutschland*, 2 vols. (Berlin, 1840), I, 108.

25 Among many versions of the King's words this one, recorded by Prince Ferdinand of Brunswick and cited in O. Herrmann, "Prinz Ferdinand von Preussen ueber den Feldzug im jahre 1757," *Forschungen zur brandenburgisch-preussischen Geschichte* 31 (1918), 101-102, is the least embellished and probably the most accurate.

26 Frederick to Finckenstein, Aug. 16, 1759, *Politische correspondenz Friedrichs des Grossen*, 46 vols. (Berlin, 1879-1939), XVIII, 487.

27 Quoted in Jeremy Black, *European Warfare, 1660-1815* (New Haven, CT., 1994), p. 65.

28 K.Schmidt, *Die Taetigkeit der preussischen Freibataillone in den beiden ersten Feldzuegen des siebenjaehrigen Krieges (1757-1758)* (Leipzig, 1913), gives the early history of these misbegotten formations.

29 See Lynn, *Giant of the Grand Siecle*, passim; and Ernst Redlich: *De Praeda Militari: Looting and Booty, 1500-1815* (Wiesbaden, Steiner, 1956).

30 Cited in Curt Jany, *Geschichte der Preussischen Armee*, reprint ed. (Osnabrueck, 1967), Vol. II, p. 10.

31 Duffy, *The Army of Frederick the Great*, 67-68; and *The Military Life of Frederick the Great* (New York, 1986), pp. 336 ff., base their generalizations on literally hundreds of corroborating anecdotes.

32 Archenholtz *Geschichte des Siebenjaehrigen Krieges*, II, 68. The author was present at Liegnitz as a junior officer.

33 When during the Seven Years' War Frederick ordered the destruction of the Saxon king's palaces, every regular officer refused. The deed was finally done by one of the free batallion commanders. Duffy, *Military Life*, 334.

34 Cf. H.Conrad, *Die Geistigen Grundlagen des Allgemeinen Landrechts fuer die Preussischen Staaten von 1794* (Cologne, 1958), and H.Weill, *Frederick the Great and Samuel Cocceji: A Study in the Reform of the Prussian Judicial Administration, 1745-1755* (Madison, WI., 1961).

35 Duffy, *Military Life*, 257-258.

36 Cf. Eda Sagarra, "The Image of Frederick II of Prussia in Germany in the Century before Unification," *European Studies Review* IV (1974), 23-32.

Chapter Eight

1 "Report of Training in the American Expeditionary Forces," from AEF G-5 to AEF Chief of Staff AEF, dated 04 July 1918, 29. Timberman-Fiske Papers, United States Army Military History Institute (USAMHI) collection.

2 U.S., Department of War, *War Department Annual Report for Fiscal Year Ended June 30, 1919*, Vol 1, Part 1, "Report of the Chief of Staff"(Washington, D.C.: Government Printing Office, 1920), 280. U.S. Department of War, *The War With Germany: A Statistical Summary*, compiled by Leonard P. Ayres (Washington, D.C.: Government Printing Office, 1919), 16.

3 *War Department Annual Report, 1919*, 299.

4 Edward M. Coffman, *The War to End All Wars: The American Military Experience in World War I* (Madison: University of Wisconsin Press, 1968), 55. and John G. Clifford, *The Citizen Soldiers* (Lexington: University of Kentucky Press, 1972), 228-35. The West Point Class of 1917 graduated a few weeks early in April 1917, the Class of 1918 graduated in August 1917, the Class of 1919 in June 1918 and the Classes of 1920 and 1921 both graduated on 01 November 1918. Despite these early graduations, the total number of graduates for the Classes of 1917-1919 totaled only 427 officers; not even enough to fill a single infantry division's need for junior officers. The statistics for the sources of commission come from *The War With Germany*, 22. Physicians and other specialists commissioned directly from civilian life accounted for 34% of the officer ranks, and soldiers commissioned from the ranks accounted for the remaining 6%.

5 Ralph B. Perry, *The Plattsburg Movement* (New York: E.P. Dutton and Company, 1921), 202.

6 *War Department Annual Report, 1919*, 313-314.

7 "Replies to Officers' Questionnaires" from Morale Branch of the War College and War Plans Division to the Chief of Staff, dated 5 November 1919, 52. National Archives, RG165, NM84, Entry 378, Box 6 (here after cited as Morale Branch Report). My thanks to Ty Seidule for sharing this excellent source.

8 Perry, 190.

9 General Headquarters American Expeditionary Force, *Report of Officers Convened By Special Orders No.98, GHQ AEF 09 April 1919*, 9-10. (Here after cited as the Lewis Board) in USAMHI library.

10 Morale Branch Report, 69. This was a frequent complaint from junior officers. Most blamed the army itself for failing to increase NCO pay and training.

11 W.A. Sirmon, *That's War* (Atlanta: The Linmon Company, 1929), 21.

12 328th Infantry Historical Committee, *History of the Three Hundred and twen-*

ty-eighth Infantry Regiment (No publisher, 1922), 7-8.

13 G. Edward Buxton Jr., ed. *Official History of the 82nd Division American Expeditionary Forces* (Indianapolis: Bobbs-Merrill Co., 1919), 4.

14 This was the opinion not only of Pershing but also of a number of the junior officers and enlisted men who served in France. Pershing's opinion are found in, John J. Pershing, *My Experience in the World War*, Vol. I.
    (New York: Frederick A. Stakes Company, 1931), 154. and *War Department Annual Report, 1919*, "Final Report   of Gen. John J. Pershing.," 560-561. The Morale Branch Report is rife with junior officer criticisms of the level of their soldiers' training and also contains a unexpectedly high degree of self reflection as to the officers' own complacency in these shortcomings. See 57-52 and 76-77.

15 Morale Branch Report, 77.

16 Alvin C. York, *Sergeant York: His Own Life Story and War Diary*, ed. Tom Skeyhill (New York: Doubleday, Doran and Company, 1928), 46. York noted that the officers never managed to correct this deficiency. During the St. Mihiel Offensive, he remembered that his comrades "were still mostly hitting the ground or the sky. They burned up a most awful lot of Uncle Sam's ammunition.," 210.

17 Historical Committee, *The Plattsburger* (New York: Winkoop Hallenbeck Crawford Co. 1917), 14. Obviously the author was as ill-informed of his nation's history as he was of the situation in France.

18 Pershing, *My Experience*, Vol I, 150-4 and Vol II, 237-8.

19 Memorandum from AEF G-5 to AEF Chief of Staff dated 04 July 1918, 31-32. Similar feeling were expressed by Pershing himself and other high ranking AEF officers. See, James G. Harbord, *The American Army in France: 1917-1919* (Boston: Little, Brown and Company, 1936), 407-8. and Robert L. Bullard, *Personalities and Reminiscences of the War* (New York: Doubleday, Page and Company, 1925), 100-4.

20 Ibid., 154.

21 Coffman, *The War to End All Wars*, 66.

22 The Lewis Board, Annex R, 6.

23 Morale Branch Report, 52. The same officer noted "much time wasted in learning methods of signaling, open warfare, etc. which were useless in Europe."

24 Buxton, *Official History*, 11-12. and Sirmon, *That's War*, 96-100.

25 The Americans were not happy with the confinements of the "live and let

live" system and the apparent timidity of their allies. Frank A. Holden, *War Memories* (Athens, Ga.: Athens Book Company, 1922), 103-4. Holden served as an infantry lieutenant in the 82nd Division's 325th Infantry.

26 Sirmon, *That's War*, 163, 176-80.

27 Buxton, *Official History,* 15-16.

28 In late September 1917 as the division approached full strength, the War Department order all but 783 of the units soldiers to be sent to other divisions. Two months later the War Department ordered the division to transfer another 3,000 men with certain industrial or craftsman experience to other posts. One month prior to the division's departure, the War Department removed 1,400 "enemy aliens" (immigrants from Germany or Austria-Hungary) from the units ranks and filled the 82nd with 5,000 raw recruits. One soldier, Ralph Flynt, was on a ship to France within 18 days of his induction. Buxton, *Official History*, 1-3. and Holden, *War Memories*, 27-8.

29 Sirmon, *That's War*, 104 and 119.

30 Morale Branch Report, 54. The same complaints were echoed by some senior commanders. The 7th Division commander, Major General Whittenmyer, stated that the pulling of junior officers to attend school "absolutely destroyed all results in the way of instruction in the companies and Battalions." Lewis Board, Annex R, 19.

31 An example of this opinion comes from a lecture given by Col. M.G. Spinks to the Army War College in Washington D.C. on 09 October 1933 entitled "Major Problems of the Inspector General, A.E.F., and Their Solutions." Spinks admits that "temporary officers" were "an exceptionally fine and well qualified group of men," but they were "not familiar with things military. They were uninformed and untrained in military matters." AWC 401-A-5, USAMHI., 8.

32 U.S., Department of War, *The United States Army in the World War*, 17 Vols. (Washington D.C.: Government Printing Office, 1948), Vol. 15: *Reports of Commander-in-Chief A.E.F. Staff Sections and Services*, 304-5.

33 Harbord, *The American Army in France*, 481-484.

34 "Major Problems of the Inspector General, A.E.F., and Their Solutions," 9.

35 U.S., Department of War, *The United States Army in the World War*, 17 Vols. (Washington D.C.: Government Printing Office, 1948), Vol. 14: *Reports of Commander-in-Chief A.E.F. Staff Sections and Services*, 401.

36 Morale Branch Report, 21. The report of returning officers is replete with hash and bitter invectives against the AEF's senior leadership. A field artillery officer wrote, "Many Commanding Officers were ignorant as to what their organizations were capable of doing in action. That is they expected the

impossible at times and did not take advantage of things they could do at times." While some of the comments stem from hard feelings, there can be no doubt that much of the criticism is accurate.   The lack of experience among senior officers led Pershing to retain the massive and ponderous "square" division structure within the AEF.   By placing as many soldiers in American divisions as the Allies had in a corps, Pershing believed that he was maximizing the use of his limited pool of senior command experience.   In fact, the unwieldy divisions only served to further undermine his vision of a maneuver based American Army.

37   Ibid.

38   U.S., Department of War, *The United States Army in the World War*, 17 Vols. (Washington D.C.: Government Printing Office, 1948), Vol. 14, 403.

39   Morale Branch Report., 27.

40   Sirmon, *That's War*, 145.

41   The tactical performance of the First Army was not lost on Pershing.   While he praised the doughboys for their victory and loudly proclaimed the Americans' superiority, he also sent messages to the division commanders moving towards the Meuse Argonne expressing his concern over the Americans' tendency to bunch up during attacks and his leaders' over reliance on frontal attacks.   Pershing, *My Experiences in the World War*, 286. Marshall, *Memories of My Services in the World War*, 167. "Report of Training in the American Expeditionary Forces," 36-43.

42   Justus Owens to "Mamma" (Settie Owens), 14 September 1918, contained in the Justus Erwin Owens Scrapbook, Special Collections, Hargrett Rare Book and Manuscript Library, University of Georgia, folder 2856 (M).

43   Ibid. Owens admitted that the night's fruitless wanderings had left his soldiers "wet and cold" and in bad "humor."

44   USAMHI World War I Veteran Survey (hereafter USAMHI Survey), File #1547, (George Loukides, PFC, 326 IN, 82nd DIV).   Enflade fire allows an attacker or defender the ability to shoot along the entire length (the flank) of an enemy formation. This means that the shooter can inflict very heavy casualties on the enemy formation while the enemy's' return fire is limited by their own formation.

45   York, *Sergeant York*, 208-9.

46   USAMHI Survey, File # 2705, (Harry House, SGT, 320 MGB, 82nd DIV).

47   Holden, *War Memories*, 147.

48   Morale Branch Report, 53.

49   Lewis Board, Annex R, 13 and 2.   In the same report George Marshall com-

mented that "company and battalion commanders required a long time to learn how to maneuver their troops, except by a straight ahead advance, and were even slower in learning how to combine rifle action with maneuver." He also blasted the American tendency to "bunch" under fire., Annex R, 6.

50 Buxton, *Official History*, 16, 29, 86-87, 213. The strength of an American "squire" division of the First World War was 1000 officers and 27,000 men.

51 Clarke Howell, Jr., to "Mrs. Barnes" (Mattie Owens Barnes), 15 December 1918, Owens Scrapbook.

52 York, *Sergeant York*, 220.

53 "Impressions and Recollections of Operations, C Co, 325 In" Dated 26 December 1918 from "CPT John K. Taylor, Commanding C Company to COL. Whitman, Commander 325th Infantry." contained in unpublished "History of the 325th INF, Letters from Company Commanders" in BG Whitman Papers, WWI 6052, USAMHI. Taylor's report is of his company's 11 October 1918 attack on St. Juvin.

54 Morale Branch Report, 34.

55 Lewis Board Report, 11. Infantry and machine gun officers also suffered the highest ratio of men killed in action. Eighty out of every 1000 infantry officers were killed in action. Fifty-one out of every 1000 infantry enlisted men were killed in action. Ayres, *The War With Germany*, 121.

56 BG Whitman Papers, WWI 6052, Box 1, USAMHI.

57 "Report of Training in the American Expeditionary Forces," 13-14.

58 Benjamin Heath to "Dear George and Mabel" dated 25 October 1918, WWI 2880, USAMHI.

59 Morale Branch Report, 25.

60 Ibid., 25-28. One officer noted that the enlisted men were treated "like slaves."

61 Raymond B. Fosdick, "Report to the Secretary of War on the Relation of Officers and Men in the A.E.F.," dated 17 April 1919.

62 *The Service Record: Atlanta's Military Weekly*, 5 June 1919, 57.

63 War Department, *Annual Report for 1919*, Vol. 1, Part 3, Continued., 3374-6.

64 "Report of MAJ Oliver Q. Melton, Commander K Company, 325th Infantry to COL Whitman, Commander 325th Infantry," undated, in BG Whitman Papers. In the same collection, 1LT W.G. Green reported that on 16 October the "greater part of the company was taken sick with disintery and dyreahea and we evacuated a number of men for this reason. They were to weak to perform their tasks." (Sic).

65 Coffman, *The War to End All Wars*, 332-3. and Robert C. Humber "Absences and Desertions During the First World War," Army War College Historical Section Report No. 35. USAMHI., 4.

66 Lewis Board Report, Annex S., 9. This view was also held by some officers responding to the Morale Branch Survey. An artillery lieutenant noted, "The United States Army is the best that I have had the chance to observe, but this is because of the of the high grade of its enlisted personnel, and not so much because of its officers.," 30-1.

67 "Report of Training in the American Expeditionary Forces," 44.

Chapter Nine

✱ The author acknowledges the Association of the United States Army who graciously granted copyright permission to publish "Heroism Under Fire," an article that appeared in the January, 1996, issue of *Army* magazine.

Chapter Ten

1 A number of individuals have provided crucial advice throughout the writing of this chapter. In particular, I would like to mention the assistance of Professors Fritz Stern, David Cannadine, Dennis Showalter and Linda Frey, as well as the untiring assistance of the editor of this book, Christopher D. Kolenda. Without their generous assistance, this paper would have been far worse. Any errors, however, are solely the work of the author.

2 U.S. War Department, *War Department Technical Manual TM-E 30-451: Handbook On German Military Forces* (Washington, D.C.: United States Government Printing Office, 1945), pp. 1-2. Despite asking the right questions, not all of the conclusions in the *Handbook* are supportable; nonetheless, for an analysis of an enemy while still fully engaged in operations, it is a remarkable book, and one that treats the capabilities of the Germans with greater accuracy than some recent works.

3 The groundbreaking work seeking to analyze German tactical effectiveness is Edward A. Shils and Morris Janowitz, "Cohesion and Disintegration in the Wehrmacht in World War II," *Public Opinion Quarterly* XII (Summer 1948): 280-315. Though the work is still quite useful, the works of Omer Bartov (*The Eastern Front 1941-45: German Troops and the Barbarisation of Warfare* (London: Oxford University Press, 1985) and *Hitler's Army: Soldiers, Nazis, and War in the Third Reich* (London: Oxford University Press, 1991)) have questioned many of the conclusions in the article. For an excellent and brief investigation of the motivation of the German soldier, see Stephen G. Fritz, "Ideology and Motivation in the Wehrmacht on the Eastern Front: The

View From Below," *The Journal of Military History* 60 (October 1996): 683-710. For a superb examination of German defensive doctrine, see Timothy A. Wray, *Standing Fast: German Defensive Doctrine on the Russian Front During World War II, Prewar to 1943* (Fort Leavenworth, Kansas: U.S. Army Command and General Staff College Combat Studies Institute, 1986). In Colonel Wray's words, "While it did not 'fight outnumbered and win' by achieving final victory, the German Army waged its defensive battles in Russia with sufficient skill, tenacity, and resourcefulness to merit close scrutiny" (ix). Indeed, that sentiment can be applied to unit cohesion as well as doctrine.

4   The *Waffen SS* has been a topic of great investigation. The definitive works regarding combat effectiveness, unit cohesion, greater propensity to commit war crimes, and analysis of overall cost effectiveness are Charles W. Sydnor, *Soldiers of Destruction* (Princeton: Princeton University Press, 1977) and George H. Stein, *The Waffen SS: Hitler's Elite Guard at War* (Ithaca, NY: Cornell University Press, 1966).

5   The volume of literature on the topic is growing. A good, but occasionally flawed source which investigates the conduct of army units (including *Grossdeutschland*) is Omer Bartov, *The Eastern Front 1941-45: German Troops and the Barbarisation of Warfare* (London: Oxford University Press, 1985). See also by the same author, *Hitler's Army: Soldiers, Nazis, and War in the Third Reich* (London: Oxford University Press, 1991). Bartov investigates the effectiveness of Nazi indoctrination on the German soldier in both works. He argues that the indoctrination was quite successful and accounted not only for the German soldier's fanatical resistance, but also the large number of war crimes committed by Army troops, especially on the Eastern Front. For a solid account of the current state of the field regarding ideological motivation, see Stephen G. Fritz, "'We are trying...to change the face of the world' — Ideology and Motivation in the Wehrmacht on the Eastern Front: The View from Below," *The Journal of Military History* 60 (Oct 1996), 683-710. Fritz effectively challenges many of Bartov's conclusions; see also by the same author, *Frontsoldaten* (Lexington, Kentucky: University Press of Kentucky, 1995).

6   James F. Dunnigan, "Organization of German Ground Forces," in *Strategy & Tactics Staff Study Nr. 1, War in the East: The Russo-German Conflict, 1941-45*, ed. Staff of *Strategy and Tactics Magazine* (New York: Simulations Publications, Inc), 132.

7   Paul Adair, *Hitler's Greatest Defeat: The Collapse of Army Group Centre, June 1944* (London: Arms and Armour Press, 1994), 171. The exact number of German casualties is unlikely to be known for certain due to the magnitude of the defeat — entire divisions were destroyed virtually to the last man —

but the official OKW report listed 300,000 men lost. The Soviets claimed 158,000 Germans captured and 381,000 killed along with the destruction of over 2,000 tanks, 10,000 guns and 57,000 motor vehicles. R. Ernest Dupuy and Trevor N. Dupuy, *The Harper Encyclopedia of Military History*, 4th ed. (New York: HarperCollins, 1993), 1220-1. For the definitive work on the Soviet Union's war against Germany, see John Erickson's two-volumes: *The Road to Stalingrad: Stalin's War with Germany* (Harper & Row: New York, 1975) and *The Road to Berlin: Continuing the History of Stalin's War with Germany* Westview Press: Boulder, CO, 1983). See also Earl F. Ziemke, *Stalingrad to Berlin: The German Defeat in the East* (Washington, D.C.: US Army Center of Military History, 1987), 325, who lists German losses as 25 divisions. In addition to the general surveys on the Eastern Front [Albert Seaton, *The Russo-German War 1941-45* (London: Greenhill Books, 1971) and Alan Clark, *Barbarossa: The Russian-German Conflict, 1941-1945* (New York: William Morrow, 1965)], there has been a renewed investigation of this somewhat neglected defeat, thanks especially to the translation of a number of German-language works into English. Among others, see Alex Buchner, *Ostfront 1944: The German Defensive Battles on the Russian Front 1944*, trans. David Johnston (Atglen, PA: Schiffer Military/Aviation History, 1995).

8 Dupuy and Dupuy, 1212. Although Operation Cobra assured the survival of the allied invasion force, it is important to remember that a large number of German troops, and more importantly, German armor, escaped eastward.

9 The Germans' own estimates of mid-August 1944 listed the strength of Tito's forces as 42 divisions and 120,000 men while the Chetniks were estimated to possess an additional 60-70,000 men. Department of the Army, *Department of the Army Pamphlet No. 20-243: German Antiguerrilla Operations in the Balkans (1941-1944)*, German Report Series (Washington, D.C.: Department of the Army, 1954), 66-7 (Map 6). The situation on the Eastern Front was desperate as well — from a disorganized mass of displaced, deserting and bypassed soldiers during the summer of 1941, the Soviet partisans numbered some 200,000 by 1944. Often resupplied and supported by the Red Army, German rear operations were in constant danger of partisan attack from late 1943 until the end of the war. During operation Bagration, Belorussian partisans set off 10,500 explosions and claimed to have derailed 147 trains in a three day period. From Earl F. Ziemke *et al.*, *The Soviet Juggernaut* (Alexandria, VA: Time-Life Books, 1980), 129. One authoritative estimate lists 1,933,000 partisans as being active in the Soviet Union throughout the war, Jörgen Hästrup, *European Resistance Movements, 1939-1945: A Complete History* (Westport, CT: Meckler Publishing, 1981), 471-472. See also, Matthew Cooper, *The Nazi War Against Soviet Partisans, 1941-1944* (New York: Stein & Day, 1979).

10 Cornelius Ryan, *A Bridge Too Far* (New York: Touchstone, 1974), 599. See also Cornelius Bauer, *The Battle of Arnhem* (London: Hodder and Stoughton, 1966); Christopher Hibbert, *The Battle of Arnhem* (London: B.T. Batsford, 1962); Martin Middlebrook, *Arnhem 1944: The Airborne Battle, 17-26 September* (Boulder: Westview Press, 1994).

11 Technically, the term *Wehrmacht* applies to the entire German defense forces of the Second World War, whereas *Heer* refers specifically to the army. In this paper, I will generally use the term *Heer* when referring strictly to the German Army and *Wehrmacht* when the meaning can be applied to the entire German Armed Forces.

12 Dupuy & Dupuy, 1218. For further study on the Battle of the Bulge, see Hugh M. Cole, *The Ardennes: The Battle of the Bulge* (Washington, D.C.: US Army Center of Military History, 1994); Charles B. MacDonald, *A Time For Trumpets* (New York: Bantam Books, 1984);Gerald Astor, *A Blood-Dimmed Tide: The Battle of the Bulge by the Men Who Fought it* (New York: Donald Fine, 1992); John Eisenhower, *The Bitter Woods* (New York: Putnam, 1969); Charles Whiting, *The Last Assault: The Battle of the Bulge Reassessed* (New York: Sarpedon, 1994).

13 This is a very contentious issue. A number of important works have been written on the topic that strongly disagree with my position. Recently, some military historians have argued that the notion of German tactical superiority is largely myth, especially in the later period of the war. A new release which has received wide coverage is Keith Bonn, *When the Odds Were Even: The Vosges Mountains Campaign, October 1944-January 1945* (Novato, CA: Presidio Press, 1994). The main shortcoming to this work is illustrated by the work's very title — the odds were not even in the Vosges Mountains because the American units were among the very best of any theater in the war while the German forces were, for the most part, second-rate units. For a detailed review see review essay, "Were the Odds Really Even?" in *Armor* (January-February 1998). For an analysis of the combat effectiveness of ordinary German Army divisions, see Col. Trevor Dupuy, *Numbers, Predictions and War* (Fairfax, VA: Hero Books, 1985).

14 Both authors have been heavily criticized for their methodology and conclusions; nonetheless, their work is still quite useful. See especially, Martin van Creveld, *Fighting Power: German and U.S. Army Performance, 1939-1945* (Westport, CT: Greenwood Press, 1982) and Col. Trevor N. Dupuy, *A Genius for War: The German Army and General Staff 1807-1945* (Fairfax, VA: Hero Books, 1977). Training, tactics, organization and the German General Staff consistently figure quite high (and rightfully so) in any accounting for German tactical excellence. Two recently published provocative articles highlight many of the important factors leading to this tactical excel-

lence. See John F. Antal, "The Wehrmacht Approach to Maneuver Warfare Command and Control" in *Maneuver Warfare: An Anthology*, ed. Richard D. Hooker, Jr. (Novato, CA: Presidio Press, 1993), 347-359 and M.P. Grant, "Fighting Power: The German Army of World War II and the British Army of Today: An Analysis of the Conceptual and Moral Components of German Tactical Effectiveness in World War II and the Lessons for the British Army Today," *British Army Review* (December 1996), 59-72.

15 Part of this stems from the fact that the memoirs written after the war by prominent German general officers tend to focus on the early victorious campaigns. Also many of the field commanders in later stages of the war did not survive the war to write memoirs, and many of those that did survive did not wish to recount their experiences.

16 By far, the definitive work on the Battle of Sedan is Robert A. Doughty, *The Breaking Point: Sedan and the Fall of France, 1940* (Hamden, CT: Archon Books, 1990). A brief introduction to the Küstrin-Berlin highway engagement is recounted in Department of the Army Pamphlet 20-269, *Small Unit Actions During the German Campaign in Russia*, 125-8.

17 Col. Trevor N. Dupuy, "An Analysis of the War" in *Strategy & Tactics Staff Study Nr. 1, War in the East: The Russo-German Conflict, 1941-45*, ed. Staff of *Strategy and Tactics Magazine* (New York: Simulations Publications, Inc), 101.

18 The US Army defines combat power as "A complex combination of tangible and intangible factors which are transitory and reversible on the battlefield. Combat power is comprised of the effects of maneuver, the effects of firepower, the effects of protection, and the effectiveness of leadership. The skillful combination of these elements in a sound operational plan will turn potential into actual power." Department of the Army FM 101-5-1, *Operational Terms and Symbols* (Washington, D.C.: Government Printing Office, 1985), 1-16. The US Army's official doctrine emphasizes that, "Leadership is the most essential element of combat power." Department of the Army FM 100-5, *Operations* (Washington, D.C.: Government Printing Office, 1986), 11. Historians and armies of the world alike strongly emphasize the importance of sound leadership at the tactical level.

19 Professor Dennis Showalter used this phrase to explain the effectiveness of Frederick the Great's armies during a lecture at West Point, New York, on September 5, 1997. I believe the term is equally suitable for describing the environment of organizational trust that existed in the majority of units of the German Army during the Second World War.

20 One of the lasting myths of Nazi Germany is that the regime functioned like a well-oiled machine. In fact, it is now clear that Hitler purposely encour-

aged fierce personal and departmental rivalries to solidify his own position. The best single work on the state organization of Nazi Germany is Karl Dietrich Bracher, *The German Dictatorship*, trans. Jean Steinberg (Fort Worth: Holt, Rheinhart and Winston, Inc., 1970). For a brief but masterful account of Hitler's subordination of the German Army see Gordon Craig, *Politics of the Prussian Army* (London: Oxford University Press, 1955), pp. 468-503. The number of books investigating the German Army as an organization is quite large and constantly growing, but a good place to begin is Klaus-Jürgen Müller, *Armee, Politik, und Gesellschaft in Deutschland 1933-1945* (Manchester: Manchester University Press, 1987) and Matthew Cooper, *The German Army 1933-1945: Its Political and Military Failure* (New York: Bonanza Books, 1984).

21   Prior to the start of the Second World War, the German *Reich* was divided into 15 command areas or *Wehrkreise*. These *Wehrkreise* were assigned Roman numerals I to XIII within the boundaries of Germany proper, XVII to XIX contained Austrian territory annexed by Germany in 1938, and the defeat of Poland added two additional *Wehrkreise*. From Dirk Blennemann, "Building the Beast: The World War II Training and Replacement Systems of the German Army," in *Hitler's Army: The Evolution and Structure of German Forces, 1933-1945*, ed. Staff of *Command Magazine* (Conshohocken, PA: Combined Books, 1996), 11.

22   It is interesting to note that Germany had 162 divisions in 1941 while the United States activated barely more than 90 divisions, of which 89 saw combat, despite having twice the population as Germany and fighting Japan as well as the Germany. Between September 1939 and April 1945 some 17,893,200 men passed through the *Wehrmacht* and the *Waffen SS*, truly an impressive figure. Van Creveld, p.65. Obviously, many factors contributed to this – the German use of forced labor from conquered territories and the large size of the United States Army Air Force – but it was still a remarkable achievement that Germany fielded some 16 million soldiers in the course of the war.

23   Samuel W. Mitcham, Jr., *Hitler's Legions: The German Army Order of Battle, World War II* (New York: Dorset Press, 1985), 27. The headquarters and territories of the *Wehrkreise* were as follows: I — Königsberg (East Prussia, extended in 1939 to include Memel and parts of Poland); II — Stettin (Mecklenberg and Pomerania); III — Berlin (Altmark, Neumark and Brandenburg); IV — Dresden (Saxony and part of Thuringia, later annexed northern Bohemia); V — Stuttgart (Würtemberg and part of Baden, Alsace added in 1940); VI — Münster (Westphalia and Rhineland); VII — Munich (southern Bavaria); VIII — Breslau (Silesia and Sudetenland, later Moravia and southwestern Poland); IX — Kassel (Hessen and part of Thuringia); X —

Hamburg (Schleswig-Holstein and northern Hanover, extended in 1940 to include Danish Slesvig); XI — Hanover (Braunschweig, Anhalt and the remainder of Hanover); XII — Wiesbaden (Eifel, the Palatinate, the Saar, part of Hessen, 1940 Lorraine and the Nancy area); XIII — Nuremburg (Northern Bavaria, western Bohemia added in 1938); XIV — Berlin (no territory, disbanded as a *Wehrkreis* in 1939, later became Headquarters, XIV Panzer Corps); XV — Berlin (no territory, disbanded as a *Wehrkreis* in 1939, later became Headquarters, 3rd Panzer Army); XVI — Berlin (no territory, disbanded as a *Wehrkreis* in 1939, later became Headquarters, 4th Panzer Army); XVII — Vienna (Northern Austria, extended in 1939 to include the southern regions of Czechoslovakia); XVIII — Salzburg (Southern Austria, extended in 1941 to include northern Slovenia); XX — Danzig (former Danzig Free State, Polish Corridor and western East Prussia); General Gouvernement — Warsaw (created in 1943 to include most of central and southern Poland); Bohemia and Moravia — Prague (the remainder of what had been Czechoslovakia, created in 1942). From Mitcham, 32.

24 For example, the II Infantry Corps was located in the II *Wehrkreis* and both corps headquarters and *Wehrkreis* headquarters were located in Stettin.

25 The US Army Military Intelligence Service's *German Army Order of Battle* of October 1942 listed the average age of Corps Commanders in the field as 54 while it put the average age of *General z.b.V.* commanding *Wehrkreise* at 64. *German Army Order of Battle: October 1942* (Mt. Ida, Arkansas: Lancer Militaria, n.d.), 9.

26 It is beyond the scope of this article to go into further detail regarding the *Wehrkreis* system at the national level, but an example will suffice in demonstrating the freedom granted the *Wehrkreis* commander. In the Fall of 1940 the 33rd Infantry Division of *Wehrkreis* XII was ordered to be transformed into the 15th Panzer Division, making its horses and those troops dedicated to them unnecessary while at the same time there was the need for many noncommissioned officers with motorized and armored experience. The *Allgemeines Heeresamt* (General Army Office) of the OKW dictated that a large portion of the noncommissioned officers and horses freed by the conversion be transferred to the newly created 129th Infantry Division of *Wehrkreis* IX, but otherwise the remainder were to be distributed within those units within *Wehrkreis* XII. *Ibid.,* 10.

27 The highest was *Kriegsverwendungsfähig* or *Kv* (fit for war), middle being *Garnisonverwendungsfähig* or *Gv* (fit for garrison-type duty) and the lowest classification was *Wehrunfähig* or *Wu* (unfit for defense). *Ibid.,* 66.

28 It is worth remembering that active army service often followed extensive para-military training in the National Socialist youth organizations: the *DVM* (*Deutsches Jungvolk*) from the age of 10 to 14; the *HJ* (*Hitler Jugend*) from

the age of 14 to 18; and the *RAD* (*Reichsarbeitsdienst* or labor service) which was compulsory prior to military service. Though all organizations were not military organizations *per se*, they instilled in their members a basic understanding of military living, disciplined formations, familiarity with land navigation, physical training and of course, Nazi indoctrination. The transition from the barracks of the *RAD* to the army would have not been a difficult one. For an in-depth look at the effectiveness of the paramilitary organizations on preparing young men for military service, see H.W. Koch, *The Hitler Youth: Origins and Development 1922-1945* (New York: Barnes & Noble, 1975), 162-276.

29 Fritz, "Ideology and Motivation in the Wehrmacht," 686.

30 Van Creveld, 67. This process was closely tied to German Army organization and replacements, discussed below.

31 B. Mueller-Hildebrand, "*Statistisches System*," U.S. Army Historical Division Study PC 011 (Koenigsten Trans., 1949), 68, quoted in Van Creveld, 62.

32 Grant, 65.

33 Blennemann, "Building the Beast" in *Hitler's Army*, 16.

34 Van Creveld, 44.

35 Mitcham, 15.

36 Van Creveld, 47. The author notes that in 1939 the divisional staff of a 1939 German infantry division of 17,855 men consisted of 96 men or just .53% of the entire division.

37 Grant, 61.

38 There are many works addressing the *Reichswehr* and its influence on the *Wehrmacht*. In addition to Gordon Craig, above, see also F.L. Carsten, *The Reichswehr and Politics 1918-33* (Oxford: Oxford University Press, 1966); Robert J. O'Neill, *The German Army and the Nazi Party, 1933-1939* (New York: James H. Heinemann, 1966); and Albert Seaton, *The German Army 1933-1945* (New York: St. Martin's Press, 1982) among others.

39 Richard Humble, "Das Heer – an army of strengths and weaknesses" in Simon Goodenough, ed., *Hitler's War Machine* (London: Salamander Books, Ltd., 1996), 68.

40 Again, the details of the replacement system will be addressed below; suffice it to say that each field division had its own organic *Feldersatzbattalion* (Field Replacement Battalion) and each infantry corps had a corresponding district in Germany from which all recruits and replacements were drawn.

41 As the war continued on into its third year and the activity of partisans increased, the distinction between the Field Army and the Replacement Army

diminished. The Replacement Army units moved into the occupied territories and became increasingly involved in security operations. This change had positive implications in that the training became even more realistic as actual combat often became part of training. In the fall of 1942 in an attempt to formalize the relationship, the OKW created field training divisions which were to complete the basic training of soldiers destined for the Field Army while at the same time being fully dedicated to conducting security operations in the occupied countries. The combat duties of the division ensured that they frequently went to combat with inadequately trained soldiers; it is not surprising that casualties were disproportionately high. The field training divisions were quickly disbanded in early 1943. The field training divisions were replaced by a multi-echeloned system that resembled the one in place prior to the failed experiment with field training divisions. The new system continued to place great emphasis on individual initiative and personal leadership. Divisions continued to be responsible for completing the training of recruits, noncommissioned officers, and specialists. Field Armies were responsible for the training of company, troop, and battery commanders, as well as the advanced training for noncommissioned officers and specialists. The Replacement Army still provided for the basic training of recruits, noncommissioned officers, and specialists. In addition, the Replacement Army retained the responsibility for training officer candidates. The General Staff had the responsibility for training General Staff officers, as well as the divisional and regimental commanders. This system continued until Germany surrendered. For a detailed discussion, see Van Creveld, 42-82.

42 *Ibid.,* 73.

43 *Ibid.*

44 Basically, *Auftragstaktik* meant that orders contained only essential information — clearly stated mission, objective and specific tasks — without limitations on the commanders freedom of action within these parameters. The concept aimed at forcing subordinate commanders to analyze their superior commander's mission in detail ensuring appropriate subsequent action even when additional information was not available. A major consequence of *Auftragstaktik* was the speedy transmission of orders, frequently allowing the German units to get inside the enemy force's decision cycle. For a superb and concise account of the characteristics of *Auftragstaktik*, see Christopher D. Kolenda's article, "Some Thoughts on *Auftragstaktik*." Especially helpful is Captain Kolenda's description of the organizational culture required for *Auftragstaktik* to work: "...the organization must have the cultural underpinnings of *Trust*. *Auftragstaktik* is as much a cultural doctrine as it is a tactical one, perhaps even more so. In fact, we might label it 'trust tactics.'

Seniors, subordinates and peers must have complete faith and trust in one another for *Auftragstaktik* to work. This trust is developed through training — tactical and technical competence, and education — the ability to know *how* to think, not just *what* to think, coupled with a mutual understanding how each other will likely approach and solve battlefield problems." Kolenda correctly identifies the four cultural values underpinning this trust as discipline, obedience, independence, and initiative. For additional reading on *Auftragstaktik*, see Trevor N. Dupuy, *A Genius for War: The German Army and the General Staff, 1807-1945* (Englewood Cliffs, NJ: Prentice-Hall, 1977) and John T.Nelsen, II, "Auftragstaktik: A Case for Decentralized Battle" *Parameters* Vol. XVII (September 1987), 21-34.

45 For a brief but informative account, see Karl Diefenbach *et al.*, *Grundzüge der deutschen Militärgeschichte*, Vol 1., (Freiburg, Germany: Rombach Verlag, 1993), 56-61.

46 From Seeckt's diary, quoted in George H. Stein, ed., *Fists of Steel* (Alexandria, Virginia: Time-Life Books, 1988), 20.

47 *Ibid.*, 23.

48 For the best account of Seeckt and his legacy see Carsten, above. Whether Seeckt laid the foundation for the *"Blitzkrieg"* of the Second World War is a contentious issue and not germane to this paper; what is clear is that he left a standard of exacting training discipline, initiative and quality that continued into the army of the Third Reich.

49 Albert Seaton, *The German Army 1933-1945* (New York: St. Martin's Press, 1982), 11-15.

50 Van Creveld, 121-2.

51 *Ibid.*, 122.

52 Award documents from the personal collection of the author.

53 The following account of the exploits of *Leutnant* Primozic is taken from Franz Kurowski and Gottfried Tornau, *Sturmartillerie: Die dramtische Geschichte einer Waffengattung 1939-1945* (Stuttgart: Motorbuch Verlag, 1978), 111-114

54 While the *Reichswehr* had an entrance examination, the *Wehrmacht* did not due to the exigencies created by the massive military expansion in the years following Hitler's seizure of power.

55 For a detailed discussion of the importance of combat awards and their sequence, see note 65.

56 Even then it was the case that character was still put before education; nonetheless, possession of the *Abitur* was a key consideration for gaining admittance to one of the ten cadet schools first established by Frederick the

Great, especially in the decades preceding the First World War. The *Abitur* was the certificate or diploma granted after nine years attendance at a *Gymnasium* (selective secondary school, generally limited to those of good birth with substantial resources to support the student) and passing of the difficult graduation examination. For a brief discussion of the *Abitur* and its significance in the political, cultural and military history of Germany, see Craig's *Germany 1866-1945*, 180-223: "Religion, Education and the Arts." For the impact of National Socialism on the German education, see also, David Schoenbaum, *Hitler's Social Revolution: Class and Status in Nazi Germany 1933-1939* (New York: W.W. Norton & Co., 1966).

57   This would involve having been screened by the regimental commander and possessing the proper education and background, with the express purpose of eventually gaining a commission.

58   Until 1937, the curriculum in officer school consisted of the following average breakdown per week: six hours of tactics; three hours each of weapon technology and engineering service; two hours each of topography, army organization and citizenship; one hour each of anti-aircraft defense, signals and communications and motor vehicle technology; two-thirds of an hour on sanitary service; and one-third hour on military administration. Upon graduation and entry into the branch-specific school, instruction on citizenship was dropped, while two to three hours of military history per week were added. Military history was considered second in importance only to tactics, of all of the courses taught. In addition, specialized subjects such as mathematics, physics and science were added. From Van Creveld, 137-138.

59   *Ibid.,* 138.

60   In 1942, prospective officers were first given six months' training in the Replacement Army, then spent three months at the front, returned for three months in an officer school, and then spent an additional two to four months at the front prior to being commissioned. The problem with this system was that casualties were so high among officer candidates that front-line service was reduced during the training period from 1942 to the end of the war as follows: three to four months training in the Replacement Army, two to four months noncommissioned officer training in the Replacement Army, two months' platoon leader training in the Replacement Army, promotion to *Unteroffizer* (noncommissioned officer), two months' service at the front, promotion to *Fahnenjunker* (cadet), three to four months training at the officer school, promotion to *Oberfahnrich* (senior cadet), two months advanced officer training and then commissioning. Additionally, men not originally chosen for commissioning but who had demonstrated excellence in combat or on active service could be recommended by their regimental commander for commissioning. After six months additional service, they could be eligi-

ble for officer training if they already possessed the *Abitur* and if they did not, one year's service would be required. Clearly, front-line service against the enemy counted a great deal and allowed many thousands of soldiers to receive commissions. From *Ibid.,* 138-9.

61 Over half of the officer candidates in the film are decorated with the Iron Class Second Class and their branch-respective combat badges, such as the *Infanterie Sturmabzeichen* (Infantry Combat Badge), *Panzerkampfabzeichen* (Tank Combat Badge) or the *Sturmabzeichen* (General Assault Badge).

62 Quoted in Van Creveld, 127-129.

63 The extremely high number of German general officer casualties – in excess of 600 — during the Second World War further illustrates the emphasis on combat leadership. For an interesting investigation of the individual combat leadership of German general officers, see French L. MacLean, *Quiet Flows the Rhine: German General Officer Casualties in World War II* (Winnipeg, Canada: J.J. Fedorowicz, 1996).

64 John R. Angolia, *For Führer and Fatherland: Military Awards of the Third Reich* (San Jose, CA: R. James Bender Publishing, 1987), 110-111.

65 The OKW created the special badge for the single-handed destruction of a tank on March 9th, 1942 to recognize what was becoming an increasingly commonplace event on the Eastern Front; prior to that date individual destruction of a tank was recognized with the *Sturmabzeichen* (General Assault Badge). The General Assault Badge was awarded for taking part in three separate assaults against the enemy by troops other than armor or infantry, who had their own assault badges. Here is another example of standards to receive an award actually increasing, rather than becoming inflated. The highest number of tanks destroyed by an individual soldier in single-handed action was 21. *Oberstleutnant* (Lieutenant Colonel) Günter Viezenz achieved this amazing total, and yet not even that number of tanks personally destroyed won him the Knight's Cross! Not surprisingly, however, Viezenz's bravery continued so that eventually he did earn the Knight's Cross. *Ibid.,*109. As for the Iron Cross and the Knight's Cross, there were actually several grades, with each subsequent award requiring the lower award before the higher grade could be awarded. The grades of the Iron Cross were: *Eisernes Kreuz Zweiten Klasse* (Iron Cross Second Class), *Eisernes Kreuz Erste Klasse* (Iron Cross First Class), *Ritterkreuz* (Knight's Cross of the Iron Cross), *Ritterkreuz mit Eichenlaub* (Knight's Cross of the Iron Cross with Oak Leaves), *Ritterkreuz mit Eichenlaub und Schwerten* (Knight's Cross of the Iron Cross with Oak Leaves and Swords), *Ritterkreuz mit Eichenlaub, Schwerten und Brillianten* (Knight's Cross of the Iron Cross with Oak Leaves, Swords and Diamonds). The highest grade, the *Ritterkreuz*

mit golden Eichenlaub und Schwerten (Knight's Cross of the Iron Cross with golden Oak Leaves and Swords), of which only one was ever awarded, went to the most decorated aviator of all time, Hans-Ulrich Rudel who flew 2,530 combat missions destroying 519 Soviet tanks, one battleship, one cruiser, one destroyer, 70 landing craft, nine aircraft, as well as hundreds of military vehicles and artillery pieces among other incredible feats of heroism. In addition to the Iron Cross series of awards, other awards for heroism were created so as not to dilute the standards of the existing awards but that would still recognize bravery in action, such as the *Deutches Kreuz im Gold* (German Cross in Gold) created in September 1941 which was not technically part of the Iron Cross series of awards, but came in between the Iron Cross First Class and the Knight's Cross.

66 Guy Sajer, *The Forgotten Soldier* (Washington, D.C.: Brassey's (US), 1990), 216-8. Although technically not a German due to his Alsatian birth, Sajer's work presents the best account of life for the German Army infantryman on the Eastern Front "from below."

67 Letter to the author, dated July 20, 1997. The original text in German reads: "Sicher haben Sie richtig erkannt, daß alle militärischen Erfolge auf der guten Ausbildung des Unteroffizierkorps basieren und darauf, daß der junge Leutnant Vorbild ist in jeder Beziehung. Eine Kompanie muß sein wie eine Familie und der Führer muß wenigstens von der Kampfstagfel jeden Soldaten genau kennen, auch privat. So erarbeitet er sich das Vertrauen seiner Männer. Wenn dann der Leutnant von vorne führt, bleibt der Erfolg nicht aus." For an excellent account of Otto Carius' career as a junior officer serving in the armored branch of the German Army on the Russian Front, see his autobiography, Otto Carius, *Tigers in the Mud* (Winnipeg, Manitoba: Fedorowicz, 1992). Carius took part in over 50 armored engagements and served on tanks ranging from the Czech 38-T to the Hunting Tiger from 1940 to 1945. His career is emblematic of the junior officer of the German Army.

68 Edward A. Shils and Morris Janowitz, "Cohesion and Disintegration in the Wehrmacht," in Daniel Lerner, ed., *Propaganda in War and Crisis* (New York: George W. Stewart, 1951), 390-1. Shils and Janowitz also report that this attitude towards junior officers and noncommissioned officers only broke down in the last weeks of the war, or in those units such as the *Volksgrenadier* divisions where Nazi Party hacks were assigned leadership positions.

69 Van Creveld, 165.

70 See, especially, Bartov, above.

71 French L. MacLean, *Quiet Flows the Rhine: German General Officer Casualties in World War II* (Winnipeg, Canada: J.J. Fedorowicz, 1996), 8.

72 Humble, 95.

Chapter Eleven

1 Some of this material is from the book *Bombs, Cities, and Civilians: American Airpower Strategy in World War II* (Lawrence: University Press of Kansas, 1993). Used by permission of the publisher. The views expressed herein are those of the author and do not purport to reflect the positions of the United States Military Academy, Department of the Army, or Department of Defense.

2 Henry L. Stimson and McGeorge Bundy, *On Active Service in Peace and War* (New York: Harper and Brothers), 632-633; Memo, George Marshall to Ernest King, "US Chemical Warfare Policy," 15 June 1945, Box 75, Folder 35, George C. Marshall Papers, George C. Marshall Research Library, Lexington, Va.; on American differences with the British on area bombing, see Crane, 42-46, 93-111.

3 See John Dower, *War Without Mercy* (New York: Pantheon, 1986); Michael Sherry, *The Rise of American Airpower: The Creation of Armageddon* (New Haven: Yale, 1987); Ronald Schaffer, *Wings of Judgment: American Bombing in World War II* (New York: Oxford, 1985); quote from Michael Howard, *Studies in War and Peace* (New York: Viking, 1971), 239.

4 Dower, 53-54, 77-93; Henry L. Stimson Diary, Yale University, (microfilm version), 31 Dec 1944 entry; Memos, Stimson to FDR, 17 Sep 1943 and JCS to FDR, 22 Sep 1943, Box 104, Personal Secretary File, FDR Library, Hyde Park, NY.

5 Letter, Kenney to Arnold, 1 Jan 1943, Box 121, Nathan F. Twining Papers, Library of Congress.

6 Charles F. Brower, IV, "The Joint Chiefs of Staff and National Policy: American Stategy and the War with Japan, 1943-1945," (Ph.D. dissertation, University of Pennsylvania, 1987), 209-210; Ronald H. Spector, *Eagle Against the Sun* (New York: Vintage Books, 1985), xiii.

7 Letter, Curtin to MacArthur, 7 Apr 1943, with 10 Apr reply, 1061/43; Memo, BG B.M. Fitch to Allied Commanders, "Air Attack of Objectives Within the Philippine Archipelago," 1 Nov 1944, and Msg to same from MacArthur, 2 Sep 1944, 11061/41, Records of US Army Commands, RG 338, National Archives.

8 Correspondence on Intramuros incident, 16-17 Feb 1945 in File 373.21, 11061/44 and on Rabual hospital, 23-24 May 1944 in File 373.11, 11061/41, RG 338, NA; Dower, 41; Douglas MacArthur, *Reminiscences* (New York:

McGraw-Hill, 1964), 276. The Fifth and Seventh Air Forces, part of MacArthur's Far East Air Forces, did mount three incendiary attacks in August 1945 on towns in Kyushu with industrial targets, though it is unclear whether MacArthur knew about the specifics of those missions, or that the Fifth Air Force Intelligence Officer had decreed, "There are no civilians in Japan" after finding out that all Japanese men from 15 to 60 and women from 17 to 40 were liable for defense duties as part of a Peoples Volunteer Corps. See Wesley Frank Craven and James Lea Cate, *The Army Air Forces in World War II* (Chicago: Univ. of Chicago Press, 1948-1958), V: 696-699.

9   Craven and Cate, V: 628-635; Samuel Eliot Morison, *The Two-Ocean War* (New York: Ballantine Books, 1972), 477-478.

10 Thomas M. Coffey, *HAP: The Story of the U.S. Air Force and the Man Who Built It* (New York: Viking, 1982), 358-375; Curtis LeMay with MacKinley Kantor, Mission with LeMay (Garden City, NY: Doubleday), 340-341, 370-372.

11 Coffey, *Iron Eagle* (New York: Crown Publishers, 1986), 4, 34-38, 50, 56-60, 69, 89-91, 139, 243; St. Clair McElway, "A Reporter with the B-29s: III - "The Cigar, the Three Wings, and the Low-Level Attacks," *The New Yorker* (June 23, 1945): 26.

12 Craven and Cate, II: 698-699; Schaffer, 66-67; USSTAF Air Intelligence Summary No. 50, Records of Interservice Agencies, RG 334, NA; Minutes of 3rd Bombardment Group Commanders Meeting, 15 Oct 1943, Box B8, Curtis LeMay Papers, Library of Congress; Coffey, Iron Eagle, 99.

13 Lesson Plan for Conference on Air Operations Against National Structures, 11 Apr 1939, File 248.202A-25, Air Force Historical Research Agency, Maxwell AFB, Alabama.

14 Sherry, 101-102; Memo, BG Martin Scanlon to MG Barney Giles, "Priorities: Japanese Objective Folder Material," 19 Feb 1942, File 360.02, Box 101, Henry H. Arnold Papers, Library of Congress; Jack Couffer, Bat Bomb (Austin: University of Texas Press, 1992).

15 Craven and Cate, II: 354-355; Schaffer, 110-111; Herman S. Wolk, "The B-29, the A-Bomb, and the Japanese Surrender," *Air Force* (Feb 1975): 55; "Air Plan for the Defeat of Japan," ABC 381 Japan (27 Aug 1943), File ABC 384.5, Boxes 477-478, The Army Staff, RG 319, NA.

16 "Outline of presentation of views of Commanding General, AAF, on the role of the Air Forces in the defeat of Japan," 22 Feb 1944, Naval Aide's Files, Maproom Box 167, FDR Library.

17 Coffey, *Iron Eagle*, 127-128.

18 Ibid., 121; Kenneth P. Werrell, *Blankets of Fire: U.S. Bombers over Japan during World War II* (Washington: Smithsonian Institution Press, 1996), 55-81; Brief, Pasco to Arnold, 18 Dec 1944, Box 41, Arnold Papers; Schaffer, 124.

19 Schaffer, 124; Msg, Hansell to Arnold, 16 Jan 1945; Memo, Lanasberg to Stearns, "Estimate of Possibilities of Visual Bombardment of Primary Targets," 28 Feb 1945; Memo, Seaver to Loughridge, "Ballistic Winds over Japan," 1 Mar 1945, File 762.912-1, AFHRA.

20 Craven and Cate, V: 551-567; H. H. Arnold, *Global Mission* (New York: Harper and Brothers, 1949), 541; Haywood S. Hansell, Jr., *The Strategic Air War against Germany and Japan* (Washington: USGPO, 1986), 208-215, Coffey, *Iron Eagle*, 129-132, 144-145; McElway, "A Reporter with the B-29s: II - The Doldrums, Guam, and Something Coming Up," *The New Yorker* (June 16, 1945): 32.

21 Letter, LeMay to Norstad, 31 Jan 1945, Box B11, LeMay Papers; LeMay, 344-345, 368; Letter, Norstad to Spaatz, 3 Mar 1945, File 519.9701-15, AFHRA; Coffey, *Iron Eagle*, 125-126.

22 Craven and Cate, V: 568-576; Hansell, *Strategic Airwar against Japan* (Washington: USGPO, 1980), 51; Coffey, *Iron Eagle*, 147, 157; for more on the flap over Dresden, see Crane, 113-119.

23 Forward to XXI Bomber Command Tactical Mission Report, Mission No. 40, Urban Area of Tokyo, 10 Mar 1945, prepared 15 Apr 1945, Box 26, LeMay Papers.

24 "Pacific Report #90", *The United States Strategic Bombing Survey* (New York: Garland, 1976), X: 70-73.

25 Wilbur H. Morrison, *Point of No Return* (New York: Times Books, 1979), 224; Lawrence Cortesi, *Target: Tokyo* (New York: Kensington Publishing, 1983), 233-274; Thomas R. Havens, *Valley of Darkness* (New York: W.W. Norton, 1978), 178-181; Harold H. Martin, "Black Snow and Leaping Tigers," *Harper's Magazine* 192(February 1946): 151-153.

26 LeMay, 351-352, 384; Morrison, 225; XXI Bomber Command, "Analysis of Incendiary Phase of Operations Against Japanese Urban Areas," 39-40, Box 37, LeMay Papers.

27 Robert L. Gleason, "Psychological Operations and Air Power," *Air University Review* 22(March-April 1971): 36-37; Letter, Chauncey to Giles, 16 Jul 1945, File 091.412, Box 61, Arnold Papers; 20th AF Mission Reports 297-302, 28-29 Jun 1945, File 760.331, AFHRA; Havens, 167.

28 Letter, Laurence Kuter to Frederick Anderson, 15 Aug 1944, Operational Diary, The Papers of Frederick L. Anderson, Hoover Institution on War, Revolution, and Peace, Stanford University, Stanford, California; John D.

Chappell, *Before the Bomb: How America Approached the End of the Pacific War* (Lexington, KY: University Press of Kentucky, 1997), 194n86.

29 LeMay, 373; Journal, "Trip to Pacific June 6, 1945 to June 24, 1945," 13 June entry, Box 272 and Msg, Arnold to Eaker, Anderson, and Norstad, undated, Truman File, Box 45, Arnold Papers; Coffey, *Iron Eagle*, 174-175.

30 Memo, Lovett to Stimson, 31 Jul 1945, with accompanying report, File Aircraft, Air Corps General, Records of the Office of the Secretary of War, RG 107, NA; David R. Mets, *Master of Airpower* (Novato, Cal.: Presidio, 1988), 298-299; Directive, Eaker to CG, US Army Strategic Air Forces, 26 Jul 1945, Box 13, LeMay Papers.

31 Diary of Terminal Conference, July 10, 1945 - July 30, 1945, entries for 13, 15, 17, 23, and 24 Jul, Box 249, Arnold Papers.

32 Msg, Spaatz to Eaker, 2 Aug 1945 and Diary entry, 11 Aug 1945, Box 21, Spaatz Papers; Mets, 302-303; Barton Bernstein, "The Perils and Politics of Surrender: Ending the War with Japan and Avoiding the Third Atomic Bomb," *Pacific Historical Review* 46 (1977): 16-17.

33 Craven and Cate, V: 756; Wartime History, 20th Air Force (PIO Version), File 760.01, AFHRA.

34 Hansell, *Strategic Airwar against Japan*, 74-93.

35 On the perceived vulnerability of Japanese transportation, look at "Pacific Report #53" in Volume VIII of the Garland reprint of the United States Strategic Bombing Survey and "Pacific Report #54" and "Pacific Report #55" in Volume IX; Bernstein, "Compelling Japan's Surrender Without the A-bomb, Soviet Entry, or Invasion: Reconsidering the US Bombing Survey's Early-Surrender Conclusions," *The Journal of Strategic Studies* 18 (June 1995): 101-148; Martin Gilbert, *The First World War: A Complete History*(New York: Henry Holt and Company, 1994), 256n.

36 Diary of Henry L. Stimson, 6 May, 6 June, 2 July 1945, Yale University Library(microfilm); Noam Chomsky, *American Power and the New Mandarins* (New York: Pantheon, 1969), 167; Len Giovannitti and Fred Freed, *The Decision to Drop the Bomb* (New York: Coward-McCann, 1965), 36; Stimson and Bundy, 630-633; for a good example of the press coverage of LeMay's May releases see page 1 of the 30 May 1945 *New York Times*.

37 F.M. Sallagar, *The Road to Total War*(New York: Van Nostrand Reinhold, 1975), 156-157; Maj. Robert A. Doughty, *The Evolution of U.S. Army Tactical Doctrine, 1946-1976* (Fort Leavenworth, KS: Combat Studies Institute, 1979), 12-13.

38 Crane, 136-138; Bernstein, "Eclipsed by Hiroshima and Nagasaki: Early Thinking About Tactical Nuclear Weapons," *International Security* 15(Spring

1991): 167-168; Bill Moyers, at the conclusion of "The Arming of the Earth," an episode in his 1984 Public Broadcasting System series, "A Walk through the 20th Century with Bill Moyers."

Chapter Twelve

1 See Robert A. Doughty, *The Seeds of Disaster: The Development of French Army Doctrine 1919-1939*. Archon Books, 1985, Chapter 5, for the best description of the development of French "methodical battle" doctrine between the wars.

2 It is important to remember that the term *blitzkrieg* postdates the development of the German techniques of warfare and there is no such thing, therefore, as *blitzkrieg* "doctrine." The term is use in this paper merely as a convenient shorthand for German military technique.

3 Heinz Guderian, *Achtung-Panzer!* London, Arms and Armour, 1992, P. 205.

4 *Voprosy strategii i operativnogo iskusstva*, Moscow, Voenizdat (hereafter VSOI), p. 172.

5 VSOI, p. 173. For an excellent discussion of the German development of the elastic defense, see Lupfer...

6 Those who are familiar with current American doctrinal terminology will find the Soviet definition of "deep battle" to be rather different from our own. Whereas current American "deep battle" refers to the action of artillery, aviation, and other long-range fires against units in the enemy rear *not in contact* with American forces, the Soviet concept referred to the penetration of ground forces into the enemy's operational rear. In the Soviet concept, the "deep forces" are ground units in contact with enemy ground units, just displaced into the enemy rear away from the friendly main lines; in the American concept, there are no ground forces in the enemy's rear, just the falling of artillery and rocket rounds on enemy reserves and command posts. Thus many of the engagements in what the Soviets term "deep battle" would fall under the current American concept of the "close battle" in which ground forces are in contact with the enemy, while the American concept of "deep battle" might be more aptly termed "deep strikes."

7 Richard Simpkin, *Deep Battle, The Brainchild of Marshal Tukhachevskii*, p. 141.

8 Simpkin, p. 221.

9 S. S. Kamenev, VSOI, p. 145.

10 Simpkin, p. 91.

11 Simpkin, p. 89.

12 Simpkin, pp. 92-94.

13 Vladimir Triandafillov, *The Nature of Operations of Modern Armies,* p. 90-1.

14 Simpkin, p. 92.

15 Simpkin, p. 182-3.

16 Lester Grau, *The Bear Went Over the Mountain.* NDU Press.

17 This was not true of the American Army before its professionalization in the 1970s. The weakness and greenness of the lower ranks in the American Army during World War II made possible and required the outstanding generalship of Patton and Macarthur and others. The tactical prowess of American forces in the Gulf, on the other hand, carried the day much more than any skill of the Army's senior commanders of that time.

18 It is true that Field Regulation 1936 clearly hoped that battalion commanders and commanders at even lower echelons would also be encouraged to take the initiative. The stereotyping of Soviet commanders at those levels as completely lacking in initiative is clearly overdrawn; it is, however, clearly valid to some extent as well.

19 Simpkin, p. 89-90.

20 Simpkin, p. 90.

21 It is likely that this injunction actually applies primarily to operational and large-tactical units not below division-level.

22 Simpkin, p. 238.

23 Simpkin, p. 213.

24 Isserson, VSOI, p. 397.

25 Louis Rotundo, ed., *The Battle of Stalingrad.* Brassey's, p. 97.

26 Rotundo, p. 100.

27 Rotundo, p. 110.

28 David Glantz, *From the Don to the Dnepr,* pp. 76-78.

29 Cited in Glantz, p. 78.

30 Glantz, p. 79.

31 See Glantz for a good account.

32 Ziemke, p. 321.

Chapter Thirteen

1 Respect, one of the seven core Army values, is "the regard and recognition of the absolute dignity that every human being possesses." See Sean D. Naylor, "The Core of the Matter: Army Defines Ethics in Seven Central Values," *Army Times* (December 16, 1996), 3.

2 In Alexander's army, as well as those of Greek mercenaries, officers were forbidden to abuse their subordinates. Officers, often elected by their soldiers, were considered to be leaders of equals rather than masters of subjects; equality of respect was an important part of the warrior ethos. See John Keegan, *The Mask of Command* (London: Penguin Books, 1987), 45.

3 Carlo D'Este, *Patton: A Genius for War* (New York: Harper Collins, 1995), 533-546.

4 George Armstrong Custer, for example, was court-martialed in 1867 for charges including excessive cruelty and illegal acts in executing deserters along with mistreatment of his men in the field. He was found guilty and suspended from the Army without pay for a year — General Ulysses Grant observed that the "lenient" sentence must have been a result of the Court considering Custer's distinguished war record. See Evan Connell, *Son of the Morning Star*, (New York: Harper and Row, 1985), 173-175.

5 "An address delivered by MG J.M. Schofield to the Corps of Cadets, USMA, West Point, NY, August 11, 1879," p. 7.

6 *Superintendent's Annual Report*, (West Point: USMA Printing Office, 1920), 2-3.

7 Roger H. Nye, *Challenge of Command* (Wayne, NJ: Avery, 1986), 51

8 Steve Neal, "Why We Were Right to Like Ike," *American Heritage*, XXXVII (Dec 1985): 64.

9 GEN D. Eisenhower to MG M. Taylor, Ltr, War Department, 2 January 1946, 2.

10 Nye, 51.

11 Martin Holland "Forging a New Army," unpublished, University of North Carolina master's thesis, 1996.

12 LTCs R.H. Marcrum and W.L. Golden, etc., "A Preliminary Evaluation of the Fourth Class System," Annex C "Historical Analysis," 1969, 2.

13 *Superintendent's Annual Report*, (West Point: USMA Printing Office, 1920), 2.

14 Chairman of the Joint Chiefs of Staff, "Joint Vision 2010," 1996, 29.

15 For Plato, the true "guardian" must be both "courageous" and "gentle" — fierce in battle toward their enemies, gentle and respectful toward the citi-

zens of the *polis*. Education in warfare and moral philosophy, for Plato, is the guardian of the guardians (Book V of Plato's *Republic* deals directly with this issue); see also Lloyd J. Matthews, "The Officer as Gentleman: A Waning Ideal?" *Army* (March 1997).

16 S.L.A. Marshall, *The Armed Forces Officer*, (Washington, D.C.: Government Printing Office, 1950)

17 See John C. Bahnsen and Robert W. Cone, "Defining the American Warrior Leader," *Parameters* (Fall, 1990), 1-5.

Chapter Fourteen

1 See, for instance, Charles C. Manz and Henry P. Sims, Jr., "SuperLeadership: Beyond the Myth of Heroic Leadership," *Organizational Dynamics* (Spring 1991), 21. The authors refer in passing to Peter Drucker's argument that charisma becomes the undoing of leaders because they become inflexible, convinced of their own infallibility, and are reluctant to develop their subordinates.

2 Bernard M. Bass, *Transformational Leadership: Industrial, Military, and Educational Impact* (Mahwah, NJ: Lawrence Erlbaum Associates, 1998), 5.

3 Jay A. Conger and Rabindra N. Kanungo, *Charismatic Leadership in Organizations* (London: Sage Publications, 1998), 49.

4 Max Weber, the noted German sociologist, describes three pure types of social authority based on separate sources of legitimacy. Among these were rational, traditional and charismatic grounds. Weber used these concepts to analyze the transition of society away from traditional and charismatic grounds toward the more formal and rational grounds found in modern bureaucracy. See Max Weber, *The Theory of Social and Economic Organization*, trans. A.M. Henderson and Talcott Parsons, ed. Talcott Parsons (Glencoe, Ill.: The Free Press, 1947) 328-9. See also, Max Weber, *On Charisma and Institution Building* (Chicago: University of Chicago Press, 1968), 46; and Jay A. Conger and Rabindra N. Kanungo and Associates, *Charismatic Leadership*, (San Francisco: Jossey-Bass Publishers, 1988).

5 See John Keegan, *The Face of Battle* (New York: Penguin Books, 1976), 56-89.

6 For a more in-depth discussion on how good leaders care for their soldiers and families, see John C. Bahnsen and Robert W. Cone, "Some Thoughts on Taking Care of Your Soldiers," *Armor* (July-August 1987), 36-41. Caring for soldiers and their families demonstrates a long-term investment in peacetime that will help to sustain a unit in combat.

7 The warrior leader possesses three distinct qualities: a sincere recognition of the privilege of *special trust and confidence* accorded to those whose respon-

sibility it is to defend our democracy, the *mental readiness* that places a primacy on intellect to find solutions to complex problems, and the *inspiring* leadership manifested in the leader's exceptional character and competence — given a free choice, soldiers would elect the warrior leader as their captain. See John C. Bahnsen and Robert W. Cone, "Defining the American Warrior Leader," *Parameters* (Fall 1990), 1-5.

Chapter Fifteen

1 Department of the Army, Field Manual 22-103, *Leadership and Command at Senior Levels* (Washington, DC: U.S. Government Printing Office, 1998), pp. 9-14, 27-38, 81-83.

2 General Andrew J. Goodpaster uses this phrase to emphasize the importance of setting goals.

3 For a description of the role of the commander's estimate in the tactical planning process, see Department of the Army, Field Manual 101-5, *Staff Organization and Operations* (Washington, DC: U.S. Government Printing Office, 1997), p. C-2.

4 In the standard Army operations plan, the mission statement is followed immediately by the "concept of the operation" (essentially the commander's vision) which then leads to schemes for synchronizing battlefield functions such as maneuver and fire support, and eventually to specified tasks for subordinate units (i.e., programs for implementing the vision).

5 The core of Army training doctrine is in two manuals: Department of the Army, Field Manual 25-100, *Training the Force* (Washington, DC: U.S. Government Printing Office, 1988); and Department of the Army, Field Manual 101-25, *Battle Focused Training* (Washington, DC: U.S. Government Printing Office, 1990). See page 1-9 of FM 25-100 for a description of the training management cycle.

6 This phrase is widely attributed to LTG (Retired) Arthur S. Collins, Jr. The point is made throughout his book, *Common Sense Training* (Novato, CA: Presidio Press, 1978).

7 Harold G. Moore, "After Action Report, IA DRANG Valley Operations, 1st Battalion, 7th Cavalry, 14-16 November 1965," 9 December 1965, p. 19.

8 For a moving description of these events, see Lt. Gen. Harold G. Moore (Ret.) and Joseph L. Galloway, *We Were Soldiers Once ... and Young* (New York: Random House, 1992).

Chapter Sixteen

1 K.E. Hamburger, "Leadership in Combat: A Historical Appraisal," An internal study conducted by the Department of History, U.S. Military Academy, 1984, p. 3.

2 Phillip Longworth, *The Art of Victory* (New York: Holt, Rinehart and Winston, 1965), 36.

3 K. Osipov, *Alexander Suvorov* (London: Hutchinson and Company, 1945), 30.

4 Edward L. Fox and Donald Mathews, *The Physiological Basis of Physical Education and Athletics*, (New York: Saunders Publishing, 1981), 105.

5 David Bodanis, *The Body Book*, (Boston: Little, Brown and Company, 1984), 204-205.

6 H. Benson, J.F. Beary and M.P. Carol, "The Relaxation Response," *Psychiatry* (February, 1974), 43.

7 Gwendolyn Drew, "An Historical Study of the Concern of the Federal Government for the Physical Fitness of Non-Age Youth with Reference to the Schools, 1790-1941," *Research Quarterly* (October, 1945), 202.

8 Field Manual (FM) 21-20, *Physical Training*, 1946, 1-56.

9 Robert M. Nideffer, "Attention Control Training." In R.N. Singer, M. Murphey and L.K. Tennant (ed.), *Handbook of Research on Sports Psychology* (New York: Macmillan Press, 1994), 542-556.

10 3d Armored Division After Action Review, 1984 Canadian Army Trophy (CAT) Competition, 14 September 1984.

Chapter Seventeen

1 Headquarters, Department of the Army, *FM 25-100: Training the Force* (Washington, D.C.: U.S. Government Printing Office, 1988), 2-1.

2 Headquarters, Department of the Army, *FM 25-101: Battle Focused Training* (Washington, D.C.: U.S. Government Printing Office, 1988), 2-2.

3 Ibid.

4 Sergeant's Time, in many units, is a four or five hour block of time each week, free of distractions, specifically devoted to the noncommissioned officers so they can train their individual squads or crews on a set of tasks that they select.

Chapter Nineteen

1 In discussions between the author and General William Depuy.

2 William Cohen, *Report of the Quadrennial Defense Review* (Department of Defense, May, 1997), iv.

3 Lynne Joy McFarland, L. E. Senn, and J. R. Childress, *21st Century Leadership.* (New York: The Leadership Press, 1994), 93.

4 *Ibid.*, 103.

5 John Gardner, *On Leadership* (New York: The Free Press, 1990), 124.

6 James C. Collins and J. Porras, *Built To Last* (New York: Harper Collins, 1994), 9.

7 Gardner, *On Leadership*, 136.

8 McFarland et al, *21st Century Leadership*, 9.

9 Collins, *Built to Last*, 141.

10 *Ibid.*, 187. Not surprisingly, 3M and J&J are two of the eighteen companies featured in *Built to Last*.

11 Stephen Ambrose, *Citizen Soldiers* (New York: Simon and Schuster, 1997), 425-32.

12 Charles Barnard, *The Functions of the Executive* (Cambridge: Harvard University Press, 1972), xi.

13 Ronald Heifetz, *Leadership Without Easy Answers* (Harvard University Press/Belknap, 1997).

14 Tom Clancy, and Frederick Franks, *Into the Storm, A Study in Command* (New York: Penquin Putnam Inc., 1997), 487, 515.

15 Collins, *Built to Last*, 68-79.

16 Ibid., 69.

17 Ibid.

18 James Collins, *Inc. Magazine*, Oct 97, 40.

19 McFarland et al, *21st Century Leadership*, 138.

20 Collins, *Built to Last*, 59.

21 Ibid., 58-60.

22 See Richard Pascale, *Fast Company* (August/September 1996), 65. Also R. Pascale, M. Hillemann. and L. Giosa, "Changing the Way We Change," *Harvard Business Review 97* (November-December 1997), 127-137. The article analyzes the successful change efforts of Sears, Roebuck, Royal Dutch Shell, and the U.S. Army. The National Training Center and the After Action Review are showcased in the article.

23 Norman Douglas, in Gardner, *On Leadership,* 173.

24 Discussions between the author and Captain Paul F. Able, commander of B Co., 708th Maintenance Support Company, 8th Infantry Division, the US Army Europe winner of the General Douglas MacArthur Leadership Award for 1988.

25 V Corps, "Breakdown on Health Risks by Age and Sex," 18 April 1989. 40% of the women and 36% of the men appraised themselves as having four or more indicators of stress. 18% of the men indicated that they had 13 or more alcoholic drinks per week. 17% of the women, age 25 or less, indicated that they had seriously consider suicide in the last two years. Sample size for the men was 21,881; for women 2,890.

Index